A

HISTORY

OF

THE NEW SCHOOL,

AND OF

THE QUESTIONS INVOLVED IN THE DISRUPTION OF THE PRESBYTERIAN CHURCH IN 1838.

BY

SAMUEL J. BAIRD, D.D.

PHILADELPHIA:
CLAXTON, REMSEN & HAFFELFINGER,
Nos. 819 & 821 MARKET STREET.
1868.

WESTCOTT & THOMSON,
STEREOTYPERS, PHILADA.

TO

ROBERT J. BRECKINRIDGE,

AUTHOR OF THE ACT AND TESTIMONY,

JAMES LENOX AND NATHAN L. RICE,

MEMBERS OF THE CONVENTION OF 1835,

FRANCIS McFARLAND, GEORGE W. MUSGRAVE,

CHARLES HODGE, DAVID ELLIOTT,

JOSEPH McELROY, NATHANIEL EWING,

WILLIAM L. BRECKINRIDGE, WILLIAM S. PLUMER,

AND THE OTHER SURVIVORS

OF

A GENERATION TRIED AND FAITHFUL

THIS TRIBUTE

TO

THE PRINCIPLES WHICH THEY DEFENDED,

AND

THE MEMORIES OF THE SAINTED DEAD,

IS,

WITH AFFECTIONATE VENERATION,

INSCRIBED.

CONTENTS.

CHAPTER XXX.

CHAPTER XXXI.

CHAPTER XXXII.

CHAPTER XXXIII.

CHAPTER XXXIV.

CHAPTER XXXV.

PREFACE.

WHEN the Pelagian Controversy in the Presbyterian Church came to an end, in the division of 1838, a history of it was announced by my father, the Rev. Thomas D. Baird. No person in the Church was more favorably situated or competent to execute the work thus undertaken. His ministry ran parallel with that controversy. It began in South Carolina, in 1811, amid the excitement then prevailing in connection with the case of W. C. Davis. He first sat in the General Assembly in 1814, and witnessed the beginning of agitation there, in connection with the case of Dr. Ely. He was a member again, in 1817, the next occasion on which the controversy came into that court. Subsequently, he sat in the Assemblies of 1826, 1832, 1837, and 1838, and was a member of the Missionary Convention, in Cincinnati, in 1831, and of the Old School Conventions of 1835, 1837, and 1838, of each of the latter of which he was an officer. These facts were pledges of his profound interest in the questions involved in the controversy, and of abundant opportunity of becoming thoroughly familiar with the facts; whilst his integrity and candor were constantly attested by his most zealous antagonists. He had collected large materials; but had written nothing, when, on the 8th of January, 1839, he received a summons to lay off the harness; and departed, with the song of the cherubim on his lips.

From my boyhood, a deeply-interested observer of the controversy, and in my youth, a witness of the Convention and Assembly of 1835, and of the Assembly of 1836, and the Old School conferences of that year, I was early led to plan the fulfillment of my father's unfinished work, and to seize every opportunity to add to the materials already collected by him. Twenty-five years have elapsed since I began to write with that view. But as my studies and researches progressed, the plan was enlarged; and for many years, it has been the cherished

A *

hope of my life to prepare and publish a full history of the Presbyterian Church in this country. In this hope, I have been encouraged and stimulated by the sanction and urgency of a number of the most honored and eminent men in our Church, most of whom now rest from their labors. The requisite preparations have been pretty fully made, and all that now remains to the accomplishment of the enterprise, is the enjoyment of necessary leisure to finish the composition, from materials already digested and upon plans fully matured.

In the mean time, the question now engrossing our Church, touching reunion with the New School, has developed a necessity for information, which is inaccessible to the Church at large, and which is of vital importance, in order to wise decisions and action, at the present time. I have, therefore, employed some brief leisure redeemed from laborious official engagements,—chiefly during a month's midsummer vacation,—in giving the present form to a portion of my materials. Neither my time, nor situation, has been such as to enable me to give that critical revision to the style and the minuter historical details which I should have desired. But I have no fear that the essential accuracy of the history can be successfully impeached, and the reader will make due allowance for any minor defects, which may be discovered.

There are doubtless many who will greatly deprecate the present publication, upon a principle which is near akin to the Romish maxim, that ignorance is the mother of devotion. To such, I have only to say, that, if there are any lessons clearly taught in the Word of God, one of them is, the duty of the Church to live in the light of her own history, and give constant and anxious heed to the lessons of instruction and admonition which it conveys. If an individual would be inexcusable, who, in circumstances of peculiar emergency, should deliberately disregard and ignore the lessons of his own experience, bearing directly upon his present case, lest they should interfere with the dictates of the moment's impulses and interests,—much more would the Church of God be guilty, should she,—entrusted with the great interests of Immanuel's kingdom, close her eyes and stop her ears, to the facts of her own past history; because they may run counter to the plans and passions of the hour. The voice of history is the voice of God speaking by his providence; and let him beware, who refuses to listen and to heed.

Throughout these pages, the two parties into which the Church was divided, are designated by their well-known titles of Old and New

School. The titles are not only appropriate, but originated with the New School themselves. In New England, the Edwardean Theology early claimed to itself the name of, the New Divinity. Dr. Dutton in his history of the North Church in New Haven, states himself to have been informed by the younger Edwards, that, in 1777, there were in Connecticut, three parties,—"Arminians, who, he said, were a small party; the New Divinity gentlemen, of whom he was called one; who were larger; but still small; and the main body of the ministers, which were Calvinistic." In March, 1826, a gentleman who spent a short time in New Haven, found the phrases, "Dr. Taylor's views," "Our views," "the New Divinity," familiarly used to indicate the theology which was afterward proclaimed from that institution.

The first use of the designations, Old and New School, in our reading of the literature of the controversy, occurs in a writer signing himself, Zeta, in Dr. Ashbel Green's magazine, the Christian Advocate, for 1824. The editor, in a notice of a new edition of Marck's Medulla Theologiæ, then just out, had remarked that "the author, it is well known, was a stanch Calvinist, of the old school;"* using the phrase, as yet free from any party significance, in a well-understood and obvious sense. Thereupon, Zeta says to the editor—"The distinction between 'a Calvinist of the Old School' and one of the New, is recognized, I see, in page 129, of your March number. You know that our Presbyterian community are in fact divided—technically, I hope, not essentially, not inimically, not *toto cœlo*,†—on the subject of systematic theology. The difference is not at all so great as the common enemy would misrepresent it; nor even as some sincere brethren have supposed. It is, also, conscientious on both sides; and, therefore, piety to our common and glorious Lord, ought to constrain us to mutual forbearance. If ever there was a proper sphere for the exercise of this lovely grace, it exists, at present, in our Church; and I am persuaded that in proportion as the two Schools become acquainted with each other, animosity, jealousy, and scorn,—those unlovely passions of 'the old man,'—will subside, and be gradually superseded by sensations at once more pleasant and more pure.—'And Abram said unto Lot, Let there be no strife between me and thee,—FOR WE BE BRETHREN.'"‡

* Christian Advocate, 182[illegible] † By the whole heavens.

‡ Ibid, p. 208.

Zeta, thus commences a series of articles on the atonement, in which he recognizes the two parties by the names here given. The articles seem to have been terminated abruptly, by the editor, at a point where the writer began to develop a serious departure from the Confession of Faith, as to the nature of the atonement. The style of this writer and his sentiments seem clearly to identify him with the Rev. S. H Cox, D. D., who, in the Princeton Review for October, 1831, uses the same designations.

In the discussions of the Assembly of 1831, and connected there with, these names began to be familiarly employed, and have con tinued, since, in general use.

One word is necessary, as to the theological stand-point from which the controversy is viewed in this history. The author is *not* a philo sophical realist, as has been assumed of late. He is simply and only a disciple of the theology of the Reformation, as set forth in the stand ards of Westminster and the writings of the old standard divines. A firm and unwavering faith in those doctrines has determined the light in which every fact has been viewed, and every doctrine stated in this work.

In making quotations, it has been a rule of inflexible observance to *retain without modification the emphasis of the original.* Where it was desirable to call special attention to a clause in such a passage, it has been done, in a few instances, by *repeating* the passage with the neces sary emphasis.

As the work is designed as much for the common people of God, as for the learned, marginal translations are given of all phrases derived from the learned languages.

Under the designation of "Hewit MS.," references are made to a volume of copies of an original correspondence with which I was favored by my late venerated friend, the Rev. Dr. Nathaniel Hewit, of Bridgeport, Connecticut.

With profound devotion to the welfare of our beloved Church, and prayer for the peace of Israel, this history is now submitted to the candor of the reader.

STAUNTON, VA., *July* 30, 1868.

INTRODUCTION.

THE New School controversy arose from the introduction into the Church of new doctrines, which threatened the overthrow of the whole system of saving faith, contained in our standards. Strictly and fundamentally, the issue was doctrinal. The question dependent was not, indeed, as to the truth or falsehood of the theology of the New School. Upon that issue, the number of adherents of the party would have been comparatively small. But it was, as to the allowance of those doctrines, in the Church. In this light, it was viewed by the Old School, from the beginning, and set forth in their various documents, particularly in the Memorial and Testimony of 1837. It was in this light that, during the controversy, the subject was treated by the New School, always, and officially expounded in their "Declaration" of 1839. It was upon this issue of doctrinal toleration, that they were able to rally the whole strength of the party, in every instance, for the defence of those who were impeached of unsoundness in the faith. The disorders introduced by the Plan of Union were held in comparatively light regard, viewed as mere departures from the order of our Church. It was, as the means of introducing and giving currency to doctrinal errors that they became the occasion of anxiety and alarm. The question between the boards and institutions of our Church and those of voluntary origin and constitution, originated, and derived [illegible] significance, from the fact that the former were set for the promulgation and defence of the gospel as exhibited in our standards; whilst the latter were devoted to the propagation of the undefinable principles of "liberal Presbyterianism."

For a number of years after the division, the distinctness with which these facts were recognized, and the vivid memories cherished of the unhappy scenes of controversy, inevitably consequent upon such doctrinal diversities as existed, precluded any idea of reunion, unless upon condition of an agreement in doctrinal sentiments and policy, which all felt to be,for the present generation,beyond hope.

But, as years rolled on, the actors in the controversy have generally passed off the stage. The memories of false doctrines and their unhappy consequences have faded away; and the separation of the two bodies has prevented that intimacy of intercourse, by which a knowledge would have been retained in the common mind of the Church, of current errors, still cherished and disseminated, as of old. On the contrary, the pressure of embarrassments resulting, in various respects, from the division, has been increasingly felt; inducing a growing disposition to disparage the grounds of separation, and to exalt the desirableness, and insist upon the practicability,of a reunion.

In consequence, the subject had been, from time to time, presented, with more or less earnestness, to the consideration of the Assembly. At length, in 1866, it came under consideration, in the Committee of Bills and Overtures, in consequence of memorials received from the Presbyteries of Leavenworth, Muncie, New Lisbon, Madison, Erie and Oxford. If the proper time had come for action on the subject, the resolutions reported by the committee were unexceptionable, and the principles therein stated were such as must commend themselves to every true friend of the Church and of the cause of Christ.

"1. This Assembly expresses its fraternal affection for the other branch of the Presbyterian Church, and its earnest desire for reunion, at the earliest time consistent with agreement in doctrine, order and policy, on the basis of a common standard and the prevalence of mutual confidence and love, which are so necessary to a happy union, and to the permanent peace and prosperity of the united Church.

"2. That it be recommended to all churches and church courts, and to all ministers, ruling elders, and communicants, to cherish fraternal feelings, to cultivate Christian intercourse, in the worship of God, and in the promotion of the cause of Christ, and to avoid all needless controversies and contentions.

"3. That a committee of nine ministers and six ruling elders be appointed, provided that a similar committee be appointed by the other Assembly, now in session in this city, for the purpose of conferring in regard to the desirableness and practicability of reunion; and if, after conference and inquiry, such reunion shall seem to be desirable and practicable, to suggest suitable measures for its accomplishment, and report to the next General Assembly."

To these resolutions, the Rev. Dr. Van Dyke proposed an amendment, to include in the negotiations the Southern Presbyterian Church. The amendment was laid on the table and the resolutions were adopted.

The committee, appointed by the Moderator, in pursuance of these resolutions, consisted of the Rev. Drs. J. M. Krebs, C. C. Beatty, J. T. Backus, P. D. Gurley, J. G. Monfort, W. D. Howard, W. E. Schenck, V. C. Reed, and F. T. Brown, and Elders J. M. Ray, R. McKnight, S. Galloway, H. K. Clarke, G. P. Strong, and O. Beatty.

The overture was accepted by the New School Assembly, and a like committee appointed. When the committees met, they seem to have ignored altogether the primary object of their appointment, which was, "to confer in regard to the desirableness and practicability of reunion." Only after ascertaining these points, upon conference and inquiry, were they authorized "to suggest suitable measures for its accomplishment." But the committee seem to have jumped, at once, to the conclusion, that the consummation was both desirable and practicable; and thereupon proceeded to enter into the constructing of a treaty of union.

Nor, in the provisions of the plan adopted, did the committee pay any more regard to the instructions under which it was appointed, than with respect to the preliminary question. Those instructions contemplated union, only upon condition of "agreement in doctrine, order, and policy, on the basis of the common standards." A very different basis was adopted by the committee.

When the two committees met, that of the Old School proposed as the basis of union, a strict conformity to the standards, in doctrine and order. This basis was urged, with great earnestness, upon the New School members; but was firmly and utterly repudiated by them. The Old School insisted that the Confession of Faith should be adopted in its obvious, fair, historical sense. The New School claimed that it should be adopted in the sense in which it has heretofore been received in the two churches.

Finding that this, and nothing less, would be acceptable to the New School, it might have been supposed that the Old School members would accept this as a demonstration that, for the present, reunion is impracticable; and so report to the Assembly. But, instead of this, the New School conditions were accepted, and a plan of union formed, on that basis. During the controversy, whilst the charges of Arminianism and Pelagianism were brought home with demonstration, to New School divines, the attempt was once or twice feebly made, by way of foil to these charges, to impeach the Old School of Antinomianism and Fatalism; although no case was ever specified, and no proof ever attempted. Deriving the suggestion of its language from these facts, the committee recommended the following as the doctrinal basis of union, in its report of 1867.

"1. The reunion shall be effected on the doctrinal and ecclesiastical basis of our common standards; the Confession of Faith shall continue to be sincerely received and adopted 'as containing the system of doctrine taught in the Holy Scriptures;' and its fair, historical sense, as it is accepted by the two bodies, in opposition to Antinomianism and Fatalism on the one hand, and to Arminianism and Pelagianism, on the other, shall be regarded as the sense in which it is received and adopted." If, the fact that, in the joint committee, this paper was adopted after, and because of, the refusal of the New School members to accept the standards strictly, and the very language of this article, itself, were together insufficient to prove that its intent was to establish in the united Church the "liberal" principles of subscription contended for by the New School, it was only further necessary to point to the fact that these precisely were the terms of subscription set forth by Mr. Barnes, on his trial, and sanctioned by the New School in his acquittal.* The historical sense in which the two parties have respectively adopted the Confession, will very fully appear in the following pages; the Old School always insisting upon the strict maintenance of the doctrines of that formulary, and the New, from the first, claiming an indefinite liberty of divergence from it.

The terms of union provided for consolidating the Boards and committees of the two churches. In doing this, the lists of the Boards of Publication were to be examined by a joint committee of seven from each body; and if three of either committee objected to any publication, it should be stricken from the list. That is, in the committee of fourteen, all the Old School members, and four out of seven of the New School, might vote to retain Boston's Fourfold State. But if a minority of three of the New School committee should happen to dislike the emphasis therein given to the doctrine of imputation, and object to the book, it could not be retained;—a scheme well adapted to render the publications of our Church as indefinite, "catholic" and valueless, as those of any "unsectarian" voluntary society in the land.

Respecting the Seminaries of the Church, it was provided that those of the General Assembly should be permitted to place themselves under Synodical control, if at any time, they should desire it. Those belonging to the New School were, also, to be allowed, when they choose, to place themselves under ecclesiastical control. It will be found, in the following history, that the New School seminaries originated in jealousy of ecclesiastical control, and in opposition to the doctrinal strictness enforced upon those established by the Assembly. The plan, in fact, provided that they should retain that independence, unless they should see fit voluntarily to surrender it. In other words, the Old School seminaries were to come, at once, under the joint control of the New School; and they were authorized to retain exclusive control of the others, as long as they chose.

One additional point, of fundamental importance, was provided for, in the treaty. During the controversy, the right and

* See below, p. 480.

duty of the Presbyteries to be fully satisfied as to the qualifications of ministers, coming to them for admission, even though bringing "clean papers," or regular testimonials, were insisted upon by the Old School, and denied by the New School. The cases of Messrs. Barnes and Beecher, gave signal interest and importance to the question. The doctrine of clean papers was effectually employed by Dr. Peters to fill the Presbytery of Cincinnati, with the supporters of the American Home Missionary Society. Prior to the rise of the controversy, the right of Presbyteries, though unquestioned, was seldom exercised for lack of occasion. The cases, however, of the Cumberland and New Light heresies in Kentucky, illustrated the principle held by our Church from the beginning.* The constitutional right of Presbyteries to make examination of applicants for admission, was denied by the New School Assembly of 1834, but reaffirmed, in 1835. In 1837, it was made imperative on Presbyteries "to examine all making application for admission into their bodies, at least, on experimental religion, didactic and polemic theology, and church government." Such has continued to be the law and practice of our Church, ever since.

No sooner, however, did the New School separate themselves from the Assembly, in 1838, than they decreed, that "Whereas, it is the inherent right of Presbyteries to expound and apply constitutional rules touching the qualifications of their own members, therefore,—

"Resolved, That the action of the last General Assembly, making it imperative on the Presbyteries to examine all who make application for admission to their bodies, not excepting ministers coming from other Presbyteries, is null and void."†

If the doctrine of this resolve be true, that of the Form of Government is false, which expressly assigns to the Assembly the prerogative of "deciding in all controversies respecting doctrine and discipline." Should any Presbytery see fit to fill up the ranks of its ministry with Pelagians, Arians and Socinians, and its eldership with unordained "committee-men," it would, according to this act, be in the exercise of its "inherent

* See below, p. 136; and Baird's Assembly's Digest, pp. 633, 641.

† Moore's "New Digest," p. 117.

right," and no superior court would be entitled to interfere. The doctrine is, in fact, Presbyterial Independency; and is much nearer akin to Congregationalism than to the system of our standards. Such is the theory; and the practice, as experience has fully illustrated, enables one unsound Presbytery, at its own discretion, to infuse poison into the whole Church.

On this subject, the treaty of union was couched in general terms, which, however, to those who understood the history, were profoundly significant. It provided that, "in order to avoid the revival of past issues, by the continuance of any usage in either branch of the Church, that has grown out of our former conflicts, it is earnestly recommended, to the lower judicatories of the Church, that they conform their practice, in relation to all such usages, as far as consistent with their convictions of duty, to the general custom of the Church, prior to the controversies that resulted in the separation."

It was not pretended that this very adroitly phrased paragraph had reference to any other question than that of the examination of ministers; and when reduced to plain English, it was a provision that, "in order to avoid the revival of that issue," the Old School should surrender the point.

Such were the essential points in the plan of reunion, submitted to the Assembly of 1867. By the Assembly, the plan was sent down to the Presbyteries, without any expression of approbation or disapprobation, in order to afford the Church "a full opportunity to examine the subject, in the light of all its advantages and difficulties, so that the committee may have the benefit of any suggestions which may be offered, before making a final report for the action of the next Assembly."

Already, it was evident that, on this subject, there were two parties in the Church;—one composed of those who hold the union to be of paramount importance, and the maintenance of Old School principles of altogether secondary consideration; and the other, embracing those who admitted the eminent desirableness of union; but regarded it as proper and justifiable, only upon condition that it could be accomplished, without the sacrifice of the distinctive principles maintained by the Old School, during and since the controversy. It was, further, evident, that, whatever might be the private sentiments of the members of the committee, there was not one of them, whom the latter class could regard as a reliable representative of their views and principles. When, therefore, the Moderator was about to fill a vacancy in the committee, occasioned by the illness of Dr. Krebs, it was hoped that the claims of this party would be regarded, and a name was suggested, of one of the most worthy and respected pastors in the Church, as a representative of that class. The suggestion, however, was disregarded, and the committee retained its one-sided character.

By a strong majority of the Presbyteries, the Plan of reunion was disapproved, as involving a surrender of sacred principles, for the defence of which our Church has been set by the King of Zion.

The joint committee again assembled, and spent several days in consultation. Upon the adjournment, it was announced that the conclusions arrived at would not be published until laid before the two Assemblies. It was, however, soon rumored abroad, that, for two or three days, the Old School members of the committee had insisted upon terms, in accordance with the mind of the Church, as ascertained by the action of the Presbyteries. Such terms had been utterly refused, by the New School, and the committee was about to adjourn, in despair; when the same hand by which was written the doctrinal basis of 1867, again proposed a doctrinal article, upon which all united. The terms thus proposed were submitted to the Assemblies of 1868, and are now before the churches for acceptance or rejection. The doctrinal article is in the following words:—

"1. The reunion shall be effected on the doctrinal and ecclesiastical basis of our common standards; the Scriptures of the Old and New Testaments shall be acknowledged to be the inspired word of God and the only infallible rule of faith and practice; the Confession of Faith shall continue to be sincerely received and adopted, 'as containing the system of doctrine taught in the Holy Scriptures,' it being understood that this Confession is received in its proper historical, that is, the Calvinistic or Reformed sense; it is also understood that various methods of viewing, stating, explaining, and illustrating the doctrines of the Confession, which do not impair the integrity of the Reformed or Calvinistic system, are to be freely allowed in the united Church, as they have hitherto been allowed in the separate churches; and the Government and Discipline of the Presbyterian Church in the United States shall be approved as containing the principles and rule of our polity."

The reader will find, upon comparing this with the doctrinal basis of 1867, that it is precisely the same thing, couched in different phrases; this being, if possible, more precise and unequivocal in repudiating the Old School, and adopting the New School, principles and phraseology. The básis of 1867, conforms to the platform of Mr. Barnes' "Defence," as we have already seen. That of 1868, covers the same ground, but is conformed, rather, to the position of the New Haven professors, as set forth in their "Statement" on the subject.*

On the disposition of the Seminaries and Boards, the new terms corresponded with those of the preceding year. Respecting the publications of the two churches, it was referred to the Board of Publication of the united Church, to revise them, "and perfect a catalogue for the joint Church, so as to exclude invidious references to the past."

As to the examination of intrant ministers, there is a seeming improvement, by which, however, nothing is gained to the cause of sound doctrine.

"10. It is agreed that the Presbyteries possess the right to examine ministers applying for admission from other Presbyteries; but each Presbytery shall be left free to decide for itself when it shall exercise the right.

"11. It shall be regarded as the duty of all our judicatories, ministers, and people, in the united Church, to study the things which make for peace, and to guard against all needless and offensive references to the causes that have divided us; and, in order to avoid the revival of past issues, by the continuance of any usage in either branch of the Church that has grown out of our former conflicts, it is earnestly recommended to the lower

* See below, p. 209.

judicatories of the Church, that they conform their practice in relation to all such usages, as far as is consistent with their convictions of duty, to the general custom of the Church prior to the controversies that resulted in the separation."

Of no value, for the maintenance of the doctrinal purity of the ministry, will be the abstract right, thus acknowledged in the Presbyteries; a right thus expressly removed from the category of duties, and from the right of supervision and enforcement by the higher courts; whilst it is stigmatized with odium, by this fundamental law of the Church, and discountenanced, as in such circumstances, it would be, by the common custom of the Church. The basis of 1867 recommended the Presbyteries to waive their prerogative. That of 1868, deprives the Assembly of all power over the subject.

The true character of the doctrinal basis, was promptly recognized and hailed by the New School Assembly. It was referred to a committee of which the Rev. Dr. Hickok was chairman. Of the doctrinal terms, this committee reported, and the Assembly adopted, the following exposition.

"'Various methods of viewing, stating, explaining, and illustrating' the doctrines of the Confession of Faith are to be freely allowed in the united Church, as they have hitherto been allowed in the separate Churches, only they must not impair the integrity of the Calvinistic system. And now who shall decide whether the views do impair the integrity of the system? If there be a strenuous and rigid umpire, such will doubtless be found intolerant of opinions and interpretations contrary to its own. A mind cautious and jealous of all encroachment on religious liberty will doubt, and in proportion to his fears he will hesitate or object.

"But is the danger here really formidable? Admit the majority of the ecclesiastical body must decide; but in the way the members of our Presbyteries now will have their standing in the united Church, then, will they be unsafe and exposed to oppression? Aside from the manifest liberality and confidence and love which there must be in the members of the opposite branch, before three-quarters of its Presbyteries shall vote us together, there are three quite impregnable safeguards. The man whose sentiments do not violate the Calvinistic system cannot be hurt. And if the fear still is, that in the opinion of the judicatory, the sentiment may be in violation of the integrity of the Calvinistic system, and that the opinion of the judicatory must rule, the answer at once is, not the judicatory on its own opinion, but the judicatory as convinced that the opposite branch of the Church has allowed or not allowed the sentiment to be in consonance with the Calvinistic system. If the man is not out of the pale of his former Church's orthodoxy, he cannot be in danger from any ecclesiastical court's rigidity or bigotry. Danger from this cannot be further pressed without directly questioning the candor and honesty of the judicatory, and then we are at once beyond all Christian redress or regulation."

After the adjournment of the Assemblies, the Rev. George Hill met with Dr. Hickok, and conversed with him on this subject. "In that conversation," says Mr. Hill, "he (Dr. Hickok) said 'as they (the New School) regarded the basis as binding them to tolerate the Old School doctrine of immediate imputation, so they regarded it as binding us to tolerate—well (said he) to give it a definite form—Taylorism.' He farther said that 'it was the belief that the basis bound us to tolerate everything that they had tolerated, that finally reconciled many of the members of the New School Assembly to vote for the basis, notwithstanding their opposition to the tenth Article.' I expressed to him the conviction that the present basis is more latitudinarian than the one of last year, and he answered that 'he so regarded it, and was surprised—not grieved, but surprised—that the Old School committee consented to it.'"

The attention of Dr. Hickok was called to Mr. Hill's statement, by a member of the committee on reunion. He replied, that he remembers the conversation referred to, but does not remember the remark respecting Taylorism. He does not, however, pretend to deny it; but proceeds to reiterate an equivalent statement.

"I am willing to stand publicly responsible for the opinion, that the said first Article will bind the united Church to tolerate such doctrines and explanations as have been allowed as orthodox by either branch, and that any particular Presbytery, must judge not merely from its own opinion of the orthodoxy of the same, but in view of what has been allowed by either one or the other of the separate branches. I do not choose to say of any doubtful, specific doctrine or explanation, whether it has or has not been so allowed by either branch. Certainly I should not wish to be understood as saying that 'Taylorism' in any 'definite form' had been so allowed."

Nor, we suppose, would Dr. Hickok deny it. It is, however, clear in what sense the New School Assembly and Church understands and accepts the basis of reunion; and it is certain that their understanding is fully sustained by a strict interpretation of the language of the paper, and confirmed by reference to the history of the question, both in the old time of the controversy, and in the discussions of the joint committee.

This report, moreover, of Dr. Hickok, was, upon motion of Dr. R. J. Breckinridge, formally read in our Assembly, after which, the Assembly proceeded to adopt the plan of union,—rejecting and laying on the table, every proposition which looked toward repudiating or guarding against the sense thus put upon it.

So far, the majority of the Assembly had, manifestly, accepted and committed itself to the New School understanding of the basis. Knowing, officially, the sense in which the covenant was understood by the other party, and accepting the terms thus interpreted, to the express exclusion of all cautionary or explanatory amendment, they were bound alike in law and morals by the sense thus acquiesced in.

After the adoption of the doctrinal basis, Dr. Monfort moved that "while the Assembly has approved of the Report of the joint committee on reunion, it expresses its preference for a change in the first item on the basis, leaving out the following words, viz.:—

'It being understood, that this Confession is received in its proper, historical, that is, the Calvinistic or Reformed sense; it is also understood, that various methods of viewing, stating, explaining and illustrating the doctrines of the Confession, which do not impair the integrity of the Reformed or Calvinistic system, are to be freely allowed in the united Church, as they have hitherto been allowed in the separate Churches.' The Assembly believe that by leaving out these clauses, the basis will be more simple, and more expressive of mutual confidence."

The real nature and effect of this overture for amendment will appear in view of the reasons which made it so acceptable to the New School, who had been so firm in insisting upon liberty as to doctrine. These are apparent. Before the adoption of the basis of union the Rev. Dr. Eagleson had moved to amend it by striking out the above-cited clause. Had that motion carried, it would have been recognized as a rejection of the latitudinarian principles of the basis. And had the members of the Assembly generally understood the precise effect of the course taken, they would, no doubt, have thus acted; for it is not supposable that a majority of the members designed to sanction the principles contained in the "Gurley basis;" as the result most signally proved. Probably, the leading managers of the business understood precisely what they were doing.

After the committee's basis had been adopted, in response to the action of the New School Assembly, and with the distinct and official view to the tenor of that action, the proposed amendment, *couched in the terms in which it was framed, and enforced by the arguments which accompanied it*, was so far from correcting the false principles of the basis, that it constituted a most effectual recognition and confirmation of them. It was proposed to the New School Assembly, as an alternative, at their option, to the committee's basis. No intimation was given, or implied, of dissatisfaction with the principles of the basis, nor with the New School interpretation of it. On the contrary, the reason, the only reason, stated in the proposition itself, for the change, is that it will render the basis "more simple and *more expressive of mutual confidence.*" And when the commissioners from the Assembly laid the amendment before the Harrisburgh Assembly, they were careful to state that this proposal originated with "*the friends of reunion*," that they were perfectly satisfied with the basis as it was, and only suggested this amendment, as being expressive of greater mutual confidence, and likely to strengthen the overture in the Presbyteries. Upon this ground they threw themselves upon the magnanimity of our New School brethren, pleading "in earnest appeals to the Assembly to aid them in the coming struggle."* When it is considered, that there was no party in the Assembly, nor in the Church, opposed to reunion, provided the fundamental principles distinctive of our Church are protected,—it is evident what meaning the New School were expected to attach to the phrase, "friends of reunion," and in what sense they were to understand the proposed amendment, as coming from those "friends," rather than from others.

The New School Assembly, thus appealed to, was ready, by a large majority, to have accepted the proffered amendment; but was precluded by the fact that so many members had left, that there were not enough remaining to justify an orderly reconsideration.

In the mean time, the members of our Assembly would seem to have been awakening to a just sense of the position, into which, by eminently skillful management, they had been led, and the attitude in which these transactions had placed the Assembly and the Church. Reflection on the impressive arguments of Hodge and Breckinridge, Backus, Humphrey, Woods and others, could not fail of inducing conviction in many minds. The unanswerable arguments of the protest of the minority were about to be spread on the records and go forth to the Church, with names affixed, which have always and most justly commanded the affectionate reverence, not of our Church only, but of the whole Church of God.

It was when this protest was about to be read, that Dr. Hall rose, and proposed to offer a resolution which would obviate the necessity for the protest. The resolution was unanimously adopted, as follows:—

"*Resolved*, That this Assembly desires it to be understood that the first Article of the report of the joint reunion Committee, which is the doctrinal basis of union, and which was adopted on Friday last by this Assembly, is not to be interpreted as giving license to the propagation of doctrines which have been condemned by either Assembly, nor to permit any Presbytery in

* Harrisburgh correspondent of the Pittsburgh Banner, June 10, 1868.

the united Church to license or ordain to the work of the ministry any candidate who maintains any form of doctrine condemned by either Assembly."

This resolution was substantially the same as an amendment which Dr. Humphrey had proposed, pending the motion to adopt the first Article. But, as now adopted, the resolution, as Dr. Humphrey justly remarked, was "no part of the terms sent to the New School Assembly; and, hence, does not meet the case, nor obviate the necessity for the protest, which I now offer."

After the protest had been read, the Rev. Dr. J. C. Backus moved to send by telegraph to the Assembly at Harrisburgh, a copy of the paper of Dr. Hall, just passed by the Assembly. There was a cry of "No! no!" and a motion made to lay the proposition on the table. This motion was lost, and the resolution of Dr. Backus was adopted. Of the reception of this communication, by the New School Assembly, the Harrisburg correspondent of the Pittsburgh Banner gives this account:—

"Just before the final adjournment a despatch was received from Albany, announcing the passage of a resolution by the Old School Assembly as to the construction of the first Article of the basis, which, at first, created quite a sensation. Upon reflection, however, it was supposed that its object was to conciliate the minority; and that as it was proposed by a friend of reunion, and unanimously adopted, *it meant nothing very serious.* I do not wonder that it aroused suspicion; and with my present light upon the subject I cannot but regard its adoption as entirely superfluous."

The italics were made by the correspondent himself. The intimation conveyed by the whole statement is so offensive that it would be justly regarded as grossly slanderous, had it proceeded from any other than a "friend of reunion." It seems that the action of our Assembly "aroused suspicion" in the minds of our New School brethren, who, at first, apprehended that the Assembly really meant what the Hall resolution said. But this unpleasant impression was obviated, by the consideration that the proposition came from a "friend of reunion," to whom it seems is conceded the privilege of saying the most serious things "to conciliate the minority," without meaning anything serious thereby.

The idea that such was the design of our Assembly, is not to be tolerated for a moment; and it is to be hoped that the action of our Presbyteries will be such, as will cause all men to understand that they do seriously mean to be faithful to that testimony which God has committed to our beloved Church; and it becomes them to ponder the fact that the adoption of the proposed basis of union would place us in a position of doctrinal defection unspeakably worse than was ever imputed to the New School. Whatever else may be chargeable against them, they have never entered into a formal contract to grant harbor and protection to heresy. However lax may have been their views and practice on the subject, they have retained the matter under the control of their own consciences, reserving the right of acting upon each case on its own merits, as it arose. To us it is now proposed to enter into a solemn covenant, which will be paramount to the Constitution itself, to tolerate and protect all such "explanations" and teachings as our New School brethren have been accustomed to permit. How much this means, no man on earth can tell. That it does include the teachings of Messrs. Barnes and Beman, and Finney and Taylor, we do know. History records it, and the Presbytery of Tioga attests it. But what else may prove, upon investigation, to have found shelter under the broad ægis of New School toleration, the future only can discover.

It will be said, as it was upon the floor of the Assembly, that every New School member of the committee of reunion repudiated the position taken by that Presbytery. But that fact has no bearing, whatever, on the issue. As we have seen, the doctrinal basis, as justly interpreted by Dr. Hickok and the New School Assembly, entitles any sentiments to impunity, which have been heretofore tolerated in either Church. The members of the New School committee may not like it; but the fact is, that the Presbytery of Tioga had openly taken its position on this subject, before the adoption of this basis, unrebuked by any competent authority in the body. Its dictum, therefore, constitutes a precedent, in the contemplation of the Gurley basis, to which any impleaded Pelagian will be entitled to appeal, in his vindication, if the basis is adopted ; and it is scarcely necessary to say, that, if the Tioga Presbytery has been the only one to avow this position, pending these negotiations, it is not the only one which has practically occupied it. The Taylorism of Mr. Finney never prevented his being a cherished member of the New School party; and it was not until his withdrawal from the Church and embrace of perfectionism, the logical sequence of his previous sentiments, that he ceased to be recognized by them, as entitled to all confidence and respect. The avowed Pelagianism of the Rev. Dr. Edward Beecher, and Professors Sturdevant and Kirby, received judicial sanction from the Presbytery of Illinois,* and Dr. Beman and Mr. Barnes, with many others of like sentiments, are, to this day, cherished ministers of the New School Church. Their sentiments it has a perfect and unquestionable right to sanction, in all honesty. But the Old School must abandon the principles for which our Church has always contended, before they can consent to union, on such terms.

It is asserted that our New School brethren have changed on the doctrinal question. The only question that has ever divided us, on that subject has been the propriety of tolerating and shielding error. If, on that subject, they have changed, what means the interpretation, given by Dr. Hickok and adopted by their Assembly, to the basis of union. What mean the gratulations of the Moderator, Dr. Stearns, a member of the reunion committee, that "under this basis, with its conceded rights of stating, explaining and illustrating doctrine, Albert Barnes never could have been tried for heresy." What meant the Rev. Dr. H. B. Smith, another member of the committee, in urging that according to the basis, neither branch of the Church had a right to say that its own interpretation was the only correct one; "and that if he supposed that the basis would prevent free inquiry or new views of the Bible and the Confession, he should not vote for that basis. Liberty was the very life of the Church. It should not be bound finally to any particular interpretation."

In fact, it seems that even the "Hall resolution" is found sus-

* See below, p. 472.

ceptible of an interpretation, in consonance with this principle of liberty. So, it appears to be explained by Dr. Hall, himself; and so, the author has been informed by a very excellent New School brother, he understands it,—as perfectly consistent with the honorable recognition of Messrs. Barnes and Beman, in the united Church.

Whatever else, however, may be ambiguous, the negotiations so far, have made it clear that the errors against which the Old School testimonies were addressed are still cherished in the bosom of the New School Church; and that that body is as determined as it was in 1837, in claiming for those errors unmolested status.

The whole matter is thus reduced to a very simple issue. There is a fundamental and irreconcilable difference of principle between the two bodies, on this subject of liberty of doctrinal divergence from the standards. The question for the Old School to determine is, whether we are prepared to ignore all the past, surrender the principles on which our Church has heretofore stood, furl up the banner of testimony which she has borne, and enter into covenant to abandon the precious doctrines of grace to the mercy of every theological empiric who may fancy that his "free inquiries" have found a new and better way.

HISTORY OF THE NEW SCHOOL.

CHAPTER I.

THE ENGLISH HEADS OF AGREEMENT.

Presbyterianism was never organized in England—Nominal Presbyterians in 1688—Union of 1690—Its origin—The Heads of Agreement—The resulting system—Baxter's Neonomian scheme—Mather's estimate of it—The Pinners' Hall controversy—False moderation—Doctrinal teaching decried—Laxity of subscription—Bourn's Catechisms—Arian defection—Mainly among the Presbyterians—The origin and end of the development—Appeals of Congregationalists and the New School to this history.

THE standards of Westminster were the products of the piety, learning and researches of English divines. But the authors were never privileged to witness the action of the system in their own churches. The Long Parliament did, indeed, enact a polity which purported to be based on that of the Assembly. But the whole system was so modified as to be altogether subservient to the designs and subordinate to the power of Parliament, to which, in all cases, the ultimate decision of ecclesiastical questions was reserved. Thus were the divines of Westminster thwarted in their labors, and the prelatic historian, Echard, scornfully but truly says, that "the Presbyterians never saw their dear Presbytery settled in any one part of England." Even the Parliamentary system was not brought into general operation. It was altogether unacceptable to the Presbyterians, opposed by the Independents, and unsatisfactory even to the Parliament itself, in which the Independents were gaining the ascendancy. At length, Cromwell seized the reins, and the Parliamentary discipline at once fell into disuse.

In some instances the Presbyterian ministers voluntarily united themselves in organizations formed after the scriptural model. But they were under the frown of Cromwell, and upon his death became the objects of the most unrelenting persecutions of the restored house of Stuart. In 1688 the tyranny and misrule of that family came to an end. The exhausted patience of England drove James the Second from the throne, and the nation threw itself into the arms of the illustrious William of Orange, a Presbyterian prince. With him came respite from persecution, and, after long delay by a reluctant Parliament, the Act of Toleration. Now, at length, might have been realized the hopes so long deferred—the development on the soil of England of the polity so fitly framed by the wisdom of England's best divines. But the nominal Presbyterians, who hailed the accession of William to the throne, were not the same who nearly half a century before had met in Westminster and composed those formularies. A new generation had arisen, which had been cradled in the licentious reign of Charles the Second, and surrounded by influences every way unfavorable to the maintenance and transmission of sound principles.

It was, in fact, scarcely possible that the men of 1688 should have felt any peculiar interest in the distinctive principles of Presbyterian church government, or possessed any intelligent acquaintance with them. In this respect they were at a disadvantage which was not shared by their brethren, the Independents. The Presbyterian system involved features requiring extended co-operation, which implies more or less publicity and consequent exposure to the agents of persecution. But the other, offspring of a bloody period, is pre-eminently fitted for perpetuation at such a time; for, wherever a little company of believers is associated for worship, it is complete in itself for all the purposes of their system. The Independents, therefore, emerged from the dark period which preceded the revolution of 1688 fully organized, familiar with the practical working of their system, and prizing it the more for all they had endured on its account, and for the blessings they had experienced in the stolen enjoyment of its ordinances.

The Presbyterians were in altogether different circumstances. During forty years of oppression and persecution they had been entire strangers to the practical operation of the Reformed polity, and it was impossible in their situation that they should have studied with any diligence, or cherished with strong attachment, the theory of a system so utterly impracticable to them. On the other hand, they were thoroughly habituated to a system which the pressure of their circumstances had moulded into essential agreement with that of the Independents. They felt an affectionate regard for that party which had so long shared with them the anxieties and scourge of persecution, and they were trained to the habit of compromise with regard to principles of order under the pressure of necessity—a habit easily degenerating into a readiness to yield them to considerations of expediency or convenience.

When to the circumstances already indicated we add that new doctrines of seeming innocence, but really pregnant with apostasy, were cherished by leading Presbyterians and gaining strength in the party, we need look no further to find causes abundantly adequate to account for the fact that a less stringent order of discipline was preferred to that of Westminster—that when the prize was just within their grasp these sons of an illustrious ancestry should reject it, and sell their birthright for a mess of pottage. The Union of 1690, though devised and executed by eminent and honored servants of Christ, was unwise in its conception, and, as demonstrated by the result, was consummated under the frown of the Head of the Church. For its origin we must look to the churches of New England.

Although a majority of the early population of the New England colonies were Independents, still many of the ministers and people who sought refuge there from the persecutions of England were, by conviction and preference, Presbyterians. Such was Wilson, one of the first pastors of Boston. Such was Hooker, the pioneer of Connecticut, "the light of the Western churches;" and Elliot, the apostle of the Indians. The Governor and Council of Connecticut, in 1680, in reply to a series of questions proposed to them by the

Lords of Trade and Plantations in regard to the character of the population, etc., state that "some are strict Congregational men, others more large Congregational men, and some moderate Presbyterians. And, take the Congregationalists of both sorts, they are the greater part of the people in the colony."* Such was the composition of the most of the Northern colonies. The commingling of these elements induced frequent debates and uneasiness, and gave occasion to the repeated assembling of councils and synods, by which schemes of discipline were constructed and plans of comprehension devised, varying from the Erastian Congregationalism of the Cambridge platform to the almost Presbyterian order of that of Saybrook. Thus, upon a vaguely-defined and varying basis, by the union of Independents and Presbyterians, were the Congregational churches of New England created.

The example thus exhibited in the colonies suggested frequent movements toward a similar union in the mother country. Baxter gives an account of three several schemes of this sort in which he was engaged, all of which failed.†

Shortly before the accession of William and Mary, the Rev. Increase Mather, being at the time President of Harvard College, was sent to England, and remained there several years on business of the province and college. Whilst there, he set himself with great zeal to bring about such a union in the mother country as had long been familiar to him in the New England colonies. His proposals were seconded by Bates, Howe,

* Hinman's Antiquities of Connecticut, p. 141.

† Orme's Life of Baxter, vol. i., p. 577.

Baxter and others. The result was, that in 1690* the ministers of the three denominations in London—the Presbyterians, Independents and Baptists—entered into articles of union with each other. These articles, or, as they were entitled, "Heads of Agreement," constituted a final and entire surrender of Presbyterian principles by the ministers of that name. The example of London was speedily imitated throughout the kingdom.

The author of Magnalia Americana, speaking of the Heads of Agreement, says, "The brethren of the Presbyterian way in England are lately come into such an happy union with those of the Congregational that all former names of distinction are now swallowed up in that blessed one of 'United Brethren.' And now, partly because one of New England, namely, Mr. Increase Mather, then resident in London, was very singularly instrumental in effecting of that union, but more because that union hath been for many lustres, yea, many decades of years, exemplified in the churches of New England, so far that I believe 'tis not possible for me to give a truer description of our own ecclesiastical constitution† than by transcribing thereof, the articles of that union shall be here repeated."‡

The system developed in the articles gives the Independent definition of the particular congregation. It declares that "In the administration of church power,

* In some recent discussions the date is given as 1691. The above is according to Bogue and Bennet, vol. i., p. 381.

† The articles were formally adopted by the Association of Connecticut in 1708 (Upham's Ratio Disciplinæ, p. 311), and are usually published along with the other traditional standards of the New England churches.

‡ Magnalia Americana, vol. ii., p. 233.

it belongs to the pastor and other elders of every particular church, if such there be, to rule and govern, and to the brotherhood to consent according to the rule of the gospel." It states the office of deacon to be "of divine appointment, and that it belongs to their office to receive, lay out and distribute the church's stock to its proper uses by the direction of the pastor and brethren, if need be. And whereas divers are of opinion that there is also the office of ruling elders, who labor not in word and doctrine, and others think otherwise; we agree that this difference make no breach among us." No provision was made for stated meetings of church officers, but it was agreed, "1. That, in order to concord, and in other weighty and difficult cases, it is needful, and according to the mind of Christ, that the ministers of the several churches be consulted and advised with about such matters. 2. That such meetings may consist of smaller or greater numbers, as the matter shall require. 3. That particular churches, their respective elders and members, ought to have a reverential regard to their judgment so given, and not dissent therefrom without apparent grounds from the word of God." But to preclude any assumption of authority in these councils it was agreed, "That none of our particular churches shall be subordinate to one another, each being endued with equality of power from Jesus Christ. And that none of the particular churches, their officer or officers, shall exercise any power or have any superiority over any other church or their officers."

Thus, for no case that could arise in regard to the discipline of members or ministers was there any tribunal other than the particular church, and for possible dereliction of churches no remedy whatever was provided. It is not necessary to enter more into detail in order to demonstrate that by these articles of union the nominal Presbyterians of England definitively abandoned every feature distinctive of the Westminster polity. Of the system now inaugurated in its stead we have some illustrations in the observations of our own Samuel Davies, whose visit to England on behalf of the College of New Jersey enabled him to witness the operation of the system in its heyday of success. In his journal, writing in London, he says: "In the evening I went to the Amsterdam Coffee-house, where the Independent ministers meet for friendly conversation and to consult about the affairs of the churches, for they have no other Associations, as the Presbyterians have no other Presbyteries. Indeed, there seems to be no government exercised jointly among either of them. The English Presbyterians have no elders nor judicatories of any kind, nor seem to me to agree but in very few particulars with the Church of Scotland. I find," he further remarks, "the Calvinistic Presbyterians, as well as the Baptists, choose to frequent the Independent coffee-house, rather than associate with their Presbyterian brethren of Arminian or Socinian sentiment at Hamlin's."*

In view of the state of these churches thus developed, we might leave them, with the language of Orme, the biographer of Baxter, himself a Congregationalist. Having given a history of the union, he adds, that "from the date of this agreement Presbyterianism may

* Davies, in Foote's Sketches of Virginia, vol. i., p. 250.

be said to have existed but in name in England."* But there are lessons in the subsequent history of these churches upon which we shall briefly linger.

We have mentioned the existence of incipient heresy as one of the causes which indisposed the nominal Presbyterians of King William's time to organize their churches after the Westminster model. Arminianism had for a half century been dominant in the Established Church, and was also gradually infecting the churches of the Continent. Richard Baxter, a man eminent among the Presbyterians, alike for his talents and piety, for his invaluable practical writings, and for his sufferings under the persecutions of the Second James, had attempted to open a "middle way" between the harshness of the Reformed theology and the laxity of Arminius. The following, from Mather's Magnalia Americana, not only exhibits some of the leading features of the new system, but also the esteem in which it was held by the fathers of New England: "As in those elder days of New England the esteem which our churches had for that eminent man (Mr. Baxter) did not hinder them from rejecting that new covenant of works, with which they thought he confounded that most important article, upon the notions whereof the Church either stands or falls; thus it is a grief of mind unto our churches at this day to find that great and good man, in some of his last works, under the blinding heat of his indignation against some which we also account unjustifiable, yea, dangerous opinions and expressions, of Dr. Crisp, reproaching some of the most undoubted points of our common faith. We read him

* Orme's Life of Baxter, vol. ii., p. 350.

unaccountably enumerating among errors, which he says have corrupted Christianity and subverted the Gospel, such things as these:

"'They *feign* that God made a covenant with Adam, that if he stood God would continue him and his posterity, and if he fell God would take it as if all his posterity then personally sinned in him.' '*Feigning* God to make Adam not only the natural father and root of mankind, but also arbitrarily a constituted representer of all the persons that should spring from him. Whence they infer that Christ was, by God's imposition and his own sponsion, made the legal representative person of every one of the elect, taken singularly; so that what he did for them God reputeth them to have done by him. Hereby they falsely make the person of the Mediator to be the legal person of the sinner.' 'They *forge* a law that God never made, that saith, "Thou, *or thy surety*, shall obey perfectly, or die."' 'They *feign* God to have made an eternal covenant with his Son.' 'They *feign* Christ to have made such an exchange with the elect that having taken all their sins he hath given them all his righteousness, not only the fruit of it, but the thing in itself.' 'They say that by the imputation of Christ's righteousness, habitual and actual, we are judged perfectly just.' 'They talk of justification in mere ignorant confusion. They say that to justify is not to make righteous, but to judge righteous.' 'They err grossly, saying, that by "faith imputed for righteousness" and our "being justified by faith," is not meant the act or habit of faith, but the object, Christ's righteousness, not stickling thereby to turn such texts into worse than nonsense.'

"All these are Mr. Baxter's words, in his 'Defence of Christ,' ch. ii. These things which our churches, with amazement, behold Mr. Baxter thus calling fictions, falsehoods, forgeries, ignorant confusions and gross errors, were defended by Mr. Norton as the faith once delivered to the saints; nor do our churches at this day consider them as any other than glorious truths of the Gospel."*

The reputation of Baxter's learning and piety, and the fame of his sufferings under the persecutions of the High Commission, gave ready and extensive currency to his views, although they were met with determined opposition from the beginning. Soon after the institution of the Pinners' Hall Lectures, in 1672, the introduction there of these opinions created uneasiness, and induced some controversy with the adherents of the evangelical theology. It was not, however, until after the death of Baxter that the seeds which he had profusely sown germinated in an open rupture. About that time a work was published by the Rev. Daniel Williams, one of the most eminent of the Presbyterian party, which, under pretence of opposition to Antinomianism, strove to obscure and overturn the received doctrines of grace, and to substitute Baxterianism in their stead. The result was a heated controversy and the ultimate exclusion of Dr. Williams by the patrons of Pinners' Hall from the lectureship which he there held. The partisans of the new theology, together with many others who aspired to a character of moderation and "candor," now united in establishing a rival lectureship, which was instituted at Salters' Hall in 1694. In

* Magnalia Americana, vol. i., p. 266.

consequence of this separation, the meeting at Pinners' Hall, where the Independents were predominant, became the rallying-point of the defenders of the Calvinistic theology, whilst that at Salters' Hall was the head-quarters of the United Brethren, where the new theology was cherished and propagated.

But the pregnant character of the heresies, which had now obtained foothold and recognition, was not the only ominous indication in the United Churches. A false moderation had, in the minds of many, usurped the place of zeal for the truth. By this not a few were ensnared who were still free from the infection of doctrinal error. Under the pretence of superior "candor" and liberality of sentiment was veiled a real intolerance toward those who felt that they were set for the defence of the Gospel; and this was associated with a slothful indifference to the errors of its assailants. Carried away by this influence, some of the most eminent and excellent men of the age, themselves sound in the faith, gave their countenance to the authors of innovation, and thus lent themselves to weaken the hands of the witnesses for the truth. Such was Henry, the commentator, himself untainted with heresy, yet the biographer of Dr. Benion, to whose Neonomian theology he gives the implied sanction of publication without censure. Such was Howe, the chaplain of Cromwell, the most prominent of the Independents, who withdrew with Williams from Pinners' Hall, and aided in establishing the rival lecture. "He had truly a great soul," says Calamy, his biographer, "and at the same time a very cool and moderate spirit, and was an utter enemy to that uncharitable and censorious humor that is visible in so many. He did not look upon religion as a system of opinions, or a set of forms, so much as a divine discipline to reform the heart and life. In lesser matters he could freely give others the liberty of their own sentiments, and was as unwilling to impose as to be imposed on."* So says Dr. Calamy, his contemporary and biographer; and in describing Howe he expresses his own and the prevailing sentiments of the age. Opposition to error was stigmatized as intolerance and persecution, and earnestness in defence of the truth was looked upon as indicative of bigotry and narrowness of soul.

Near akin to this was a growing disposition to decry doctrinal preaching, and substitute in its stead the enforcement of practical duties. Since "religion was not a system of opinions, or a set of forms, so much as a divine discipline to reform the heart and life," as Calamy insists, it immediately followed that the preaching of doctrinal truth—the promulgation of systems of opinions—was unprofitable, and the preacher's business ought rather to be the laying down of appropriate rules of discipline for the reformation of the feelings and conduct.

An illustration of this disposition to supersede all doctrinal instruction presents itself in a volume of catechisms, of which we shall say more presently. In the preface parents are thus admonished: "They are considerable errors in the method of education that parents take more pains to teach their children the doctrines than the duties of religion, though the doctrines are

* Howe's Life, prefixed to his works, New York, 1835, super-royal 8vo., p. 51.

revealed for the sake of the duties; that they are more careful to instruct them in the abstruse and darker than in the plain doctrines of Christianity, though these are always the most important; that they too much neglect duties to men and those inward virtuous tempers which are the spring of these duties, though duties to men who need our love and service are as strongly insisted on in Scripture as duties to God who needs them not."*

Another circumstance conspired to facilitate the process of declension. The Heads of Agreement declared, that "As to what appertains to soundness of judgment in matters of faith, we esteem it sufficient that a Church acknowledge the Scriptures to be the word of God, the perfect and only rule of faith and practice, and own either the doctrinal part of those commonly called the Articles of the Church of England, or the Confession, or Catechisms, Shorter or Larger, compiled by the Assembly at Westminster, or the Confession agreed on at the Savoy, to be agreeable to said rule." Thus, with abounding liberality, the United Churches esteemed it sufficient to acknowledge either of five several documents to be agreeable to the word of God. But even this rule, moderate as were its demands, applied only to the churches. For the ministry no provision whatever was made. In practice the candidate drafted his own creed, on presentation of which, if satisfactory to the selected council, he was ordained. Ultimately, as liberal principles became prevalent, even this was omitted, and the whole matter was reduced to a mere profession of faith in the Scriptures as being the word of God.

A very interesting illustration of the process here

* Bourn's Catechisms, p. 23.

indicated is presented in a work to which allusion has already been made—a volume of catechisms for the instruction of children and youth, published during the progress of the apostasy by Mr. Samuel Bourn. It consists of a short and a large doctrinal and an historical catechism from the pen of Mr. Bourn, to which is added an edition of the Westminster Shorter Catechism, altered and amended. In the preface we are informed that "'Tis now generally thought that the religious principles set forth in the Bible have been better understood in this present age, through the free and diligent researches of the learned, than they had been in any since the primitive times. As there are still farther advances made in critical learning, and by the later annotations on the Scriptures great improvements are made upon those that went before, no considerate person can reasonably think that in ninety years' space men of letters and study should see no cause for giving such accounts of the doctrines of revelation as would some way or other vary from what had been taught before that period, especially considering that the teachers of Christianity in this nation had been no very long while out of the Antichristian darkness; how much of their time had been taken up in defending the Reformation against the Romanists, as well as in their ordinary ministerial work, and how little they had left for thoroughly studying the inferior points of gospel divinity."*

A few of the questions of the Shorter Catechism, as here amended, will serve as a clue to the whole system. In answer to the fundamental question, What is sin? we read that "Sin is any voluntary want of conformity

* Bourn, p. 276.

to or transgression of the law of God." "The fall brought mankind into a state of sin, as in consequence of the fall men are born with less perfect constitutions than Adam was created with, were more liable to do evil and less able and disposed to do good, which became an unhappy inlet to actual transgressions and habits of wickedness." "God having out of his mere good pleasure purposed from eternity to show special favor to mankind, did enter into a covenant of grace," etc. "Effectual calling is the work of God's Spirit, by which in concurrence with his Word and providence and our own sincere endeavors he so convinceth us of our sin and misery, and enlightens our minds in the knowledge of Christ, and renews our wills, as to persuade and enable us to embrace Jesus Christ freely offered to us in the Gospel." "Justification is that act of the free grace or favor of God wherein he pardoneth all our sins and accepteth us as righteous in his sight, through Jesus Christ, upon our believing in him." "Faith in Jesus Christ is such a firm and hearty persuasion of the truth of his Gospel as is productive of obedience to it." One additional answer will complete the outline and reveal the landing-place of this scheme. Instead of the Westminster question on the Trinity we have the inquiry, "Do not the Scriptures give an account of more divine persons than one? The Scriptures give an account of Father, Son and Holy Ghost, and that this holy Trinity were entirely united in completing the most glorious of all God's works."

The first open avowal of Arianism was in Exeter, where the Rev. James Pierce, after much trouble and the call of repeated councils, was excluded from the church of which he had charge for refusal to preach the doctrine of the Trinity. He had previously maintained an obstinate silence on that subject, but immediately upon his exclusion erected a separate congregation, and proclaimed his Arian sentiments. In London the defection was less rapid and extensive than in the country, although the poison was, there, too, spreading its secret infection. In 1730, of forty-four Presbyterian ministers in the city, nineteen were professed Calvinists, twelve Baxterians, and thirteen Arminians—not one avowed Arian. Yet among them was Lardner, who became an Arian and died a Socinian. Others followed in the same course.

As the defection originated in the doctrinal views of leading Presbyterian divines, so several circumstances conspired to induce its development, particularly among the churches of that name. Their union with the Independents had stripped them of every safeguard of their own system, without compensating them with even the feebler barriers of Independency. The moral power of the latter system is essentially dependent upon a conscientious conviction of the divine right, and consequent duty of each congregation to exercise the functions of government and discipline over its own officers and members, irrespective and independent of any other tribunal. Repudiating as they did this opinion, it was not to be expected that the Presbyterian churches should assume the exercise of functions and the burden of responsibilities, such as those of persecution for heresy, which were odious in themselves, and not enforced by their own conscientious opinions as to the order of God's house. Hence, the authors of innovation were much less liable to be brought to account in a Presbyterian than in an Independent Church.

The respectable social rank of the Presbyterian body,* and the rich endowments which it gradually accumulated, were also a snare to its own people and an inducement to the corrupt and designing to unite with it. The reputation of tolerance and "candor" naturally caused the erroneous to coalesce with the Presbyterian churches rather than with the stricter Independents, with whom, on the other hand, the faithful ministers and people of God everywhere sided. Any churches, of whatever antecedents, in which the new doctrines became prevalent, readily arrayed themselves under the respectable and tolerant banner, on the folds of which was inscribed the Presbyterian name. On the contrary, individuals who loved the truth withdrew from the backsliding churches, and united with Independent congregations. Sound parts of Arian congregations, separating themselves, formed Independent churches, and whole congregations, as their pulpits became vacant, sought Independent pastors and assumed that name.

Such is the history of the Socinian apostasy of the nominal Presbyterians of England. Beginning in the theological aberrations of the sainted Baxter, it ended in blasphemies against the Son and Spirit of God. Starting out with a denial of the imputation of Adam's sin, of the vicarious satisfaction of Christ, and of the imputation of his obedience and sufferings, nourished by lax principles on the subject of subscription to the

* See Davies' Journal, in Foote's Virginia, pp. 245, 253.

Confession, and free from the trammels of a scriptural discipline, its fatal career was quickly run. Traversing the systems of Arminius and Pelagius, its nominal results were reached in the utter denial of the divinity of Christ and of the existence of the Holy Spirit of grace.

That apostasy is the constant appeal of Congregational writers in proof that Presbyterianism is no protection against fatal heresies, and the Heads of Agreement are the favorite resort of our New School brethren in tracing the origin of that liberal policy which they so much admire. The facts of this history preclude both of these appeals. The "liberal Presbyterianism" of England originated in a compelled Independency. Its organization never was Presbyterian, but was the original of Congregationalism, and it resulted in Socinian heresy and a return to Independency.

CHAPTER II.

THE GENERAL PRESBYTERY.

Makemie — His times in Ireland and Scotland — Persecutions — Effects on his character—Scene of his labors—Variety of his employments—Rev. Nathaniel Taylor—Ninian Beall and Upper Marlborough—Religious liberty in the Middle Colonies—Rev. John Wilson—His Scotch correspondence—Rev. Samuel Davis—Rev. Jedidiah Andrews and the church in Philadelphia—They were Presbyterians—Rev. John Hampton and Rev. George Macnish—Occasion of forming the Presbytery—Its constituents—No constitution adopted—Designed as an evangelic society.

At a meeting of the Presbytery of Lagan, in the north of Ireland, held in December, 1680, a communication was received from "Colonel Stevens, in Maryland, beside Virginia," asking for a minister for that region. In the preceding January the Rev. T. Drummond had introduced to the Presbytery Mr. Francis Makemie, of the neighborhood of Ramelton, in Donegal, as a candidate for the ministry. He was probably now a graduate of Glasgow University. "*Franciscus Makemius, Scoto-Hybernus*,"* was enrolled a student therein in 1675. He was licensed by the Presbytery in 1681, and subsequently ordained, says Reid, "on the call of Colonel Stevens." The date of his ordination is unknown, as the records of the Presbytery are a

* A Scotch-Irishman.

blank for several years after his licensure.* That was the darkest hour in the history of the martyr Church of Scotland. When Makemie entered the university of Glasgow in 1675, Lauderdale and Sharpe were busy devising and executing those atrocious measures against the Church which even Sir Walter Scott asserts might have been suggested by Satan himself, and which pressed more and more heavily in the following years. In 1678 the "Highland Host" was brought down upon the people, and its atrocities may have been witnessed by Makemie himself, as they passed through Glasgow. Grahame of Claverhouse began his bloody career the next year, and when Makemie was licensed, in 1681, the Duke of York, afterward King James, was himself in Scotland superintending and stimulating the zeal of the persecutors, and feasting his own eyes with the personal inspection of the agonies of his victims under the tortures of the boot.

Ireland was at this time comparatively at rest. But the Presbytery of Lagan having, in 1681, appointed a fast, no doubt with reference to the state of public affairs, they were harassed with prosecutions, fines and imprisonments, and in consequence there remain for several years no records of their proceedings. During this interval Makemie was ordained, and from the mode in which in a passage presently to be cited he refers to that service as performed by "godly, learned and judicious discerning men," without speaking of the Presbytery distinctively, it seems probable that the meeting was not a regular session of that body, but a private

* Reid's History of the Presbyterian Church in Ireland, vol. ii., p. 324.

assembly of such of the members as were able to convene.

Of the ordination services the only information we have is contained in his own "Answer to George Keith's Libel on a Catechism published by F. Makemie." In this publication he says: "I am constrained to justify my office from these uncharitable calumnies, and, that grace might be magnified, by giving this relation, in the sight of an all-seeing and all-present God; that, ere I received the imposition of hands, in that scriptural and orderly way of separation unto my holy and ministerial calling, I gave requiring satisfaction, to godly, learned and judicious discerning men, of a work of grace and conversion wrought in my heart, by the Holy Spirit, in my fourteenth year, by and from the pains of a godly schoolmaster, who used no small diligence in gaining tender souls to God's service and fear; since which time, to the glory of God's free grace be it spoke, I have had the sure experiences of God's dealings with me, according to his infinite and unerring wisdom, for my unspeakable comfort."*

Thus early grounded in the faith by a personal experience of its power, educated amid the scenes of a bitter persecution, trained and brought forward by a pastor, Mr. Drummond† who had lain in prison six years for the testimony of the Gospel; ordained to the work of missions upon a call to go to the far-off wilds of the new world,—Makemie went forth at the voice of God,

* Webster's History of the Presbyterian Church, p. 299.

† Whence did Drummondtown, Accomac county, Va., the scene of Makemie's early labors, derive its name, if not from that of this gentleman?

not knowing whither he went, but strong in faith, and bearing aloft the banner of the cross, inscribed with that noble legend most fitting to become the motto of the Church which his labors founded: *Preces et lachrymæ arma sunt ecclesiæ:* "*Prayers and tears are the arms of the Church.*"*

In this, his early history we have the secret of the devotion to the doctrines of our standards which inspired Makemie's noble testimony in the presence of Cornbury: "As to our doctrines, my lord, we have our Confession of Faith, which is known to the Christian world, and I challenge all the clergy of York† to show us any false or pernicious doctrines therein." Here, too, is the source of that lofty and magnanimous spirit which dictated his memorable reply to the demands of the petty tyrant, that he and Hampton should give bond and security for their good behavior, and "also bond and security to preach no more in my government."‡ "As to our behavior," said Makemie, "though we have no way broke it, endeavoring always so to live 'as to keep a conscience void of offence toward God and man,' yet, if your lordship requires it, we would give security for our behavior; but to give bond and security to preach no more in your Excellency's government, if invited and desired by any people, we neither can nor dare do."§ Noble words! Worthy of record beside those of the great Reformer at Worms! Such

* The motto of Makemie's sermon in New York, for preaching which he was imprisoned by Cornbury.—*Presbyterian Magazine*, vol. ii., p. 37.

† That is, of New York, called York throughout his "Narrative."

‡ Makemie's Narrative, in Hill's History, p. 177.

§ Makemie, in Hill, p. 178.

was the man who laid the foundations of our Church. May she ever be true to his devoted spirit!

Makemie's ordination and removal to America probably occurred in 1682, or early in 1683, as it took place in response to the application of Colonel Stevens, which was received in December, 1680. On the 2d of April, 1682, he preached for the Rev. William Hampton, of Burt, in Donegal,* and on the 22d of July, 1684, writes a letter from Elizabeth River, Va., to the Rev. Increase Mather, of Boston, from the tenor of which it is evident that he had been already some time in America.†

Colonel William Stevens, at whose invitation Makemie came, was a resident of Rehoboth, Md., a judge of the county court, deputy-lieutenant of the province, and one of the lord proprietary's council. The lower part of the eastern shore of Maryland was early settled by refugees from the persecutions in Scotland.‡ It was on their behalf that Stevens' letter was written, and probably among them Makemie's first labors were employed. "There is record evidence of the fact that there were five church edifices and as many organized Presbyterian congregations in Somerset county on the 13th day of May, 1705"§—those of Snow Hill, Pitt's Creek, Wicomico, Monokin and Rehoboth—gathered, without doubt, by the labors of Makemie, as there is no evidence of any other minister preceding him there. In Virginia his stated ministrations ex-

* Reid, vol. ii., p. 324. † See the letter in Webster, p. 297.

‡ Spence's Letters on the Early History of Presbyterianism in America, p. 80.

§ Spence, p. 82.

tended to Accomac county, on the eastern shore, and to Lynnhaven, on Elizabeth River, in Princess Ann county. Here was a church organized some years before Makemie's coming. Its nameless Irish pastor died in August, 1683, and Makemie being providentially driven into that port on a voyage of exploration from Maryland to Ashley river, in South Carolina, he was induced "to stay that season." He was still there in the summer of 1685, and at his death had property in the place.*

Abundant thus in his ministerial labors Makemie supported himself by commerce, in which he seems to have been extensively engaged. In fact, if we may believe Cornbury, his employments were even still more various. "He is a Jack-of-all-trades. He is a preacher, a doctor of physic, a merchant, an attorney, a counsellor-at-law, and, which is worst of all, a disturber of governments."† "You, sir, know law?" demanded Cornbury of him, in surprise at the clearness of his defence when impeached of preaching contrary to law. "I do not, my lord, pretend to know law; but I pretend to know this particular law, having had sundry disputes thereon."‡ He needed to know the law, for "it is a matter of tradition that he suffered often under the laws of Virginia. 'He durst not deny preaching, and hoped he never should, while it was wanting and desired.'"§ Thus he became "a disturber

* Webster, pp. 297, 298. Foote's Sketches, i., p. 45.

† Cornbury to the Lords Commissioners of Trade and Plantations, in Webster, p. 307.

‡ Makemie's Narrative, in Hill, p. 179.

§ Foote's Sketches, part i., p. 47.

of governments," a true follower of Him who "came not to send peace on the earth, but a sword."

One of the earliest of Makemie's fellow-laborers was Nathaniel Taylor, of Upper Marlborough, Maryland. Colonel Ninian Beall had fled from persecution in Scotland and found a refuge in Maryland. As early as 1689 he was already a prominent man in the colony.* "Some years after his arrival he made a purchase of several large tracts of land from the tribe of Piscataway Indians. On one of these tracts he laid out the town of Upper Marlborough, and there fixed his residence. Remembering that he had a large number of relations at home subjected to the same sufferings from which he had escaped, he wrote to his friends to come over to Maryland and participate in his happiness, urging it upon them, at the same time, to bring with them a faithful minister of the Gospel. They arrived some months afterward, accompanied by the Rev. Mr. Taylor, their pastor."† The date of his arrival is unknown. All the circumstances would indicate it to have been some time before the beginning of the seventeenth century. His church was known on the records indifferently as Marlborough and Patuxent.

In Virginia toleration was allowed to Dissenters only where the sterile soil refused a sufficient crop of tobacco to stimulate the cupidity of the parsons of the Establishment. "'Tis observed," says Beverly, writing in 1705, "that those counties where the Presbyterian meetings are produce very mean tobacco, and for that

* Webster, p. 68, note.

† Rev. Dr. Balch, in the Princeton Review, 1840, p. 346. Mrs. Balch was descended from Colonel Beall.

reason can't get an orthodox minister to stay among them."* In Maryland religious liberty, secured by a charter from a Protestant king to a Catholic proprietary, invited extensive immigration from Ireland and Scotland. In Pennsylvania, too, and the Jerseys religious liberty, a fertile soil and a salubrious climate attracted the steps of many of the exiles of persecution.

At New Castle, Delaware, which was then attached to Pennsylvania, was a congregation of which the Rev. John Wilson was the pastor. His coming must have been at an early date, as already, in 1686, William Huston had by will left to Wilson and his successors a tract of land of three hundred acres on Christiana Creek, four or five miles from New Castle.†

About 1702, having some cause of dissatisfaction, he withdrew from the church at New Castle; but, in 1703 returned. His Scotch origin is indicated by his being appointed by the Presbytery in 1707 to correspond with Scotland for the purpose of securing a minister for Lewes, Delaware. He and Mr. Makemie were appointed to write to Scotland to Mr. Alexander Coldin, minister of Oxam, of the Presbytery of ——, to signify the earnest desires of the people in and about Lewestown for his coming over to be their minister. "The Presbytery appoints Mr. John Wilson to write to the Presbytery of —— to the effect aforesaid, and make a report of his care herein against the next Presbytery."‡

Mr. Makemie may have been personally acquainted

* Beverly, in Foote, i., p. 51.

† Colonial Documents, in Webster, p, 311.

‡ Records of the Presbyterian Church, p. 10.

with Mr. Coldin, who was reported to the Scotch Assembly, in 1689, as a minister in regular standing in the Irish Church; and enumerated with others who were then supposed to be in Scotland.*

Again, when, in 1710, the General Presbytery opened correspondence with the Presbytery of Dublin and the Synod of Glasgow, the Rev. John Henry, who had been received, the previous year, from Dublin Presbytery, was appointed to write to that body; and Mr. Wilson and Mr. James Anderson were the committee to correspond with the latter.† Mr. Anderson had been ordained and sent out, as a missionary to America, by the Presbytery of Irvine, in the Synod of Glasgow.

It is impossible to account for the prominent position given to Wilson in this Scotch correspondence,—preferred to all the other members of the Presbytery, and placed in marked precedence over Makemie and Anderson, unless we suppose him to have been from Scotland.

Samuel Davis was another Presbyterian minister, residing in Delaware, at the close of the seventeenth century. He was, however, so absorbed in trade as to prevent his fulfilling the duties of a pastor. He preached occasionally at Lewes, and was present at the organization of the Presbytery; which, however, he attended but once afterward. Of his origin and history but little further is known.

Philadelphia was visited by Makemie, in 1692, but no marked results seem to have followed. It was not

* Reid, ii., p. 513.

† Records of Presbyterian Church, p. 19.

until the summer of 1698, that Mr. Andrews removed to that place and commenced his labors. He was from Massachusetts, a graduate of Harvard, in 1695. He was probably ordained by an occasional Presbytery, in the fall or winter of 1701. His Record of Baptisms and Marriages, begins, 1701, tenth month,* fourteenth day. Says Talbot, the Church missionary at Burlington, writing April 24, 1702,—"The Presbyterians, here, come a great way, to lay hands on one another. . . . In Philadelphia one pretends to be a Presbyterian, and has a congregation to which he preaches."† In 1703, Keith writes from Philadelphia, "They have here a Presbyterian meeting and minister,—one called Andrews, but they are not likely to increase here."‡ It thus appears, that, although Andrews was from New England, he and his people were avowed Presbyterians some years before the organization of the Presbytery.

Two other names make up the list of those who were connected with the Presbytery in its origin. In the summer of 1704, Makemie sailed for Great Britain, from whence he returned the next year, bringing with him John Hampton and George Macnish. Mr. Hampton may have been a relative of the Rev. William Hampton, of Burt, before mentioned. Macnish is stated by Reid to have been from Ulster, a representation which is perfectly consistent with the unquestionable evidence that he was a native of Scotland. So intimate was the relation between the churches in the

* "Tenth month,"—December. The year formerly began with the 25th of March.

† Hawkins' Missions of the English Church, in Webster, p. 314.

‡ Keith, in Gillett's History of the Presbyterian Church, vol. i., p. 21.

two countries, that such translations were of constant occurrence.

Probably, the return of Makemie from this voyage was the occasion for the organization of the Presbytery. He had brought with him a considerable reinforcement to the ministry in the field, including, it is believed, not only Messrs. Hampton and Macnish, but Mr. John Boyd, a licentiate, who was soon after ordained. He had secured the promise of the London ministers, "to undertake the support of two itinerants, for the space of two years, and, after that, to send two more, on the same conditions, allowing the former, after that time to settle."* These were considerations which could not but stimulate the scattered Presbyterians to new interest and encouragement in their labors, and suggest to them the importance of organization, in order to avail themselves efficiently of the advantages thus presented, and to exercise a judicious supervision over the itinerant labors about to be bestowed upon the field.

The first leaf of the records of the Presbytery is lost, so that we are uninformed as to the time and place of the first meeting, and the members then present. As it appears in the defective record, the body, in 1706, consisted of Messrs. Francis Makemie, Moderator, Jedidiah Andrews, John Hampton, John Wilson, Nathaniel Taylor, George Macnish, and Samuel Davis. The first remaining minutes are occupied with the trials and ordination of Mr. John Boyd, which took place in December, 1706. He was a native of Scotland, and

* Records of Presbyterian Church, p. 20.

labored at Freehold and Middletown, New Jersey, where he died, in 1708.*

About fifteen congregations were, at first, connected with the Presbytery; of which two were in Virginia, six in Maryland, five in Pennsylvania and Delaware, and two in New Jersey. With one exception, these all seem to have been composed of Scotch and Irish emigrants. Mr. Andrews' church was "made up of divers nations."†

It has been common to represent the Presbytery as originally organized, by a compromise between Presbyterians and Congregationalists. But, there is not a trace of evidence that any member of the body was a Congregationalist, or, that any one of them, except Andrews, was from New England; and he was an Old Side Presbyterian.

Of any defined principles or terms of union, or formal constitution, adopted by the Presbytery, we have no intimation. Certainly, there was no act or record formally adopting the Westminster Standards.‡ "As far as I know," said the Rev. John Thomson, "we have not any particular system of doctrines, composed by ourselves or others, which we, by any judicial act of our Church, have adopted to be the articles or confession of our faith, etc. Now, a church without a confession, what is it like? It is true, as I take it, we all generally acknowledge and look upon the Westminster Confession and Catechisms to be our confession, or what we own for such; but the most that can be said is, that

* Webster, p. 323.

† Andrews' Letter to Colman, in Webster, p. 105.

‡ See Assembly's Digest, p. 25.

the Westminster Confession of Faith is the confession of the faith of the generality of our members, ministers and people; but, that it is our confession as we are a united body politic, I cannot see, unless it hath been received by a conjunct act of the representatives of the Church."*

In fact, the transaction in which our Church organization, on this continent, originated, seems to have been of the simplest and most unpretending nature. Certain brethren, who knew each other, as Presbyterians of the Westminster Confession, and who had been accustomed to meet and consult together, occasionally and informally as on occasion of Andrews' ordination, now found the interests of the cause of Christ to demand more formal and stated deliberations, and, therefore, determined to meet annually, for the transaction of business, without alluding to the circumstance,—or, perhaps, even in their own minds adverting to it,—that they were, in fact, marking the lines of a new and distinct division of the camps of Israel. They knew and mutually recognized each other, as men sworn and faithful to the truth, as set forth in the Westminster symbols. And the very unquestioned familiarity of the fact precluded the suggestion of its being formally placed upon record, until the circumstances of the growing Church, and dangers threatening from without, called attention to the necessity. They regarded themselves, in fact, as only a branch of the Church of Scotland, subject to its constitution, and dependent upon its patronage, and therefore did not need to adopt a constitution for themselves.

Whilst the records are silent on this point, there is

* Digest, p. 28.

another on which they are explicit. The distinct design of the fathers of our Church, in organizing themselves into a Presbytery, was the erection of an evangelic society,—an executive organ for the propagation of the Gospel. In a letter, addressed to Sir Edmund Harrison, of London, in May, 1709, they set forth the deplorable condition, spiritually, of the colonies; and urged the Christian people of London to come to their help. "The negotiation begun and encouraged by a fund, in the time when our worthy friend, Mr. Makemie, now deceased, was with you, for evangelizing these colonies, was a business exceeding acceptable to a multitude of people, and was likely to have been of great service, if continued; which makes us much grieved that so valuable a design was so soon after its beginning, laid aside. The necessity of carrying on the same affair being as great, if not greater, now, than it was then, we hope that our patrons in London will revive so good and important a work, and not let it lie buried under the ashes. . . . That our evangelical affairs may be the better managed, we have formed ourselves into a Presbytery, annually to be convened at this city; at which times, it is a sore distress and trouble unto us, that we are not able to comply with the desires of sundry places, crying unto us for ministers, to deal forth the word of life unto them. Therefore, we must earnestly beseech you, in the bowels of our Lord, to intercede with the ministers of London, and other well-affected gentlemen, to extend their charity and pity to us, and to carry on so necessary and glorious a work."*

Let it never be forgotten that our Church was des-

* Letter in Records of Presbyterian Church, p. 16.

tined, in its very origin, and erected, to be an evangelical society, to conduct under its own supervision, the business of giving the Gospel to the world. In this capacity, and with this intent, not only were the labors of these men of God multiplied and untiring, but their applications for ministers and the means of their support, until settled here, were assiduous and importunate, to the London ministers, and to the Presbytery of Dublin, and the Synod of Glasgow; to the former of whom, they through Sir Edmund Harrison of London first wrote in 1709, and to the latter, in 1710; and repeatedly afterward.

CHAPTER III.

THE ADOPTING ACT.

Growth of the Presbytery—Twelve Glasgow collegians—Scotch ecclesiastical order observed—Synod subdivided—Subscription controversy, in Ireland—The Belfast society—Defections in Switzerland, England and Scotland—The Irish Pacific Act—Controversy—Exclusion of the non-subscribers—They lapse into Unitarianism—Subscription in New Castle Presbytery—New elements in the Synod—Thomson's overture—What he proposed—Causes of distrust among the "English and Welsh"—Surmises of Andrews—Dickinson's opposition—Moderation of the Synod—The Synod of 1729—Thomson's overture committed—Preliminary Act—Adopting Act—The Directory and Discipline recommended.

THE troubles to which the Irish Church was subjected, from the machinations of the High Church party, under the countenance of Queen Anne, operated greatly to increase the strength of the infant Presbytery in America. On the 1st of August, 1716, the Rev. James Anderson writes to Dr. Sterling, Principal of Glasgow College,—"In this country there are, since I came here, (seven years,) settled three other Presbyterian ministers, two of which are from your city of Glasgow. There are, in all, of ministers who meet in a Presbytery once a year, sometimes in Philadelphia, sometimes here, in New Castle, seventeen; and two probationers from the north of Ireland, whom we have under trial for ordination; twelve of which have had the most and best of their education at your famous university of Glasgow. We are mostly but young, raw, hands; yet, glory to our God! he magnifies and perfects his strength in our weakness, and makes it evident that he can work wonders of grace, by poor means and insignificant instruments.

"As to our proceedings, in matters of public worship and discipline, we make it our business to follow the Directory of the Church of Scotland, which, as well as we may, we own as our mother Church. We make it our business to settle, and to make settlements for, ministers of our persuasion, that join with us, in places where the Gospel has either never at all been preached, or else, in places where there are wretched, profane, debauched, careless creatures of the Bishop of London, of which there has been not a few, and yet are, within the bounds of these provinces, whence some of our brethren meet;* which is the reason of our meeting with many hardships and difficulties, both from the inconveniences of our congregations and the opposition of inverate enemies."†

A few weeks after the writing of this letter, the Presbytery erected itself into a Synod. On the 21st of September, 1716, it recorded that, "it having pleased Divine Providence so to increase our number, as that, after much deliberation, we judge it may be more serviceable to the interest of religion, to divide ourselves.

* Dr. Hawks, in his "Contributions to the Ecclesiastical History of the United States," fully confirms and illustrates the justice of this account of the early clergy of Maryland and Virginia.

† See the letter in Presbyterian Magazine, vol. i., p. 278.

into subordinate meetings or Presbyteries, constituting one annually as a Synod, to meet at Philadelphia or elsewhere, to consist of all the members of each subordinate Presbytery or meeting, for this year at least,—therefore it is agreed by the Presbytery, after serious deliberation, that the first subordinate meeting or Presbytery, to meet at Philadelphia or elsewhere, as they shall see fit, do consist of the following members, viz.: Masters Andrews, Jones, Powell, Orr, Bradner, and Morgan. And the second, to meet at New Castle or elsewhere as they shall fit, to consist of these, viz.: Masters Anderson, McGill, Gillespie, Wotherspoon, Evans, and Conn. The third, to meet at Snowhill or elsewhere, to consist of these, viz.: Masters Davis, Hampton and Henry. And, in consideration that only our brethren, Mr. Macnish and Mr. Pumry, are of our number upon Long Island, at present,—we earnestly recommend it to them to use their best endeavors with the neighboring brethren, that are settled there, which, as yet, join not with us, to join with them in erecting a fourth Presbytery. And as to the time of the meeting of the respective Presbyteries, it is ordered that it be left to their own discretion.

"Ordered, that a book be kept, by each of the said Presbyteries, containing a record of their proceedings, and that the said book be brought, every year, to our anniversary Synod to be revised."*

The endeavors of the Long Island brethren were successful. The Rev. George Phillips, of Setauket, joined with them, and the Presbytery was organized. On the other hand, the Rev. Mr. Henry died within

* Records of Presbyterian Church, p. 45.

the year and the Snowhill Presbytery was merged in that of New Castle.

At this time, questions had arisen in the Irish Church, which were destined to have an important bearing upon the interests of the infant Church in America.

We have seen the development, among the English Presbyterians, of a tendency to lax theology, spreading its contagion from the Continent, about the beginning of the eighteenth century. In the Irish Church, the adoption of the Westminster standards, by intrants into the ministry, had been universally customary, but the old book of Minutes having been lost, there was no recorded regulation on the subject, until 1698, when it was made a rule, by unanimous vote of the General Synod of Ulster, that no young man be licensed to preach the Gospel, till "he subscribe the Confession of Faith, in all the articles thereof, as the confession of his faith."*

For some years, this rule continued to be observed, without question or hesitation. But, in 1705, the Belfast Society was formed, consisting of a number of talented young ministers and others, all of whom were more or less tainted with the "liberal" spirit of the age.

"In this society were first promulgated many opinions, hitherto new in Ireland, which, being at variance with both the doctrine and constitution of the Presbyterian Church, naturally excited, so soon as they became known, much attention; and gradually created no little disaffection and alarm. The opinions did not directly impugn any of the leading doctrines of the Gospel, as embodied in the Church's Confession of Faith; but

* Reid, vol. iii., p. 12.

they tended to undermine the entire system of a sinner's acceptance, as taught therein; by placing that acceptance, mainly, on sincerity; by inculcating the innocency of error, when not willful; and by undervaluing all belief in positive doctrines, as uncertain, or, at all events, as non-essential. In reference to ecclesiastical discipline, the members of the society taught, among other things, that the Church had no right to require candidates for the ministry to subscribe a confession of faith, prepared by any man or body of men; and that such a required subscription was a violation of the right of private judgment, and inconsistent with Christian liberty and true Protestantism."*

Most of these opinions were already prevalent in the Presbyterian churches of Switzerland; and became the precursors of the Socinian apostasy of these churches. In England, the writings of Whiston, Clarke and Hoadley, and the discussions at Salters' Hall, were preparing the way, by the prevalence of these sentiments, for the extensive dissemination of Arian and Socinian doctrines, both in the Establishment, and among the Presbyterians. And, in Scotland, the proceedings against the Rev. John Simpson, professor of divinity in the university of Glasgow, for teaching Arminian and Pelagian errors; and the culpable lenity exercised toward him, announced the beginning of the reign of Moderatism, in that once glorious Church. That trial was terminated in the Scotch Assembly of 1717.

The agitation caused in Ireland by the debates and publications of the Belfast Society, brought the subject to the notice of the General Synod, in 1720. By it, a

* Reid, iii., 158.

paper was adopted, which is known as the Pacific Act. This Act bestowed elaborate eulogies upon the Confession, and reproved any who might have disparaged it. Then, citing an act of the General Synod, in the year 1705, which required simple subscription to the Confession,—it declared that this act was "thus to be understood, as now is practised by the Presbyteries,—that if any person, called upon to subscribe, shall scruple any phrase or phrases in the Confession, he shall have leave to use his own expressions; which the Presbytery shall accept of, providing they judge such a person sound in the faith, and that such expressions are consistent with the substance of the doctrine; and that such explications shall be inserted in the Presbytery books." *

This compromising expedient was the beginning of a bitter controversy, continued for six years, between subscribers and non-subscribers; many of whom refused to assent to any profession of faith whatever, unless couched in the very words of Scripture. At length, the General Synod, in 1726, excluded the non-subscribers from its communion. "The instructive experiment which was now tried of a non-declaring church ended in Independency, real or virtual, and what was much more deplorable, in Unitarianism. And, just in proportion as certain Presbyteries of the Synod relapsed into non-subscription, the same doctrinal errors prevailed in them; until, at the distance of a century, this state of things led to another separation,"† in 1828, resulting from extensive Socinian defection, anew developed, in the Synod.

* Reid, iii., 171. † Reid, iii., 248.

The protracted agitation in Ireland could not but arrest the attention and affect the policy of the Church in America. The movement, here, for subscription to the Westminster standards, originated with the Presbytery of New Castle. Several of the ablest members of the Synod were natives of Ireland, connected with that Presbytery. One of these, Thomas Craighead, was brother to Robert Craighead, moderator of the General Synod of Ulster, in 1719. Whilst the subscription controversy was at its height, in Ireland, that Presbytery, in 1724, entered on their records a formula, which their candidates for licensure were required to sign:—"I do own the Westminster Confession as the confession of my faith." What may have been the course of the other Presbyteries, on this subject, is unknown; as their records are lost.

Originally, as we have seen, the General Presbytery was composed almost wholly of Scotch-Irish ministers and people. But, after the distribution of its members into local Presbyteries, considerable accessions were received, particularly in New Jersey, and on Long Island, of congregations of English, Welsh, and New England people; and of ministers from New England and Wales. The connection of these ministers and churches, comparatively ignorant, as they were, of usages and questions which were familiar to the other members, rendered the matter of subscription much more delicate than, otherwise, it would have been.

In 1726, the Irish Synod excluded the non-subscribers. In 1727, the Rev. John Thomson, an Irish member of New Castle Presbytery, brought to Synod an overture, for the adoption of the Confession by the body: "We are now likely to fall into a great difference," says Andrews, (April, 1729,) "about subscribing the Westminster Confession of Faith. An overture for it, drawn up by Mr. Thomson, of Lewestown, was offered to our Synod, the year before last; but not then read in the Synod. Measures were taken to stave it off; and I was in hopes we should have heard no more of it. But, last year, it was brought again, recommended by all the Scotch and Irish members present; and, being read among us, a proposal was made, prosecuted and agreed to, that it should be deferred till our next meeting, for further consideration. The proposal is, that all ministers and intrants should sign it, or be disowned as members. Now, shall we do it? They will certainly carry it, by numbers. Our countrymen say, they are willing to join in a vote to make it the Confession of our Church; but to agree to making it a test of orthodoxy and term of ministerial communion, they will not. I think all the Scotch are on one side, and all the English and Welsh on the other, to a man." * In the interval between the Synods of 1728 and 1729, the overture was printed,† and "Remarks" upon it were published by Dickinson.‡

Thomson, in the appendix to his work on the Government of the Church, published in 1740, states the motives which actuated him in this affair:—"When it pleased our glorious and almighty King, Jesus, who has the hearts of the kings of the earth in his hands, that, as the rivers of waters are turned, he can turn them whithersoever he pleaseth, to move the hearts of our

* Letter to Colman in Hodge's History, p. 168.

† See the Overture, in Hodge, p. 162, and Assembly's Digest, p. 28.

‡ Webster, p. 106.

Synod, with such a remarkable unanimity, to adopt the Westminster Confession and Catechism, etc., it was matter of very great satisfaction to most of us, and to myself in particular, who had been, for some time before, under no small fears and perplexities of mind, lest we should be corrupted with the new schemes of doctrine, which, for some time, had prevailed in the north of Ireland; that being the part from whence we expected to be, in a great measure, supplied with new hands, to fill our vacancies in the ministry, within the bounds of our Synod." *

In the overture, Thomson represents the Church as "too much like the people of Laish, in a careless, defenceless condition, as a city without walls. (Or perhaps my unacquaintedness with our records may cause me to mistake.) For, as far as I know, though we be an entire particular Church, and not a part of a particular Church, yet we have not any particular system of doctrines, composed by ourselves or others, which we, by any judicial act of our Church, have adopted to be the articles or confession of our faith, etc. Now, a church without a confession, what is it like? It is true, as I take it, we all generally acknowledge and look upon the Westminster Confession and Catechisms to be our confession, or what we own for such. But the most that can be said is, that the Westminster Confession of Faith is the confession of the faith of the generality of our members, ministers, and people. But, that it is our confession, as we are a united body politic, I cannot see; unless, First, it hath been received by a conjunct act of the representatives of our Church; I

* Thomson's Government of the Church of Christ, p. 116.

mean, by the Synod, either before or since it hath been *sub formâ synodi*:* Secondly, unless due care be, and hath been taken that all intrants into the ministry among us have subscribed the said Confession, or, by some equivalent solemn act, *coram auctoritate ecclesiastica*,† testified the owning it as the confession of their faith; which, how far it is observed within the bounds of our Synod, I am ignorant. Now, if this be so, (for upon this supposition I speak,) I think we are in a very defenceless condition. For, if we have no Confession, which is ours by synodical act; or, if any among us have not subscribed or acknowledged the Confession, *ut supra*,‡ then, First, There is no bar provided to keep out of the ministry those who are corrupt in doctrinals; they may be received into the ministry, without renouncing their corrupt doctrines. Secondly, Those that are in the ministry among us may propagate gross errors, and corrupt many thereby; without being discovered to preach anything against the received truth, because, *supposito ut supra*,§ the truth never was publicly received among us."

He urges the danger resulting from the fact that "Arminianism, Socinianism, Deism, Free-thinking, etc., do, like a deluge, overflow even the Reformed churches, both established and dissenting;" and that the poverty of the Synod forbade its being able to plant a seminary, for the education of its own candidates; so that she must depend on other places for men to fill the vacancies; "and so are in danger of having our minis-

* In the form of a Synod.

† In the presence of ecclesiastical authority.

‡ As above.

§ Upon the above supposition.

try corrupted, by such as are leavened with false doctrine before they come among us."

"Fourthly, I am afraid there are too many among ourselves, who, though they may be sound in the faith, themselves, yet have the edge of their zeal, against the prevailing errors of the times, very much blunted; partly, by their being dispirited, and so, by a kind of cowardice, are afraid, boldly, openly, and zealously, to appear against those errors that show themselves in the world, under the patronage and protection of so many persons of note and figure; partly, by a kind of indifference and mistaken charity, whereby they think they ought to bear with others, though differing from them in opinion, about points which are mysterious and sublime, but not practical nor fundamental, such as predestination. Now, although I would grant, that the precise point of election and reprobation be neither fundamental nor immediately practical; yet, take predestination completely, as it takes in the other disputed points between Calvinists and Arminians, such as universal grace, the non-perseverance of the saints, foreseen faith and good works, etc., and I think it such an article in my creed, such a fundamental of my faith, that I know not what any other articles would avail, that could be retained without it."

For these reasons, he urges that "the Synod would, by an act of its own, publicly and authoritatively, adopt the Westminster Confession of Faith, Catechisms, etc., for the public confession of our faith, as we are a particular organized Church." That it would "make an act to oblige every Presbytery within our bounds, to oblige every candidate for the ministry, to subscribe or otherwise acknowledge, *coram presbyterio*,* the said Confession of Faith, etc., and to promise not to preach or teach contrary to it:"—"To oblige every actual minister coming among us to do the like:"—and "to enact, that, if any minister within our bounds shall take upon him to teach or preach anything contrary to any of said articles,—unless, first he propose the said point to the Presbytery or Synod, to be by them discussed,—he shall be censured, so and so."

In this paper, the suggestion that some members of the Synod were suspected of timidity and time-serving, with regard to unpopular doctrines, was naturally calculated to excite anxiety as to the design of the movement. There was, however, another intimation even more alarming. The overture urges "that secret bosom enemies of the truth, (I mean those who, being visible members of a church, do not openly and violently oppose the truth professed therein; but, in a secret covert way, endeavor to undermine it,) are as dangerous as any whatever; and, therefore, the Church should exercise her vigilance, in a special manner, against such; by searching them out, discovering them, and setting a mark upon them, whereby they may be known, and so not have it in their power to deceive."

This language, which persons familiar with the Ulster discussions, would at once recognize as being suggested by the aspects of that controversy, was, by the "English and Welsh" members of the Synod, suspected to be indicative of designs hostile to them. The "Scotch" being settled principally in Pennsylvania and southward, whilst the others were generally located in

* Before the Presbytery.

New York and New Jersey,—their intercourse was comparatively limited, and their personal knowledge of each other not sufficient to constitute a basis of perfect mutual confidence, in the presence of such issues as were here presented. What peculiar interpretations may not these Scotch brethren put upon the Confession? Is not the purpose to use the adoption of it as a means of enforcing upon the Synod whatever peculiar views they may hold on points of no significance? Or, is the design to enforce the *ipsissima verba*,* the minutest phraseology, of the Confession, in all things, on the consciences of members, and thus exclude those who cannot so receive it? "Some," says Andrews, "say the design of this motion is, to spew out our countrymen; they being scarce able to hold way with the other brethren in all their disciplinary and legislative notions. What truth there may be in this, I know not. Some deny it; whereas others say there is something in it. I am satisfied, some of us are an uneasiness to them; and are thought to be too much in their way, sometimes; so that, I think, it would be no trouble to lose some of us. Yet, I can't think this to be the thing ultimately designed; whatever smaller glances there may be at it."†

Andrews does not seem to imagine the possibility, even, of any doctrinal difference. All he is afraid of is, that some of the others may not be able to come up to the requirements of the Scotch and Irish, in "their disciplinary and legislative notions." And these, precisely, are the points that were guarded, in the proceedings connected with the Adopting Act.

* The very words. † Letter to Colman, in Hodge, p. 168.

Dickinson, in his "Remarks" upon the overture, insisted that Laish will not be bettered by the wall of subscription; that her true defence consists in a thorough examination of candidates on the work of grace in their hearts; in reviving discipline, bringing offenders to account, and being diligent in preaching the whole counsel of God.' He urges, that the Synod had already a bond of union, in the general acknowledgment of the truth; and that the enforcing of subscription is the fruitful cause of controversy and division. "Subscription, therefore, is not necessary to the being or the well-being of a church; unless hatred, variance, emulation, wrath, strife, sedition and heresies are necessary to that end."*

This would seem to have been a hasty and inconsiderate publication. The positions therein taken cannot be reconciled with Dickinson's subsequent action, and are impliedly repudiated, in publications afterward issued by him. At the erection of the Synod of New York, he and his brethren made subscription a term of union with the New Brunswick brethren. His attitude, at this time, is not, however, to be confounded with that of the non-subscribers of Ulster. They utterly refused to subscribe to any human formula of faith; as being a violation of the rights of conscience. The objections of Dickinson were grounded in expediency. To his Remarks, no reply seems to have been made. In fact, the majority of the Synod acted with great moderation and forbearance. Whilst, confessedly, an overwhelming majority were in favor of the overture,—they not only consented to waive its introduction, when first

* Webster, pp. 106, 107.

brought to the Synod, but, the next year, unanimously agreed to postpone the decision for a twelvemonth longer,—thus allowing two full years for consideration, before final action. This fact, of itself, must have convinced the other brethren, upon reflection, that no secret designs were cherished, and no extreme policy contemplated.

The minutes of 1728 record that "there being an overture presented to the Synod, in writing, having reference to the subscribing of the Confession of Faith, etc., the Synod, judging this to be a very important affair, unanimously concluded to defer the consideration of it till the next Synod; withal recommending it to the members of each Presbytery present to give timeous notice to the absent members; and it is agreed, that the next be a full Synod."* The meetings were sometimes by delegation.

When the Synod met, in 1729, although the attendance was comparatively large, Morgan, Pemberton, Webb, and Pumry, all of them New England men, were absent, a fact, which, of itself, seems to indicate that the delay, and consequent opportunity for information and mutual understanding, had induced the quieting of apprehensions, and a restoration of confidence.

Messrs. Andrews, Dickinson, Thomson, Pierson, Craighead, Conn, Budd, and the moderator, Anderson, were appointed "a committee for the fund, or any other business that the Synod shall recommend unto them."

"Ordered that the committee for the fund meet at three o'clock, P. M., together with the commissioner of

* Records, p. 91.

the Synod. Masters Andrews, Cross, Dickinson, Pierson, Craighead and Gillespie were appointed to be the Commissioners of the Synod for the ensuing year. The affair relating to the Confession, under our consideration, since our last, is referred to the committee, to draw up an overture on it." *

The engagement of the committee with the Commissioner of Synod did not prevent their being prepared to report at the opening of the sessions, next morning, a paper which received the unanimous approval of the body. "It was agreed to, *in hæc verba.*†

"Although the Synod do not claim or pretend to any authority of imposing our faith upon other men's consciences, but do profess our just dissatisfaction with, and abhorrence of such impositions, and do utterly disclaim all legislative power and authority in the Church, being willing to receive one another as Christ has received us, to the glory of God, and admit to fellowship in sacred ordinances, all such as we have grounds to believe Christ will at last admit to the kingdom of heaven, yet we are undoubtedly obliged to take care that the faith once delivered to the saints be kept pure and uncorrupt among us, and handed down to our posterity; and do, therefore, agree that all the ministers of this Synod, or that shall hereafter be admitted into this Synod, shall declare their agreement in, and approbation of, the Confession of Faith, with the Larger and Shorter Catechisms of the Assembly of Divines at Westminster, as being, in all the essential and necessary articles, good forms of sound words, and systems of Christian doctrine, and do also adopt the said Confession and Catechisms as the

* Records, p. 93.

† In these words.

confession of our faith. And we do also agree, that all the Presbyteries within our bounds shall always take care not to admit any candidate of the ministry into the exercise of the sacred function, but what declares his agreement in opinion with all the essential and necessary articles of said Confession, either by subscribing the said Confession of Faith and Catechisms, or by a verbal declaration of their assent thereto; as such minister or candidate shall think best. And, in case any minister of this Synod, or any candidate for the ministry, shall have any scruple with respect to any article or articles of said Confession or Catechisms, he shall, at the time of his making said declaration, declare his sentiments to the Presbytery or Synod; who shall, notwithstanding, admit him to the exercise of the ministry within our bounds, and to ministerial communion, if the Synod or Presbytery shall judge his scruple or mistake to be only about articles not essential and necessary, in doctrine, worship, or government. But if the Synod or Presbytery shall judge such ministers or candidates erroneous in essential and necessary articles of faith, the Synod or Presbytery shall declare them uncapable of communion with them. And the Synod do solemnly agree, that none of us will traduce, or use any opprobrious terms, of those that differ from us, in these extra-essential and not-necessary points of doctrine; but treat them with the same friendship, kindness, and brotherly love, as if they had not differed from us in such sentiments." *

This paper was adopted, says the record, "after long debating." The entire discussion, however, was closed

* Records, p. 94.

and the paper passed during the morning session, between nine and the midday adjournment.

The above paper is, on the records of the Synod, designated as its 'First, or Preliminary Act."* In the afternoon was enacted the Adopting Act.

" All the ministers of this Synod now present, except one, that declared himself not prepared, viz.: Masters Jedidiah Andrews, Thomas Craighead, John Thomson, James Anderson, John Pierson, Samuel Gelston, Joseph Houston, Gilbert Tennent, Adam Boyd, Jonathan Dickinson, John Bradner, Alexander Hutchinson, Thomas Evans, Hugh Stevenson, William Tennent, Hugh Conn, George Gillespie, and John Wilson, after proposing all the scruples that any of them had to make, against any articles and expressions in the Confession of Faith and Larger and Shorter Catechisms of the Assembly of Divines at Westminster, have unanimously agreed in the solution of those scruples, and in declaring the said Confession and Catechisms to be the confession of their faith; excepting, only, some clauses in the twentieth and twenty-third chapters; concerning which clauses, the Synod do unanimously declare, that they do not receive those articles in any such sense as to suppose the civil magistrate hath a controlling power over Synods, with respect to the exercise of their ministerial authority; or power to persecute any for their religion; or, in any sense contrary to the Protestant succession to the throne of Great Britain."

"The Synod, observing that unanimity, peace, and unity, which appeared in all their consultations and determinations relating to the affair of the Confession, did

* Records, p. 126.

unanimously agree in giving thanks to God, in solemn prayer and praises."*

Subsequently, a motion being made to know the Synod's judgment about the Directory; they gave their sense of the matter in the following words;—viz.:

"The Synod do unanimously acknowledge and declare that they judge the Directory for Worship, Discipline and Government of the Church, commonly annexed to the Westminster Confession, to be agreeable in substance to the Word of God, and founded thereupon; and therefore do earnestly recommend the same to all their members, to be by them observed, as near as circumstances will allow, and Christian prudence direct."†

Here, a significant discrimination is observable. With one specific exception, the Confession and Catechisms are adopted absolutely, without reservation, as "the confession of their faith." But respecting the Directory, they speak in different style. It, they pronounce to be "agreeable, *in substance,* to the Word of God;" and therefore, to be observed, "as near as circumstances will allow, and Christian prudence direct." The meaning of this we shall see, hereafter.‡

* Records, p. 94. † Records, p. 95. ‡ See below, p. 121.

CHAPTER IV.

THE PRELIMINARY ACT.

Diversity of opinions respecting the Act—Principles of strict and liberal subscription—The Act was no compromise—Thomson obtained just what he asked—Dickinson surrendered the only point he made—He denied the power of making laws—No one claimed it—The Preliminary Act unambiguous on some points—Why ambiguous on others—It was cautionary, till a mutual understanding could be had—The distinction of essential and non-essential true and necessary—The Adopting Act was designed to be strict—Force of the exception—Design as to adoption by candidates—Adoption in the next year's Synod—Inquiry as to compliance of Presbyteries.

No other document of our Church has elicited more discussion, as to its meaning and intent, than has the Preliminary, commonly called the Adopting Act. It has been represented as a compromise,—as ambiguous in its terms,—and as designed to admit of a considerable latitude of doctrinal sentiments among the ministry of the Church. Before entering upon the discussion of these points, it will be proper to ascertain, if possible, what is the precise question at issue, between the advocates of a liberal, and of a strict, adoption of the Confession of Faith.

The great body of the doctrines of the Confession and Catechisms, constitute a logical system, the several parts of which are so related to each other, that they must stand or fall together. The question, for example, between the doctrine of the utter inability of man since the fall, to keep the law of God, to repent of sin, or turn to God, and the doctrine that he has the natural ability, but wants the moral,—that his inability is wholly of the will, and that men could turn to God, if they would, may seem, at the first glance, a very trivial matter. Yet, when traced out to its ultimate consequences, it involves almost every doctrine of theology, every truth of the Gospel. The one view supposes the fall and ruin of the whole nature of man, in Adam; and it implies a necessity for the immediate and omnipotent agency of the Holy Spirit, creating the man anew in Christ Jesus. This, again, implies the union, by this Spirit, dwelling in them, of Christ and the believer. Thus, he, then, became responsible for his people's sins, as the sins of his own body; and standing, in this light, at the bar of justice, he was made a true and proper vicarious satisfaction for their sins, and wrought for them a perfect righteousness. They, on the other hand,—by virtue of this same union his members,—are robed in his very righteousness; and, in it, stand justified at the bar of God, and admitted to the adoption of sons, by virtue of oneness with the First-born. In every direction, we might thus trace the ramifications of this system.

The other view implies and springs from the notion, that the fall was not a depravation of man's entire nature, but only a perversion of his affections and his will; whilst his understanding and conscience are unimpaired. It involves the conclusion, that no omnipotent transforming agency is necessary, in order to the restoration of man,—that all that is requisite is, that the truth be brought convincingly before the mind, so as to determine the will, in favor of the claims of God,—that to this purpose, the Spirit is only necessary as an enlightening and persuading agent, exercising no transforming new creating power, nor acting immediately on the heart, but only, mediately, through the Word. Thus, the spiritual union of the believer and Christ is ignored and excluded, his vicarious satisfaction is thereupon denied; the doctrine of justification rejected; and the whole gospel scheme overthrown. The very nature and holiness of God, himself, are presented in a false and distorted light, from these premises; as, his is conceived to be a justice that may be set aside, and a mercy that strives against and overcomes justice; for sin is supposed to be pardoned, without satisfaction to the law; and sinners are saved, although the records of justice still for ever exhibit the uncanceled charges against them.

Such are the logical connections of these several opinions respecting the question of man's inability by nature. And these diverse consequences, not only result from the specific positions taken upon that point, but each several proposition, in these two schemes implies and logically demands all the others, in them respectively. If the skillful naturalist is able, from a single bone, to reconstruct the entire animal to which it belonged, even though, before, nondescript,—much more certainly, can the intelligent theologian from any specific proposition, on what may be regarded, popularly, as the minor points in systematic theology, determine the system to which it belongs, and reconstruct the entire scheme. Not only is this the case; but, it is farther true, in the history of doctrine, that all departures from the faith, perhaps, without exception, have originated in error on some one of these subordinate points. Men do not, at once, apostatize from the great cardinal truths of the Gospel, until, first, their faith has been perverted and the foundations removed, by error cherished on some of the subordinate related truths.

It is in view of these facts and principles that their position is taken, by those who advocate the enforcing of a strict adoption of the Confession of Faith, by the ministry of the Church. They do not mean to assert, that everything contained in the Confession is infallibly true. The question, for example, whether the production of the universe out of nothing, took place within the six natural days of the Mosaic record,—the question of the marriage of a deceased wife's sister,—such as these, are questions, simply, of biblical interpretation, as to points of history and law, the decision of which, however made, affects in no wise, any one doctrine of the sytem of revealed and saving truth; whether as to the nature of God or of man, the nature and demerit of sin, or the plan of salvation. Some errors, therefore, on such points may be tolerated without danger to the Gospel.

Strict subscribers, further, do not mean to assert that the language of the Confession is, in all cases, unquestionably the best that could be selected, to state the scriptural truth, on the subjects presented. This idea is precluded by the fact that the same doctrines are stated in the Constitution, in three several forms,—in the Confession and the two Catechisms;—to which the Westminster Assembly, and the Scotch Church added a fourth, in "The Sum of Saving Knowledge," which they appended to the other standards.

But the position taken by those who insist upon a strict adoption of the Confession is, that, whilst due allowance is made for the imperfection of man, which attaches to all he does, yet the doctrines, all of them, of the connected system set forth in the Confession, are the very and infallible truth of God, and gospel of salvation. In this view, they comprehend, not only the confessedly great truths, but those of minor consideration; as divinely revealed, necessary to the others, and parts of the system; which, without them, must fall to pieces. Besides these, another consideration enters into the position thus stated. When the Church shall have been supplied with a ministry, who have been admitted on the ground of permitting some unimportant departures from the system of the standards, these will be bound, in consistency, to admit others, whose position is a little farther removed than their own. Otherwise, they set up their own schemes, as more sacred and binding than that of the Confession itself; as they claim for themselves the right to go beyond the bounds set by it. The second generation would therefore depart a little farther than the first; and so on, until utter apostasy is the inevitable result; as is demonstrated, by too many lamentable instances.

Thus, the position of those who require strict adoption, is easily ascertained and defined. Those, on the contrary, who insist upon more liberal terms—rejecting the standard given in the Confession, are set afloat, without the possibility of defining, or taking, any specific position, as to the extent to which divergence is to be allowed. Whilst some would resist any very serious departure, others would claim the right to reject everything, but "the great doctrines." Of this, we shall have, in the subsequent history, abundant illustrations.

We return to the consideration of the Preliminary Act. Was the paper a compromise? If, by this word, it is intended that the language was carefully weighed and guarded, so as to avoid just objections from those who hesitated upon the measure, it is readily conceded. But if, by compromise, it be meant that, in deference to opposing sentiments, the supporters of Thomson's overture waived any of their claims, or accepted, or were supposed to accept, less than was asked in that paper, we see not a shadow of ground for the assumption. What was the question at issue between the author and opposers of the overture? Thomson's proposal was that the Confession be adopted as the confession of faith of the Church; and that if any minister take upon him to teach or preach anything contrary to any of its articles, "*unless first he propose the said points to the Presbytery or Synod to be by them discussed*," he shall be censured. Here, evidently, it was distinctly contemplated, that more or less diversity of sentiment must be expected to exist, upon some points, among those who could cordially unite in the adoption of the Confession. It is assumed that disagreement with that standard, within certain limits, was allowable; whilst greater departures would be censurable; and the extent of allowable departure was left, as yet, undefined. Further, the Presbytery and Synod are designated, to the exclusion of individual private judgment, as entitled, first, to determine that question, in each case, as it should arise. Such was the whole extent of the demand of the Scotch members; in precise accordance with what we have above stated, as to the difference between questions of systematic theology and those statements of the Confession which relate to history, law, ethics, and order.

On the other hand, as we have seen, Dickinson arrayed himself, absolutely, against subscription, in any form whatever; a position which was, no doubt, hastily taken; and which was undoubtedly surrendered, altogether, by him, in consenting to the Adopting Act. This point being given up, there was really no further room for controversy. When the parties came to understand each other, the whole matter reduced itself to a question of words. The author of "Dickinson on the Five Points" had not acted in the interest of a lax theology. His objection was not to the importance and necessity of soundness in the faith, nor to the authority of the Church to insist on and enforce it. This he strenuously urged, in his very argument against the overture. What he denied was the efficacy of adopting the Confession, as a public standard, in securing this. And, the question on that point being yielded, he only further required that the adoption should be in such form as would not tend to infringe the liberty of God's people, by any seeming usurpation of the regal authority of Christ. This was accomplished by the distinct repudiation of any such authority, stated in the preamble to the Preliminary Act; and by the allowance that absolute agreement with the Confession was not necessary, on non-essential points; guarding, at the same time, the door thus opened, by the express provision that the Presbyteries and Synod were to be the judges of what, in the Confession, is immaterial, and what essential. But, in all this, there was no compromise, on the part of the advocates of subscription. They had not asked the Synod to assume to itself power to add to the law of Christ; nor proposed to exalt the Confession to a level with his Word. As promptly as any, would they have united in resisting, even to death, any such attempt. What was granted in the Adopting Acts, was precisely what the overture proposed; and it was, therefore, so cordially accepted by the authors of that paper.

But the Preliminary Act is charged with ambiguity. There are certain points in it, set forth, it will be admitted, with unambiguous clearness.—That the Confession, as a whole, is in accordance with the Word of God. —That it is not infallibly true, in all its details.—That all the doctrines therein contained are not of equal importance; but that whilst some forms of error are comparatively harmless, there are others of more serious import.—That there is, therefore, room for allowable and innocent diversity of sentiment, among the ministry, on some points; and necessity for agreement on others; and that no individual is at liberty to oppose any doctrine, whatever, of the Confession, upon the assumption that it is non-essential, without first submitting the question to the adjudication of the church courts, and conforming himself to their judgment.—All this very clearly appears in the paper.

The ambiguity of the document consists in its failing

to indicate the line of demarcation between the essential and non-essential doctrines. A regard to the precise object of the paper, itself, and its position in the series of transactions will shed light on this point. The paper was cautionary in its design and origin. The suspicions of sinister motives, which, Dickinson and his friends entertained, at first, against the authors of the movement, were now, no doubt laid aside. But the reputation of the Scotch for pertinacity and exclusiveness, on small points, was as great then as now. Situated as "the English" members of the Synod were, they could not anticipate what minute point might be forced into undue prominence by their brethren, when the Confession should have been established as the standard of the Church. The Westminster articles, on the relations of Church and State and the powers of the civil magistrate in sacred things, which have since been altered by our Church, then stood in their original form. The attempt might be made to put the most objectionable sense upon these articles, and to thrust them upon the Synod as essential parts of the book, and terms of ministerial fellowship. And, further, when the members of the Synod should be called on to declare their acceptance of the Confession, it was impossible to anticipate which of the most valuable members might prove to hold some opinion as to "doctrine, worship or government," not in strict accordance with the teachings of the Confession; and which, however unimportant, might be made the ground of his exclusion. Thus, at so early a date as 1707, a difference of sentiment as to "worship," had been developed between the Presbytery and Mr. Andrews, respecting the stated expository reading of the Scriptures, as part of the Sabbath morning services; and it is doubtful whether he ever, on this point, conformed to the Scotch mode. The difficulties in New York, involved many questions between the stricter discipline of the Scotch, and the looser views of others.

It was, as the breakwater, erected for protection against a possible tide of violence, coming in at the close, on points such as these,—as a safeguard to the minority, until the designs and ends of the majority were more fully known, that the ambiguous phrases of the Preliminary Act were adopted. And when, after free and full conference, the entire Synod proved to be perfectly harmonious, in the interpretation given to the questionable clauses of chapters twenty and twenty-three, and the unqualified adoption of the rest, the ambiguous expressions had already fulfilled their design, and were cast aside, as obsolete; the unanimity of the Synod in the unqualified adoption of the Confession, being recognized, as we shall presently see, as superseding the vague and ambiguous generalities of the Preliminary Act.

Further, it is to be considered that, even apart from the special and obvious intent of the indefiniteness of the expressions of the Preliminary Act, it is impossible, from the very nature of the case, to be much more precise and definite than are the phrases in question. That there is just ground for the distinction of essential and non-essential doctrines of religion is conceded by all the parties. But to trace by anticipation, the line of demarcation between them, and state precisely how far and upon what points diversity may be tolerated, and where it becomes censurable; is beyond the skill of human intelligence. The Synod declined to attempt it; but left each case, as it should arise, to be determined on its own merits.

The question remains, whether the Adopting Act was designed to establish a rule of strict conformity to the connected doctrines of the Confession, or to allow a liberal margin of departure from them. On this point, the only information contained in the Preliminary Act, is included under two heads;—that, as the Confession then stood, there were in it articles not essential and necessary; respecting which, diversity of sentiment would not necessarily operate exclusion from the ministry;—and, that, even on these points, parties must make known, to the proper court of the Church, any such opinions, and submit themselves to its judgment, respecting them.

In the Adopting Act, itself, we do not find the members to have availed themselves of this provision, on any point, except those having reference to the civil magistrate. They unanimously agreed in the solution of all the scruples that any of them had to make against any articles and expressions in the Confession and Catechisms, and in declaring the said Confession and Catechisms, to be the confession of their faith, "*excepting only*" those clauses.

Here, the comprehension and the exception are both significant. The members did not reject the excepted clauses. But those clauses were obscure and susceptible of an obnoxious sense. This sense is specified, in order to its rejection. The scrupulous particularity, here, is significant as to the unqualified manner in which, otherwise, the book was received.

The Synod, then, started out with the adoption, without exception or reservation, of every chapter and article of the Confession and Catechisms, by the unanimous voice of the members; a caution only being entered against what many others, as well as Blair, believed to be a false interpretation of two or three clauses, which are now no longer in the book.

For themselves, this was their only recourse to the distinction between necessary and non-necessary articles. Otherwise, they asked no relaxation of the strictest rule of interpretation. What did they require of others? Were candidates to be indulged with a larger liberty than, thus, the members required for themselves?

In the proceedings of 1729, this point is left undetermined. The next Synod adopted the following minute: "Whereas, Some persons have been dissatisfied at the manner of wording our last year's agreement about the Confession, etc., supposing some expressions not sufficiently obligatory upon intrants:

"*Overtured*, That the Synod do now declare, that they understand these clauses that respect the admission of intrants or candidates, in such a sense as to oblige them to receive and adopt the Confession and Catechisms, at their admission, in the same manner and as fully as the members of Synod did, that were then present:—Which overture was unanimously agreed to by the Synod."*

The Synod which thus *unanimously* expounded the Adopting Act was a full meeting, and of as high author-

* Records, p. 98.

ity as that of the preceding year. And its interpretation of the Act, even although it had been mistaken as to the intention of the authors of it, is of equal authority, and therefore, fixes unequivocally the effect of the Act, with respect to intrants. They, too, must receive and adopt it as did the members of Synod, at the first, without reservation, except as to the designated clauses. Nor have we any reason to imagine that this interpretation of the intent of the Adopting Act was at all erroneous. Of the eighteen ministers who united in adopting the Act, twelve were now present, and unanimously concurred in the interpretation here given; and of the seventeen now in attendance, but seven could be counted as of the stricter Scotch party. The exposition now given was not, therefore, in the interest of that party, nor in violation of the wishes and sentiments of the others; but must be taken as a true account of the understanding of the members, at the time of the passage of the Adopting Act, as to its effect, with relation to intrants.

When the members originally united in the Act, "one declared himself not prepared." This was Mr. Elmer, a new member, who now, with Mr. Morgan and Mr. Pemberton, who were before absent, reported "that they have declared before the Presbytery, and desire that their names be inserted in our Synodical records."

Also, "Mr. David Evans, having withdrawn from the Synod three years ago, upon a protest put in by him and some other brethren, declared his hearty concern for his withdrawal, and desired to be received as a member again. And, he having proposed all the scruples he had to make about any articles of the Confession and Catechisms, etc., to the satisfaction of the Synod, and declared his adopting the Westminster Confession of Faith and Catechisms, agreeably to last year's Adopting Act, he was unanimously received in, as a member again; and for his ease, is joined to the Presbytery of Philadelphia."* The occasion of his former protest and withdrawal does not appear. The Minutes of 1727, only state that "a paper of protest was brought into the Synod, after all business was done, by Messrs. Jones, David Evans, Webb, and Hubbell, which was ordered to be kept, *in retentis*."†

Thus, with patient forbearance and prudence, but firmly and decidedly, were the lines drawn, and the bounds of the camp fixed and marked.

For two or three years, without any special order on the subject, reports came up of the compliance of incoming ministers with the Adopting Act. It was then, in 1734;—

"Ordered, that the Synod make a particular inquiry, during the time of their meeting every year, whether such ministers as have been received as members, since the foregoing meeting of the Synod, have adopted, or have been required by the Synod or by the respective Presbyteries to adopt, the Westminster Confession and Catechisms, with the Directory, according to the Acts of the Synod made some years since, for that purpose; and that, also, the report made to the Synod, in answer to said inquiry, be recorded in the minutes."‡

From this date, the inquiry here indicated was regu-

* Records, p. 97. † Ibid., p. 88. "*In retentis*,"—On file.
‡ Records, p. 109.

larly made, and the result recorded. At least, until the schism of 1741, no man was admitted into the ministry of the Church, without his adoption of the Confession, according to the strict terms of the final Act of 1729, being ascertained and entered upon the records of Synod.

It is, here, further worthy of notice, that while the doctrinal standards were thus strictly adopted and enforced, a different rule was applied to the Discipline and Directory. These, as we have seen, were pronounced, by the Synod, to be agreeable, "*in substance,*" to the Word of God. The meaning of this significant distinction, we shall hereafter see stated by a most competent committee of the Synod itself.

CHAPTER V.

THE EXPLANATORY ACT OF 1736.

Misunderstandings of the Act, among the people—Entered in Presbytery books—Explanations of 1736—Misrepresentations of that minute—Gillett's History—Preposterous ground there taken—Position of the "New Side" men—Blair's statement, in reply to Craighead—He views the Acts of 1729 and 1736, as entirely consistent and true—At least, this was the accepted interpretation—All parties were alike zealous in behalf of the strictest orthodoxy.

WHILST, thus, the Synod was using every means to establish the Westminster symbols, as the standards of the Church and the confession of faith of its ministers,—occasion of misapprehension and suspicion had occurred. The Preliminary Act had been printed and circulated, alone, without the Adopting Act, itself. Whether an enemy had done this, we are uninformed. But the effect was, to excite apprehension that the body had adopted latitudinarian principles. The Synod therefore, in 1735, "ordered, That each Presbytery have the whole Adopting Act inserted in their Presbytery book."*

Still, uneasiness prevailed, in some quarters, and, in 1736, "An overture of the committee, upon the supplication of the people of Paxton and Derry, was brought in, and is as followeth:—

"That the Synod do declare, that inasmuch as we

* Records, p. 115.

understand that many persons of our persuasion, both more lately and formerly, have been offended with some expressions or distinctions, in the First or Preliminary Act of our Synod, contained in the printed paper, relating to our receiving or adopting the Westminster Confession and Catechisms, etc., that, in order to remove said offence, and all jealousies that have arisen, or may arise, in any of our people's minds, on occasion of said distinctions and expressions, the Synod doth declare that the Synod have adopted, and still do adhere to the Westminster Confession, Catechisms, and Directory, without the least variation or alteration; and without any regard to said distinctions. And we do further declare that this was our meaning and true intent in our first adopting of said Confession, as may particularly appear, by our Adopting Act, which is as followeth:—'All the ministers of the Synod now present, (which were eighteen in number, except one that declared himself not prepared,) after proposing all the scruples any of them had to make against any articles and expressions in the Confession of Faith, and Larger and Shorter Catechisms of the Assembly of Divines at Westminster, have unanimously agreed, in the solution of these scruples, and in declaring the said Confession and Catechisms to be the confession of their faith, except only some clauses in the twentieth and twenty-third chapters; concerning which clauses, the Synod do unanimously declare, that they do not receive those articles in any such sense as to suppose the civil magistrate hath a controlling power over Synods, with respect to the exercise of their ministerial authority, or power to persecute any for their religion, or in any sense contrary to the Protestant succession to the throne of Great Britain;'—And we hope and desire that this our Synodical declaration and explication may satisfy all our people, as to our firm attachment to our good old received doctrines, contained in said Confession, without the least variation or alteration; and that they will lay aside their jealousies, that have been entertained, through occasion of the above hinted expressions and declarations, as groundless.

"This overture approved *nemine contradicente*."*

Here, it will be observed, that the Synod, after declaring that they have adopted, and do still adhere to the Confession, etc., "without the least variation or alteration, and without any regard to said distinctions," at once cites the language of the Act, in which, apparently, a very signal exception is specified. How is this? Did the Synod stultify itself in thus speaking? No! but the members denied the repudiated sense of the specified articles to be their true meaning;—a denial in which they were sure of being sustained by the common voice of their people.

This very harmless paper, has elicited an extraordinary amount of displeasure and misrepresentation. The New School Assembly of 1839, in a solemn Declaration, issued by it, asserts, that "in 1736, that party who were in favor of the strong measures of the Scottish Church, had gained so much ascendancy that they brought a majority of the Synod to follow the example of the two Presbyteries of New Castle and Donegal, and adopt the Confession, Catechisms, and Directory of the Westminster Assembly of Divines, without altera-

* No one dissenting. Records, p. 126; Digest, p. 31.

tion or exception; thus establishing the power of the civil magistrate to control Synods and persecute the Church."* And Dr. Gillett says, of the Synod's statement, as to the original adoption of the Confession,—"As a matter of fact, this was not true; as a matter of right, it was a gross injustice, to attempt to change the constitutional basis, upon which the Synod had deliberately, and with full notice of its intention, placed itself. In spite of this action, the Adopting Act still stood as the fundamental and constitutional basis of the Synod; and no possible *interpretation* could supersede it."† By "the Adopting Act," he means the Preliminary Act.

A glance at the paper will satisfy the reader how utterly groundless the assertion that the Synod of 1736, established the power of the civil magistrate to control Synods and persecute the Church. That its statement of the facts is true, we have already seen. The desperate assertion of the unquenchable vitality of the Preliminary Act and of its paramount obligation, in spite of all subsequent determinations, by the same authority, is merely ludicrous; and the charge of falsehood and injustice, recorded against the fathers of our Church, arouses a just indignation.

A statement which corresponds with all the facts of previous record; which was made within seven years of the occurrence; entered upon record by the unanimous voice of every man in the Synod, English and Welsh, Irish, Scotch and New Englanders, Old Side and New! A statement confirmed by every contemporaneous fact and witness, and which was questioned by

* Minutes, N. S. Assembly, 1839, p. 57.

† Gillett's History, i. 58.

no one, until a century had elapsed!—The writer, who will venture to brand the fathers of our Church with falsehood in such a statement as this, may claim the meed of courage. But it is awarded at the expense of the higher virtues of impartial fidelity to the facts of history.

Gross injustice is charged. But against whom? Not a voice in the Synod, then or subsequently complained or protested. Not a hint of dissatisfaction is heard, there or elsewhere, on the subject. Were those who subsequently formed the New Side party the persons injured? They utterly refuse to occupy that position; but expressly confirm the declaration of the Synod of 1736. In fact two of the Tennent's (William, the father, and his son, of the same name,) were present, when the Synod unanimously made that declaration. If it was false, they are as deeply implicated as any others.

Samuel Blair, too, will be acknowledged competent to testify for that party; and he certainly had the means of knowing whereof he affirmed. His evidence we have; given under circumstances demanding the strictest accuracy. Alexander Craighead had withdrawn from the Synod, with the New Brunswick party. But he immediately separated himself from them, upon their declining to adopt the Solemn League and Covenant. In reply to cavils, thereupon, published by him, Blair speaks in the following terms:—

"Now,—whether Mr. Craighead could suppose so or not, that neither Synod nor Presbytery, in this province, did ever receive the Westminster Confession of Faith, in every chapter of it,—the thing, itself, is manifestly false in fact both ways. There never was any scruple, that ever I heard of, made by any member of the Synod, about any part of the Confession of Faith; but only about some particular clauses in the twentieth and twenty-third chapters; and those clauses were excepted against, in the Synod's act receiving the Confession of Faith, only in such a sense, which, for my part, I believe the reverend composers never intended in them; but which might, notwithstanding, be readily put upon them. Mr. Craighead, to prove what he supposes, dwells much on what is called the Synod's Preliminary Act about the Confession of Faith, made in 1729. But let that Act be thought as insufficient as it can possibly admit, and granting that it was not sufficient for the securing of a sound orthodox ministry; yet that is no argument but the Confession of Faith has been sufficiently received by other Acts. And so, in fact, it has been, by the Synod's Act for the purpose, I think in the year 1730, [1729] wherein the Synod declares, 'All the ministers of the Synod now present,'"—(Here Mr. Blair copies the Adopting Act in full. He then continues,—) "Here you see, the Synod have received the whole of the Westminster Confession of Faith and Catechisms, as the confession of their faith, save only some clauses in the twentieth and twenty-third chapters."

Again, Mr. Blair proceeds to cite this very act of 1736. "Moreover, in the year 1736, the Synod declare that they adopted and do still adhere to the Westminster Confession, Catechisms, and Directory, without the least variation or alteration, and without any regard to the distinctions in the aforesaid Preliminary Act. It seems, some people were jealous, from the first Preliminary Act, (without knowing or considering that the Synod had afterward agreed in the solutions of all scruples, which any of them had, concerning any articles or expressions in the Confession of Faith; and so, unanimously adopted and received it, in a fixed, determinate, manner, as before related;) that the Synod were about to vary and alter the Confession and Directory, and to set up new principles of religion and government, contrary thereto. In answer to which jealousies, the Synod declares that they adhere to the Westminster Confession, Catechisms, and Directory, without the least variation or alteration; which view of the case takes away all Mr. Craighead's pretence for calling this declaration notoriously false. Mr. Craighead may readily remember, that when our two Presbyteries met together, June 3, 1741, after the separation of the Synod, we declared and recorded that we adhered to the Westminster Confession of Faith, Catechisms, and Directory, as closely and fully as ever the Synod of Philadelphia, in any of their public acts or agreements about them."*

It was above stated, that all contemporary testimony confirms the truth of the Synod's statement in 1736. Possibly, Mr. Craighead must be excepted; to whom however, and to our historian, Blair's answer may be held sufficient. And further, it is to be observed, that Craighead's assertion applies no more directly to the Act of 1729 than to that of 1736. Even the latter, he denies to have involved such an adoption as would,

* Animadversions on the Reasons of Mr. Alexander Craighead's receding from the judicatures of this Church, together with its Constitution. By Samuel Blair. In Hodge, p. 198.

in his estimation, have been sufficient. The suggestion of a scruple, as to the meaning of the excepted clauses, was probably offensive to him; and, in fact, he would have accepted nothing short of the unequivocal adoption of the entire book without reservation, including the Solemn League and Covenant; which was then found in all editions of the Westminster standards.

A careful regard, to Blair's statement, will make it evident, that he viewed the several stages in the proceedings of 1729, in precisely the light, in which we have exhibited them. The members, at first, cautiously felt their way, until they came to a mutual understanding, as to the extent of the objects of the movers of the overture; and the real sentiments of those who, at first, opposed it. This once attained, all difficulty was at an end, and opposition ceased.

That the declaration of 1736 did truly interpret that of 1729, is evident. It is, further, unquestionable, that, true or false, that declaration determined the sense in which, thenceforward, the Confession was adopted by candidates. At least, until the withdrawal of the New Brunswick party, in 1741, no man was admitted into the ministry of the Synod, who had not, in this strictest mode, adopted the entire Confession, and, of whose adoption notice was not taken on the record of Synod.

They were masters of the theology of that Confession. They appreciated fully, and none more fully than the New Brunswick brethren, the symmetry of its structure, the justness of its proportions, and the accuracy of its details. They could not, therefore, fail to realize how fatal to the whole structure might be the opening of a single joint,—the loosening of the smallest stone of the building. Themselves grounded in the system, they, therefore, permitted no secret doubts or scruples on any teaching of the book. If any such were entertained, they must be made known to the Church, and its decision thereon obeyed.

Such are the facts, as to this first period in the history of our Church; and such the position in which it stood, at the close of that period, as to its public Confession. Not, as articles of comprehension; not, for substance of doctrine; not as a "system," merely; but, in all the articles thereof, with that one exception, which so strongly establishes the comprehensiveness of the obligation, as to every clause besides, the Westminster standards were received and set forth, as the confession of their faith, individually and as a body. Cherishing that whole system, as the truth of God; and, in that faith, looking for eternal life, their preaching was a testimony to its doctrines. And, in their writings, they, being dead, yet speak the same testimony, with demonstration and power.

CHAPTER VI.

THE NEW SIDE SCHISM.

Prior state of the churches—Prevalence of Irreligion—The Great Awakening—Disorders—The Tennents—Intrusions into churches—Act of Synod on the subject—Act on examination of candidates—New Brunswick Protest—Old Side protest of 1741—The schism—New Brunswick Adopting Act—Their Declaration—New York members labor for reunion—Their amicable withdrawal—Erection of New York Synod—Basis of it—New Side no liberalists—Claim Scotch affiliation—They held the Confession as a test of Orthodoxy—Letter to Scotch Assembly—New Haven Adopting Act of 1753.

WE have seen the history of the Adopting Act, and the attitude of the Church on the subject, down to the schism of 1741. Let us now inquire, whether the subsequent history corresponds with the foregoing.

The tendency which manifested itself in the churches of Europe, in the first half of the eighteenth century, to lapse into fatal heresies, was not so fully developed, in this country. Yet all the evidence assures us of the exceedingly low state of religion, and the abounding of worldliness and licentiousness, among the people at large.

"I doubt not but there were some sincerely religious persons, up and down," says the Rev. Samuel Blair; "and there were, I believe, a considerable number, in several congregations, pretty exact, according to their education, in the observance of the external forms of religion; not only, as to attendance upon public ordinances on the Sabbath, but, also, as to the practice of family worship, and, perhaps, secret prayer, too; but, with those things, the most part seemed, to all appearance, to rest contented, and to satisfy their conscience with a dead formality in religion. A lamentable ignorance of the essentials of true practical religion, and of the doctrines relating thereto very generally prevailed. The nature and necessity of the new birth, were little known or thought of; the necessity of a conviction of sin and misery, by the Holy Ghost opening and applying the law to the conscience, in order to a saving closure with Christ, was hardly known at all, to most. The necessity of being first in Christ, by a vital union, and in a justified state, before our religious services can be well pleasing or acceptable to God, was very little understood or thought of; but the common notion seemed to be, that, if people were aiming to be in the way of duty, as well as they could, as they imagined, there was no reason to be much afraid."*

Such was the state of religion, in the most favorable circumstances, both in Europe and America, when that remarkable work of grace began, which is known as The Great Awakening. Among the churches of the Synod, it commenced in 1730, in the pastoral charge of the Rev. John Tennent, in Freehold, New Jersey. Great blessings followed, in many places. Believers were quickened, and the ungodly awakened and converted, in great numbers. But, soon, grievous disorders marred the work. A diversity of sentiment arose respecting it, among the best men in the Synod. Those

* Blair's Works, p. 336.

who were not prepared to go all the lengths of extravagance were denounced as "blind leaders of the blind," "dry, sapless, unconverted, ministers," "babbling, ignorant priests," "the devil's advocates," "diabolical reasoners," "ministers of Satan and enemies of all righteousness." Their congregations were intruded upon; their people seduced, and distraction and division prevailed.

Especially conspicuous for zeal and success, in gathering in the abundant harvest of that day, were the Tennents and the other pupils of the patriarch of the Log College, at Neshaminy. But the Petrine impetuosity and fervor of spirit, which were chief elements of their power, in thundering the terrors of the law upon the impenitent, and pressing the claims of the gospel on the consciences of the awakened, operated, at the same time, to induce a spirit of censoriousness toward others, and a contemptuous disregard of the rights of their brethren, and of the regulations of the Synod for their protection.

So great were the inconveniences and distractions consequent upon the proceedings of the New Lights, as the patrons of extravagance were called, that the Synod was at length constrained to interpose. Ministers claimed to have such a special and extraordinary illumination and guidance of the Spirit, as to free them from responsibility to the ordinary rules of propriety, and the regulations of the Church. They professed to have the gift of discerning spirits, and readily pronounced such of their brethren as could not approve their rash and violent proceedings to be unregenerate men; and "it was no sin" to denounce and vituperate such. Their pastoral charges, therefore were entered; the people taught to despise their ministers; pastors unsettled, and congregations rent asunder.

Not only were such measures prevalent, in the immediate vicinity of the active supporters of the work; but their ministers and licentiates traveled in all directions, and, by similar proceedings, threw the entire Church into a ferment.

In view of these disorders, the Synod, in 1737, passed an act for preventing intrusions. By this Act, ministers, and, especially, probationers, were forbidden to intrude into churches, outside their own Presbyteries, without the concurrence of the brethren of the Presbytery of the bounds.* This Act, however, was by the offending brethren, utterly disregarded.

Another occasion of difference arose. Hitherto, the Synod had derived its supplies of ministers from abroad; of men who had already been thoroughly trained, in the colleges of Britain and New England. As the candidates from Tennent's school began to multiply, attention was called to the necessity of some measures being taken by the Synod, to ascertain the adequate education of those who, thus, without a regular collegiate degree, were entering the ministry. Apprehension was felt, and not without reason, that the zeal of the Tennents was in danger of hurrying forward a number of youths, whose training was essentially defective.

An act was therefore passed, in 1738, to provide for the emergency. It declared that "natural parts, however great and promising; for want of being well improved, must be marred of their usefulness," and that

* Records, pp. 134, 137.

"want of due care and pains paves the way for ignorance, and this for a formidable train of sad consequences." To prevent this evil, it was provided, that every student who had not graduated in some college, before being encouraged by any Presbytery for the work of the ministry, should "apply himself to this Synod; and that they appoint a committee of their members, yearly, whom they know to be well skilled in the several branches of philosophy, and divinity, and the languages, to examine such students, in this place, and finding them well accomplished in those several branches of learning, shall allow them a public testimonial from the Synod, which, till better provision be made, shall, in some measure, answer the design of taking a degree in the college."*

Against these Acts of the Synod, the New Brunswick brethren entered a protest, and proceeded in entire disregard of them. In addition to the charges of thus denying the authority of the courts of the Church, and of engaging in the disorders already mentioned, the New Light party were accused of departure from the doctrines of the Confession, in several particulars; as, in asserting "that every true Christian is sure of his own conversion; every adult person, when he is converted, must be able to tell the time, place and manner of his conversion; that no adult person is converted, without first undergoing an high degree of legal, ungracious, preparatory, convictions and terrors; with several other points of doctrine which have no foundation in the Word of God, nor are they agreeable to our Confession, etc."†

* Records, p. 141. † Thomson's Church Government, p. 32.

At length the controversy reached a crisis, and in 1741, the Synod was rent asunder. A protestation was brought in, by those who felt aggrieved by the course of the New Brunswick party.

"1. We protest," said they, "that it is the indispensable duty of this Synod to maintain and stand by the principles of doctrine, worship and government of the Church of Christ, as the same are summed up in the Confession of Faith, Catechisms, and Directory, composed by the Westminster Assembly, as being agreeable to the Word of God, and which this Synod have owned, acknowledged and adopted; as may appear by our Synodical records, of the years 1729 and 1736, which we desire to be read publicly.

"2. We protest that no person, Minister or Elder, should be allowed to sit and vote in this Synod who hath not received, adopted, or subscribed, the said Confessions, Catechisms, and Directory, as our Presbyteries respectively do; according to our last explanation of the Adopting Act; or who is either accused or convicted, or may be convicted, before this Synod, or any of our Presbyteries, of holding or maintaining any doctrine, or who act and persist in any practice, contrary to any of those doctrines, or rules contained in said Directory, or contrary to any known rights of Presbytery, or orders made or agreed to by this Synod, and which stand yet unrepealed; unless, or until he renounce such doctrine, and, being found guilty, acknowledge, confess, and profess his sorrow for such sinful disorder, to the satisfaction of this Synod, or such inferior judicatory as the Synod shall appoint or empower for that purpose."*

* See the Protestation, in the Records, p. 157; Digest, p. 597.

Upon these and other like grounds the protesters asserted that the disorderly members had forfeited their right to be acknowledged "as members of this judicatory of Christ; whose principles and practices are so diametrically opposite to our doctrine, and principles of government and order, which the great King of the Church hath laid down in his Word."

Upon the reading of this paper, the New Side party took the ground that, as the signers of the protest were a minority of the body, (but twenty out of forty-four), and had declared that they could not remain united; they should withdraw. The protesters, on the contrary maintained that the New Side had forfeited their seats, even though a majority. A scene of confusion ensued. The New Side insisted on a count. A tumultuary count took place, during which the Moderator, Mr. Andrews seems to have left the chair. The New Side proved to be a minority; as several who did not sign the protest were in hearty sympathy with its authors. Great excitement prevailed; in the midst of which, the moderator resumed the chair, and, in hopes of securing calmer deliberation and action, commanded silence, and called upon the Synod to unite in an appeal to the Head of the Church, in prayer. At this moment, the New Side party withdrew from the house. They, at once, met in a Presbyterial capacity; took measures to perpetuate their organization; and, among other proceedings, adopted the following minute as to the charge of departing from the Confession: "Inasmuch as the Ministers who have protested against our being of their communion, do, at least, insinuate false reflections against us, endeavoring to make people suspect that we are receding from Presbyterian principles;—for the satisfaction of such Christian people as may be stumbled at such aspersions, we think it fit unanimously to declare that we do adhere as closely and fully to the Westminister Confession of Faith, Catechisms, and Directory, as ever the Synod of Philadelphia did, in any of their public acts or statements about it."*

Shortly afterward, the same body issued to the public a "Declaration" of their views and principles, in which they thus announced themselves:—

"We think it proper, for the satisfaction of all, concerning us, and as a due testimony to the truth of God, to declare and testify to the world our principles and sentiments in religion, according to which we design, though divine grace, ever to conduct ourselves, both as Christians and as Ministers and Ruling Elders.

"And, *first*, as to the doctrines of religion, we believe with our hearts, and profess and maintain with our lips, the doctrines summed up and contained in the Confession of Faith, and Larger and Shorter Catechisms, composed by the reverend Assembly of Divines at Westminister, as the truths of God, revealed and contained in the holy Scriptures of the Old and New Testaments; and do receive, acknowledge, and declare the said Confession of Faith and Catechisms to be the confession of our faith; yet so as that no part of the twenty-third chapter of said Confession shall be so construed as to allow civil magistrates, as such, to have any ecclesiastical authority in Synods, or church judicatories, much less the power of a negative voice over them in their ecclesiastical transactions; nor is any

* Digest, p. 32.

part of it to be understood as opposite to the memorable revolution, and the settlement of the crown of the three kingdoms in the illustrious house of Hanover."*

These declarations, it will be observed, were made with specific reference to the insinuation made in the protest, that these brethren did not conform to the Acts of 1729, and 1736.

Ten ministers withdrew with the New Side party; of whom but two were from New England. Dickinson and the rest of the Eastern members, whilst rejoicing in the work of grace wrought through the instrumentality of the New Brunswick brethren, disapproved of the disorders with which they were chargeable; and had cordially concurred in the propriety of the acts, on intrusion, and the examination of candidates. But, regarding the proceedings, by which those members had been separated from the Synod, as being irregular and disorderly, they labored, for some years, to induce the Philadelphia Synod to recognize and readmit them. At length, failing in this, they determined to retire from the Synod, and join with the New Brunswick brethren, who had, in the mean time, been led to a juster view of the impropriety of many of their former proceedings.

The New York members, therefore, having applied for and received the consent of the Synod to their so doing, amicably withdrew, in 1745, and united with the excluded brethren in erecting the Synod of New York. In forming this union, however, they were careful to incorporate in its terms a distinct assertion of the authority of the Confession of Faith, and a repudia-

* Hodge, ii., p. 229; Digest, p. 33.

tion of the disorderly principles and practices which had led to the division.

This subscription, thus enforced by Dickinson and the New York brethren upon the New Brunswick men, is the more significant, in view of the position taken by him on the subject, at the time of the Adopting Act.

"1. They agree that the Westminister Confession of Faith, with the Larger and Shorter Catechisms, be the public confession of their faith, in such manner as was agreed unto by the Synod of Philadelphia, in the year 1729; and to be inserted in the latter end of this book. And they declare their approbation of the Directory of the Assembly of Divines at Westminister, as the general plan of worship and discipline."

"2. They agree that in matters of discipline, and those things that relate to the peace and good order of our churches, they shall be determined according to the major vote of Ministers and Elders; with which vote every member shall actively concur or pacifically acquiesce;"* and if any one cannot conscientiously do so, in a case deemed necessary by the Synod, he shall peaceably withdraw, without disputation or contention.

From the history thus carefully traced, it is evident that Blair did not speak ignorantly, nor without consideration, when he so emphatically denied the assertion of Craighead, that the minute of 1736 was false, as to the intention of the Act of 1729. It also appears that the unequivocal language of the expository minute was not too strict for the New Side men, the only ones whom it can be supposed to have offended. In full view of

* Records, p. 233.

it, they declare that they adopt the Westminster standards, as fully as the Synod of Philadelphia had ever done. They, thus stand voluntarily and fully committed to the strictest rule of subscription. "Substance of doctrine" had no favor with them.

At a subsequent date, the Synod of New York adopted a minute designed to obviate misapprehensions among the Dutch churches:—"We do hereby declare and testify our constitution, order, and discipline to be in harmony with the Established Church of Scotland. The Westminster Confession, Catechisms, and Directory for Public Worship and Church Government, adopted by them, are in like manner adopted by us. We declare ourselves united with that Church, in the same faith, order, and discipline. Its approbation, countenance, and favor, we have abundant testimonies of. They, as brethren, receive us; and their members we, in like manner, as opportunity offers, receive as ours," etc.*

Again, the Synod replied to an insulting letter from some disaffected members,—"Though we might justly refuse to take any further notice of what is offered in said paper, yet as we would condescend to the weakness, and, as far as can consist with duty, bear with the imperfections, of those who are under our care, for the sake of their edification; we therefore inform them, that, by adopting the Westminster Confession, we only intend receiving it as a test of orthodoxy in our Church;† and it is the order of this Synod, that all

* Records, p. 245.

† It was expressly as "a test of orthodoxy" that the New England members of Synod hesitated to adopt the Westminster Confession,

who are licensed to preach the gospel, or become members of any Presbytery in our bounds, shall receive the same as the confession of their faith, according to our constituting act; which we see no reason to repeal."*

The affinity of the Synod to the Church of Scotland was again asserted, in a letter to the General Assembly of that Church, on behalf of the college of New Jersey. In it, they say,—"Your petitioners conform to the constitution of the Church of Scotland, and have adopted her standards of doctrine, worship, and discipline." And unfolding their necessities they "most earnestly pray that this reverend Assembly would afford the said college all the countenance and assistance in their power. The young daughter of the Church of Scotland, helpless and exposed, in this foreign land, cries to her tender and powerful mother for relief."†

Scotch Presbyterianism was no object of alarm or repugnance to these fathers of our Church. Their position, on this question, was distinctly defined and consistently maintained, from the beginning.

At this era in the history, occurs a curious coincidence. New England seems to be regarded as the early patron of liberal principles of subscription. At New Haven, the officers of the college had, heretofore, been required to give their strict adoption of the Saybrook Platform, which included the Savoy Confession. But now, in 1753, five years before the reunion of the divided Synod, not only the officers, but the Trustees of the college, were required to subscribe the Westmin-

when that measure was originally proposed; as we have already seen.

* Records, p. 274. † Letter, in Records, p. 257.

ster Confession and Catechisms, in the most unqualified sense, and to renounce all doctrines and principles contrary thereto. No class of Presbyterians, Scotch or American, ever were more rigid, on this point, than the New England churches, in all their history, prior to the rise of the school of Edwards.

CHAPTER VII.

LATER DOCTRINAL HISTORY.

Old Side subscription—Amicable withdrawal of the New York members—Correspondence opened between the Synods—New York proposals for reunion—Conference of commissioners—"That paragraph about essentials"—Doctrinal errors charged on the New Side—Proposed testimony to the revival—"That paragraph" had reference to acts of church courts—The New Side affiliated with Scotland—The doctrinal basis of reunion—Controversy of Tennent and Cowell, on the motives of seeking God—Harker's doctrinal errors—His book censured—He is suspended from the ministry—Doctrinal position stated in the ecclesiastical convention of 1785—Authority of the Synod—Adoption of the Confession, after the revision of 1788.

Of the sentiments of the Old Side Synod of Philadelphia, it is scarcely necessary to speak. None question their strict conformity to the Scotch type. Immediately upon the withdrawal of the New Side, in 1741, it was "overtured, That every member of this Synod, whether minister or elder, do sincerely and heartily receive, own, acknowledge, and subscribe, the Westminster Confession of Faith and Larger and Shorter Catechisms, as the confession of his faith; and the Directory, as far as circumstances will allow and admit, in this infant Church, for the rule of church order. Ordered that every session do oblige their elders, at their admission to do the same.

"This was readily approved, *nemine contradicente*."*

When the New York members, with the consent of the Philadelphia Synod, withdrew, to unite with the other party, one of the motives determining their action undoubtedly was, to facilitate the reunion of the two bodies. In submitting their proposal to separate, they say:—"This they desire to do, with the consent of this body, that they may not be thought to set up, and act in opposition to this, and that there may be a foundation for the two Synods to consult and act in mutual concert with one another hereafter, and maintain love and brotherly kindness with each other."†

The Synod replied, that, "though we judge they have no just ground to withdraw from us, yet seeing they propose to erect themselves into a Synod at New York, and now desire to do this in the most friendly manner possible, we declare, if they or any of them do so, we shall endeavor to maintain charitable and Christian affections toward them, and show the same, upon all occasions, by such correspondence and fellowship as we shall think duty, and consistent with a good conscience."‡

In accordance with the intention thus expressed, the Synod of New York at its first meeting appointed a committee, to correspond with the Synod of Philadelphia, which promptly responded to their communication.§

In pursuance of the same pacific policy, an overture was introduced into the New York Synod, and adopted, in 1749, proposing that negotiations be opened with the

* Records, p. 159. † Ibid., p. 181.
‡ Ibid., p. 181. § Ibid., p. 234.

Philadelphia Synod, upon the following fundamental terms.

"1. To preserve the common peace, we would propose, that all names of distinction, which have been made use of, in the late times, be for ever abolished.

"2. That every member assent unto and adopt the Confession of Faith and Directory, according to the plan formerly agreed to by the Synod of Philadelphia in the years ——.

"3. That every member promise, that after any question has been determined by the major vote, he will actively concur or passively submit to the judgment of the body; but if his conscience permit him to do neither of these, that then he shall be obliged peaceably to withdraw from our Synodical communion, without any attempt to make a schism or division among us. Yet this is not intended to extend to any cases but those which the Synod judges essential, in matters of doctrine or discipline.

"4. That all our respective congregations and vacancies be acknowledged as congregations belonging to the Synod, but continue under the care of the same Presbytery as now they are, until a favorable opportunity presents for an advantageous alteration.

"5. That we all agree to esteem and treat it as a censurable evil, to accuse any of our members of error in doctrine or immorality in conversation, any otherwise than by private reproof; till the accusation has been brought before a regular judicature, and issued according to the known rules of our discipline."*

In conformity with this overture, committees of the

* Records, p. 239.

two Synods met. But the New York brethren, waiving all other matters, immediately insisted that the protest of 1741 should, by some authentic and formal act of the Synod of Philadelphia, be made null and void. The result was a heated discussion, and a reference to the respective Synods, to prepare and exchange, at their next sessions, specific proposals for union. "At the same time, these three principal things were especially recommended to the consideration of the respective Synods. 1. The protest. 2. That paragraph about essentials. 3. Of Presbyteries."*

"That paragraph about essentials," has been supposed to allude to the Preliminary Act of 1729. But there is, here, no allusion to that paper. The phrase refers to the above third article of the fundamental terms proposed by the New York Synod, as the basis of negotiation. The point presented in that article involved the principle on which the New Brunswick brethren had been excluded; and presented, therefore, a material point to be adjusted, before reunion.

As we have already seen, the Old Side had charged the New with doctrinal error; and, on that ground, held them bound to withdraw, as having forfeited their right to sit in the Synod. But wherein did these doctrinal errors consist? In the use of some unguarded expressions, as to the necessity of "preparatory ungracious convictions," in order to conversion; assurance of grace, which the believer must possess; a consciousness of the time of his conversion; and the rights of conscience, in opposition to the authority of the Church, etc.; points upon which diversity disappeared, as soon

* Records, p. 241.

as the excitement had cooled, and men came to a dispassionate estimate of each other's language. When the negotiations for union took place, the only difference of "doctrine" that survived was, as to the nature of the work, of which the churches had been recent witnesses. While the one party, looking only to the blessed results, in conversions multiplied, did not hesitate to pronounce it a glorious work of God's grace,—the others, looking too exclusively upon the unhappy concomitants, declared themselves unable to join in the high testimony, which their brethren earnestly sought to elicit from them. "You seem to insist," said they, "on a joint testimony for such a glorious work of God, in the late religious appearances, as a term of union; by making it one of your proposals for peace and union, that you hope both Synods will go into such a testimony. How is this consistent with your former professed sentiments of the duty of forbearance, in said case, and with your declared sentiments, that no difference in judgment, in cases of plain sin and duty, and opinions relating to the great truths of religion, is sufficient reason why the differing member should be obliged to withdraw, unless the said plain duty or truth be judged, by the body, to be essential, in doctrine or discipline?"*

To this, the New York Synod replied, that there was no inconsistency between their hoping to secure a joint testimony and "their declared sentiments that difference in judgment should not oblige a dissenting member to withdraw from our communion; unless the matter were judged, by the body, to be essential in doctrine or dis-

* Records, p. 207.

cipline. And this we must own is an important article with us, which we cannot any way dispense with; and it appears to us to be strictly Christian and scriptural, as well as Presbyterian; otherwise, we must make everything that appears plain duty to us, a term of communion, which, we apprehend, the Scripture prohibits. And it appears plain to us, that there may be many opinions relating to the great truths of religion, that are not great themselves, nor of sufficient importance to be made terms of communion. Nor can these sentiments "open the door to an unjustifiable latitude in principles and practices," any more than the apostolic prohibition of receiving them that are weak to doubtful disputations. What is plain sin and plain duty, in one's account, is not in another's; and the Synod has still in their power to judge what is essential and what is not."*

In a word, the question involved in these discussions, was not with respect to points of doctrinal theology, in the ordinary acceptation of the term, as those doctrines are defined in the Confession; but as to questions of duty arising, from time to time, in the changing circumstances of the Church, such as those that connected themselves with the former state of awakening; and opinions on such questions as those mentioned above, opinions which have no formal determination in the Confession. In fact the whole discussion grew out of "that paragraph" in the New York fundamental terms, above cited, and related to acquiescence in decisions,—not, of the Confession,—but, of the judicatories of the Church, upon questions arising in the course of their administration.

* Records, p. 254.

It is to be remembered, that it was pending these very discussions between the two Synods, that the Synod of New York affiliated itself, as we have seen, with the Church of Scotland, having already committed itself, so fully and variously, to the strictest maintenance of the doctrines of the Westminster standards.

The result of the negotiations between the Synods was their reunion, in 1758, on a basis which exhibits the "paragraph about essentials," in its true position, and contained a recognition of the Westminster standards, even much stricter than that passed by the Synod of Philadelphia, immediately after the separation. The latter it will be remembered, was adopted, in response to the demand of the protestants, that the Acts of 1729 and 1736 should be enforced on all members of the Synod. The following are three of the articles of reunion of 1758.

"I. Both Synods, having always approved and received the Westminster Confession of Faith, and Larger and Shorter Catechisms, as an orthodox and excellent system of Christian doctrine, founded on the Word of God, we do still receive the same as the confession of our faith, and also adhere to the plan of worship, government, and discipline, contained in the Westminster Directory; strictly enjoining it on all our members and probationers for the ministry, that they teach and preach according to the form of sound words in said Confession and Catechisms, and avoid and oppose all errors contrary thereto.

"II. That, when any matter is determined, by a major vote, every member shall either actively concur with, or passively submit to, such determination; or, if, his conscience permit him to do neither, he shall,—after sufficient liberty modestly to reason and remonstrate,—peaceably withdraw from our communion, without attempting to make any schism. Provided, always, that this shall be understood to extend only to such determinations as the body shall judge indispensable in doctrine or Presbyterian government.

"VI. That no Presbytery shall license or ordain, to the work of the ministry, any candidate, until he give them competent satisfaction, as to his learning, and experimental acquaintance with religion, and skill in divinity and cases of conscience; and declare his acceptance of the Westminster Confession and Catechisms as the confession of his faith, and promise subjection to the Presbyterian plan of government in the Westminster Directory."*

Another element of the evidence, as to the theology of this period, is found in the two cases of doctrinal controversy, which arose and were adjudicated by the Synod. They illustrate, in a very striking manner, the strictness of the doctrinal position maintained.

The first of these originated in some speculations of a minister from New England, on a subject which has been much discussed in that region,—the lawfulness of seeking our eternal happiness from selfish motives. Gilbert Tennent was the life and soul of the New Side party,—the party supposed to be advocates for liberal terms of subscription. Yet he it was who assailed Cowell for unsoundness on this subject, and brought him before the bar of Synod, on that ground.

The Rev. David Cowell had been called to the church

* Records, p. 286.

in Trenton. Upon his trials for ordination, he submitted an exegesis on the question, "*An lex naturæ sit sufficiens ad salutem.*" (Is the light of nature sufficient to salvation?)* Perhaps, in this paper, or in the examination which followed, he expressed himself in such terms as led to the imputation that he held that self-love is the foundation of all obedience. Tennent opened a correspondence with him, on the subject; and, after a protracted discussion, called the attention of the Synod to the matter.

That body referred it to a committee, at the head of which was Dickinson. The committee reported, that though there were some incautious and unguarded expressions used by both the contending parties, yet they have ground to hope "that the principal controversy between them flows from their not having clear ideas of the subject they so earnestly debate about." The committee then proceeded to make a statement of doctrine on the subject; to which both parties declared their assent, and the matter was dropped. The next year, however, Tennent declared himself dissatisfied with the conclusion of the affair, and requested that it be reopened; which the Synod declined to do. This was in 1749; and, at the same meeting, Mr. Tennent made this one of the principal grounds on which, in a paper, read by him to the Synod, he declared his suspicions that some of the members were unconverted.— "First, their unsoundness in some principal doctrines of Christianity, that relate to experience and practice; as, particularly, in the following points:—

"1st. That there is no distinction between the glory

* Hall's History of the Presbyterian Church in Trenton, p. 70.

of God and our happiness;—that self-love is the foundation of all obedience. . . .

"2d, That there is a certainty of salvation annexed to the labors of natural men." . . .

Of these points, Thomson justly says, "Although I will not take upon me to justify these expressions, as sound, in their most obvious meaning, yet I think it's a very strange stretch of censoriousness and rash judging, to conclude the person unregenerate who useth them."*

But, judged by this criterion, and that of Tennent's published works, what would have been his voice, as to unessential doctrines? What feature of recent improvements upon the Westminster system would he have tolerated, under that head?

The other case of doctrinal controversy, originated in New Brunswick Presbytery, in 1758, just before the re-union. The Rev. Samuel Harker was charged with having vented some erroneous doctrines, and the case was referred to the Synod of New York, by which a committee was appointed to deal with him, as they should have opportunity, for his conviction. Every member of this committee belonged to the original New Side party. The efforts of the Synod were ineffectually continued, for five years after the union, to recover this member. In the mean time, he published a book entitled, "An Appeal to the Christian World,"† in which his sentiments were developed. This book was, by the Synod in 1762, referred to a committee, to examine and report upon it. They reported the next year, where-

* Thomson's Church Government, pp. 9, 11.

† Webster, p. 623.

upon "the Synod proceeded to consider Mr. Harker's principles, collected from his book, by the committee, which are in substance as follows:

"1. That the covenant of grace is in such a sense conditional, that fallen mankind, in their unregenerate state, by the general assistance given to all under the gospel, have a sufficient ability to fulfill the conditions thereof, and so, by their own endeavors to ensure to themselves regenerating grace and all saving blessings.

"2. That God has bound himself by promise, to give them regenerating grace, upon their fulfilling what he, (Mr. Harker,) calls, the direct conditions of obtaining it; and, upon the whole, makes a certain and an infallible connection between their endeavors and the aforesaid blessings.

"3. That God's prescience of future events, is previous to and not dependent on his decrees; that his decrees have no influence on his own conduct, and that the foresight of faith was the ground of the decree of election.

"It is further observed, that he often uses inaccurate, unintelligible, and dangerous, modes of expression, that tend to lead people into false notions of several important matters; as, that Adam was the federal father of his posterity, in the second covenant, as well as in the first; that the regenerate are not in a state of probation for heaven; and several such like.

"The Synod judge that these principles are of a hurtful and dangerous tendency, giving a false view to the covenant of grace, perverting it into a new modeled covenant of works, and misrepresents the doctrine of the divine decrees, as held by the best Reformed

Churches; and, in fine, are contrary to the Word of God and our approved standards of doctrine."*

The Synod called in Mr. Harker, and "questioned him in many particulars;" and, after mature deliberation, suspended him from the ministry, and ordered "that all be duly warned not to receive his doctrines, nor admit his ministrations, until it shall please God to convince him of his mistakes, and to bring him to the acknowledgment of the truth, and recover him from the error of his ways."†

It would seem an easy matter to decide, from these two judicial cases, alone, as to the attitude of the Church, at that time, on the question involved in the phrasing of the Preliminary Act.

There was a signal occasion in her subsequent history, when the Synod was called upon, in a most responsible manner, to declare herself on this point.

In October, 1785, a convention met at New York, composed of commissioners from the Reformed Dutch, the Associate Reformed, and the Presbyterian Synods, for the purpose of making arrangements for more intimate relations between the several bodies. At this convention the Reformed Dutch committee asked for an explicit statement, by each committee, of the formulas of doctrine and worship received by the churches, severally. The commissioners of the Synod of New York and Philadelphia were Drs. John Rodgers, Alexander McWhorter, and Samuel Smith, and Rev. Messrs. Nathan Kerr, and John Woodhull; men surely competent to speak on the subject. Their answer was approved by the Synod, and was in the following terms:

* Records, p. 329. † Ibid, p. 329.

"The Synod of New York and Philadelphia adopt, according to the known and established meaning of the terms, the Westminister Confession of Faith as the confession of their faith; save that every candidate for the gospel ministry is permitted to except against so much of the twenty-third chapter as gives authority to civil magistrates in matters of religion. The Presbyterian Church in America considers the Church of Christ as a spiritual society, entirely distinct from the civil government, having a right to regulate their own ecclesiastical policy, independently of the interposition of the magistrate.

"The Synod also receives the Directory for public worship and the form of Church Government, recommended by the Westminster Assembly, as in substance agreeable to the institutions of the New Testament. This mode of adoption we use, because we believe the general platform of our government to be agreeable to the sacred Scriptures; but we do not believe that God has been pleased so to reveal and enjoin every minute circumstance of ecclesiastical government and discipline, as not to leave room for orthodox churches of Christ, in these minutæ, to differ, with charity, from one another.

"The rules of our discipline and the form of process in our church judicatures, are contained in Pardovan's (alias Steuart's) Collections, in conjunction with the acts of our own Synod; the power of which, in matters purely ecclesiastical, we consider as equal to the power of any Synod or General Assembly in the world. Our church judicatures, like those of the Church of Scotland, from which we derive our origin, are church Sessions, Presbyteries and Synods: to which it is now in contemplation to add a National or General Assembly."*

Here is a distinct recognition of the authority of the Confession, in the sense of the minute of 1736; and a further most significant discrimination between the standards of doctrine and the rules of government. The latter may be adopted by candidates "for substance." But no such liberty is allowed respecting the former.

In this paper, the Synod reports the contemplated erection of a General Assembly. It was, at the time, engaged in a revision of the standards, with that view; and the above statement is of peculiar significance in its bearing upon the events immediately following.

In the revision, the excepted clauses were corrected, and after amendment of the Form of Government, and the Directory, the whole was adopted as the Constitution of our Church, the Confession of our faith, and the "standard of our doctrine, government discipline, and worship."†

The purpose of this laborious inquiry has been to ascertain, from the authentic records, what has been the real attitude of our Church, as to the doctrines set forth in her standards. Has she received them strictly, as being a true and reliable exposition of the teachings of the Scriptures, in accordance with which she would have her people instructed, and her testimony maintained before the world? Or, has she held them as the point of departure; from the definitions of which her ministers are at liberty to diverge, according to the vagaries of their own fancies, provided they do not

* Records, p. 518. † Ibid., p. 547.

depart "essentially" from the system of truth. In a word, are they criteria of the orthodoxy of our ministry and the fidelity of their teachings; and, if they are not, how are the courts of the Church to determine what she holds to be necessary and essential, and what she allows to be indifferent; who are orthodox, and who heretical?

The facts are, that even the Preliminary Act did not allow any divergence, whatever, from the standards, without submitting it to the courts of the Church, and conforming to their judgment respecting it;—that the minute of 1736, is in perfect harmony with the face of the record of 1729; that it was confessedly enforced until the division; that the Old Side party always adhered to it, and the New Side with reiterated emphasis endorse it; and that, in 1785, it was recognized, without question, as the established and universal law of the Church. The Rev. Samuel Blair, in 1741, had never heard of a minister of the Synod who scrupled anything in the Confession, except the clauses as to the magistrate. Tennent could not even tolerate a crude or ambiguous sentiment, on the efficacy of self-love in impelling men to seek salvation: and when Harker published sentiments, innocent, compared with many which now find harbor under the Presbyterian name, he was, apparently, without a dissenting voice, excluded from the ministry.

CHAPTER VIII.

THE ASSEMBLY AND THE CONFESSION.

Organization of the Assembly—Powers of the General Synod—Powers of the General Assembly—Constitution of the Assembly—The Barrier Act—Articles of the Constitution—The Constitution did not emanate from the Presbyteries—The Barrier Act changed—Doctrinal position of the Assembly—Case of Balch—Craighead's doctrines—New Light schism—The Cumberland Presbytery—W. C. Davis' case—Case of Craighead—Doctrinal attitude of the Church, as seen in these histories.

WE have seen the origin of the General Presbytery, about 1705, and its expansion in 1716, into a Synod, having charge over several subordinate Presbyteries. During its Synodical existence, as before, the body usually convened in "full Synod;" but it sometimes met by delegation of commissioners from the Presbyteries. The year 1788, witnessed a further expansion of the system. The sixteen Presbyteries, into which the body had been subdivided, were distributed into four Synods; the name of the supreme court changed to the General Assembly, and provision made in the Constitution that it should be composed of commissioners, of equal numbers of ministers and elders, elected according to a fixed ratio by the Presbyteries.

Prior to this change in the constitution of the

supreme court of the Church, its powers had been unlimited by any constitutional restrictions. The commissioners of the Synod, in 1786, in the convention with the Dutch and Associate Reformed Churches, asserted its power, "in matters purely ecclesiastical," to be "equal to the power of any Synod or General Assembly in the world."* This representation was true, and received an illustration from the measures then in progress, for the reorganization of the Church. These consisted in a revision of the Confession of Faith and Catechisms, the Form of Government, Discipline and Directory; a readjustment of the Presbyteries; the erection of four Synods; and the reconstruction of the supreme court itself. All this was done by the Synod, of its own motion, and by its own sole and supreme authority.

In this process of revision, however, the supreme court was divested of some of the prerogatives which it had previously possessed. The necessity of this grew out of the change in the composition of the body. It was no longer a full assembly of the ministry and representative elders of the churches, but a delegation from these. And yet, as the court representative of the whole Church, it was invested, of necessity, with the immediate charge of her highest interests. Careful provision was, therefore, made in the revised Constitution, in two respects, to secure the best interests of the Church, under such a system, from possibly corrupt or hasty and improvident action by the Assembly.

The first of these had respect to the constitution of the body itself. It was provided that "the General

* Records, p. 519.

Assembly shall consist of an equal delegation of bishops and elders from each Presbytery," in a prescribed ratio.* The various regulations of the Constitution determine that the qualifications of the members of the Assembly are,—constitutional ordination and good standing in the ministry or eldership of the Church,—a lawful constituency, that is, a constitutional Presbytery,—and legal election and commission. All those who are possessed of these qualifications,—they, and no others, are authorized and required to sit in the Assembly, "to consult, vote, and determine, on all things that may come before the body, according to the principles of the Constitution of this Church, and the Word of God."

The other cautionary provision, contained in the revised Constitution, consisted in a limitation imposed upon the powers of the Assembly. In the early struggles of the Church of Scotland with the house of Stuart, she was greatly embarrassed by the action of Assemblies, in which, by corruption and violence, the government had secured control. By them, acts and regulations were passed, which changed the Constitution, and bound the Church hand and foot, and placed her at the disposition of the king and his ministry. When, afterward, the liberties of the Church were recovered, the Barrier Act was passed, as a protection against similar attempts. This Act provided that "before a General Assembly of this Church pass any acts which are to be binding rules and constitutions to the Church, the same Acts be first proposed as overtures to the Assembly; and, being passed, as such, be remitted to the consideration of the several Presbyteries of the Church, and

* Form of Government, xii. 2.

their opinions and consent reported to the next Assembly, following; who may then pass the same into Acts, if the more general opinion of the Church, thus had, agree thereto."*

This Act was, by the General Synod, transcribed into the revised Constitution, and defined as a "restriction upon the powers of the Assembly."

In another respect, the Assembly was divested of powers possessed by the Synod. That body, whilst modeling the Constitution at its own discretion, provided that the book, as thus amended, should continue to be the Constitution of the Church, unalterably, "unless two-thirds of the Presbyteries under the care of the General Assembly shall propose alterations, or amendments, and such alterations or amendments shall be agreed to, and enacted by the General Assembly."†

Subject to these restrictions, the powers formerly held by the Synod passed to the Assembly, under the two general heads of stated duties to be performed; and occasional prerogatives to be exercised. These regulations stood in the Constitution, as thus originally revised and published, in the following form:—

Powers of the Assembly.

"SECT. IV. The Assembly shall receive and issue all appeals and references, which may be regularly brought before them from the inferior judicatories; they shall review the minutes and proceedings of every Synod, to approve or censure them; they shall give advice and instructions, in all other cases submitted to them; and they shall also constitute the bond of union, peace, cor-

* Compendium of the Laws of the Church of Scotland, ii. 205.

† Records, p. 546.

respondence, and mutual confidence, among all the churches.

"SECT. V. To the General Assembly also belongs the power of consulting, reasoning, and judging, in all controversies respecting doctrine and discipline; of reproving, warning, and bearing testimony against, error in doctrine, or immorality in practice, in any Church, Presbytery or Synod; of corresponding with foreign Churches; of putting a stop to schismatical contentions and disputations; and, in general, of recommending and attempting reformation of manners; and of promoting charity, truth, and holiness, through all the churches; and of erecting new Synods, when they judge it necessary.

Other powers of the Assembly.

"SECT. VI. Before any overtures or regulations, proposed by the Assembly, to be established as standing rules, shall be obligatory on the churches, it shall be necessary to transmit them to all the Presbyteries, and to receive the returns of, at least, a majority of the Presbyteries, in writing, approving thereof."*

Restriction of the powers of the Assembly.

Such were the powers which the Church, through the General Synod, originally conveyed to its lineal successor, the General Assembly; and such the restrictions imposed

* "Constitution of the Presbyterian Church," etc., MDCCLXXXIX. p. 147. A comparison with the present Form of Government, will discover the emendations, made in these articles, in 1820. The titles to the chapters, in this first edition, are significant. "Chapter viii. Of the Congregational Assembly, or Judicatory usually styled, the Church Session." "Chapter ix. Of the Presbyterial Assembly." "Chapter x. Of the Synodical Assembly." "Chapter xi. Of the General Assembly."

upon it. The common impression that it was, by the Presbyteries, that all these changes were made, is erroneous. The Presbyteries were not called to take any part, whatever, in the transaction; except that the General Synod sent them, for perusal, a copy of the first Draught of the Constitution it was about to establish, and invited them to submit their remarks upon it. But it was not framed by their instrumentality, nor submitted to their vote; but, by the Synod, ordained, as the fundamental law of the Church, to which the Presbyteries were required to conform themselves.

In one important respect, these provisions of the Constitution have been modified. In 1798, the Assembly passed an Act, regulating the mode of receiving foreign ministers and licentiates into the Presbyteries, and enjoined its observance upon them. To this, the Presbytery of New York objected the article restrictive of the power of the Assembly to establish standing rules, without a vote of the Presbyteries. The Assembly denied that the restrictive clause, could have been meant for such rules as the Presbytery supposed; and asserted that it was designed to indicate the way in which the constitutional rules contained in the Form of Government, Discipline, and Directory, should be altered. That the design of the Scotch Barrier Act was, merely, to prevent any alterations in the fundamental laws and Constitution of that Church, is certain; and it seems probable that Witherspoon and the fathers, who transferred it to our Constitution, intended it in the same sense; although they inadvertently failed to harmonize it with the fundamental ordinance, which required two-thirds of the Presbyteries to consent to any amendment whatever, whether of the doctrinal standards, or, constitutional rules.

The result of this discussion was the submission to the Presbyteries of an amendment of the controverted clause; so that instead of "standing rules," as formerly, it should read "constitutional rules." The alteration was allowed by the requisite number of Presbyteries; there being twenty-two, ayes, seven nays, and two not voting.* This amendment was made in 1805. By it, the Assembly was released from any previous restraint; and distinctly recognized as endowed with power to enact any standing laws and rules, not in conflict with the provisions of the Constitution. The changes which were made in the constitution of the supreme court, and in the standards of the Church, in 1788, brought with them no change in her doctrinal position. The only amendments introduced into the doctrinal formularies, were those by which the ambiguity of the passages respecting the civil magistrate was obviated, by the substitution of language in accordance with the constant sentiments of our Church, on that subject. The clauses, to which exception was heretofore allowed, being thus rectified, exception was no longer permitted; but the Constitution was erected as "the standard of our doctrine, government, discipline, and worship;"† and every candidate for the ministry is required to declare his reception of the doctrinal formularies "as containing the system of doctrine taught in the Holy Scriptures."‡

Of the sense in which these expressions were used by

* The Digest, p. 49, inaccurately gives these numbers 22, 6, and 3.

† Digest, p. 36; Records, p. 547.

‡ Form of Government, xv. 12: 2.

the authors, we have already had a very clear illustration, in the statement made by the Synod's commissioners, in the convention of 1786, to the Dutch and Associate Reformed commissioners. Occurrences, of a date immediately subsequent to the reorganization of the Church, shed further light on the subject.

Seven years after the amended Constitution had been promulgated, the Rev. Hezekiah Balch, of Greenville, Tennessee, in a trip to New England, imbibed some of the doctrinal views of Dr. Hopkins of Newport, who had published his "System of Doctrines," two years before, in 1793. Upon his return, Mr. Balch engaged with all the zeal of a new proselyte in the propagation of these opinions. He published them in the Knoxville Gazette, in the form of Articles of Faith. In propagating his views, he was overbearing and violent. The matter was brought into the Presbytery of Abingdon, and caused much perplexity and trouble; for a time, rending the body asunder. The attention of the General Assembly was arrested; and it addressed a letter to the ministers and churches of the Presbytery. "We perceive with pain,"—said the Assembly,—"that novel opinions,—or, at least, opinions presented in a novel dress, and appearance, have been openly and extensively circulated amongst you. . . . . We take the present occasion of declaring our uniform adherence to the doctrines contained in our Confession of Faith, in their present plain and intelligible form; and our fixed determination to maintain them against all innovations. We earnestly wish that nothing subversive of these doctrines may be suffered to exist, or to be circulated amongst the churches; we hope that even now explanations of our known principles, by unusual and offensive phrases, will be cautiously guarded against."*

At the next meeting of the Assembly, Balch's case came up, by reference, from the Synod of the Carolinas. His creed was examined, and besides some minor matters, to which exception was taken, he was found guilty of false doctrine, in the following particulars:—

"In making disinterested benevolence the only definition of holiness or true religion." "In representing personal corruption as not derived from Adam; making Adam's sin to be imputed to his posterity, in consequence of a corrupt nature already possessed, and derived from we know not what; thus, in effect setting aside the idea of Adam's being the federal head or representative of his descendants, and the whole doctrine of the covenant of works." "It is also manifest that Mr. Balch is greatly erroneous, in asserting that the formal cause of a believer's justification, is the imputation of the fruits and effects of Christ's righteousness, and not the righteousness itself; because righteousness, and that alone, is the formal demand of the law; and consequently, the sinner's violation of the divine law can be pardoned, only in virtue of the Redeemer's perfect righteousness being imputed to him and reckoned as his."

In view of these errors, the Assembly determined to require Mr. Balch to acknowledge in its presence that he was wrong in the publication of his creed; and "that, in the particulars specified above, he renounce the errors pointed out; and that he engage to teach nothing hereafter of a similar nature." The Assembly also directed the Moderator to admonish him of the

* Minutes 1797, p. 129; Digest, p. 630.

divisions, disorders, and trouble which he had given the Church.

From this decision Mr. Langdon, the delegate from Connecticut, and one member of the Assembly, dissented. Mr. Balch read an open acknowledgment and retraction, was solemnly admonished, and was then declared to be in good standing. Upon his return home, however, he was reported as saying that "he was fifty thousand times stronger in belief of that definition of holiness than he was before." This he admitted, before the Synod of the Carolinas; only, instead of fifty thousand, he would say five hundred thousand. The Synod, thereupon, suspended him from the ministry. He was afterward restored. The region of East Tennessee ultimately became infected to a considerable extent, with the leaven thus introduced.

The New Light and Cumberland Schisms, in Kentucky, gave new occasion for the fidelity of the Church, in protecting the purity of her doctrines and order. In the former of these cases, the trouble arose from the dissemination of Hopkinsian errors, in the midst of a protracted religious excitement; and in the latter, from Arminian views, originated in similar circumstances. The Cumberland Presbytery, received the Confession of Faith; except that they denied the doctrine of fatality which they held it to contain, and supposed a sufficiency of grace to be given to every man, for his attaining to repentance and salvation.

The New Light heresy was an ultimate result of the theological discoveries which Dr. Balch had imported to East Tennessee from New England. The Rev. Thomas B. Craighead, a native of North Carolina, and pastor of a church in Middle Tennessee, with less critical acumen than Dr. Taylor, but with almost equal fertility of genius, and fullness of development, anticipated, by a quarter of a century, some of the main features of the theology of New Haven. "God never was the author of sin, by will or by contrivance. He used every means consistent with the freedom of the human will, and his [man's] moral agency, to prevent the entrance of sin into the world. He never willed the destruction of any man, only on account of sin. He never rejects the sinner, who does not reject the counsel of God, against his own soul. And, to that rejection, we are neither compelled by any necessity of nature, by any dispensation of Divine Providence, nor secret purpose of his heart." The saints of the primitive Church were in a different position from us; as the inspired canon was not yet completed, to which the immediate presence and agency of the Spirit were necessary. But "while this Spirit dwelt in the hearts of his people, it seems to have been his whole office to supply the want of records. He never infringed the liberty of the human will. He never infused such dispositions, made such impressions, shed such light on the mind, or otherwise laid such constraints or restraints on their natures, as to render their actions necessary, or to force them to keep God's law." "It is contended by many, that it is the immediate power of the Spirit that renders the Word effectual, to produce either faith or holiness.... Can anything dwell in our minds but thoughts or ideas? . . . Your pretensions to immediate agency are inadmissible, on gospel principles. . . . Do you pretend that you are enlightened, to understand the Scriptures, by the Spirit? How comes it, then, that good men differ in their interpretation of the same passage?" "The power of believing, in every intelligent creature, consists in the strength of the testimony. Believing is never either an independent or voluntary act.* No man can believe without testimony. No man can resist the force of credible testimony, if he suffers it to enter into the view of his understanding. Neither disposition, nor will, nor motives, have the least effect. Believing is an intellectual, not a moral act. Dispositions, or moral principles may affect suffering the testimony to enter into the view of the understanding; but when it enters, the desire of life, temporal or eternal, nor the fear of death, can affect it. In the licentiousness of your freedom, you may refuse to hear or obey God, and destroy your own soul; but if you admit his word to enter into the view of your understanding, as his word, it is the highest, most coercive and irresistible cause in the universe. . . . Faith acquaints us with the divine attractives, without which we cannot come to him. But when we are acquainted with these, we can never rest without devoting ourselves to him and his service."†

These doctrines of Craighead, which were published to the world in 1809, had been instilled, by their author, into the mind of Barton W. Stone, in 1799 or 1800; by whom they were imparted to McNemar and Dun-

* "Voluntary," here, is manifestly used in the sense of self-determined.

† "A Sermon on Regeneration, with an Apology and an Address to the Synod of Kentucky, together with an Appendix, by T. B. Craighead, A. B., V. D. M., Lexington, Ky., 1809, pp. 28, 4, 11, 26.

lavy. Matthew Houston was also a disciple of Craighead.* In 1803, the Synod of Kentucky, found, on review of the records of the Washington Presbytery, that two of its members, Messrs. McNemar and Thompson, had been, in a memorial, charged with holding dangerous errors, and that the Presbytery had passed slightly over the matter. The Synod censured the negligence of the Presbytery, and determined to examine the accused. At this juncture, Messrs. Marshall, Stone, McNemar, Thompson, and Dunlavy, denied the jurisdiction of the Synod and withdrew. They immediately organized themselves into a Presbytery, which was afterward joined by Houston. They were all deposed from the ministry.

Of these men Marshall and Thompson ultimately returned to the Church; Houston, McNemar, and Dunlavy, before the end of the year, joined the Shakers; Stone repudiated the divinity of Christ, and ultimately joined the sect of the Campbellites.

The course of the Synod, with respect to the Cumberland Presbytery, was similar to that in the New Light case. Proposing to examine the erroneous members, they withdrew, and were at once suspended from the ministry. From them, has sprung the large and respectable denomination of the Cumberland Presbyterians.

In both of these cases, the action of the Synod of Kentucky was, after mature inquiry and deliberation, fully approved, and commended by the Assembly.

In 1810, the case of the Rev. Wm. C. Davis came before the Assembly. For some years, there had been

* Davidson's Kentucky, p. 271.

uneasiness felt, among the churches of South Carolina, on account of the doctrines preached by Mr. Davis. In 1809, he published a treatise on systematic theology, entitled, "The Gospel Plan," the examination of which the Synod of the Carolinas referred to the Assembly. That body appointed a committee to examine the book. The report specified the following errors, which the Assembly declared to be contrary to the Confession of Faith:—"The active obedience of Christ constitutes no part of that righteousness by which a sinner is justified." "Obedience to the moral law was not required, as the condition of the covenant of works." "God could not make Adam, or any other creature, either holy or unholy." "Regeneration must be a consequence of Faith. Faith precedes regeneration." "Faith, in the first act of it, is not a holy act." "If God has to plant all the principal parts of salvation in the sinner's heart, to enable him to believe, the gospel plan is quite out of his reach, and consequently, does not suit his case; and it must be impossible for God to condemn a man for unbelief; for no just law condemns or criminates any person, for not doing what they cannot do."

Some other expressions and sentiments the Assembly pronounced to be unguarded and dangerous. On the whole, it judged that the preaching or publishing of the sentiments here specified "ought to subject the person or persons so doing, to be dealt with, by their respective Presbyteries, according to the Discipline of the Church, relating to the propagation of errors."*

Under this decision, Mr. Davis was cited to trial, by the Presbytery of Concord. Failing to appear, after

* Minutes, p. 448, 452; Digest, p. 645.

repeated citations, he was suspended from the ministry, for contumacy; and finally deposed.

During the pendency of the Cumberland difficulties, in Kentucky, a Commission of the Synod was appointed to visit the Cumberland Presbytery, respecting those matters. It was also instructed to investigate the truth of reports which prevailed as to the propagation of erroneous doctrines, by Mr. Craighead. The Commission, accordingly, communicated with him, and received such statements as were, on some points, ambiguous, but upon the whole, satisfactory. At the next meeting of the Synod, Mr. Craighead preached a sermon, which produced much dissatisfaction, on account of the erroneous views therein set forth, and the inconsistency between them and his answers to the Commission. The Synod, thereupon, passed a resolution, "That the Rev. Thomas B. Craighead be entreated, to be cautious, in future, as to the matter of his sermons; and careful not to offend against the doctrines of the Confession of Faith, and the feelings of his Christian brethren; and that the Moderator be directed to read this minute to Mr. Craighead."

Three years afterward, Mr. Craighead set at naught this admonition, by publishing the sermon, much enlarged, with additional offensive matter. Some of its leading features have been already given. The Presbytery of Transylvania took up the subject, and, after an investigation, referred it to the Synod, by which Mr. Craighead was suspended from the ministry. The charges, under which this sentence was pronounced were two: "Denying and vilifying the real agency of the Spirit in regeneration, and in the production of faith and sanctification, in general;" and "denying, vilifying, and misrepresenting, the doctrine of divine foreordination, and sovereignty, and election."

Mr. Craighead gave notice of appeal to the next Assembly, which met in 1811. But, failing to appear, to prosecute his appeal, the Assembly pronounced the decision of the Synod to be final. In 1822, a memorial from him induced the Assembly to reopen the case; which was, finally, taken up for hearing, in 1824. The lapse of time however, the age and infirmities of the appellant, the irregularity which had cut him off from an earlier hearing, and other causes, induced a disposition to leniency in the case. The Assembly decided "that the charges were not so clearly proved, but that he might possibly have meant only to deny the immediate agency of the Spirit, whilst admitting his mediate operation by and with the Word; such being the sense which he seems now to have given to the language. But upon the most favorable construction, the doctrines of the sermon were pronounced different from those of the Reformed churches and our Church, and erroneous, although the error is not of fundamental importance." The spirit of the discourse and of the publication of it was also condemned; and the Assembly declared that "Mr. Craighead ought so to retract or explain his sentiments, as to afford reasonable satisfaction to his brethren."

The whole case was, therefore, referred to the Presbytery of West Tennessee, where Mr. Craighead then lived, with authority, upon his giving satisfactory retractions or explanations, to restore him to the ministry. This was accordingly done.

The history of this case closes the record of doctrinal questions, in our Church, prior to, and apart from the New School controversy.

Of this whole history, two remarks present themselves. In no one instance, is there any intimation of appeal being made to the distinctions of the Preliminary Act of 1729; or, to any such supposed policy of our Church, to justify departure, on any point, from the doctrines of the Confession. In no one case, when such departure was brought to the knowledge of the Church, did it fail to elicit the infliction of judicial censures.

CHAPTER IX.

THE NEW ENGLAND CHURCHES.

Independents in the Westminster Assembly—Savoy Confession—Early New England standards—Presbyterians in New England—Cambridge Platform—Heads of Agreement—Saybrook Platform—The Connecticut churches claimed to be Presbyterian—Early intercourse of the General Synod and the Congregational churches—The American Episcopate—Conventions on the subject—Correspondence with New England, after the Revolution.

AMONG the members of the Westminster Assembly, there were a few individuals, who harmonized in their doctrinal sentiments with the other members, but rejected the Presbyterian system of church organization and government, and advocated the principles of Independency. Some time after the dissolution of the Assembly, a conference of Independent ministers and lay messengers from their churches met at the Savoy, London, for the purpose of adopting standards of faith and order for their churches. The document framed and published by this assembly thence received the name of the Savoy Confession. This formulary, was merely the Westminster Confession, slightly altered, in some places, so as to express, more distinctly, the truth, on points on which later errors seemed to indicate the propriety of more specific statements. Those chapters, also, were omitted which relate to church order and discipline, instead of which one was inserted in accordance with their own system. Of the doctrinal amendments, that on justification will illustrate the character and tendency. Chapter eleven, section one, was made to read as follows:

"Those whom God effectually calleth, he also freely justifieth, not by infusing righteousness into them; but by pardoning their sins, and by accounting and accepting their persons as righteous; not for anything wrought in them, or done by them, but for Christ's sake alone; nor, by imputing faith itself, the act of believing, or any other evangelical obedience, to them, as their righteousness; but by imputing Christ's active obedience unto the whole law, and passive obedience, in his sufferings and death, for their whole and sole righteousness, they receiving and resting on him and his righteousness, by faith; which faith they have not of themselves, it is the gift of God."

In this Savoy article, the clause, "by imputing Christ's active obedience unto the whole law, and passive obedience in his sufferings and death, for their whole and sole righteousness,"—comes in the place of the following clause in the Westminster Confession:—"by imputing the obedience and satisfaction of Christ unto them." This alteration has evident reference to the Neonomian error, of which we have already given account; and was, therefore, very offensive to Baxter, the great patron of that error. It illustrates the extent of the difference between the Westminster and Savoy Confessions.

The Westminster Confession had been adopted by a Synod of the New England churches, at Cambridge, in

1648. "We do judge it," said this Synod, "to be very holy, orthodox, and judicious, in all matters of faith, and do, therefore, freely and fully, consent thereunto, for the substance thereof; only, in those things which have respect to church government, and discipline, we refer ourselves to the platform of church discipline agreed upon by this present assembly,"*—the Cambridge Platform.

After the publication of the Savoy Confession, "it was twice publicly read, examined, and approved;" at a Synod held in Boston, in 1680, "and some small variations made from that of Savoy, in compliance with that at Westminster; and so, after such collations, but no contentions, voted and printed, as the faith of New England."†

We have already mentioned, that many of the early colonists of New England were Presbyterians; amounting, in 1680, in Connecticut, to nearly one-half of the entire population. Early efforts were made by them to organize themselves according to their Presbyterian principles. But the government was against them; and its power was used, without scruple, to suppress such attempts; so that they were never permitted to develop the Presbyterian system of order.

Their influence, however, was powerfully felt in the form early given to the constitution of the New England churches. Cotton's book "Of the Keys," is stated by Mather to have been, next to the Bible, the early platform of the New England churches; and he quotes Rutherford, speaking of that treatise as "well sound

* Mather's Magnalia, Hartford, 1820, vol. ii., p 155.

† Ibid., p. 156.

in our way, if he had given some more power to Assemblies, and in some lesser points."

In the Cambridge Platform, itself, of 1648, a system is described to which the same language may justly be applied. "Of elders, (who are also in Scripture called bishops,)" it states that "some attend chiefly to the ministry of the Word, as the pastors and teachers; others attend especially unto rule, who are, therefore, called ruling elders." "The office of the deacon is instituted in the Church by the Lord Jesus Christ. . . . The office and work of the deacon is, to receive the offerings of the church, gifts given to the church, and to keep the treasury of the church, and therewith to serve the tables, which the church is to provide; as, the Lord's table, the table of the ministers, and of such as are in necessity; to whom the deacons are to distribute with simplicity."

"Church government or rule is placed by Christ in the officers of the Church." "Synods, orderly assembled, and rightly proceeding according to the pattern, Acts xv., we acknowledge as the ordinance of Christ; and, though not absolutely necessary to the being, yet many times, through the iniquity of men and perverseness of the times, necessary to the well-being of churches, for the establishment of truth and peace therein." "The Synods' directions, so far as consonant to the Word of God, are to be received with reverence and submission; not only for their agreement therewith, (which is the principal ground thereof, and without which they bind not at all,) but also, secondarily, for the power, whereby they are made, as being an ordinance of God, appointed thereunto in his Word."

Mather, in his Magnalia, written about the close of the seventeenth century, states the following, among other points, determined "by a late assembly of our ministers at Cambridge."

"Synods duly composed of messengers, chosen by them whom they are to represent, and proceeding with due regard unto the will of God in his Word, are to be reverenced, as determining the mind of the Holy Spirit, concerning things necessary to be received and practiced, in order to the edification of the churches therein represented."

"The power of church government belongs only to the elders of the church."

"There are yet certain cases wherein the elders, in the management of their church government, are to take the concurrence of the fraternity."*

The Heads of Agreement of 1690, do not seem ever to have been formally adopted by the New England churches at large. They have been recognized, however, from their first publication, as true exhibitions of Congregational principles. The Saybrook Platform was formed, in 1708, by a Synod of the Connecticut ministers; who, at the same time, owned and consented to the Savoy Confession and the Heads of Agreement. These three documents, thenceforth, became the standards of the Connecticut churches.

The Saybrook Platform provided that the elders of a particular church, with the consent of the brethren, have power and ought to exercise discipline, in all cases within that church. The churches, in each county,

* Mather, vol. ii. p. 213.

form a Consociation. The council of this body consists of all the teaching and ruling elders of the churches; which are, also, at liberty to delegate lay messengers, who are entitled to deliberate and vote, as members; provided, however, that no matter shall be determined without a majority of the elders. This court is empowered to try and decide all questions of scandal coming up from any of the churches.

The Platform also appointed that all the teaching elders in each several county, shall form a county Association, with power to consult respecting the duties of their office, to resolve questions submitted to them; to examine and recommend candidates for the ministry; to enter proceedings, before the appropriate council, against any of their number, for scandal or heresy; and to look after vacant churches, and take measures to have them supplied. The Platform also provided for a General Association, composed of one or two delegates from each county Association in the State, to meet once a year. In the Associations, lay delegates were not admitted.

In 1799, the Old Hartford North Association, in reply to certain inquiries, made the following statement, as to the constitution of the Connecticut churches.

"This Association gives information to all whom it may concern, that the constitution of the churches in the State of Connecticut, founded on the common usages, and the Confession of Faith, Heads of Agreement, and Articles of Church Discipline, adopted at the earliest period of the settlement of the State, is not Congregational, but contains the essentials of the government of the Church of Scotland, or Presbyterian

Church in America, particularly, as it gives a decisive power to ecclesiastical councils; and a Consociation, consisting of ministers and messengers, or a lay representation from the churches, is possessed of substantially the same authority as a Presbytery. The judgments, decisions, and censures in our churches and in the Presbyterian are mutually deemed valid. The churches, therefore, in Connecticut, at large, and in our district, in particular, are not now, and never were, from the earliest period of our settlement, Congregational churches, according to the ideas and forms of church order contained in the Book of Discipline, called the Cambridge Platform. There are, however, scattered over the State, perhaps ten or twelve churches (unconsociated) who are properly called Congregational, agreeably to the rules of Church Discipline in the book above mentioned. Sometimes, indeed, the Associated churches of Connecticut are loosely and vaguely, though improperly, termed Congregational. While our churches, in the State at large, are, in the most essential and important respects, the same as the Presbyterian,* still, in minute and unimportant points of church order and discipline, both we and the Presbyterian Church in America acknowledge a difference."†

In these facts, we have the key to the circumstance that many of the churches of New England, are, to this day, known by the name of "Presbyterian." And, of the many ministers who, formerly, from New England, entered our church, Edwards was not the only one who could have written, as did he,—"I have long been per-

* *Quere*—[Church of Scotland.]

† Van Ransselaer's Presbyterian Magazine, 1856, p. 172.

fectly out of conceit of our unsettled, confused way of church government in this land; and the Presbyterian way has ever appeared to me most agreeable to the Word of God, and the reason and nature of things."*

The identity of the theology of the two denominations, and the comparative agreement on the subject of order and government, early induced intimate and confidential relations between the New England churches, and those of the General Synod. In Connecticut, so strong were the tendencies toward a thorough adoption of Presbyterianism, as to encourage the hope of actual union. In 1723, occasion of correspondence with the Connecticut ministers having arisen out of difficulties in the church in New York, the Synod appointed a committee to confer with them on that subject; "and if the good ends proposed, relating to New York, be at the conference happily accomplished, the Synod recommends it to those of their members afore appointed to said conference, to treat with said ministers of Connecticut about a union with us; and empower them to concert and conclude upon any methods that may conduce to that end."† The condition precedent failed, and the overture for union does not seem to have been communicated. The middle of the eighteenth century witnessed a time of much controversy and trouble in Connecticut, arising out of the Presbyterian tendencies which prevailed, and the anxious exertions which were employed to prevent their acquiring general control.

The first stated intercourse between the Synod and the New England churches, arose out of the question

* Dwight's Life of Edwards, p. 412. † Records, p. 76.

of the American Episcopate, and the parties to it were, the General Synod and the General Association of Connecticut.

Among the measures devised, by the patrons of British supremacy in the colonies, with a view to secure uniformity in religion, the general establishment of the Church of England, and the entire subordination of the colonies to the British Government, one of the most cherished was that of establishing, by act of Parliament, an American Episcopate.

It was imposible that the people of New England and the Presbyterian Church should regard such a project with indifference. They had fled to this country, expressly, to find refuge from the oppressions and persecutions which they had suffered in Great Britain, for refusal to conform to that Church. They had realized, in the land of their exile, enough of the same policy from that Church, to satisfy them, that only the power was wanting to enact the English St. Bartholomew, and the oppressions by which the Presbyterians of Ireland and Scotland had been trodden and peeled. The objection was not to the enjoyment, by those who preferred them, of the rites of religion according to the order of the Episcopal Church. But it was, to the power of Parliament to assume jurisdiction over the ecclesiastical affairs of the colonies. That this was the point where the whole question hinged, is not only apparent, on the entire face of the discussions on the subject, but is demonstrated by two facts ; first, that the great body of Episcopalians, themselves, were as active in opposition to the scheme as any others ; and second, that as soon as the Revolution had obviated any apprehensions from Parliament, all opposition was withdrawn, and the consecration of the first American bishops was hailed, with general congratulations, by the other denominations in America.

Of the controversy on this subject, John Adams, writing to Dr. Morse, Dec. 2, 1815, says,—that "the apprehension of Episcopacy contributed, fifty years ago, as much as any other cause, to arouse the attention, not only of the inquiring minds, but of the common people, and urge them to close thinking on the constitutional authority of Parliament over the colonies."

"The objection was not merely to the office of bishop, though even that was dreaded; as, to the authority of Parliament, on which it must be founded. The reasoning was this:—The archbishops and bishops, in England, can neither locate and limit dioceses in America, nor ordain bishops, in any part of the dominions of Great Britain, out of the realm, by any law of the kingdom, or any law of the colonies, nor by any canon law acknowleded by either. The king cannot grant his *conge d'elire** to any people out of the realm. There is no power, or pretended power, less than Parliament, that can create bishops in America. But, if Parliament can erect dioceses, and appoint bishops, they may introduce the whole hierarchy, establish tithes, forbid marriages and funerals, establish religion, forbid dissent, make schism heresy, impose penalties extending to life and limb, as well as to liberty and property."

Such considerations excited universal apprehension, when it was known that Archbishop Secker had been zealously laboring to secure the obnoxious measure.

* Permission to elect.

In Virginia, a convention of the clergy was called, to consider the propriety of petitioning for a bishop. But twelve out of one hundred attended; and, of these, four protested against the petition; whereupon the house of burgesses tendered the protesters their unanimous thanks, "for the wise and well-timed opposition they had made to the pernicious project of a few mistaken clergymen, for introducing an American bishop."*

It was with a view to the exertions, at this time, making on this subject, that the General Synod, in 1766, addressed a letter to the brethren in Connecticut, proposing a convention of delegates from the two churches. The Synod, at the same time, appointed eight commissioners to act on its behalf, in such convention.

Mr. Rodgers, one of these commissioners was pastor of the church in New York, which at this very time, was making a renewed but unavailing effort to secure a charter. The opposition of the Episcopal clergy had prevented its obtaining this privilege; which had been pursued by repeated applications, beginning as early as 1719. The last petition was now pending, before the Lords Commissioners of Trade and Plantations, in London. Before them the Bishop of London appeared, personally, in opposition, and defeated the petition, which, after long delay, was rejected, in August, 1767.† Such facts stimulated the zeal of the colonists against the increase of Episcopal power. It was not until after the Revolution that a charter was obtained by that Church.

* Hawk's Contributions, vol. i. p. 127–130.

† Webster, p. 579.

The proposal for a convention was accepted by the General Association of Connecticut. At the first meeting, a plan of intercourse between the two churches, was agreed upon, which was adopted by both. It provided for an annual convention of delegates from the two bodies; which should, however, have no power over pastors, churches, or any of the internal affairs of the churches. They were to remain entire and independent of each other. The objects prescribed to the convention were, "to gain information of the public state of this united cause and interest; to collect accounts relating thereto; to unite our endeavors for spreading the gospel and preserving the religious liberties of our churches; to diffuse harmony and keep up a correspondence thoughout the united body, and with our friends abroad; to recommend, cultivate and preserve, loyalty and allegiance to the king's majesty; and, also, to address the king or the king's ministers, from time to time, with assurances of the unshaken loyalty of the pastors comprehended in this union, and the churches under their care; and to vindicate them, if unjustly aspersed."*

Aspersions of their loyalty were, at that time, rife; and were employed in resisting such applications as that of the New York church.

The plan provided for inviting the other New England churches, and the Reformed Dutch brethren to join the convention. They do not, however, seem to have acceded to it. The convention, at once, opened correspondence with influential parties in Britain, and maintained a vigilant watchfulness over the interests of the

* This Plan of Union, in Green's Christian Advocate, vol. xi. p. 496.

churches, as involved in the policy of the British government, the Society for propagating the gospel in foreign parts, and the advocates of the American Episcopate. The last meeting was held in 1776, when the independence of the United States precluded the apprehensions out of which they had originated, and they ceased to meet.

After the Revolution, stated intercourse with New England was not resumed until 1791. In that year, the General Assembly made overtures, for correspondence, to the Congregational churches. They were immediately accepted, by the General Association of Connecticut; and, ultimately, by all the New England churches. The plan, first adopted with the Connecticut Association, provided that the two parties should, each, annually appoint three delegates to attend the sessions of the other, with a right to deliberate on all questions coming before the body, but not to vote. In 1794, the Assembly proposed, and the Association agreed, that the delegates be allowed to vote; and the plan, thus amended, was adopted in the subsequent treaties with the other New England churches.

CHAPTER X.

THE PLAN OF UNION.

Origin of the Plan—Its provisions—It was less in harmony with Presbyterianism than the Saybrook Platform—Its unconstitutionality—Its imprudence—The Plan of 1808—Admission of the Middle Association—Its subdivision—Erection of the Synod of Geneva—Synod of Genesee—Presbytery of Chenango—Synod of Utica—Practical working of the Plan of Union—Synod of the Western Reserve—Presbyterianism enervated by the Plan—Prevalence of Hopkinsianism in New England—Consequent reaction toward Independency.

In 1801, the Assembly adopted what is popularly known as the Plan of Union, with the Association of Connecticut.

The Presbyterian tendencies of the ministers of Connecticut were the originating cause of this plan. Emigrants from New England, and from the Presbyterian Church, were filling up the wilderness of western New York and Ohio. They were brought into intimate contact, in circumstances which indicated the propriety and duty of their endeavoring to unite in Christian fellowship, and in maintaining the ordinances of religion. To facilitate this object, the proposition for a system of co-operation was made, by the General Association of Connecticut, to the General Assembly. The latter referred the proposition to a committee, consisting of the Rev. Drs. Edwards, McKnight, and Woodhull, the Rev. Mr. Blatchford, and Elder Hutton. Of this committee, Mr. Blatchford was the delegate appointed by the Association of Connecticut, to confer on this subject, and Dr. Edwards had recently been received from that Association.

The committee soon reported the Regulations, which were approved by the Assembly, sent to the Association and adopted by it. This important paper is entitled to a place, in full, in these pages. It is as follows:—

"Regulations adopted by the General Assembly of the Presbyterian Church in America, and by the General Association of the State of Connecticut, with a view to prevent alienation, and to promote union and harmony in those new settlements which are composed of inhabitants from these bodies.

"1st. It is strictly enjoined on all their missionaries to the new settlements, to endeavor, by all proper means, to promote mutual forbearance, and a spirit of accommodation, between those inhabitants of the new settlements who hold the Presbyterian, and those who hold the Congregational, form of Church government.

"2d. If, in the new settlements, any church of the Congregational order shall settle a minister of the Presbyterian order, that church may, if they choose, still conduct their discipline according to Congregational principles, settling their difficulties among themselves, or by a council mutually agreed upon for that purpose. But, if any difficulty shall exist, between the minister and the church, or any member of it, it shall be referred to the Presbytery to which the minister shall belong, provided both parties agree to it; if not, to a council consisting of an equal number of Presbyterians and Congregationalists, agreed upon by both parties.

"3d. If a Presbyterian church shall settle a minister of Congregational principles, that church may still conduct their discipline according to Presbyterian principles, excepting that if a difficulty arise between him and his church, or any member of it, the cause shall be tried by the Association to which the said minister shall belong, provided both parties agree to it; otherwise by a council, one half Congregationalists and the other Presbyterians, mutually agreed upon by the parties.

"4th. If any congregation consist partly of those who hold the Congregational form of discipline, and partly of those who hold the Presbyterian form, we recommend to both parties, that this be no obstruction to their uniting in one church and settling a minister; and that, in this case, the church choose a standing committee, from the communicants of said church, whose business it shall be to call to account every member of the church who shall conduct himself inconsistently with the laws of Christianity, and to give judgment on such conduct. That if the person condemned by their judgment be a Presbyterian, he shall have liberty to appeal to the Presbytery; if he be a Congregationalist, he shall have liberty to appeal to the body of the male communicants of the church. In the former case, the determination of the Presbytery shall be final, unless the church shall consent to a further appeal to the Synod, or to the General Assembly; and, in the latter case, if the party condemned shall wish for a trial by a mutual council, the cause shall be referred to such a council. And provided the standing committee of any church shall depute one of themselves to attend the Presbytery, he may have the same right to sit and act in the Presbytery as a ruling elder of the Presbyterian church."*

We have already described the Saybrook Platform, by which the order of the Connecticut churches was regulated. A comparison of the two will show that the Regulations of 1801 did not even conform as closely to the principles of Presbyterian government as did the Platform. The theory, distinctly stated in the latter, was, that the power of discipline belongs to the elders, whom all the churches were expected to elect. And although it provided for the admission into the judicial councils of the Consociations, of lay messengers, authorized to sit and vote,—yet, a majority of the elders was necessary, in order to a decision. Further, this presence of lay messengers was limited to the county Consociations, which correspond to our Presbyteries, except that their business is mainly, if not exclusively confined to cases of controversy and discipline, arising in the churches of their bounds. On the other hand, the Associations,—which had charge of the more important duties of Presbyteries and Synods, such as consultations as to the duties of the ministry and the common interests of the churches, the supplying of vacant churches, and the examination and recommending of candidates for the ministry, were composed exclusively of ministers; neither ruling elders nor lay messengers being admitted to their deliberations. The Councils appointed by the provisions of the Platform were, furthermore, invested with sole jurisdiction, over all cases, to the exclusion of special mutual councils, called for the par-

* Minutes, 1801. p. 124; Digest, p. 570.

ticular occasion, which were used in the strictly Congregational churches.

In none of these respects, was the Plan as much in accordance with our principles and order as was the Platform. In judicial cases, instead of Consociation or Presbytery, it authorized mutual councils of mixed materials, Presbyterian and Congregational. In churches composed of a mixed membership, it set aside the elders, which both Confession and Platform demand, and substituted a standing committee, consisting of persons who were subjected to no examination, and held to no pledge, neither of adherence to the doctrines of the Confession, nor of devotion to its system of order. They were neither called, nor tried, nor ordained, to any office in the church. Yet they were empowered to sit, as sole judges, in the first instance, of all cases arising in the church. They were authorized to send delegates to Presbytery, with power, not only to sit in the determining of judicial cases,—the only power which, under the Platform they could pretend to claim in the Consociation,—but also to deliberate and act on all questions which might come before the body. And, whilst the Platform expressly excluded all laymen from the deliberations of the Associations of their own Church, respecting its great interests; and, even in judicial cases, gave their votes no power, unless sustained by a majority of the elders,—the Plan gave them an equal voice with the most venerable ministers and elders, over the greatest interests of the Church, to which their very attitude indicated that they were probably alien, and possibly hostile.

In this system, the disregard of the plainest requirements of the Constitution, which, expressly and unequivocally, prescribed the organization of Presbyteries and qualifications of their members, is less surprising. For, the fathers of our Church, having so recently been accustomed to see the General Synod exercise powers, unrestricted by a constitution, were not yet able to realize that the General Assembly was bound to conform to the provisions of the Constitution, which the Church, through the General Synod, had established, for her own protection and the ordering of all her courts, higher and lower.

The imprudence of allowing such a breach in her walls, as that involved in the Plan of Union, might have been expected to arrest a more prompt attention, and secure its rejection. But the Assembly was seduced by the siren of union and peace. The Plan was adopted, and the way thus prepared for corrupting the doctrines of the Church, the utter defacing of her order, and the introduction of protracted controversy and strife, and final schism.

The principal field, contemplated in the Plan of Union, was the western part of the State of New York, which was, then, rapidly filling with a population, by whom the wilderness was subdued and the institutions of civilization and Christianity established. In 1807, the Synod of Albany, meeting at Cooperstown, received delegates from two Congregational bodies, located in that region;—the Middle Association in the Western District, and the Northern Associated Presbytery. Their mission was, to treat of "union and correspondence" with the Synod. In response to their overtures, the Synod addressed a letter to the two bodies, proposing that they should enter into organic union with the Presbyterian Church. "Nor do we confine our invitation," said the Synod, "to you, as ministers; but we also extend it to delegates from your churches; whom we are willing to receive, as substantially the same with our ruling elders; to assist us in our public deliberations and decisions. Knowing the influence of education and habit, should the churches under your care prefer transacting their internal concerns in the present mode of Congregational government, we assure them of our cheerfulness in leaving them undisturbed, in the administration of that government, unless they shall choose to alter it themselves."*

This proposition was made, subject to the approval of the General Assembly. The Assembly granted the desired permission, in 1808, whereupon the Middle Association accepted the plan and was received by the Synod, "retaining their own name and usages, in the administration of the government of their churches, according to the terms stated in the plan."

The sixth article, in the Constitution of the body thus received by the Synod, provided, that "nothing should be construed in opposition to the accommodating articles agreed upon between the General Assembly of the Presbyterian Church, and the General Association of Connecticut."†

In 1809, the year after the reception of this Association, it reported to the Synod, twenty-one churches, all of them, it would seem, Congregational. At the next meeting of the Synod, a joint request was received from the Middle Association and the Presbytery of Geneva,

* Assembly's Digest, p. 574. † Ibid., p. 572.

to be subdivided into three Presbyteries. In compliance with this request, a part of the territory of the Geneva Presbytery was detached from it, and joined to the Middle Association, which was divided into the two Presbyteries of Cayuga and Onondaga. These both, at once, in written constitutions, planted themselves upon the Plan of Union, and were Presbyterian only in name.*

In 1812, these three Presbyteries, Geneva, Cayuga, and Onondaga, were erected into the Synod of Geneva. This body received an early enlargement, in consequence of the dissolution of the Congregational Association of Onondaga, the ministers and churches of which connected themselves with its Presbyteries, on the "accommodating plan."

In 1821, the Synod of Genesee was erected out of four Presbyteries detached from the Synod of Geneva. Springing from that body, which traced its origin so directly to the plan of 1808, and the Middle Association, this Synod was, like its parent, largely composed of Congregational materials; and the Plan of Union was recognized as paramount to the Constitution of the Presbyterian Church.

The Synod of Geneva, at a later period, received a new accession from the Congregational churches. In 1826, an overture came before the Assemby, "for the promotion of a new Presbytery, in the county of Che-

* For the facts here presented, respecting the Synods of Geneva, Genesee, and Utica, we are indebted mainly to "Facts and Observations concerning the organization and state of the churches, in the three Synods of Western New York and the Synod of Western Reserve;" by the Rev. Dr. James Wood, 1837.

nango and adjacent parts, in the State of New York." The overture was granted, and the Assembly constituted the Presbytery of Chenango, to be composed of five enumerated ministers. Not a church was, at first, connected with the body. It was attached to the Synod of Geneva.*

In September of the same year, at the second meeting of this body, it adopted an accommodation plan, grounded on that of 1808; allowing churches to govern themselves mainly upon Congregational principles. Two churches then joined it. Some time afterward, the Union Association was broken up, and its ministers and churches mostly came into the Presbytery.

The Synod of Utica was erected, in 1829, by a division of the Synod of Albany, and was, from the first, largely composed of Congregational materials, under the operation of the Plan of 1801. The Presbyteries of which it was constituted, had already received repeated accessions of Congregational ministers and churches, under the Plan. In 1819, the Presbytery of Oneida received eleven Congregational ministers and nine congregations, in consequence of the dissolution of the Oneida Association; the ministers of which desiring to join the Presbytery, persuaded their churches to acquiesce in the step. During the three following years, nine churches were added to the Presbytery; the most of them Congregational.

It will be recognized, at once, from this history, that the system contemplated in the Plan of Union of 1801, was essentially modified in its actual operation. Instead of being used, strictly, as a temporary expedient, for

* Assembly's Minutes, 1826, p. 21.

the organization of mixed churches, where both parties were too feeble to attempt independent action, and for enabling the churches, in their infant condition, to avail themselves of the services of such ministers as might be accessible, whether Presbyterian or Congregational, without affecting the ecclesiastical relations of the churches,—the Plan was made the occasion of filling our church with Congregational ministers and churches; retaining all their denominational attachments and usages; with but slight modifications, or none. Their congregational affairs were managed, in a great measure, independently of Presbyterial control; and yet they did not hesitate to send delegates,—"committee men," to sit in Presbytery, to administer a Constitution to which they themselves refused to submit, and govern a Church, to which they felt no attachment, and with the destinies of which they refused to be identified.

Whilst such was the development in progress, in western New York, a similar process was going on in the northern part of Ohio. The following history of the Synod of the Western Reserve, is given by the Rev. J. Seward, one of its earliest pioneers.

"The Presbytery of Grand River, agreeably to the order of the Synod of Pittsburgh, was organized in the autumn of 1814; and, as it covered ground on which a union had been established between Presbyterians and Congregationalists, according to Regulations adopted by the General Assembly of the Presbyterian Church, it was deemed necessary, that this Presbytery should be so organized as to consolidate and perpetuate this union, and thus carry out the recommendations and injunctions of the General Assembly. To accomplish this object, a number of articles, adapted to the peculiar situation of the churches in this region, was adopted by this Presbytery, and afterward by the Presbyteries of Portage and Huron, as they were respectively organized. The design of these articles was, to secure to all connected with these Presbyteries, the rights and privileges pledged in the Regulations adopted by the General Assembly and the General Association, in 1801. As the Congregationalists had, from their childhood, been instructed in the Westminster Assembly's Shorter Catechism, and, as this was the basis of the Presbyterian Confession of Faith, they had no material difficulty in coming together on the distinguishing doctrines of the Christian religion, as embraced in the Calvinistic system. Nor had they any objection to the Discipline of the Presbyterian Church, so far as it was applicable to them, in their peculiar situation. Hence, in their preamble to their constitution, they express their approbation of the Confession of Faith and Discipline of the General Assembly of the Presbyterian Church in the United States of America; and, in the articles of the constitution, there is nothing that does not perfectly harmonize with the standards of the Presbyterian Church, excepting those particulars which are designed to carry out the principles of the Plan of Union, to which allusion has so often been made.

"The distinguishing particular, of this description, was, that individual ministers and churches may adopt either the Congregational or Presbyterian mode of government and discipline; and that this article shall never be affected by any additions or alterations which these regulations may receive. Here is the grand charter of contract to perpetuate the Plan of Union. The minister and churches forming these new Presbyteries supposed that they were bound to make this covenant with each other, by the express direction of the General Assembly of the Presbyterian Church. They made it. They inserted it prominently in their books of records. The records of the Presbytery of Grand River, containing this contract, were presented to the Synod of Pittsburgh, at their meeting in 1815, for examination. The peculiar circumstances of the Presbytery being understood, a committee of the most wise and judicious members were appointed to examine the records. The committee reported and the records were approved. Thus did the Synod of Pittsburgh ratify and confirm, in 1815, the covenant, proposed and adopted by the General Assembly, in 1801, and which had been in successful operation, in the new settlements, for the period of fourteen years. In 1819, the records of the Presbytery of Portage, and in 1824, the records of the Presbytery of Huron, each containing the same contract, went through with a similar process, and were approved by the Synod of Pittsburgh. The time at which these records were approved was at the first meeting of the Synod after the formation of the respective Presbyteries of Grand River, Portage, and Huron. At a meeting of the General Assembly, in 1825, a petition was presented for a division of the Synod of Pittsburgh, and the erection of a new Synod, to be composed of the three Presbyteries above named, and to be known by the name of the Synod of the Western Reserve. The request was granted, and, in compliance with the order of the General Assembly, the Synod of the Western Reserve was organized, at Hudson, September 27, 1825."*

Whilst, thus, in four great Synods, the Plan of 1801 had wholly superseded the constitution of the Church, similar results, although to a more limited extent, were realized in other parts of the Church. Its energies were gradually relaxed, its authority weakened, and instead of the Plan converting Congregationalists into Presbyterians, the opposite result was imminent,—the Congregationalizing of the entire Presbyterian Church.

When the Regulations were adopted, the ministers of New England, and especially those of Connecticut, were supposed to be thoroughly sound in the theology of the standards of Westminster, and favorable to the Presbyterian order, set forth by that Assembly. The leaven of Hopkins was but beginning to work. But within a third of a century afterward a great change had taken place. The system of New Haven was fully matured and diffusing its poison everywhere. With the prevalence of lax and unsound theology, there occurred a reaction from the strictness of the Presbyterian discipline,—the counterpart of a purely Calvinistic theology,—and a disposition was strongly developed, hostile even to the milder forms of the Consociational polity of Connecticut. The multiplication, therefore, of Congregational ministers, in the Presbyterian Church, was no increase of strength; but the introduction of an element of weakness, division, and heresy. For the present, it seemed to be a pledge of prosperity and peace. But time only was requisite, to reveal its true character.

* Seward's letter to the Ohio Observer, in Woods' Facts and Observations, p. 29.

CHAPTER XI.

NEW ENGLAND THEOLOGY.

Influence of Edwards—His theory of imputation—Realistic and Reformed doctrines—Edwards' doctrine of sin and holiness—Logical development of Hopkinsianism—Hopkins a pupil of Edwards—The system of New Divinity—Results of the doctrine of sin and holiness seen in the younger Edwards' doctrine of the atonement—Relation of Edwards to New Haven—Its logical development.

PRIOR to the rise of Edwards, the theology of New England had always been strictly conformed to that of the body of the Reformed Churches. His own theological views, as to the doctrines of the Reformed confessions, were in general harmony with the Westminister divines. In two respects, however, he must be recognized as the spring, whence have flowed many heresies, to plague the Church of God, which he loved;—in the nature of some of his opinions; and in the mode of discussion which he introduced. Holding, in accordance with the Cartesian philosophy, then prevalent, that God himself is the only cause of all phenomena and events, he hence deduced his extraordinary theory of identity, and incorporated it with the fundamental doctrines of theology. There is no such thing, according to this view, as real continued existence among the creatures. The moon that now is, is not really the same that was a moment ago. That, has fled into nothingness; and this, is a new creation, which is in the act of giving place to another; and so on continually. Upon this assumption, he proceeds to reason thus.—"If the existence of created substance, in each successive moment, be wholly the effect of God's immediate power, in that moment; without any dependence on prior existence; as much as the first creation out of nothing,—then, what exists at this moment, by this power, is a new effect; and, simply and absolutely considered, not the same with any past existence; though it be like it, and follows it according to a certain established method. *And there is no identity or oneness in the case, but what depends on the arbitrary constitution of the Creator*, who, by his wise sovereign establishment, so unites these successive new effects, that he treats them as one, by communicating to them like properties, relations and circumstances; and so leads us to regard and treat them as one." This divine constitution, he says is "the thing which makes truth, in affairs of this sort." By such a "constitution," he asserts that God made Adam and his posterity to be one, so as to involve the imputation of his sin to them.

That is, when "he spake, and it was done, he commanded and it stood fast," God did not give permanent existence to anything. He only arranged matters so as to mislead the popular mind into that belief, by a "constitution" of so strange a character, that whilst the divine sovereignty "makes truth" out of the really false appearances, it is truth of a texture so flimsy that the acuteness of this philosophy detects and exposes it, as unreal and deceptive. And so in regard to our relation to Adam.

On this subject, two diverse views had obtained more or less currency, in the Reformed Church, prior to Edwards. The first was the doctrine of the mediæval realists, who held, that human nature is an impersonal substance, created in Adam and diffused from him to his posterity, each individual being a mere phenomenon or mode of this substance. This nature had a will of its own, which apostatized from God, and carried with it, in the fall, Adam and all the race.

The other view was more generally prevalent; and was embodied in all the Reformed confessions. According to it, we "being in Adam's loins, as branches in the root, and comprehended in the same covenant,"* "sinned in him and fell with him, in his first transgression." As Boston clearly expresses it, "We are not only made liable to punishment, by this disobedience, but we are made sinners by it. Not only is the guilt ours, but the fault is ours: we not only die in Adam, 1 Cor. xv. 22, but we sinned in him, as our federal head, Rom. v. 12; we broke the covenant in him; that breach, in law reckoning, is ours; and is reckoned ours, because it is ours, by virtue of our being one with him, in his loins, as our natural and federal head."†

"It is reckoned ours, because it *is* ours." Here, precisely, is the point of difference between the old, the true, Reformed theology, and the Edwardean theory. The former teaches that we are, by generation one with Adam, and, therefore, so treated in the covenant. Edwards inverts this order, and teaches that we are regarded and treated as one with him; and are thus,

* Westminster Assembly's "Sum of Saving Doctrine," Head i. § 3.
† Boston on the Covenant of Works, Head iii.

contrary to the real fact, "constituted" one with him, and, therefore, legally, so recognized and dealt with.

In addition to Edwards' metaphysical gloss upon the doctrine of imputation, he held and propagated two or three pregnant errors. The first was, that all sin consists in selfishness; and all holiness or virtue, in disinterested benevolence. The second grows out of this.—If holiness consists in disinterested benevolence, God, when he brought creation into existence, was, bound, as a holy being, to produce that system which would secure the greatest possible amount of happiness to the universe. Edwards also insisted upon the distinction between natural and moral ability. Of the latter, only, is the sinner devoid, with respect to evangelical obedience.

The peculiarities of Edwards have, in themselves, a very harmless appearance. But, not only did they involve consequences which he would have utterly repudiated,—they were, moreover, so incorporated by him into his doctrinal system of theology, that, when they are taken away, nothing but a wreck remains. In this respect, his influence has been most disastrous, leaving his disciples afloat on the deep, without guiding star or compass. "New England theology," in all its phases, is characterized by the adoption of Edwards' definitions of sin and holiness; and by a rejection of the doctrine of imputation; identified as it was supposed to be with his doctrine of identity.

The first fruits of Edwards' speculations were seen in the teachings of Hopkins, West, Spring, Emmons, the younger Edwards, and their followers. The school of Emmons, with unflinching courage and logic, followed out the premises to their legitimate consequences. The larger number of Edwardeans stopped short, in the milder system, which goes by the name of Hopkins. The logical process was brief and simple, and the conclusions inevitable. If the creatures be no causes,—if God be the sole and immediate cause of all effects, he and he only is the cause of sin, in Adam and in us. If there be no powers in man's nature,—if the phenomena of his affections and actions are the immediate effects of the power of God,—there can be, in him, no native tendencies and dispositions, either sinful or holy. These qualities can only be predicated of exercises or acts of the will and affections. If Adam's nature is no cause to his posterity, it does not cause their depravity; God, the only cause, must in some way, be its author. If we are one with Adam, only by a "constitution," making seeming truth out of a falsehood, then he was only seemingly, and not really and truly, our head; and, hence, could not have been, and was not, our covenant head and representative. No covenant, therefore, was made with him, for his posterity. His sin was not their sin. They did not, in him, break the covenant, and justice cannot, therefore, exact its penalty of them. God may, in sovereignty, act toward us as he would toward sinners, but the inflictions so visited upon us, on account of Adam's sin, cannot be, in any proper sense, punitive nor judicial. For the same reason, Christ could not so unite himself to us as to covenant for us, or to be held accountable to justice for our sins. Nor, on the other hand, can we, by union with him, acquire a property in his righteousness. The consequence is, that Christ's atonement is denied any properly vicarious character. It was a govermental display, not a satisfaction; it was made for sin, in general, and not specifically for the sins of his elect; and his work was not determinate of the redemption of a covenant people, but only made way for the salvation of those who shall believe. The system ignores and precludes the spiritual union of Christ and the believer,—that union which fills so large a place in the old theology of the Church, and a knowledge of which our fathers thought of so much importance to the maintenance of vital religion.

Such were the teachings of the earlier disciples of Edwards. Some of them still clung to his untenable appeal to the distinction between a privative and a positive cause, to account for God's agency in the production of sin. Untenable,—for, if God be the only cause, as Edwards insists, what avails the distinction? Privative, or positive, God is the cause. From this difficulty, many took refuge in ambiguous phrases; whilst others did not hesitate to attribute all their sins directly to the efficiency of God. But they fell back upon the optimistic theory, and maintained that, since God was bound to produce the best possible system, and is a most powerful and excellent being, we are shut up to the conclusion that the present system is the best; and, sin being found in this system, we must conclude it to be an incident of the best system, and necessary to it. Sin, therefore, is not, upon the whole, an evil, but a good. Hence, it is consistent with God's holiness to produce it. It is only evil, in that the sinner is actuated by no such apprehension, but by selfish and malevolent feelings. Retaining partially the old forms of speech, these theologians utterly rejected the old doctrines of original sin,—the atonement and justification.

The new divinity was first presented to the public, in systematic form, in Hopkins' "System of Doctrines," which was published in 1793. Its author, the Rev. Samuel Hopkins of Newport, was not only a personal pupil of the elder Edwards, with whom he resided, as a student of theology,—but was also, his literary executor.

"Upon the death of Mr. Edwards, Mrs. Edwards, in consequence of verbal directions, given to her by Mr. Edwards, in his life-time, put all his manuscripts and his library into my hands and care," says Hopkins, in his autobiography; "his manuscripts to be disposed of by me, and two other ministers. And Mrs. Edwards solicited me to write the life of Mr. Edwards, to be published, with a number of sermons, to be selected from his manuscripts." He complied with the request, and says that "as these manuscripts were in my hands a number of years, I paid my chief attention to them, until I had read them all; which consisted of a large number of volumes, some of them large, besides sermons; of which sermons, I did not read the whole. In doing this, I had much pleasure and profit. My mind became more engaged in study, rising, great part of my time, at four o'clock in the morning, to pursue my study, in which I took great pleasure."* So intimately were Edwards and Hopkins related; and so thoroughly was the mind of the latter imbued and moulded by the teachings of the former.

The following were some of the leading points of

* Hopkins' Autobiography, edited by West, Hartford, 1805, p. 57.

peculiarity, in the system, which, in contradistinction to Old Calvinism, was, by its advocates, early styled, the New Divinity.

1. Holiness consists altogether in disinterested benevolence.

2. All sin consists in selfishness.

3. All holiness and sin consist in voluntary exercises or actions.

4. The moral law is the rule of duty, because it is founded in the nature and fitness of things; and, therefore, God could not but promulgate and enforce it.

5. Adam's sin is not imputed to his posterity; but by a divine "constitution" it was determined that if he, the father, should sin, all his posterity should also become sinners.

6. The depravity into which man is fallen is wholly of his will; and is total, because the will is entirely prone to evil. But it is not universal, inasmuch as the understanding and conscience remain, at least, partially unimpaired.

7. Men are possessed of a natural ability to do all the will of God. They are sinners, only because of indisposition of will, to what is right.

8. Christ's obedience and sufferings were fulfilled by him, not distinctively, as the Head of his body, the elect; but as, in general, the substitute for sinners; in whom is made an *exhibition* of divine justice, in consequence of which God can safely and consistently bestow pardon on whomsoever he will. It is not, however, such in its nature as to involve a demand of justice for the salvation, specifically, of any.

9. In order to true faith, we must feel perfect ac-

quiescence in the will of God, though it demand our perdition.

10. Faith implies a right taste and disposition. It thus shows the heart to be in harmony with the mind of Christ; and, so, renders it fit and proper that the Mediator's righteousness should be reckoned in the party's favor. Christ's righteousness does not, however, become the property of the believer, but it constitutes the meritorious ground for the acceptance of his faith for righteousness.

11. God, as a holy being, is bound, in all his works, to do that which is wisest and best; whence we may conclude the present system, sin included, to be the best possible system.

12. Hence, upon the whole, sin is not an evil; but incident to the greatest good; and, as such is caused by the efficient agency of God. Moral good and evil are equally the consequences of the divine disposal. Here, division arose. While Hopkins and others talked obscurely, and left it undecided, whether the divine efficiency employs different modes of operation, concerning the production of good and evil, Emmons did not hesitate to accept the logical conclusion from the premises; and to insist that sin and righteousness are, in the same manner, the results of the agency of the Only Cause.

In another line of deduction, the teachings of Edwards were, in their consequences, fatal to the gospel. No point of theology can be more important and vital than that which is involved in the exposition of the moral character of God. An exhaustive answer to the question, What is God? would contain all theology; and a false definition of any one of the divine attributes, as it would infuse poison into the fountain-head, must convey death through all the streams. How evidently must this be the case, if such a definition should obscure or obliterate some of the most conspicuous attributes of the divine nature! Yet this, and no less, was done by Edwards, in his definitions of sin and holiness. "All sin is selfishness;" and "All holiness or virtue is disinterested benevolence." The holiness of God is the consummate attribute, comprehensive of all the moral perfections of the divine nature. If this all-embracing attribute is adequately described by disinterested benevolence, it is manifest that the divine character is divested of every moral perfection not included in this definition. If disinterested benevolence covers and controls the whole case, then, justice and truth are subordinate, and their exercise must be determined, not by their own several claims, but by the demands of benevolence. In a word, they are excluded from among the essential attributes of God. The divine administration, determined by disinterested benevolence, may sometimes seem to conform to their requirements, but may also utterly disregard them, if benevolence should require it. The doctrine, therefore, that God is "a just God and an avenger," means nothing, and is ignored; whilst the fact that he "is of great kindness" is supposed to determine every issue in his moral government.

Now, whilst it is true that the loving-kindness of God is largely insisted on in his Word, it is also true that his truth and justice or righteousness are exhibited as entirely distinct from the other, and every way as essential, conspicuous and prevalent, in determining the plans and administration of the Most High. If mercy goes before his face, it is in the companionship of truth; while justice and judgment are the habitation of his throne. And the whole problem of the gospel was, to discover how God could be just, and yet good to men; and its glory is that on behalf of sinners, mercy and truth have met together, righteousness and peace have kissed each other, in the Lord Jesus Christ.

As relating to systematic theology, Edwards' definitions were effectual, in the hands of his son, the younger Edwards, in essentially modifying the doctrines of the atonement and justification. On this subject, three sermons, preached by him, were of signal importance. "They did much toward changing the previously common mode of thinking and teaching, on the subject; and led to the adoption of those consistent and scriptural views," says Dr. Pond, "which have since generally prevailed among the evangelical clergy of New England."*

The discourses, which occupy so important a position in the history of New England doctrines, have in view the obviating of a Socinian objection, which the author thus states: "If we be, in the literal sense, forgiven, in consequence of a redemption, we are forgiven on account of the price of redemption, previously paid. How, then, can we truly be said to be *forgiven;* a word which implies the exercise of grace? And, especially, how can we be said to be forgiven, according to the *riches of grace?* This is, at least, a seeming inconsistency. If our forgiveness be purchased, and the

* Dr. Pond, in Biblical Repository, 1844, p. 379.

price already paid, it seems to be a matter of debt and not of grace."

To this, the true and scriptural answer is found in the words of Christ,—"I and my Father are one." True, justice is fully satisfied; the debt is paid; and so, justification is by process of law, at the tribunal of justice. But it is God who has paid the debt. And, not content, merely to blot out the handwriting of condemnation,—not satisfied with a mere removal of the curse,—he has procured for us a perfect righteousness, not only sufficient to secure acquittal at the bar, but to confer a full title to life and glory. And is not this riches of grace? "He hath raised us up together and made us sit together, in heavenly places, in Christ Jesus; that, in the ages to come, he might show the exceeding riches of his grace, in his kindness toward us, through Christ Jesus."

The objection was anticipated and answered by the Westminster divines.* But, in the estimation of Dr. Edwards, there is no grace, if the law and justice of God are satisfied. Justice, he discriminates as of three kinds. The first is *commutative justice*, "which respects property and matters of commerce, solely; and secures to every man his own property." But, although the Scriptures use the terms, redemption, ransom, bought with a price,—these "are metaphorical expressions, and therefore not literally and exactly true. We had not deprived God of his property; we had not robbed the treasury of heaven. God was possessed of as much property, after the fall as before; the universe and the fullness thereof still remained his. Therefore,

* Confession of Faith, xi. 3.

when Christ made satisfaction, he refunded no property."

Does this mean, that there can be no property in anything that does not have a money value? And, that there can be no debt nor payment that is not pecuniary? Do we owe God nothing at all? Commutative justice is, of course, by Dr. Edwards, put out of the account. Christ paid no money for us.

The second kind of justice, named by Edwards, is *distributive justice*, by which a man is treated according to his personal character or conduct. "Nor is distributive justice satisfied. If it were, there would be no more grace in the discharge of the sinner, than there is in the discharge of a criminal, when he hath endured the full punishment, to which, according to law, he had been condemned."

If, then, the judge were to take the condemned criminal's place, in the dungeon, that the transgressor may go free, there would be no grace in this!

The third kind of justice, is *general* or *public justice*, and comprehends all moral goodness. "To practice justice in this sense, is to practice agreeably to the dictates of general benevolence." This it is, which, according to Dr. Edwards, is satisfied in the atonement of Christ. But of this third kind of justice, he states that "as this is improperly called justice, as it comprehends all moral goodness, it is not at all opposed to *grace;* but comprehends that, as well as every other virtue; as, truth, faithfulness, meekness, forgiveness, patience," etc. So, then, this all-comprehending grace, of general, or disinterested, benevolence, does *not* include justice, properly so called. To save appearances, the name is given to an attribute, to which Edwards admits it does not belong. It is not *justice;* and that attribute is formally excluded from the scheme, as inconsistent with grace. The end of the whole matter is, either, that justice is not an attribute of God; or, that, in the salvation of men, by the blood of Christ, violence is done to it, and for ever, even in heaven, must the blood-bought throng be under its frown. In either case, justice is excluded from any part in the administration of God. "Justice and judgment are" no longer "the habitation of his throne!" Then, woe, to the universe! woe to his own people!

To this theory of the atonement, Dr. N. S. S. Beman is fully committed; while it, more or less pervades and enfeebles all the writings of Mr. Barnes, on the subject.

The New Divinity, by degrees, spread through the churches of New England, during the closing years of the last, and the first quarter of the present century. Then arose the school at New Haven, for the propagation of the system, developed by the professors there; and it is a significant fact, that the first formal announcement of a new school of doctrine, by those divines, addressed a challenge to the optimists of the prevalent school, to justify themselves in assuming that God could prevent all sin in a moral system. Thus, the fatalism, which was involved in the Edwardean theory of divine efficiency, induced a recoil to the opposite extreme, in the assertion of the Pelagian heresy of free-will; and, by both, the whole system of biblical theology was corrupted, with doctrines having no pretence, even, to a scriptural basis; but growing wholly out of false philosophy.

The divines of New Haven found, in the very heart of the Hopkinsian system, some of the fundamental and most efficient principles of the Pelagian heresy.—That Adam was not the cause of his posterity;—that, consequently, they were not in him, in the covenant;—that they are not, therefore, punishable for the first sin; nor is depravity derived from him to them; and, that sin consists, only, in exercise, or action. Accepting these, as unquestionable principles, and recoiling, with just abhorrence, from the idea that God is the author of men's sins, they adopted the alternative, deducible from the same premises; and concluded that men are created without moral character; and that their depravity and sins are the result of circumstances, and beyond the control of God; and that regeneration is the effect of moral suasion, and not wrought by the immediate agency of the Spirit of God.

Boldly repudiating the system of "constituted" relations and fictitious intendments, which the Hopkinsians generally insisted on, the New Haven school, openly and unequivocally, denied Adam to have been the representative of his race, or Christ of his people. They held that every man comes into the world in the same moral and legal attitude in which Adam was created. Each one sins and falls, for himself, by his own free will. Christ died,—not as a legal substitute for his people, a vicarious expiation for their sins,—but as an exhibition of the love of God to sinners, and a display of the evil of sin, its just desert, and the goodness of God, in passing it by; so that, consistently with the welfare of the universe, he may forgive sin. Thus, the sinner is pardoned, and not justified; sin is forgiven, not blotted out; and justice is waived, not satisfied. Again, inasmuch as man's free will sins, and can sin, in spite of God's opposing power, it follows, that the regeneration and conversion of the sinner are beyond the power of the Spirit of God. All he can do, is to present the motives to the sinner's mind, which should induce him to turn from his sins. The rest must be the product of man's free will. Regeneration is, therefore, to be accomplished only by means of moral suasion. Man is thus induced to exert his own powers, which are altogether adequate to turn from sin unto God.

Such is the nexus of the system, the seeds of which were planted in the theology of New England by the genius of Edwards. Germinating, under the stimulus given by his writings, to metaphysical speculations in theology, the scheme has reached a position where it is impossible to remain, and, upon which, logically, the only advance can be to the open adoption of the more specious heresy of Arius, or the avowed Deism of Socinus. Already, an infinite atoning Priest and King and an almighty Renewer and Sanctifier are eliminated from the system; and the divinity of the Son and Spirit of God, although acknowledged, is meaningless and inane. The whole history, is a mere rehearsal, in slightly modified form, of the process through which the Church of Geneva, the English Presbyterians and the non-subscribers of Ulster, in the eighteenth century and the nineteenth, passed; and from whence they plunged into the abyss of apostasy. Such, in fact, was the result of the ministry of the younger Edwards, himself; who was, by many, held to have been as much the author of the Hopkinsian system as was he whose name it bears. For twenty-six years, Edwards ministered to a church in New Haven; and was then constrained to leave, by the prevalence of Unitarian and other fatal heresies among his people,—the proper fruits of a quarter of a century's training in the new theology.

CHAPTER XII.

NEW HAVEN THEOLOGY.

Early history of Dr. Taylor—Professor Goodrich's doctrines—Nettleton's protest—A new seminary contemplated—Theological department of Yale enlarged—Dr. Taylor professor of Didactic Theology—"New Divinity"—Fitch's Discourses on Sin—Taylor's Concio ad Clerum—Can God prevent sin?—Taylor on the means of regeneration—Beecher's interposition—The Andover conference.

As early as 1808, Dr. Taylor, whilst yet a student of theology, under Dr. Dwight, had given occasion for anxiety to the friends of sound doctrine, by his views, then developed. Dr. Nettleton, who was, at the time, a member of the senior class, in Yale College, says of him:—"We then differed in regard to the nature of the doings of the unregenerate. He also read me a dissertation on the doctrine of the divine decrees, and the free agency of man, which I then regarded as a virtual denial of the former, and an avowal of the self-determining power of the will."*

Dr. Taylor was subsequently settled as a pastor of a church in New Haven, in which he continued, until called to the professorship of theology. In 1820 and 1821, a discussion was in progress, on the Socinian controversy, between Professor Woods of Andover and Dr. Ware, the Unitarian professor of divinity in Har-

* Letter from Nettleton, April 30, 1839, in Hewit MS.

vard. Dr. Taylor, and others of the New Haven brethren, expressed great dissatisfaction with the positions taken by Dr. Woods, especially on the subject of native depravity, and were understood to approve the views of Dr. Ware.

Prior to this date, the students of Yale, who were destined to the ministry, had, generally, and, almost, as a matter of course, gone to Andover, to study theology. But, about this time, dissatisfaction began to prevail in Yale College, on this subject. Through the Bible-class of Professor Goodrich, sentiments were instilled into the minds of the pious youth, which purported to be a reproduction of the doctrines of the elder Edwards and Bellamy; from which the professors at Andover were charged with departing. Thus, insidiously, was the way prepared for the full developments which followed.

The apprehensions, which these indications tended to excite, were aggravated by the report of doctrines more formally enunciated in a lecture by Professor Goodrich, to his pupils in Yale, on Saturday evening, December 15, 1821. He commenced by stating that he was about to present a different view of the subject of his lecture,—original sin,—from that which was commonly held. He then proceeded to set forth a doctrine, which the better-informed students recognized as bearing a striking resemblance to that with which Dr. Ware had opposed Dr. Woods. During the preceding winter, Dr. Nettleton had been occupied some time preaching in New Haven, in an extensive revival. With him, Dr. Beecher spent a number of days, laboring in the work. "In all our social intercourse," says Nettleton,* "the

* Letter from Nettleton, April 24, 1839, in Hewit, MS.

arguments of Woods and Ware seemed to form the principal topic of conversation. Dr. Beecher, at that time, did not fully agree with Dr. Taylor, and they were often, as I expressed it, 'like two cocks, by the gills,'—Dr. Taylor clear over the mark, and Dr. Beecher so far over that I could agree with neither."

When the report went abroad of Professor Goodrich's lecture, Nettleton was laboring in Dr. Beecher's church, at Litchfield, Connecticut. The latter wrote to Dr. Taylor on the subject of the lecture. He did not fully approve of the views of New Haven; yet made such concessions as greatly dissatisfied Dr. Nettleton, who wrote to Dr. Taylor, "With all my love and respect for brothers Taylor, and Goodrich, and Beecher, I must say that neither my judgment, nor conscience, nor heart, can acquiesce; and I can go with you no farther. Whatever you may say about infants, for one, I solemnly believe that God views and treats them, in all respects, just as he would do if they were sinners. To say that animals die, and therefore death can be no proof of sin, in infants, is, to take infidel ground. The infidel has just as good a right to say,—Because animals die, without being sinners, therefore adults may. . . . You may speculate better than I can; but I know one thing, better than you do. I know better what Christians will, and what they will not, receive; and I forewarn you, that, whenever you come out, our best Christians will revolt. I felt a deep interest in the controversy, between the Orthodox and the Unitarians, while it was kept out on the open field of total depravity, regeneration by the Holy Spirit, divine sovereignty, and election. For this was taking the enemy by the heart, and I knew who would conquer. But you are giving the discussion a bad turn, and I have lost all my interest in the subject, and do not wish my fellow-sinners to hear it."*

This letter of warning was written in December, 1821. The next spring, it began to be understood that a seminary was about to be founded, in the interest of the new divinity. At the meeting of the Hartford North Association, the Rev. Dr. N. Perkins "spoke of Drs. Taylor, Beecher, and others, as associates in founding a new seminary; being apprehensive that Andover might not be what they desired it to be." Dr. Perkins remarked, with some emotion, "Dr. Beecher says, 'We,' (meaning Dr. Beecher, Taylor, and others,) 'We must have another seminary; and then, if we lose one, we shall have one left.' Dr. Perkins said, 'This is good logic,'—but, like all other men who had seen Stuart's letters to Channing, or Woods' letters to Unitarians,—he did not seem disposed to think, that the cause of orthodoxy was, at that time, in such peril as to demand another seminary; and appeared to suspect their meaning to be,—'If Andover will not inculcate our views, we must have a seminary that will.'"†

In the summer of 1822, mainly through the exertions of Prof. Goodrich, measures were taken to enlarge the theological department of Yale College, upon the plan of adding one professor for the theological class, to be assisted by the other professors, then existing. An endowment was raised for the chair of Didactic Theology,—the founders requiring the Professor to sign a

* In Letters on the Origin and Progress of New Haven Theology, (anonymously,) by Dr. Tyler, 1837, p. 8.

† Letter from Rev. J. J. Foot, May 2, 1839, in Hewit MS.

declaration that "I hereby declare my free assent to the Confession of Faith and Ecclesiastical Discipline, agreed upon by the churches of this State, in 1708,"—(that is, the Saybrook Platform.) It was provided that "If, at any future period, any person, who fills the chair of this Professorship, holds or teaches doctrines contrary to those referred to, it shall be the duty of the Corporation of the college to dismiss him forthwith; and, if they do not dismiss him, then, we reserve to our heirs the right to demand the several sums which we have paid, or may, hereafter, pay respectively."

The Corporation made record of this requirement, and voted that "this Board doth, accordingly, found and establish, in this college, on said fund, a professorship of Didactic Theology, on the terms, conditions, and limitations expressed in said instrument." Dr. Taylor was elected to the newly-founded chair, signed the required declaration, and was inducted into office. This action was afterward vindicated, by the faculty of the college, in a published statement, upon the ground that the subscription required at Yale, to articles of faith, is only binding "for substance of doctrine;" and that Dr. Taylor "had certain knowledge, from personal intercourse with the founders [of that professorship] that, had he embraced every minute doctrine of the Confession, it would have been considered a decisive disqualification for the office." Was it, then, the design of the founders to mislead the public?

For some time after the organization of the theological department, the professors were occupied in the quiet propagation of their sentiments, through the instruction of their classes, without any public demonstration, on the subject. But, soon, the students of the institution began to issue forth, eager to disseminate the new discoveries which they had received. Says a writer who, in March, 1826, spent two or three weeks in New Haven,—"I had much conversation with several theological students, and some interviews with tutor Edward Beecher, and also with Professors Gibbs and Fitch. Such phrases were very common, as,—'Our views,' 'New divinity,' 'Dr. Taylor's views;' and there seemed to be a general opinion that New Haven had made some advances in theology."*

At this time the Rev. Eleazer T. Fitch occupied the chair of Divinity, in Yale College. It was one of the duties of his office, to preach, statedly, in the college chapel, to the students. In the summer of this year, he preached, on one Sabbath, in fulfillment of this office, two sermons, on the nature of sin; which, at the request of the theological students, were published.† In these discourses, the Professor undertook to establish "the unlimited proposition, that sin, in every form and instance, is reducible to the act of a moral agent, in which he violates a known rule of duty." Having endeavored to establish this position, he hence deduced, among others, the following conclusions. "2. That the truth which we have considered shows us that there is not a *sinful heart* in any moral agent, *distinct from* his own *sinful choices, determinations*, or *preferences*." "I have not denied," says the preacher, "and do not deny, that one purpose, choice, or preference of the agent, may

* Rev. Jos. J. Foot, in Hewit MS.

† Two discourses on the Nature of Sin, delivered before the students of Yale College, July 30, 1826, by Eleazer T. Fitch, 8vo., pp. 46.

have influence over him, in regard to another; but what I deny is, that any such disposition, itself moral, which is supposed to influence the agent to a given resolution, is itself, in its origin and continuance, at all distinct from a determination of will in the agent."

"3. We learn, from the present subject, that, in the connection of Adam with his posterity, no sin of his is reckoned theirs."

"4. The subject may assist us in making a right explanation of original sin." The explanation however is very vague, and amounts to this,—that "the Scriptures intend not to teach, that men are individually the subjects of sin, by imputation of guilt; or, by vitiosity of constitution, *previous* to moral and accountable action, or *separate* from such action. We are led, therefore, to the conclusion that, although man may be so affected, at his origin, in his constitution, as to render certain his commencing moral agency in sinful action, yet, that nothing can with truth be called his original sin, but his first moral choice or preference being evil; which original determination of will, or moral purpose, operates, in addition to his original susceptibilities, as a ground of his succeeding acts being sinful."

These discourses excited comparatively little attention, in New England, where the imputation of Adam's sin had been almost universally repudiated, from the time when the writings of Edwards acquired authority and his theory of identity became identified with the doctrine; and where many of the "orthodox" held the Hopkinsian position, that all sin and holiness consist in exercise, or action. They were reviewed by the Rev.

Dr. Ashbel Green, in the Christian Advocate;* to whom the Professor replied, in a pamphlet of ninety-five pages, characterized by an extraordinary display of arrogance and hauteur.† He scouts the absurdity "of carrying our views of guilt beyond the voluntary agency of man, to (we know not what,) the *nature* of man, the *seat* of the affections." A self-determining power of the will,—a power in the sinner to make him a new heart,—is also urged with great emphasis, (although not directly asserted;) by holding up to scorn the opposite doctrine. "Will he,"—the preacher on that text,—"say, 'You know,—and the King knoweth, that none ever do make them new hearts?' Where is his warrant for this? Who has told him, that men cannot and do not 'work out their own salvation,' when the Spirit of God is influencing them to will and to do?"

At the commencement of Yale College, in 1828, Dr. Taylor preached the "Concio ad Clerum,"‡ in the college chapel, to a large assembly of the clergy of Connecticut. The text was from Eph. ii. 3. "And were, by nature, children of wrath." The doctrine announced was, "that the entire moral depravity of mankind is by nature." From this good beginning, the professor proceeded to develop a doctrine essentially identical with that set forth in Fitch's discourses. He defined moral depravity as, in general, the entire sinfulness of man's moral character,—that state of the mind and heart to which guilt and the desert of wrath pertain. This, he says, "does not consist in any essential attribute or property

* Christian Advocate, 1826, pp. 136, 162.

† An Inquiry into the Nature of Sin. New Haven, 1827.

‡ The charge to the clergy.

of the soul,—not in anything created in man by his Maker." "Nor does it consist in a sinful nature, which they have corrupted, by being *one* with Adam, and *acting in his act.*" Nor "in any *constitutional propensities* of their nature." "Nor does any degree of *excitement* of these propensities or desires, not resulting in choice, constitute moral depravity." "Nor does the moral depravity of men consist in *any disposition or tendency* to sin, which is the *cause of all sin.*"

In what then does it consist? "I answer, it is man's own act, consisting in a free choice of some object, rather than God, as his chief good; or a free preference of the world and of worldly good, to the will and glory of God." In support of this statement, he pretends to appeal to Calvin, Bellamy, Edwards, and the Westminister Assembly, itself! "The Westminister divines say that 'every sin, both original and actual, being a transgression of the righteous law of God,' etc. I ask, Is not transgression action? Is it not something done, and done knowingly and voluntarily?"

The second head of the discourse is, "that this depravity is by nature." What does this mean? "I answer, that such is their nature, that they will sin and only sin, in all the appropriate circumstances of their being." "When I say that mankind are entirely depraved by nature, I do not mean that their nature is itself sinful, nor that their nature is the physical or efficient cause of their sinning; but I mean that their nature is the occasion, or reason of their sinning; that such is their nature, that, in all the appropriate circumstances of their being, they will sin and only sin."

The discourse closes with two or three "remarks."

"1. It is consistent with the doctrine of this discourse, that infants should be saved through the redemption of Christ. They belong to a race who, by nature, and in all the appropriate circumstances of their being, will sin. . . . Do you ask when he will begin to sin? I answer, I *do not know* the precise instant. The Scriptures do not tell us,—and I can see no possible use in saying that we *do* know, what it is most palpably evident we do *not* know. Is it then said, that we sin before we are born? But there is no such thing as sinning without acting; and an apostle has told us of two infants, who, while 'not yet born,' had done 'neither good nor evil.'"

Another "remark," whilst carefully avoiding any express assertion of the self-determining power of the will, and the ability of the sinner to make himself a new heart, very earnestly intimates that doctrine to be true, and urges precisely the same arguments which had been employed before, by Professor Fitch; of whose discourses, the Concio ad Clerum was a more elaborate reproduction.

One new point, however, was now introduced into the controversy. The Professor challenged proof that God could have adopted a moral system, and prevented all sin. "Do you say, that God gave man a nature, which he knew would lead him to sin? What if he did? Do you know that God could have done better,—better, on the whole; or, better, if he gave him existence at all, even for the individual himself? The error lies in the gratuitous assumption, that God could have adopted a moral system, and prevented all sin, or at least, the present degree of sin. For no man knows this; no man can prove it. . . . I say then, that, as ignorance is incompetent to make an objection, and as no one knows that this supposition is not a matter of fact, no one has a right to assert the contrary, or even to think it."

In a long marginal note, he assails two "common but groundless assumptions:"—"First. That sin is the necessary means of the greatest good, and, as such, so far as it exists, is preferable, on the whole, to holiness in its stead. Secondly, That God could, in a moral system, have prevented all sin; or, at least, the present degree of sin." In opposition to the latter dogma, he says,—"If holiness, in a moral system, be preferable, on the whole, to sin, in its stead, why did not a benevolent God, were it possible to him, prevent all sin, and secure the prevalence of universal holiness? Would not a moral universe of perfect holiness, and of course, of perfect happiness, be happier and better than one comprising sin and its miseries? And must not infinite benevolence accomplish all the good it can? Would not a benevolent God, then, *had it been possible to him, in the nature of things*, have secured the existence of universal holiness in his moral kingdom? . . . Is there, then, the least particle of evidence that the entire prevention of sin, in moral beings, is possible to God, in the nature of things? If not, then, what becomes of the very common assumption of such possibility?"

The Concio ad Clerum was ably reviewed by the Rev. Dr. Harvey,* to whom a reply was published, in the Christian Spectator, from the pen of Professor

* A Review of a Sermon Delivered in the chapel of Yale College, Sept. 10, 1828, by Nathaniel W. Taylor, D.D., by Joseph Harvey. 8vo. pp. 40.

Goodrich; who incorporated therein the substance of his own lecture of 1821.

In the course of the year 1829, the successive numbers of the Christian Spectator contained a series of articles, from Dr. Taylor, on regeneration. Taking occasion from a recently published treatise on the means of regeneration, by Dr. Spring, of New York,* which was briefly noticed, in the first article, the professor proceeded to develop fully and boldly the views, on that and the connected subjects, which had only been implied or cautiously suggested, in the previous disclosures, from New Haven.

These articles completed the development of the essential features of the New Haven system. The writer undertakes to analyze regeneration, and show what it is, and what the means by which it is accomplished. The definition, and the process indicated, alike ignore the scriptural doctrine of regeneration, and exclude it. There is, in the scheme, no room, and no occasion, for the renewing of the Holy Ghost,—the new creation of the elect in Christ Jesus.

"Regeneration, considered as a moral change, of which man is the subject,—giving God the heart,—making a new heart,—loving God supremely, etc., are terms and phrases which, in popular use, denote a complex act. Each, in popular use, denotes what, in a more analytical mode of speaking, may be viewed and described, as made up of several particular acts and states of mind; or, as a series of such acts and states; which are, yet, so related and connected, that, for all

* A Dissertation on the Means of Regeneration, by Gardiner Spring, New York, 1827, pp. 50.

ordinary purposes, they are sufficiently defined when spoken of in combination, and as constituting *one act*, under one name. Indeed, it is of this combination or series of mental acts, only, that moral quality can be predicated; since no one act of the process, viewed abstractly from the other acts, can be a *moral* act. The act of the will, or heart, viewed abstractly from the acts of the intellect, is not moral; nor are the acts of the intellect, viewed abstractly from the will or heart."*

"When we speak of the means of regeneration, we shall use the word, regeneration, in a more limited import than its ordinary popular import; and shall confine it, chiefly for the sake of convenient phraseology, to the act of the will or heart, in distinction from other mental acts, connected with it; or, to that act of the will or heart, which consists in a preference of God to every other object; or, to that disposition of the heart, or governing affection or purpose of the man, which consecrates him to the service and glory of God."† It is "that ultimate act of the will, in which the soul, under the influence of the Holy Spirit, chooses God, as its supreme good."‡

"We affirm that there are certain mental acts and states, which, in the order of nature, at least, precede regeneration; or which precede,—as we propose to use the term, regeneration,—that act of the will or heart, in which God is preferred to every other object. Of these mental acts and states, our object does not require that we give an accurate analysis. It is sufficient for our purpose, to show that there *are* such acts and states, and that we so far describe them, that it may be under-

* Christian Spectator, 1829, p. 16.

† Ibid., p. 18.

‡ Ibid., p. 210.

stood, what class of mental acts we designate, as preliminary to regeneration, and as constituting using the means of regeneration. We proceed then to say, that before the act of will, or heart, in which the sinner first prefers God to every other object, the object of the preference must be viewed or estimated as the greatest good. Before the object can be viewed as the greatest good, it must be compared with other objects; as both are sources or means of good. Before this act of comparing, there must be an act dictated, not by selfishness, but by self-love; in which the mind determines to direct its thoughts to the objects, for the sake of considering their relative value, of forming a judgment respecting it, and of choosing one or the other as the chief good. These acts, also, imply, under the presentation of the objects to the mind, an intellectual perception of their adaptedness to the nature of man, as sources or means of happiness; and, also, an excitement of constitutional susceptibilities, in view of the objects; *i. e.*, involuntary propensities, inclinations, or desires, toward each object respectively."*

"Divine truth does not become a means to this end, until the selfish principle, so long cherished in the heart, is suspended, and the mind is left to the control of that constitutional desire for happiness which is an original principle of our nature. Then it is, we apprehend, that God and the world are contemplated by the mind as objects of choice, substantially as they would be by a being who had just entered on existence, and who was called upon, for the first time, to select the one or the other, as his supreme good."†

* Christian Spectator, 1829, p. 19. † Ibid., p. 210.

"The sinner is the subject of that constitutional desire of happiness, called self-love; to which no moral quality pertains. Let the sinner, then, as a being who loves happiness and desires the highest degree of it, under the influence of such a desire, take into solemn consideration the question, whether the highest happiness is to be found in God, or, in the world; let him pursue the inquiry, if need be, till it result in the conviction that such happiness is to be found in God only;—and let him follow up this conviction, with that intent and engrossing contemplation of the realities which truth discloses, and with that stirring up of his sensibilities, in view of them, which shall invest the world, when considered as his only portion, with an aspect of insignificance, of gloom, and even of terror, and which shall chill and suspend his present active love of it; and let the contemplation be persevered in, till it shall discover a reality and an excellence in the objects of holy affections, which shall put him upon direct and desperate efforts to fix his heart upon them; and let this process of thought, of effort, and of action, be entered upon as one which is never to be abandoned, until the end proposed by it is accomplished; until the only living and true God is loved and chosen, as his God for ever; and we say, that in this way, the work of regeneration, through grace, *may be* accomplished."*

Such is the plan devised at New Haven to make regeneration so easy that men may not be discouraged from attempting to do it. It has one defect. We are not told how to get rid of selfishness; which is the first and essential step in the whole case. Further, it will

* Christian Spectator, 1829, p. 32.

be remembered that "all sin is selfishness;" and, according to this New Haven means of regeneration, self-love, which is to be the motive power, in the process described, has no moral quality; nor have any of the series of acts enumerated, abstractly from the final act of the will, by which, as a result of the whole process, God is chosen. In the mean time, is the man in a neutral state, neither sinful nor holy?

Surely there is a better way than this. There are those who "were born, not of blood, nor of the will of the flesh, nor of *the will of man*, but of God."

Dr. Taylor's closing number was a designed modification of the previous ones; partly, at the suggestion of Dr. Beecher. The latter told him that he had employed terms badly, in speaking of the "suspension of selfishness." "All that Dr. Taylor means," said he, to Dr. Porter of Andover, is, that "the carnal mind is held in check, or does not *act*, and not that it is extinct." "While this carnal mind is thus checked, has it moral qualities?" said Dr. Porter. "Doubtless," he replied. "Is it sinful, or holy, or neither?" (Pause.) "The man is doubtless a sinner" said he. "Can one who pugnaciously and ostentatiously maintains that all sin consists in *action*, maintain that a carnal mind is sinful, when its action has ceased?" (No reply.)*

While the articles on regeneration were publishing, a conference was held, at Andover, at the house of Dr. Porter, with a view to see whether mutual explanations might not result in a restoration of confidence. There were present, the Andover professors, Professors Taylor and Goodrich, Drs. Beecher, Church, Spring, Cogswell,

* Dr. Porter, of Andover; in Tyler's Letters, p. 23.

Hewit, Mr. Nettleton and others. The explanations given, by the New Haven professors, however, only served to increase the anxiety. In the course of the interview, Dr. Woods said to Dr. Taylor, "Does the infant need regenerating grace, in the first month of its existence?" Dr. Taylor replied, "No." "Does he need this grace in the second month?" Again, he answered, "No." "Does he need it in the third month?" He replied as before. Dr. Woods pursued his inquiry, to the fourth, the fifth or sixth month of the child's age; and at one of these points, Dr. Taylor said, "I don't know but that the child may then need renewing grace."*

* Letter from Rev. Dr. John H. Church, April 30, 1839, in Hewit MS.

CHAPTER XIII.

THE CONTROVERSY IN NEW ENGLAND.

The Hawes correspondence—Beecher's letters—He was identified with Taylor—East Windsor Seminary—Dow's report on Taylor's theology—Statement of the Professors—Distinction of Primary and Secondary doctrines—"The system" and the surplusage—Theology of Dr. Woods of Andover—The Andover Professors subscribe the Catechism—Stuart and Park—Tendency to Universalism—General tendency in New England to defection—Its cause—New divinity and vital religion—Taylor and Beecher, and Nettleton.

THE "Hawes correspondence" appeared, in the Connecticut Observer, of February 20, 1832. In this correspondence, Dr. Hawes, of Hartford, in a letter to Dr. Taylor, enumerates some leading doctrines of theology, and informs him, that "there are not a few in the community who, from some cause or other, are apprehensive that you are not sound on those doctrines, and much alarm has been expressed, lest, as a teacher of theology, you should introduce heresy into our churches." He therefore tells him, "I cannot but feel that you owe it to yourself, to the institution with which you are connected, and to the Christian community in general, to make a frank and full statement of your views of the doctrines above mentioned;" and calls on him for "a clear and full expression" of his sentiments on these subjects.

Dr. Taylor, in reply, acknowledges, that "an impression has been made, to some extent, that I am unsound in the faith. This impression, I feel bound to say, in my own view, is wholly groundless and unauthorized." He appeals to "the repeated and full statements" of his opinions, already before the public, as "sufficient to prevent or remove such suspicions. The course you propose, however, may furnish information to some, who may desire it before they form an opinion, as well as the means of correcting the misrepresentations of others. I, therefore, readily comply with your request, and submit to your disposal the following statement of my belief, on some of the leading doctrines of the gospel." He then proceeds to give his creed, on the controverted points, in eleven articles, couched in language which would indicate but slight deviation from the theology of the orthodox ministry of New England. But, to these articles were added certain explanatory statements, which left no room to doubt, that the orthodox language of the articles was employed in an altogether different sense from that in common use.* It further transpired that, as at first communicated, Dr. Taylor's letter contained some things which Dr. Hawes thought unfit for publication; and that he had obtained Dr. Taylor's permission, and altered the paper, with his own hand, thus omitting the most "frank and full" statements in the whole paper. The conclusion was

* Dr. Taylor's letter appears in the Christian Spectator for March, 1832, p. 171.

inevitable, that the correspondence was a device to hoodwink the public.

In 1833, another effort to quiet apprehension, was made by Dr. Beecher, who, addressing himself in a series of letters to Dr. Woods of Andover, undertook to show, among other things, that in New England, "there are, among evangelical men no differences in *principle,* upon any fundamental point; and no *shades* of differences which do not admit of an easy and peaceful comprehension within the acknowledged limits of sound orthodoxy." He stated himself to have had "the deliberate opinion, for many years, derived from extensive observation, and careful attention to the elementary principles of the various differences which have agitated the Church, that the ministers of the orthodox Congregational Church, and the ministers of the Presbyterian Church, are all cordially united in every one of the doctrines of the Bible, and of the Confessions of Faith, which have been regarded and denominated fundamental."

It was, in fact, a matter of no little importance to this ingenious and eccentric divine, to be able to establish the position thus so confidently stated. His relation to the publication and defence of the New Haven speculations, was most intimate and responsible.

Dr. Taylor was in the habit of submitting his controversial pieces to the revision of Dr. Beecher, before publication. "This was the fact, in regard to the review of Dr. Tyler's remarks, published in the Christian Spectator, for September, 1832,"*—one of the most exceptionable productions of the author's pen; in which

* Tyler's Letters, p. 94.

he misrepresents and denounces the doctrines of a real corruption of the nature of man, incurred in the fall; of the possibility that God could have prevented sin in the universe; and of the necessity of the immediate transforming agency of the Holy Spirit, in regeneration. It was true, in regard to Dr. Taylor's communications for the Spirit of the Pilgrims, in his controversy with Dr. Tyler; in which all the peculiarities of the New Heaven system were brought under discussion. In one instance, Dr. Beecher took so much liberty with a communication, that Dr. Taylor, in a subsequent number, had occasion to make the following remark:—"Here I shall first advert to an error in phraseology, which, though not my own, occurred in some instances, in my reply to Dr. Tyler's Remarks. This arose from the insertion of a passage, while my reply was passing through the press, by one of the conductors of the Spirit of the Pilgrims. For the liberty thus taken, I am not disposed to censure my friend, considering our long intimacy, and the coincidence of our views on theological subjects, and the desire from which it sprung of giving an additional illustration of my opinions." That Dr. Beecher was the "friend" here referred to, was well understood, and it will be perceived that Dr. Taylor, here, in this public manner, claims a "coincidence of views" with Dr. Beecher, on theological subjects. This was published, under Dr. Beecher's own eye, in a periodical of which he was one of the conductors; and was suffered to pass without contradiction.

The line of argument adopted by Dr. Beecher, in his attempt to harmonize differences, and of the various publications from the pens of Drs. Harvey, Woods,

Tyler, Rand, etc., in opposition to the teachings of New Haven, we do not propose to examine.

In 1833, at a convention of the ministers of Connecticut, who were opposed to the New Haven system, the Pastoral Union was formed, on the basis of agreement in the articles of a creed which was framed for the occasion. By this Union, the East Windsor Theological Institute was founded, as a barrier against the progress of error. How inadequate for the purpose, this organization and seminary, a glance at some of the articles of its creed will evince. This was neither the Westminster Confession, nor the Savoy, the Shorter Catechism, nor any of the received Confessions of the Reformed Churches; but an original paper, of which the following articles indicate the most important positions:

"9. That Adam, the federal head and representative of the human race, was placed in probation; that he disobeyed the divine command, fell from holiness, and involved himself and all his posterity in depravity and ruin. And that, from the commencement of existence, every man is personally depraved, destitute of holiness, unlike and opposed to God; and that, previously to his renewal by the Holy Spirit, all his moral actions are adverse to the character and glory of God; and that, having the carnal mind, which is enmity against God, he is, justly, exposed to all the miseries of this life, and to eternal damnation.

"10. That sin consists in the moral corruption of the heart, the perverseness of the will, and actual transgressions of the divine law.

"12. That the only Redeemer of the elect, is the Lord Jesus Christ, who being God, became man, and continues to be God and man, in two distinct natures and one person for ever.

"13. That, except a man be born again, he cannot see the kingdom of God; that repentance, faith and holiness are the personal requisites of salvation, in the gospel scheme; that the righteousness of Christ is the only ground of the sinner's justification; that this righteousness is received by faith, and that this faith is the gift of God: so that our salvation is wholly of grace; that no means whatever can change the heart of the sinner and make it holy; that regeneration and sanctification are the effects of the creating and renewing agency of the Holy Spirit; and that supreme love to God constitutes the essential difference between saints and sinners.

"14. That the atonement made by Christ, in his obedience and death, is the only ground of pardon and salvation to sinners; and that this ground is sufficently broad for the offer of pardon to be sincerely made to all men."

It was a common remark among the disciples of the New Divinity, that the Confession of Faith contained, indeed, the system of doctrines taught in the Holy Scriptures; but that it also contained much besides. An examination of this standard, erected by the soundest divines of New England, against the errors of New Haven, may illustrate the significance of the expression; which is a key to the principle on which that Confession was adopted so readily, by every class of New England theologians, in entering our Church. The doctrine of original sin,—"the guilt of Adam's first sin, the want of original righteousness, and the corruption of man's whole *nature*,"—the "sin *in Adam* and fall with him," is utterly obscured. The only difference between New Haven and East Windsor on this point, is, that the latter dates depravity from the commencement of existence, the other from the beginning of moral agency. The eternal Sonship of Christ is ignored,—a doctrine fundamental to his divinity and to the Godhead. The vicarious atonement of the Mediator, his satisfaction to justice, and justification through his imputed righteousness,—all, are either ignored, or so veiled in vague expressions that the New Haven professors would have found no great difficulty in subscribing. The good intention of the articles is neutralized by their sinister ambiguity.

It is not, therefore, strange that East Windsor has accomplished, comparatively, little, in staying the tide of error, and re-establishing the churches in their ancient faith.

A few months after the organization of East Windsor, the Rev. Daniel Dow, one of the Corporation of Yale, being on a committee to attend the examination of the theological department of that institution, stated in his report, that, in his view, there had been a departure from the doctrines on which the institution was founded, in the instructions given. He specified the Dwight Professor of Didactic Theology, (Dr. Taylor,) as having published doctrines contrary to the creed required of that professor. Upon this report, the Corporation took no action; but appointed a committee to "inquire into the usages of the institution, respecting assent to articles of faith;" and invited the professors to a conference with the Board, on the subject. The result was a "Statement" from the professors, with the publishing of which the Corporation terminated its action in the matter. From this statement, it appeared, that, since 1722, all the officers of Yale College had been required to declare their assent to the Savoy Confession. This assent was further accompanied with an exposition of their views, in detail; designed to ascertain that their adoption really meant what it purported to be. In 1753, "when a controversy respecting 'New Divinity,' arose, a stricter assent was exacted, as a safeguard against apprehended errors. Not only the officers, but the trustees of the college were required to make a declaration of their belief in the Assembly's Catechism and Confession of Faith, not for *substance* of doctrine, merely, but for all the sentiments therein contained, and to renounce all doctrines, or principles, contrary thereto."

Upon the election of Dr. Styles to the presidency of the college, in 1778, he objected to the strict rule thus adopted, which had continued, until then, in full force. In a conference with the Corporation, he stated his difficulties, and a compromise was effected, the president subscribing the following declaration:—"I do, hereby give my assent to the Confession of Faith, and rules of ecclesiastical discipline, agreed upon by the churches of this State in 1708." The professors hence argue, that the subscription, thus established, was only for substance of doctrine.

It further appeared, from this statement, that, when Dr. Taylor was inaugurated, he, in signing the pledge required by the founders of the chair, communicated to the Corporation, an additional creed, expository of his faith. "This creed was accepted by the Corporation, as affording satisfactory evidence, that the 'substance of doctrine,' in the platform, is fully maintained."

In their statement, the professors present a synopsis of the doctrines of the Reformation, which probably contains the most precise definition to be obtained, of the extent to which the plea of substance of doctrine is held to justify deviation from those doctrines which are comprehended in a strict subseription.

"It will be generally agreed that the cardinal doctrines of the Reformation were the following:

"The entire depravity and ruin of man by nature, as the result of the sin of Adam. Justification by faith, through the atonement of Christ, to the exclusion of all merit in the recipient. The necessity of regeneration, by the special or distinguishing influences of the Holy Spirit. The eternal and personal election of a part of our race to holiness and salvation. The final perseverance of all who are thus chosen unto eternal life.—These, taken in connection with the doctrine of the Trinity; of the eternal punishment of the finally impenitent; and of the divine decrees, which is partly involved in that of election, constitute what may be called the Primary Doctrines of the Reformation.

"In addition to these, we find, in the writings of some of the Reformers, and of the Puritan divines, another class of statements, whose object was to reconcile the doctrines enumerated above, with the principles of right reason; and to reduce them to a harmonious system of faith. These may be called Secondary, or Explanatory Doctrines. As example of these we may mention:—The imputation of Adam's sin to all his descendants, in such a manner as to make them guilty and punished, in the operation of strict justice, on account of his act. The imputation of Christ's righteousness, to the believer, as the ground of his participating, on the same principles of strict justice, in the benefits of his death. The doctrine of particular redemption, or the limitation of the atonement to the elect. The doctrine of man's entire want of power to any but sinful actions, as accounting for his dependence on God for a change of heart; *et cœt.*

"Many of the old divines attached high importance to this latter class of doctrines, though differently stated by different writers; but they did so, only because they considered them essential to a defence of the primary doctrines, enumerated above. In the progress of mental and moral science, however, a great change of sentiment has taken place, in this respect. One after another of these secondary, or explanatory doctrines has been laid aside. Other modes have been adopted, of harmonizing the orthodox system of faith, and reconciling it to the principles of right reason, more conformable, it is believed, to the simplicity of the Gospel; without diminishing, but, rather, increasing, the attachment felt for the primary doctrines of the Reformation."

The former class, it will be observed, constitute "the system of doctrines." The latter are explanatory of it and may be rejected, with a good conscience, by one who declares his acceptance of the Confession, as containing "the system of doctrines taught in the Holy Scriptures." It contains "the system;" and much more!

It is significant, that the creed of East Windsor, as

already exhibited, tacitly recognized this same distinction, and ignores all but the "Primary doctrines."

For a time, Andover Seminary was looked upon as a reliable bulwark. Dr. Woods, the professor of theology, was one of the first and firmest to challenge the teachings of New Haven, and warn the churches of the dangerous character of the doctrines there promulgated. But Dr. Woods, himself, at first, denied utterly the doctrine of imputation.—"The imputation of Adam's sin to his posterity, in any sense which those words naturally and properly convey, is a doctrine which we do not believe."* At a later period in this life, he changed his views, as to the propriety of retaining the phraseology of the Catechism, on the subject. But he so explained the imputation both of Adam's sin and of the righteousness of Christ, as to harmonize avowedly with Hopkins, and Emmons, and the younger Edwards, who openly and consistently denied it. Speaking of the younger Edwards' account of the improvements in theology made by his father, Hopkins, and others, Dr. Woods asserts that, to the true doctrine of justification, by the imputed righteousness of Christ, the younger Edwards makes no objection. "All the improvement he mentions, is, that a mistaken idea of justification had been renounced, and a just idea adopted." "Any one, who examines the matter, will find that Willard and the old Calvinists explain and defend the doctrine of imputed righteousness, much in the same manner with Edwards, both father and son." Hopkins and Emmons, he says, "Professedly rejected the doctrine of imputed righteousness." But he insists that it was not

* Woods' Letters to Unitarians, p. 44.

the genuine doctrine which they repudiated; but a caricature. They really held the doctrine; only they were not aware of it!*

One thing is certain, that if the doctrine of Hopkins and the younger Edwards, as thus endorsed by Woods, be the true doctrine of imputation, the Reformers and Assembly of Divines were strangers to it.

The position of Dr. Woods, of itself, implies a remarkable state of sentiment, among those who founded and governed the institution at Andover. The Constitution, ordained by the founders, provides that every professor in the seminary shall be a man of sound and orthodox principles, according to the system of doctrines denominated the Westminster Assembly's Shorter Catechism. Every professor must, on the day of his inauguration, publicly make and subscribe a solemn declaration of his faith in divine revelation, and in the doctrines of the Catechism. He must solemnly promise to defend and inculcate the Christian faith, as thus expressed, in opposition to all contrary doctrines and heresies. He must repeat the declaration and promise, at the close of every five years; and should he refuse this, or, should he teach or embrace any of the proscribed heresies or errors, he shall be, forthwith removed from office.

Yet, it is doubtful whether one of the founders believed the fundamental doctrine of imputation, as stated in the Catechism; or, expected it to be taught. It is, therefore, no just matter of surprise, that, for years, whilst the instructions from the chair of Christian Theology were so indeterminate, as to be comprehensive of

* Woods' Theology of the Puritans, chap. iv.

every school of New England divinity, prior to the rise of New Haven,—if we may judge from the statements of Dr. Woods, above cited,—any orthodox tendencies, were neutralized by the more definite and brilliant prelections of the other instructors. The vague and inadequate conceptions of Professor Stuart, respecting the atonement, published in 1824, were followed by his denial of the eternal Sonship of Christ, and his doctrine on the nature of sin, put forth in his Commentary on the Romans, and his Essay on Sin, the doctrine of which differs scarcely a shade from that of the New Haven professors. And, soon, the chair of divinity, itself, was occupied by the inventor of the subtle distinction between the theology of the intellect, and the theology of the feelings; and the youth of Andover are openly taught to reject with scorn the doctrine of original sin; to regard regeneration, as a change in the balance of the susceptibilities; to deny the doctrine of the covenant of works; the satisfaction of Christ; and the justification of believers, through the merits of his righteousness, imputed to them. And, now, the ultimate and not distant point, to which all these currents tend, is plainly indicated, in the fact, recently announced, that, "In one year, five of the students of Andover lapsed into Universalism."* Similar phenomena are developing at the most of the other New England schools.

The facts here narrated lead to the conviction, that the causes of defection must have been widespread, and the defences of the ancient faith generally removed. In New Haven, itself, Goodrich, Fitch and Taylor,

* Rev. L. S. Childs, D.D., in "The Hartford Ordination," 1860, pp. 64, 8vo., p. 43.

each, independently and simultaneously, came to the same position, on the nature of sin,—the fundamental question in the whole controversy. And, at Andover, —notwithstanding the antagonism toward that institution and its former theology, in which New Haven avowedly originated; the spirit of emulation and rivalry, incident to the situation; the actual standard of opposition reared by Professor Woods; and the punctual and solemn exhibition and adoption of the Catechism, every five years; the same heresies soon gained an easy possession, and now hold undisputed control. Nor may the fact be overlooked, that no such defection in the seminaries, could have taken place, or would have been tolerated, unless the same causes had wrought similar results, among the ministry at large.

To the question, What is the secret of this most strange and lamentable phenomenon? there can be but one answer. The cause of all these doctrinal aberrations is to be found in the various features of the Edwardean system, already exhibited; especially, in the doctrine as to the nature of sin and holiness; and in the denial of the representative office of Adam, and of the fact, thence resulting, that "we sinned in him and fell with him, in his first transgression." The rejection of this fundamental doctrine carried with it, inevitably, the repudiation of the parallel doctrine of justification, by the imputed righteousness of Christ; and these two being removed, all is gone.

Upon the denial of original sin imputed, at once arose the two questions, How then did sin originate? and, What is its nature? And, from the answers to these questions,—conformed to the denial of our sin and fall in Adam, resulted a necessary reconstruction of the whole system of theology. From the subtle speculations of Taylor, and the plausible theory of Stuart, to the wild and despairing fancies of the author of the Conflict of Ages, every scheme that has been substituted instead of that of the Westminster divines, was originated in the struggle to find some means to account for sin, the efficient connection between us and Adam being denied.

And, then, the landmarks of a strict adoption of the Confession being, by common consent, removed, there remained no longer any barrier of warning or restraint. Each one claiming the right to depart from the received system, at least on that fundamental point,—no one was entitled to limit his brother by the measure of his own aberration. Thus, conscience was satisfied, and ecclesiastical authority disarmed. At first it was but a rivulet, which stole through the embankments. But it was the letting out of waters; and the crevasse which followed was as inevitable as the relation of cause and effect.

The system of New divinity started out, professedly, in the interest of vital religion, and zeal for the salvation of souls; and, in all its history, wherever propagated, it has assumed this guise, and affected to oppose itself to a "dead orthodoxy." In this connection, the fact is of interest, that, from the origin of the New Haven heresy, the opposition of Nettleton was prompt, open and consistent, to the last day of his life. Perhaps, no other man in this country, during the present century, has been more blessed of God in winning souls. Long before the new system had been promulgated, which held forth promises so bright for the reviving of religion, the old doctrines had been well proved by Nettleton's hands; and found to be the wisdom of God, and the power of God, to salvation to many. Not only did he refuse to exchange the weapons thus tried, for the new forgings of New Haven. Not only did he urge his expostulations, personally, upon Drs. Taylor and Beecher. But he sent forth warnings to the churches, in tones so unambiguous as greatly to annoy those gentlemen; who affected to regard themselves as the authors of his character and influence. "Dr. Taylor and I have made you what you are," said Dr. Beecher to him, "and, if you do not behave yourself, we will hew you down." This language the Doctor afterward explained as a jest; a fact, however, which he seems not to have mentioned, when he told the story to Dr. Taylor, by whom it was repeated. Whether jesting, however, or earnest, this avowal was not necessary, in order to ascertain the position of the parties. The Pelagian controversy began, at the first instant, in hostilities declared, between its authors and this true representative of the scriptural piety and the pure and Spirit-born revivals of the ancient faith.

CHAPTER XIV.

PRACTICAL PELAGIANISM.

Finney's sermons—"Sinners bound to change their own hearts"—What is the change?—Sinners can do it—What part the Spirit takes in it—"*How* to change your heart"—It is to be done by certain considerations—Ability the measure of obligation—The issue between God and man a mere question of sovereignty—Effect of the system inducing self-sufficiency and irreverence—Practical object of preaching—Philosophy of the new measures—Rude style of speech—Irreverence—"Fervency" in prayer—Particularity—Telling God the truth about people—Protracted praying—Women praying in public—The "prayer of faith"—The "holy band"—Its self-confidence and arrogance—Exciting style and particularity in preaching—The process of a Pelagian revival—The results—These the legitimate fruits of the New Haven theology.

THE Rev. Charles G. Finney was the first preacher, who adequately attempted to employ the theology of New Haven, in its practical relations. His "Sermons on Important Subjects" present favorable illustrations of his practical system. Of their publication, he stated, in the preface, that, "As my health has been such as to render it probable that I shall never be able to labor as an evangelist again, I have thought that it might, in some measure, subserve the cause of Christ, to publish something, on several points, that I have found, by experience, to need discussion and explanation."*

* Preface, p. vi., 3d edition, 1836.

We have, here, therefore, the views which his maturest experience, as an evangelist, induced him to present and insist upon. The first and second of these discourses are founded upon Ezekiel xviii. 31, and are entitled, "Sinners bound to change their own hearts;" and "How to change your heart."

In the first of these, the preacher states what a "spiritual heart" is. It "is that deep-seated but voluntary preference of the mind, which lies back of all its other voluntary affections and emotions, and from which they take their character. In this sense, I understand the term, heart, to be used, in the text. It is, evidently, something over which we have control, something voluntary; something for which we are to blame, and which we are bound to alter." "A change of heart consists in changing the controlling preference of the mind, in regard to the *end* of pursuit. The selfish heart is a preference of self-interest, to the glory of God, and the interests of his kingdom. A new heart consists in a preference of the glory of God, and the interests of his kingdom, to one's own happiness." "It is a change in the choice of a *Supreme Ruler*." In the entire discourse, there is not a word of self-loathing, in view of the ineffable holiness of God, nor of recourse to the Fountain of cleansing for sin. In fact, Christ is altogether ignored, in his true character; and is only known as the preferred candidate for gubernatorial honors. As a citizen may change his politics, "so with a sinner; if his heart is changed, you will see that Christians become his friends, Christ his candidate." "Now, the language of his heart and life is, 'Let Christ rule, king of nations, as he is king of saints.'" This presents a perfectly adequate view of the whole system.—All sin is selfishness; and the whole question, involved in the matter of salvation, is, a political issue between self and God,—who shall be king,—Christ, or, Satan.

The preacher next shows the requirement of the text to be reasonable and equitable. It is so, because it is fully within man's power to make the change. "Suppose God should command a man to fly; would the command impose upon him any obligation, until he is furnished with wings? Certainly not." "As, therefore, God requires men to make to themselves a new heart, on pain of eternal death, it is the strongest possible evidence that they are able to do it."

But, how is all this consistent with the Bible statements that a new heart is the gift of God? The preacher answers:—"There is a sense in which conversion is the work of God. There is a sense in which it is the effect of truth. There is a sense in which the preacher does it. And it is, also, the appropriate work of the sinner, himself. The fact is, that the actual turning, or change, is the sinner's own act. The agent who induces him, is the Spirit of God. A secondary agent is the preacher or individual who presents the truth. The truth is the instrument, or motive, which the Spirit uses, to induce the sinner to turn." A man, in a reverie, is unconsciously approaching the verge of Niagara. You call to him,—"Stop!" He hears; sees his danger, and turns. You thus save him. The word, "Stop," saves him. But the man says, "If I had not turned, I should have been a dead man." "Here, he speaks of it, and truly, as his own act." So here, "Not only does the preacher say, *Stop*, but, through the living voice of the preacher, the Spirit cries, *Stop*. The preacher cries, 'Turn ye, why will ye die?' The Spirit pours the expostulation home, with such power that the sinner turns. Now, in speaking of this change, it is perfectly proper to say, that the Spirit turned him; just as you would say of a man, who had persuaded another to change his mind, on the subject of politics, that he had converted him, and brought him over." "Now, it is strictly true, and true, in the most absolute and highest sense, the act is his own act, the turning is his own turning; while God, by the truth, has induced him to turn, still, it is strictly true that he has turned, and has done it himself." "The striving of the Spirit of God with men, is not a physical scuffling, but a debate; a strife, not of body with body, but of mind with mind; and that, in the action and reaction of vehement argumentation."

From such premises, the conclusion is easily drawn, that "if the sinner ever has a new heart, he must obey the command of the text, and make it, himself." But, if this be so, "why does he need the Spirit of God?" For the same reason that a man who can pay his debts, but will not, needs the appliances of the law, to make him willing, as well as able.

In the second discourse, we have the answer to the great question, to which the preacher has brought us,—"*How* to change your heart." We have already seen, that, in Taylor's means of regeneration, the first step is, to bring selfishness into a passive state; after having accomplished which, he finds all else easy. But he fails to tell how selfishness is to be thus disposed of. To this point, the whole attention of Mr. Finney is now turned. First, he warns us, that the change of heart is not to be accomplished by an arbitrary calling up of a given set of feelings or emotions. To acquire these, we must look, not at them, but at considerations appropriate to induce them. "If you will give attention, I will try to place before you such considerations as are best calculated to induce the state of mind which constitutes a change of heart."

What a miserable falling off is this! We have just been assured, in the most emphatic manner, that we ourselves can work this change,—that, if it is ever done, we, and we only, must do it. Now, when we are ready to attempt this great work, we are remanded to *considerations* which may perhaps do it for us. The thing to be accomplished is, to get rid of the affection of selfishness, and to acquire that of benevolence,—love to God and man. But these *we* cannot command;—perhaps certain *considerations* may! But what are these potent considerations, which are the best calculated to change the will and turn the heart? Are they drawn from the infinite love of God, in giving his Son, to satisfy justice, and atone for sin? Are they derived from the scenes of Gethsemane, the judgment-hall, and Calvary? No; these are altogether ignored, except in a passing allusion to them, as illustrations of the self-denial of God worthy of our imitation! The considerations,—the only ones presented, are these:—"First, fix your mind upon the unreasonableness and hatefulness of selfishness." "Next, look at the reasonableness and utility of benevolence." "Again, consider the reasons why God should govern the universe." Such are the considerations, by means of which the inquiring sinner is instructed that he can make himself a new heart. Such, the practical theology, which, emanating from New Haven, became the legitimate parent of the wildest extravagance and fanaticism, in New England and the Presbyterian Church.

The fundamental principle of all the teaching was, that ability is absolutely the measure of obligation. The argument proceeded to the assumption that, such being the case, a just God will not hold us under obligation, unless we have the corresponding ability. Hence, the conclusion was deduced, that, whatever the Bible exhibits as a duty, we now can do. The point considered in the above discourses was only one application of this general principle. "As God requires men to make to themselves a new heart, on pain of eternal death, it is the strongest possible evidence that they are able to do it. To say that he has commanded them to do it, without telling them they are able, is consummate trifling. Their ability is implied as strongly as can be, in the command itself."

This heresy involved with it a corresponding view, as to the office of the preaching of the gospel and the other means of grace. The word preached was not only different from that of the orthodox Church of God, in all ages, with respect to this point of ability, but, also, as to the matter, otherwise, of the gospel preached. In order to sustain the doctrine of ability, sin was relieved of its radical and inveterate nature, and reduced to a mere perversity of will, completely within man's control. Not only, therefore, was the office of the Spirit obscured and lost, but the precious blood of Calvary became comparatively valueless, and the doctrine of the cross of no repute,—disparaged, alike, by the denial of the infinite evil of sin, and the assertion that Christ did not, in fact, suffer its penalty. In a word, the whole issue between God and the sinner,—justice being ignored,—was reduced to a question of sovereignty, debated between the will of man and the rights of God. It is no longer, an issue between infinite holiness and unspeakable vileness and depravity; but a conflict between selfishness and benevolence,—a contest waged at the bar of man's free will, between God and Satan, who shall be sovereign;—a contest, the decision of which is with the will of man; whilst God's only remedy is, to avenge himself, by making man "as miserable as he can."

The result of all this was, that the preaching of the cross became foolishness; the announcement of the Spirit, as the omnipotent and sovereign Renewer, was condemned, as calculated to encourage men in indifference and ungodliness; and the preaching and other instrumentalities, devised and employed, were directed to one object,—by arguments, by terrors, by entreaties, by vituperation, by clamor and excitement, by protracted and exhausting exercises, by *any* means,—to *break down* the sinner's will, and induce him to "submit to God."

Another result, directly flowing from these doctrines, was the cultivation of a spirit of the most shocking irreverence and profanity. The theory professed to enthrone God. But the throne accorded to him was not his own seat of unapproachable majesty and glory; but, an exaltation conferred upon him by the free suffrages of those who prefer him as "candidate," for governor. In the Spirit, they did not recognize a creative energy, "according to the working of his mighty power which he wrought in Christ Jesus, when he raised him from the dead,"—but only a debater, skillful, indeed; but not so much so, that they had not long resisted his arguments; and could have done so for ever, had they chosen.

The disciple of this system, having tested and proved his own powers,—by resisting the Spirit, as long as he pleased, and withholding sovereignty from Jehovah; and then, by a voluntary surrender, and making himself a new heart,—felt entitled to take great liberties with the adorable Godhead, and to be very familiar with Heaven. He claimed to "have power with God,"—power to ask and receive whatever he chose.

The picture is revolting; but it is real; and the warning it conveys is one to which the Church should give solemn heed.

The system attained to its logical results, in the perfectionism which sprang up, broadcast, as an after-crop, in Western New York; and which Mr. Finney, himself, at length embraced, and transplanted to the congenial soil of Oberlin, Ohio,—soil, in both regions, fallowed for such harvests, by the operation of the Plan of Union. If the divine commands are criteria of our ability, the words, "Be ye perfect, even as your Father which is in heaven is perfect," are an assurance that we can be perfect, as God.

It is not our design to trace the history of this system of doctrines and measures, as it triumphed, in a succession of misnamed revivals, in New England, and especially among the mixed congregations of the Plan of Union, in Western New York. That region was swept, as with wild-fire, by the excitement of the new gospel; and left barren and parched, an easy prey to every form of fanaticism and satanic delusion.

Some illustrations of the system of new measures, born of the new theology, are now to be presented. In perfect harmony with the principles already stated, as determining the whole development, was the dictum, which was avowed by Mr. Finney as deciding the selection and use of means of grace. "The object of the ministry, is to get all the people to feel that the devil has no right to rule this world; but that they ought all to give themselves to God, and vote in the Lord Jesus Christ, as governor of the universe. Now what shall be done? What measures shall we take? Says one, 'Be sure and have nothing that is new.' Strange! The object of our measures is to gain attention, and you *must have* something new. As sure as the effect of a measure becomes stereotyped, it ceases to gain attention, and you must try something new." By skillful use of these new means, he thinks attention may be kept awake for a long course of years, "until our *present* measures will, by and by, have sufficient novelty in them, again, to attract and fix the public attention. And so, we shall never want, for something new."*

If the work of regeneration is one to be performed by men themselves, all this is evidently most proper. At the same time, it involves the introduction of a great diversity of measures, as the wit or fancy of different preachers happens to be more or less inventive. The following were some of the leading measures employed by Mr. Finney and his immediate followers.

* Finney's Lectures on Revivals of Religion: Boston, 1835.

Conspicuous to the first glance of observation, was a rude and vulgar dialect, ornamented with a selection of slang expressions, enforced by grimaces, and theatrical gestures. "Dignity, indeed!" cries Mr. Finney, "Just the language of the devil!" "Let hell boil over, if it will, and spew out as many devils as there are stones in the pavement," etc.

Akin to this, are the irreverence and profanity which were characteristic, not of Mr. Finney alone, but of the whole class of Pelagian revivalists. Says Mr. Finney, "Perhaps it is not too much to say, that it is impossible for God himself to bring about reformations, but by new measures." "God cannot sustain this free and blessed country, which we love and pray for, unless the Church will take right ground" in regard to politics. Many expressions thus used are too shocking to repeat. Mr. Nettleton quotes the exclamation of a pious colored woman of Troy,—"I do wonder what has got all the ministers to swear so, in the pulpit."

Another revolting feature of the system was the style of prayer employed. "Father Nash, the praying man," was a special favórite and co-laborer with Mr. Finney, in Troy. "He perhaps exceeded all others in the frequent repetition of,—'O God Almighty,—Come, God Almighty,—Come down,—break in upon them.' After continuing these strains, sometimes for a whole hour, alternately upon his knees, but more frequently sitting back upon his heels; writhing, as in an agony, throwing himself as far back as he could and recover, and then bringing his head forward into his chair; rising and bringing the weight of his fists to bear upon it, and give emphasis to his expressions; after continuing thus agonized in prayer, as he called it, for a whole hour, he would sometimes pitch forward into his chair, sometimes throw himself backward; sometimes rise and walk, as though hurried with a resistless impetus, and cry, 'O God! O God! O God!'"*

Connected with this *wrestling*, was what was much insisted upon,—particularity in prayer; that is, the naming and describing those to be prayed for. "The first thing, to be regarded as indispensable, is, to introduce the individual by name, and, in this, great care is to be taken, that the name be rightly called; as a misnomer has, it is said, been the occasion of disappointment, in the looked-for result. The next thing in order is, to tell what God knows of the individual. If perchance, the subject be a female, her sex must first be noticed, followed with, 'O Lord, thou seest this hardened enemy of thine,' (for it has been considered wickedness to call a sinner by a softer name, than God's enemy.) 'Thou seest how she has raised her female hands against thee, and how she is stretching out her puny female hands to lay hold of thee and pull thee from thy throne! See, Lord, how full her hands are of sharp arrows, to fight thee! Thou seest how she is hurling her defiance at thee. Thou knowest how black her heart is, and how her enmity to thee rankles and burns like the malice of a demon;'—and, if she be present, it must be added, 'Thou seest how she has come in here, with thy little ones, too proud to kneel before thee. Thou knowest that she has come in here on purpose to mock thee, and insult thee to thy face.' After completing

* "Delineation of the characteristic features of a revival of religion in Troy, in 1826 and 1827." By J. Brockway, p. 54, note.

this description; which, by the by, was often drawn out far beyond what I have here quoted, then might follow the petition or imprecation,—'Now, Lord God Almighty! come down upon this enemy of thine; break in upon her; break her down, O Lord, break her down.' (This could not be too often repeated.) 'Break in upon her. And if thou hast one thunderbolt in store, heavier than another, come, God Almighty, and break it over her head. Break her down. Crush her at thy feet. Slay her before thee.'"

"But, in case the subjects be males; (for, from six to twelve names were frequently introduced in the same prayer,) then the description and petition must vary with circumstances; as, 'O Lord, thou knowest he is a hardened wretch. Thou seest how he has raised his crest against thee. Thou knowest, Lord, how vile his heart is; and how nothing is wanting to make him a perfect devil, but for thee to strip the covering of his heart. Now, Lord, don't let him boast himself against thee; but draw thy sword and come down upon him. Drive it through his heart, and let him bleed at thy feet; that thine enemies may see it and be afraid.'

"This," says Dr. Brockway, an intelligent and candid eye-witness, "is a fair, though faint, specimen of the kind of praying which has been so abundant in Troy. I say, a faint specimen; because, to render it any way complete, it should be accompanied with loud groans, and with all that kind of action which denotes extreme distress. It is a *fair* specimen, because I have not introduced a single expression but what has been common; and many of them have been introduced more than twenty times in a single prayer; besides the addition of a long similar list, to fill out a prayer of half or three-quarters of an hour."*

This was particularity in prayer; and prayer that was not particular was of no value. This was fervency, and the admonition was familiar,—"Don't let us have any *cold* prayers." This was telling the truth about people; and, said Dr. Beman, when expostulated with, about it,—"Ah, well! we ought to pray the truth about folks. People are too apt, when they pray for individuals, not to tell God the truth about them. They will call them the servants of God; when, in fact, they are the servants of the devil. We ought to pray the truth about folks."†

A just conception of this part of the system, however, will not be had, until we include in it the custom of ten or twelve in succession uttering these pretended prayers, without a word besides being said, read, or sung; and several praying at the same time, whilst, perhaps, others were exhorting the impenitent to "submit to God," while the prayers were being made for them. Add to this, the promiscuous praying of women, in these assemblies,—a measure eminently adapted to "arrest attention," and create excitement. It was admitted, by some, to be wrong for women to pray in *public*. But, in mixed *social* meetings, it was altogether allowable, although fifty to a hundred persons might be present.

The "prayer of faith" filled an important place in the system. If they would only believe, they might have anything they chose to ask of God, and all other prayer was held up as an abomination to him.

As it was commonly difficult, at first, to find, in any

* Brockway, p. 23. † Ibid., p. 57.

community, a sufficient number of persons, qualified to carry on the machinery of this system, the evangelist was usually accompanied by several experts, who were represented as full of the Holy Ghost. These and the evangelist were "the holy band," whose business it was, by any means, to create and keep up an excitement, and, especially to take charge of the prayer-meetings, and the inquiry-room; from which, ordinarily, all others were excluded. The pastor was usually admitted an honorary, though subordinate, member of the band. One conspicuous trait characteristic of the band, was the indulgence of a spirit of the most arrogant pride and self-righteousness, commonly exhibited in the denunciation of Christians and ministers. "There is, to be sure," said Father Nash, addressing the people of Dr. Beman's church, in a prayer-meeting, "There is something of a revival, in Troy; but no thanks to any of you old professors, for it. No!—no thanks to any of you. You only hinder the work. If you were all removed out of the way, entirely; yes, I say,—every one of you; if you were all removed entirely out of the city, and out of reach, so that your influence would be out of sight, the work would go on a great deal better. Yes, let two or three faithful ministers come in here from abroad, and take the whole management of the work, it would go much better. There is, to be sure, some of the young converts who would help some. Yes, I could name one young convert, who is worth more than all of you. Come, now, pray, some of you. But don't make any of your cold prayers."

Intimately connected with this trait was the disposition to arrogate the gift of discerning spirits, and to pronounce all those, and especially ministers, who would not give active countenance to their proceedings, to be unconverted men. As such, they were made the subjects of prayer, in which all the approved characteristics of particularity, fervency, and "speaking the truth to God," respecting them, were liberally displayed.

Like the prayers, was the preaching of this system. Designed to excite and "break down" the hearers, it was characterized by the selection of the most alarming themes, and the presentation of them in the most startling style and with the use of the most shocking imagery. "Look! look!" cries Mr. Finney. "See the millions of wretches, biting, and gnawing their tongues, as they lift their scalding heads, from the burning lake! See! see! how they are tossed and how they howl, as the tempest beats; blown up, by the breath of the Almighty. Hear them groan, amidst the fiery billows; as they *lash*, and *lash*, and *lash*, their burning shores."*

Particularity was cultivated in preaching, as well as in prayer. Persons were described in such a manner as to leave no room to doubt who were intended; perhaps, with the eye fixed upon them, or the finger marking them, and the exclamation, "Thou art the man," accompanied with the grossest vituperations and impassioned threatenings of hell, already exemplified.

Let us suppose this system of means in full operation. The report goes abroad that the man who has been so wonderfully blessed, in the conversion of souls, has come; and that a great work of the Spirit has begun. Believers hear it with joy, and crowd to the house of God. The unconverted throng the assembly, influenced

* Brockway, p. 40.

by curiosity or hope. After a sufficient amount of the various exciting agencies has been employed, a call is made for sinners to come to the anxious seat; and the assurance is pressed upon them that now, and by this step, they must decide, for or against the claims of God. The excited throng rush to the appointed seats. Father Nash, or some other skilled in "fervent prayer," is called to lead; and the anxious are assured that it is for them, now, if they choose, to make themselves new hearts; that is, to elect the Saviour to be Governor of the universe; and that they must do it, while the prayer is being offered. The prayer is uttered, amid groans and cries; whilst the anxious, it may be, are personally addressed by parents or friends, or by one of the "holy band." At the close of the prayer, those who have "submitted to God" are called to rise, or retire to the conference-room. A number respond. The same process is renewed, again and again, until the night is far spent, and the morning hours are encroached upon. This course is continued, night after night, for weeks, or even months; as long as material remains, to be operated upon, or the susceptibilities to excitement continue.

At first, a judicious pastor and intelligent Christians may be startled, and alarmed. But souls are at stake. The revivalist has a reputation and experience, in which they fondly confide; and, soon, the power of effectual resistance is gone. The minister is "broken down," and his unwilling sanction gives an additional impulse to the revivalist's fame. Soon the papers report a great revival. Hundreds of converts are announced. Among them are numbered all who, by rising, or otherwise, in response to the oft-repeated calls, have professed themselves to have enlisted on the Lord's side. The evangelist goes his way, crowned with honor, and laden with gifts, to re-enact similar scenes, on some other stage.

But, what has been the result upon the Church? Unconverted persons, who were of a susceptible disposition and tender conscience, have been wrought up to an intense state of excitement. This, according to a well-known law of the human mind, which refuses, permanently, to sustain excessive emotion, of any kind, has suddenly given place to apathy. The subject of it is "*broken down*," and a transition is realized, which is supposed to be a change of heart. Others, more self-confident, have accepted the terms of salvation, presented to them; by electing Jesus as King, and determining, henceforward, to be on his side. They have "made themselves new hearts." Thus, the impenitent are deceived. The Church is filled with false professors. The moral susceptibilities of all are blunted and deadened,—multitudes awake out of the dream, to find themselves deceived, and to pronounce all religion a sham and a fraud. Others are the easy prey of the wildest fanatical impostures. The cause of true religion is prostrate; and the Church is doomed to years of barrenness and desolation; relieved, it may be, at long intervals, by spasms of activity, under the galvanism of similar appliances.

Such were the fruits, widely realized in Western New York, from the New Haven theology. They were its legitimate and proper results. The good taste, common sense, and piety, of many of the disciples of that school, may revolt from these exhibitions, and pause before adopting them, in their full development. But the practical system of Finney, Burchard, Myrick, and their compeers, was deduced, from the theology of New Haven, by a logic, which no ingenuity can evade.

Dr. Beecher joined, at first, with Nettleton and others in expostulations to Messrs. Beman, Finney, and the patrons of their measures. "He has set himself up," said Dr. Beman, "to oppose revivals, for fear they were getting unpopular." Whatever the motives, Dr. Beecher afterward found reason to change his position, and give the cordial sanction of his presence and voice to the preaching and measures of Mr. Finney; when laboring in Boston, at a later date.

The errors of the New Divinity may, to many, seem of no practical importance; but the results following are, the ruin of souls, and the desolation of the churches.

CHAPTER XV.

THE HOPKINSIAN CONTROVERSY.

Hopkinsianism in New York and Philadelphia—Ely's "Contrast"—The Young Men's Missionary Society of New York—Case of Mr. Cox—Division of the Society—The Triangle—Synod of Philadelphia's Pastoral letter—Case of Rev. William Gray—Whelpley's letter to two Jersey divines—Princeton suspected of "Triangular theology"—The Assembly of 1817—Moderatism—Congregational delegates voting in the Assembly—The African Institution, and the negotiations respecting it—The "New Test" discussion.

THE intimate relations existing between the Presbyterian churches and those of New England, precluded the possibility that the former could fail to be more or less affected by the radical changes which were taking place in the doctrinal principles of the other. The earliest indications of the coming troubles, occurred in New York. In that city, several ministers from New England, were settled, in connection with the Presbyterian Church. These brethren, generally, held some phase of the Edwardean, or Hopkinsian theology. Several individuals, of similar sentiments, belonged to the Presbytery of Philadelphia. None of these brethren could have gained admission into the Presbyterian Church, but for the relaxation, which the beginning of the present century witnessed in the strictness of its principles,—a relaxation of which the Plan of Union was the principal phenomenon. It was embarrassing and impracticable, after the adoption of that Plan, consistently to reject ministers from the East, on account of the peculiar doctrines which began by degrees, to be there prevalent. A footing was thus, for the first time, gained for "the substance of doctrine,"—the handmaiden of defection, always.

The propagation of the New England theology, in the churches of the two chief cities of the nation, excited much uneasiness. This was greatly increased, in 1811, by the publication of Ely's Contrast.* The author, the Rev. Ezra Stiles Ely, a native of New England, and a recent convert from the Hopkinsian system, was, at the time of this publication, stated preacher to the hospital and almshouse, in New York; a useful and indefatigable laborer among the poor and vicious in the city. At the suggestion of several of his brethren, he, in this work, exhibited, in opposite columns, the doctrines of Calvin, and the orthodox standards, in contrast with the teachings of Hopkins and his school.

The publication of the Contrast excited a hostility against the author, among the Hopkinsians of the two cities; which his vanity and imprudence did not tend to conciliate. Calls being addressed to him, from churches in each city, the Hopkinsian members of the Presbyteries made pertinacious opposition to his settlement. They proceeded to the length of a prosecution for falsehood, conducted in the Presbytery of New

* A Contrast between Calvinism and Hopkinsianism, by Ezra Stiles Ely, A. M. New York, 1811, pp. 280, 8vo.

York, with great violence and zeal. The case, however, broke down, in the midst. The members, by whom it had been urged, were indebted to the magnanimity of Mr. Ely, for exemption from the just consequences of their rashness and violence. And he was, at length, settled in Philadelphia, where he was destined, at a later day, to take so conspicuous a part in forwarding the plans of the very party, from whose early hostility he had so hardly escaped.

The uneasiness, in New York, of which the case of Mr. Ely was an incident, broke out into open controversy and division, in 1816, in the committee room of the Young Men's Missionary Society of New York. This society was devoted to the prosecution of domestic missions, and was composed of members of the Presbyterian, Associate Reformed, and Reformed Dutch Churches. Its constitution embodied a Calvinistic creed, in conformity with which the sentiments of its missionaries were required to be.

In November, 1816, the Rev. Samuel H. Cox, a licentiate of the Presbytery of New York, was proposed to the Board of Directors, as a missionary under its care. His doctrinal views were questionable; and the committee on missions refused to report him to the Board of Directors, without further evidence of his soundness. The Rev. Gardiner Spring was Mr. Cox's theological instructor, and was chairman of the committee. He refused to allow an examination of the candidate, but offered himself as a substitute. The committee, at length, consented to this curious arrangement. Three hours were spent in the vicarious examination of Mr. Cox, in the person of Mr. Spring. The result was unsatisfactory. The committee, therefore, declined to recommend Mr. Cox to the Directors.

An attempt was then made, in the Board, to have the candidate appointed, notwithstanding the unfavorable report of the committee. The motion was rejected, by a vote of six to twelve. The annual meeting was at hand. The conflict was transferred to that field. The Hopkinsian party attempted, unsuccessfully to displace the Calvinistic Directors and fill their places with others, of more congenial sentiments. Failing in this, an attempt was next made to obtain such action from the society as would prevent the exclusion of future candidates, upon the ground of Hopkinsian sentiments. The discussion was protracted through several evenings. The merits of the Hopkinsian theology were largely discussed; and as the result, the society, by a vote of one hundred and eighty-two to ninety-one, sustained the Directors, and refused to modify the policy adopted. The minority immediately withdrew, and organized the New York Evangelical Missionary Society of Young Men.

Whilst these proceedings were in progress, the public excitement was aggravated, by the publication of a series of articles, under the designation of "The Triangle." These appeared in successive numbers, in pamphlet form, over the signature of "Investigator." They were composed of caricatures of the leading doctrines of the Confession, especially on Original Sin, Inability, and the Atonement, the three points of the Calvinistic Triangle; together with violent philippics against the friends of orthodoxy, and pleas for "tolerance," and "free inquiry," on doctrinal subjects. "Orthodoxy" was held up to utter contempt, whilst Hopkinsianism was exhibited as peculiarly congenial to the spirit of revivals, and the dissemination of the gospel. The writer held a racy pen; and his pieces were admirably calculated to catch the popular ear, to which and all its prejudices he directly addressed himself. The author was the Rev. Samuel Whelpley, then residing with his son, the Rev. Philip M. Whelpley, the successor of Doctor Miller, in the First Church, New York.*

"The sentiments," says this writer, "usually denominated Hopkinsian, were never considered as heresy, by the founders of the Presbyterian Church in America, nor by the wisest and ablest divines who differed with them, in any subsequent period, in Europe or America. Nothing was ever further from their thoughts than any idea of making them at all a breaking point, in church communion and fellowship. Candidates for the ministry were never impeded in their progress, or censured, for holding them. Ordination or licensure was never refused to a man who professed them; nor was any bar laid in the way of his acceding to any vacant church, which had given him a call."†

Addressing himself to certain Hopkinsian Doctors in New Jersey, he tells them,—"That truth," by which he means Hopkinsianism, "has made progress in this country, is as evident as it is that God has poured out his Spirit on his churches,—is as evident as it is that religious freedom and toleration have here first showered

* The numbers of "The Triangle," were collected into a volume and published, in 1832, pp. 396, 8vo.

† Whelpley's Triangle, p. 160.

their blessings on mankind. The same spirit is opposed to both, and is equally free and bold to declare the latter profane licentiousness, and the former error and delusion and a departure from 'the form of sound words.' The sun, from a cloudless meridian, is not more visible, than, that a powerful diversion is making, in opposition to both; and is beginning to arm itself, not with evidence, argument, or moral suasion,—not by addressing the understandings and consciences of men,—but with varied forms of personal influence, extensive interests, and ecclesiastical censures,—with pecuniary funds, establishments, and institutions. And this incessant harping on the Reformers, and doctrines of the Reformation,—this leaning toward the established churches in Europe, [he means the Church of Scotland,] which are no models for us, but bringing round a sweep of influence, and setting up, as a mark, a kind of 'unity of the faith,' which is for ever to exterminate all freedom of opinion and inquiry, and eventually all liberty of conscience. . . . And, gentlemen, may Heaven long defend us from the yoke of the faith worn by the Protestant churches of Europe, even the best of them."*

In closing, he appeals to his correspondents,—"Your talents, your long experience, your conspicuous stations, your standing in the public confidence, and your correct sentiments, are pledges which the Church holds, that your exertions in the cause of truth will be equally distinguished and decided."†

The parties here addressed appear to have been the Rev. Drs. Richards and Griffin. They were not heed-

* The Triangle, p. 250. † Ibid., p. 255.

less of the admonition that the advocates of adherence to "the form of sound words" were "arming themselves with the means and influences of institutions;" as the subsequent history will show.

Whilst New York was agitated with this discussion, other sections of the Church began to feel the ground-swell of the coming storm. In the Synod of Philadelphia, at its meeting, in the fall of 1816, a pastoral letter, written by Mr. Ely, was adopted. In this paper, it was stated that "all the Presbyteries are more than commonly alive to the importance of contending earnestly for the faith once delivered to the saints, and of resisting the introduction of Arian, Socinian, Arminian, and Hopkinsian heresies, which are some of the means by which the enemy of souls would, if possible, deceive the very elect." A warning was uttered against "the disposition of many good men to cry, 'Peace!' when there is no peace." Presbyteries were admonished "to be strict in the examination of candidates for licensure or ordination, upon the subject of those delusions of the present age, which seem to be a combination of most of the innovations, made upon Christian doctrine, in former times. May the time never come, in which our ecclesiastical courts shall determine that Hopkinsianism and the doctrines of the Confession of Faith are the same thing." The elders were particularly exhorted to beware of those who have made such "pretended discoveries in Christian theology, as require an abandonment of the 'form of sound words,' contained in our excellent Confession."

The Pastoral also touched upon another topic:—"Three or four of our churches have experienced what is commonly called, a revival of religion; and, to them, accessions of communicants have been numerous. But, in many other congregations, a gradual, but almost constant, multiplication of the professed friends of Zion, reminds us, that, if the thunder-storm in summer excites the most attention, it is the continued blessing from the clouds which replenishes the springs, and makes glad the harvest of the husbandman. For the many, who are united in a short time, and for many who are gradually gathered to Christ, not by the great and strong wind, that rends the mountains, nor by the earthquake, but by the still small voice, which cometh not with observation, we would give our Redeemer thanks; and desire the churches to bless him, no less, for the daily dew, than for the latter and the early rain."*

From the language of this last paragraph, occasion was most unjustly taken to stigmatize the opposers of Hopkinsian errors, as enemies of revivals; advocates of "dead orthodoxy."

In the Synod of New York and New Jersey, at the same date, the subject came up, in a different form. A majority of the congregation of Goodwill, in the Presbytery of Hudson, had voted a call to the Rev. William Gray, a minister of Hopkinsian sentiments; to whom, for that reason, a strong minority were opposed. The Presbytery refused to put the call into his hands; whereupon the congregation appealed to the Synod; and by it the decision of the Presbytery was reversed. Against this decision, Dr. Alexander and others entered a protest, and an appeal was taken, by the Presbytery, to the General Assembly.

* Digest, p. 656.

These occurrences did not escape the vigilance of the Hopkinsian party, in New York. The relation of Dr. Alexander to the Theological Seminary, and the probable attitude of that institution toward their theology, was an occasion of special anxiety and apprehension. Whelpley rang out, from his "Triangle," the shrill notes of alarm. In the letter to Drs. Richards and Griffin, which we have already cited, he entered fully into the subject.

He tells these gentlemen that, "for several years past, there has been, in various places, an increasing opposition to the strain of doctrine and sentiments commonly denominated, Hopkinsian. At the present time, or within a few months, ground has been taken, on that subject, at which all those who generally adhere to that doctrine, are greatly alarmed and shocked. Direct information has been given against several young men, holding these sentiments; with a view to impede their settlement, and prevent their preaching in certain places. One has been informally cited to appear before his Presbytery, though at a great distance; to answer to the charge of preaching heresy. And I need only say, that the sentiments he preached are such as you, gentlemen, have been preaching and maintaining for many years; and that, with power and success. A whole Synod has made a firm stand, and boldly, and expressly condemned Hopkinsianism, as a heresy, and that whereby 'the enemy of souls would, if it were possible, deceive the very elect.' Corresponding with these particular acts, a combined and extensive influence has been used, and is using, to give the public mind a general strain of abhorrence and indignation against that strain of doctrine.* . . . .

"No, gentlemen, the opposition is aimed at the grand pillars of that noble and imperishable frame of doctrine which you have labored, through all your years, to establish and propagate. . . . . It is for you, reverend and beloved sirs, to consider, whether the evil has not grown to be of sufficient magnitude, and induced a state of things to require some remedy.† . . . .

"Perhaps the arrival and establishment of ministers from these churches, now called heretics, will no longer be thought necessary or consistent with Presbyterian policy. Perhaps it will be said that we now have an established ministerial Seminary; therefore it is time that the streams from that Northern fountain were dried up." . . . .

"Are we, gentlemen, to understand that young men, educated for the Church in that Seminary are to be imbued in this intolerance of spirit,—are to be sent forth to preach down Hopkinsian heresy?"‡ He supposes the triumph in the Church of the "triangular theology," reducing every minister and licentiate to a "three-square shape;" and then depicts the deplorable consequences; and "as for our Theological Seminary, it will be in the hands of men who will imbue, if possible, every candidate whom they shall instruct and send forth, in a deep abhorrence of the 'Hopkinsian heresy;' and every one will go forth under a full impression that he must beat down the odious doctrine of disinterested benevolence, and erect selfishness on its ruins."§

* The Triangle, p. 232. † Ibid., p. 233.
‡ Ibid., p. 235. § Ibid., p. 244.

The case of Mr. Gray is then taken up, and its history given, till the decision of the Synod. But "what do we see next? A large body of the Synod, headed by the very man [Dr. Alexander] whom the General Assembly has set at the head of the Theological Seminary, and, what is remarkable, the man who endeavored to distinguish himself as a friend to republican principles and the rights of mankind, rose and entered their solemn protest against this decision of the Synod; and encouraged the Presbytery to appeal to the General Assembly."*

After discussing largely the embarrassments which threaten to encounter licentiates and ministers, of Hopkinsian sentiments, he again returns to the Seminary:—

"But motives prior to all these will be effectually laid in the way of young men looking toward the ministry. They must go to a Theological Seminary; and, to the honor of that Seminary be it spoken, they have not expelled, as yet, for holding correct sentiments; but, from the appearance of things, *in progressu*, that event is soon to be expected. The principal part, nay, almost all who receive their education there, come out thoroughly and finishedly triangular. They go forth and preach all the points of *imputation*, contended for by any one;—a limited atonement;—know nothing about moral inability, and count that important distinction, as a most promising young divine of this city lately declared, before the New York Presbytery, nothing but *hodge podge;*—make all religion to consist in faith, a mystical principle, above all creature perfection

* The Triangle, p. 245.

or conception;—disinterested benevolence a scarecrow, and a little selfishness a very good thing:—that people must, by no means, be willing to be damned, in order that they may be saved;—that moral virtue is quite an Old Testament, Jewish economy, Arminian affair, and out of date;—metaphysics, ugly things:—that people must love Christ, because he is about to save them, and surely, they would be very ungrateful if they did not;—that the non-elect will be condemned for not believing that Christ died for them, because they do not know but that he did die for them. They never fail to impress the hearer that he is, in every sense, unable to do his duty; yet will be condemned for not doing it;—that he ought to believe in Christ, though faith is a divine principle implanted; and can be given to none but those whose debt to justice Christ has paid;—that men are moral agents to do wrong, but not to do right; and in a word, that sinners are not in a state of probation."*

These extracts not only illustrate the doctrinal views of the Hopkinsian party, but indicate the considerations which determined their attitude toward the institutions of our Church.

In the Assembly of 1817, the appeal, in Mr. Gray's case, came up and was sustained, and the Presbytery vindicated in its refusal to sanction the call.

The same body, however, in its review of the records of the Synod of Philadelphia, took exception to the Pastoral letter. The Rev. Dr. Miller, of Princeton Seminary, was chairman of the committee. He had been pastor of the First Church, in New York, at the

* The Triangle, p. 252.

time of the publication of Ely's Contrast. The prince of peace men,—he was much displeased with that production, and annoyed at the excitement which it occasioned in that city. He was not disposed, therefore, to regard in a favorable light, the measures of the same person, to enlist so respectable a body as the Synod of Philadelphia, in active resistance to innovation. The threatening attitude of the Hopkinsians respecting the seminary at Princeton had also, no doubt, its influence in determining his position at this time.

He, therefore, reported that the book be approved, "excepting certain parts of a pastoral letter, commencing on page 494, and a resolution on page 493, which enjoins on the several Presbyteries belonging to the Synod to call to an account all such ministers as may be suspected to embrace any of the opinions usually called Hopkinsian. On these parts of the records, the Assembly would remark, that while they commend the zeal of the Synod, in endeavoring to promote a strict conformity to our public standards,—a conformity which cannot but be viewed as of vital importance to the purity and prosperity of the Church,—the Assembly regret that zeal on this subject should be manifested in such a manner as to be offensive to other denominations; and, especially, to introduce a spirit of jealousy and suspicion against ministers in good standing, which is calculated to disturb the peace and harmony of our ecclesiastical judicatories.

"And whereas a passage in the pastoral letter, above referred to, appears capable of being construed as expressing an opinion unfavorable to revivals of religion, the Assembly would only observe, that they cannot believe that that venerable Synod could have intended to express such an opinion."*

This remarkable minute, very correctly exhibits the policy of the Moderates, who were, for some years, the dominant party in the Church,—a policy which had wellnigh been her ruin. "Strict conformity to our public standards cannot but be viewed as of vital importance to the purity and prosperity of the Church;" and zeal for it is to be highly commended, provided it expend itself in good wishes. But if any man's zeal should induce him to do anything to offend those who were destroying this vital concern, he is justly deserving of frowns and censure.

The report was adopted by the Assembly. Against this action, two protests were entered. Thus began, in the General Assembly, that struggle between the principles of our standards and the schemes of innovators, which terminated after twenty years, in the deliverance of 1837.

It is to be borne in mind, that, in consequence of the unconstitutional and suicidal policy, which had been adopted by the General Assembly, there were at this time present in that body,—voting and exercising all the rights of rulers in our church, five delegates from New England, who had no more right to such a prerogative, nor proper interest in the results, than had the bishops of the Methodist or Episcopal Church. Is it surprising, that, with such encouragement, the scheme should have been formed, and obstinately pursued, for nearly twenty years, to bring the Church fully under Congregational control?

* Minutes, 1789–1820, p. 653.

At the meeting of the Synod of New York and New Jersey, in October, 1816, a proposition was introduced, to establish a school, to train colored preachers, for the African race. That remarkable servant of God, Samuel J. Mills, was the author of the scheme. A committee was appointed to consider the proposition, upon the report of which, the overture was approved; a system of regulations was adopted, a plan formed for the African School, and a Board of Directors appointed, by whom a school was founded.

In 1818, the Board of Directors of this school, by order of the Synod, made a proposition to the Synods of Philadelphia and Albany to join in the management of the institution. In pursuance of that overture, commissioners from the two Synods met the Board, in May, 1819. The commissioners on behalf of the Synod of Philadelphia had been instructed, by that body, to propose that all persons, employed in giving theological instruction to the pupils in the school, come under the engagement taken by the professors in the Princeton Seminary. That engagement is in the following words, subscribed by the professor, on his induction into office:—

"In the presence of God and of the Directors of this seminary, I do, solemnly, and *ex animo*,* adopt, receive, and subscribe the Confession of Faith and Catechisms of the Presbyterian Church in the United States of America, as the confession of my faith; or, as a summary and just exhibition of that system of doctrine and religious belief which is contained in the Holy Scriptures, and therein revealed by God to man for his

* From the heart.

salvation; and I do solemnly, *ex animo*, profess to receive the Form of Government of said Church, as agreeable to the inspired oracles. And I do solemnly promise and engage, not to inculcate, teach, or insinuate, anything which shall appear to me to contradict, or contravene, either directly, or impliedly, anything taught in the said Confession of Faith or Catechisms; nor to oppose the fundamental principles of Presbyterian Church Government, while I shall continue a professor in this seminary."

This provision of the Princeton plan was proposed, as an article in the plan of the African School. Dr. Griffin and Dr. Spring, who were members of the Board, opposed the proposition, "because, as Dr. Griffin, distinctly avowed, they did not assent to the whole of the Presbyterian Confession of Faith, themselves." The delegation from the Synod of Albany endeavored to mediate between the opposing views. At their suggestion the phrase—"anything taught,"—was altered to read —"any doctrine of faith taught."

The article, so amended, was adopted, by the commissioners and Board, and upon that basis, a plan of union of the three Synods, in the support and management of the institution, was agreed upon. This plan was then submitted to the Board; which constituted, immediately, for the purpose of acting upon it; and was by it accepted and the union thus consummated. At a subsequent meeting, the Board in violation of the covenant thus made, rescinded their action, respecting the pledge of the professors, and rejected that article; of which action they gave written notice to the Synod of Philadelphia.

The Synod, thereupon, made record of the facts and resolved that, in view of them, "this Synod considers that resolution of the Board as a decided expression of their feelings and views upon the subject,—that they neither wish nor expect our co-operation with them in the direction of the school; and, that, on this account, the Synod do not feel themselves at liberty to act in the case; as being shut out from all co-operation with them, until further communication be had from that Board."*

At its next sessions, in 1819, the Synod of New York and New Jersey arraigned the conduct of the Board, in this matter. After a warm discussion, final action was postponed until the next year. What was the ultimate decision, we are not aware. The discussion elicited, from the pen of Dr. Griffin, an anonymous pamphlet, entitled "An Appeal, on the Subject of the New Test." The test, to which reference was had, consisted in the following words, in the Princeton pledge:—"I do solemnly promise and engage, not to inculcate, teach or insinuate, anything which shall appear to me to contradict or contravene, either directly or impliedly ANYTHING† taught in the Confession of Faith or Catechisms."

Of the negotiations, between the commissioners of the Synods and the Board of Directors of the school, Dr. Griffin makes the following statement. "Commissioners from the two Synods met the Board, in the city of New York, in May last. Those from the Synod of

* Ely's Review, vol. ii. 496.

† The emphasis here is that of Dr. Griffin, the use of which will appear below.

Philadelphia were instructed to propose the insertion of this article, in the plan of the school. A counter-proposition was made, to substitute in the room of 'anything,' (printed above in capitals,) 'any of the great doctrines,' so as to limit the promise to points really affecting the system of truth. This was not satisfactory. It was then moved to limit the operation of the promise to official instructions, in the school. But it was contended that the sermons of the principal, and his private conversations, (from house to house, was understood to be meant,) might have a serious influence on the pupils, and ought, therefore, to be restrained. This was enough to show the construction put upon the test. The Board exceedingly regretted that they were forced, by conscience, ultimately, to reject the article; and still more regret that such a circumstance should have defeated or suspended the important union proposed."*

In this statement, the writer leaves out some of the essential facts. At the suggestion of the Synod of Albany's commissioners, the phrase "any doctrine of faith," was substituted for "anything," in the pledge. As thus amended, the plan was accepted, by the Philadelphia commissioners, and by the Board, acting on behalf of the Synod of New York and New Jersey. Upon this basis, a covenant of union, for the management of the school, was at once agreed upon; and it was not until afterward, that the Board assumed the right, upon its own sole authority, to abrogate the covenant, thus solemnly closed by it, and reject,—not the test, as described by Dr. Griffin; but the amended pledge as to the "doctrines of faith."

* The Appeal, p. 4.

The real issue, therefore, was not, as the Appeal would have us suppose, upon an attempt to force the *ipsissima verba*, of the Confession upon the African school. But it was upon the proposition that the professors should not oppose any of the "doctrines of faith," contained in the Confession.

In the Appeal, Dr. Griffin states that "though the *great doctrines* of our Confession are so clearly revealed that they may reasonably be considered as settled, yet, in regard to many shades of thought and forms of expression, found in our standards, we are still at liberty to search the Scriptures daily, to see if these things are so. . . . If our standards must go so much into detail, some freedom of thought, on smaller matters, ought to be understood to be allowed to those who profess to receive them; or our Church must either be small, or contain many hypocrites."*

Again, he says, "If there *is* a case in which he [a minister] has a right to bind himself to limit his instructions by a human instrument, it is where that instrument contains nothing but the most obvious and leading doctrines of the Gospel. But even this right is questionable. It is safer to stop where our fathers stopped. But it is asked, Do not our ministers bind themselves, by their ordination vows, to believe and teach according to the Confession? Not exactly so. That assent to the Confession, which is prescribed in the Book of Discipline, is *declarative*, not *promissory;* and this is all that ever belongs to a subscription to a creed. We declare our present agreement with it; (that is, our agreement with it as a '*system*,') but we do not

* Appeal, p. 8.

pledge ourselves for agreement to-morrow, further than the creed itself shall be found to comport with the Gospel. Look at the form of engagements at ordination. The only promise exacted, respecting articles of faith, is propounded in the following words:—'Do you promise to be zealous and faithful in maintaining *the truths of the Gospel*, and the purity and peace of the Church; whatever persecution or opposition may arise on that account?' In this engagement, we promise to maintain the Confession, so far as it contains the truths of the Gospel, no farther."*

The writer tells the friends of strict subscription, that "It is merely a question whether their views, on certain minor points, shall prevail over the views of their brethren;"† and closes with the entreaty that "the test" may be "at least so modified as to respect 'the great doctrines' of our standards."‡

The reader will observe the subtle significance which Dr. Griffin attaches to the phrase "*system* of doctrine,"—a significance indicated by marking the word, "*system*," with italics and quotations. He was willing to be bound to "the great doctrines" of the standards, but claimed liberty on the "minor points." But what was to be the criterion of distinction between the greater and the less; and who was to be the judge?

Dr. Griffin's publication, it will be observed, preceded the famous "Statement" of the New Haven professors, some fourteen years. It was the first formal exposition of the "system of doctrine" theory of subscription.

* Appeal, p. 15. † Ibid., p. 25. ‡ Ibid., p. 27.

In reply to "The New Test," Dr. Janeway published a pamphlet, also anonymous, entitled—"The Appeal not Sustained." In this he vindicated the policy of strict subscription, according to the terms of the Princeton pledge. His closing sentences forecast the future, and fixed its responsibilities.

"*We proclaim it to the world, that, if the peace and harmony of our Church are to be interrupted, by the propagation of religious opinions contrary to our adopted standards of doctrines, the blame must be attached to those who introduce such opinions in violation of our constitutional engagements.*

"We deny the assertion that the differences in respect to doctrinal points that now exist, always prevailed in our Church; and in support of our denial we appeal to the condemnation of the creed of the Rev. H. B. [Balch] noticed already, in a former part of this discussion, which passed the General Assembly, with so great unanimity. We deny that ministers, in our connection dared till lately to deny the *representative* character of Adam and of Christ; to deny the *imputation* of the guilt of *Adam's first sin*, and of the *righteousness of Christ;*—to assert and maintain that the holy God is the *author of sin*, and to propagate the doctrine of an *indefinite* atonement; which represents Christ as suffering, not for the sins of his elect, who were given to him by his Father, to be redeemed; but merely for sin in general, and to make an exhibition of its evil."

A true warning and testimony, but unheeded.

CHAPTER XVI.

GROWING UNEASINESS IN THE CHURCH.

Apprehensions realized in 1814—Plan of Union, in the Synod of Pittsburgh, in 1815—Lathrop, a committee-man, in 1820—The Assemblies of 1817 and 1822 on doctrinal error—Bissell's case, in 1826—Case of Mr. John Chambers—The New England delegates to the Assembly cease to vote—Mr. Baird's view of the crisis of 1826—Overture of the Synod of Pittsburgh—Its withdrawal by Dr. Herron—Pittsburgh overture of 1831—It anticipated the Acts of 1837—The action of the Assembly upon it—Committee-men in the Assembly of 1831.

WHILST the Plan of Union and its resulting agencies were, gradually, but surely undermining the foundations of the Church, voices of admonition and alarm were occasionally uttered. But they passed unheeded. In 1814, when Ely's case was before the Assembly,—a case growing out of hostility to him, on account of his opposition to Hopkinsianism, the Rev. Dr. Beecher was present, as a delegate from the General Association of Connecticut. The questions before the Assembly, on this case, were purely of constitutional interpretation, growing out of a persistent refusal of four out of seven ruling elders, to allow a congregational meeting, in order to make out a call for Mr. Ely, who was the choice of an overwhelming majority of the Church. Yet on this question, so purely domestic, Dr. Beecher used all his eloquence and influence, against Mr. Ely, and on behalf of the recusant elders. "This," says the Rev. Thomas D. Baird, "with other things, led to a conversation among some of the brethren, about the unconstitutionality of the Plan of Union, and the expediency of its abrogation. We never, so far as we recollect, knew one man defend its constitutionality; but, as the Presbyterian Church had proved so sound and firm, in the cases of Mr. Balch, the Cumberland Presbyterians, and Mr. W. C. Davis, it was supposed that she could not be in much danger, from this quarter; and although unconstitutional, it had better be let alone."* Elias B. Caldwell, Esq., the Rev. James Magraw, and the Rev. Thomas D. Baird, were among the most decided in the expression of their apprehensions. These were thought to be sufficiently answered by retorts of, "Bigotry!" and "Intolerance!" The subject did not, however, enter into the discussions of the Assembly.

The next year, in the Synod of Pittsburgh, the records of the Presbytery of Grand River came up, for the first time, for review. The committee, to which they were referred, reported that "we doubt of their power to make Confessions of Faith, distinct from the Confession of Faith adopted by the Presbyterian Church in the United States. Perhaps, however, their circumstances may make it obvious, that what they have done was both correct and necessary; and, if they can make this appear to the Synod, we can cheerfully recommend the approbation of their records."

The Synod, thereupon, "heard the members of Grand River Presbytery, on the points alluded to, in the

* Mr. Baird, in the Pittsburgh Christian Herald, for 1837, p. 131.

above report, were satisfied with their explanations, and approved the Records."* The explanations were an appeal to the Plan of Union, and the assurance that the questionable measures, were regarded as but temporary expedients, in view of the "peculiar circumstances" of the churches in that Presbytery. Under this representation, the Synod reluctantly approved the records; although not without strong expressions of doubt, by members, as to the propriety of the action of the Assembly, which was admitted to entitle the Presbytery to exemption from censure. Such was the whole extent of the Synod's action, of which Mr. Seward in his narrative, says that it "did ratify and confirm the covenant, proposed and adopted by the General Assembly, in 1801."

In the General Assembly, the first "committee-man" that appeared, avowedly in that capacity, was Mr. Daniel W. Lathrop, who, in 1820, presented himself as a commissioner from the Presbytery of Hartford, in the Western Reserve. The case was referred to a committee, the report of which, after long discussion, and the offer of several amendments, was recommitted to an enlarged committee. The result was the introduction and adoption, "without opposition," of a compromise report. It recited the objects and provisions of the "conventional agreement" of 1801, and closed with two resolutions:—

"Resolved, In order to carry into effect the friendly object of the above agreement, that Daniel W. Lathrop be admitted, as a member of this Assembly.

"Resolved, That it be affectionately recommended to

* Printed Minutes Synod of Pittsburgh, p. 114.

the brethren who compose mixed societies of this kind, as far as expediency will allow, to conform to the letter of the constitution of the Presbyterian Church, in making their appointments and organizing their congregations."*

Of the efficacy of such resolutions, the subsequent history will give an illustration, in the person of this same "committee-man," become an ordained minister, and active member of the New School party, without ever having taken those vows which the Constitution prescribes.

In the Assembly of 1817, the subject of doctrinal error was introduced, as we have seen, through the Pastoral letter of the Synod of Philadelphia, and the attempt of the Synod to check the prevalent tendencies to defection, was visited with the frown of the Assembly.

Again, in 1822, a memorial came up to the Assembly, "complaining of the prevalence of errors in doctrine, and requesting the opinion and advice of the Assembly." It was referred to a committee, without exception, peace men; including the delegate from Vermont, besides one or two who were themselves unsound in the faith.

The report of this committee was adopted by the Assembly. That body could "never hesitate, on any proper occasion, to recommend to those who, both at their licensure and ordination, professed sincerely to receive and adopt the Confession of Faith of this Church, as containing the system of doctrine taught in the Holy Scriptures, and to all other members of our

* Minutes 1789-1820, p. 754; Digest, p. 574.

Church steadfastly to adhere to that 'form of sound words.'" There were, however, members present in that Assembly, who, neither at licensure nor ordination, nor at any other time, had officially adopted that "form of sound words," nor believed the doctrines therein taught. They, no doubt, highly approved of the rest of the reply, which declared that the Assembly is not called upon to take up abstract cases, or act upon remonstrances, as to points of doctrine, or the conduct of individuals, unless they come up in regular judicial process.*

The treatment of Lathrop's case was not likely to arrest the delegation of committee-men to the supreme court. In 1826, Mr. Josiah Bissell, appeared in the Assembly, and produced a commission as an elder, from the Presbytery of Rochester. A member of that Presbytery informed the Assembly that Mr. Bissell had not been set apart as an elder; but that he was appointed, as was supposed by the Presbytery, in conformity with the conventional agreement of 1801. In the discussion, it appeared that he was not even a committee-man. Yet, it was resolved to admit him as a member of the Assembly.

Against this action, a protest was entered, by forty-two members; in reply to whom, the Assembly stated that the reasons of its action were, "1. The commission which Mr. Bissell produced was in due form, and signed by the proper officers of Presbytery. 2. Every Presbytery has a right to judge of the qualifications of its own members, and is amenable to Synod, and not to the General Assembly; except by way of appeal

* Minutes 1822, pp. 8, 22; Digest, p. 658.

or reference or complaint, regularly brought up from the inferior judicatories; which has not been done in the present case. 3. It would be a dangerous precedent, and would lead to the destruction of all order, in the Church of Christ, to permit unauthenticated verbal testimony to set aside an authoritative written document."

The admission of Mr. Bissell was carried, by a majority of three; there being in the house, as voting members, no less than seven delegates from the Congregational Associations of New England! Another matter, which came before this Assembly, was even more calculated to arrest attention to the relations and attitude of those bodies toward our Church.

Mr. John Chambers, a candidate of the Presbytery of Philadelphia, upon examination for ordination, was rejected, on account of his doctrinal views. He, thereupon, went to Connecticut, and was ordained by the Association of the Western District of New Haven county; from which he immediately obtained a dismission to the Presbytery of Philadelphia. "We expect you to receive him as one of us:"—said they, in this paper.

The Presbytery submitted these facts to the Assembly, by which a committee of three was appointed, to visit the General Association of Connecticut and confer on this case; with instructions further, to inquire whether any, and if any what, further articles or alteration of the present terms of intercourse between the churches, may be expedient, "for the better protection of the purity, peace, and Christian discipline of the churches connected with the two bodies."

The Association appointed a committee, to confer

with this delegation. They met in New York, in August, 1826; but it appeared that the Connecticut committee had no power to do anything in relation to Mr. Chambers' ordination. It was, however, agreed, as a rule of the correspondence of the two bodies, to regard any such action as "irregular and unfriendly." It was, also, agreed that the delegates of the bodies, mutually sent to each other, should, thenceforward, have the right only to deliberate, and not to vote.

The General Assembly, the next year, addressed a letter to the other New England Associations, stating that the right given their delegates, to vote in the General Assembly, was a violation of the Constitution of our Church; and proposing that it be rescinded. The New Hampshire Association at once acquiesced in the change. The Convention of Vermont referred it to a committee, to report the next year. The result does not appear, on the minutes of the Assembly. The General Association of Massachusetts declined to consent to the change; and it was not till after four years of correspondence, that the Assembly, in 1830, received the consent of that Association to surrender her claim, thus, to trample under foot our Constitution, and exercise a potential control over the internal affairs and most sacred and peculiar interests of our Church. By that time, her attitude on this subject was no longer necessary, as a demonstration of the fixed purpose of our New England brethren to acquire possession of the Presbyterian Church, its institutions and resources.

Among the signers of the protest, in the Bissell case, was the Rev. Thomas D. Baird. He had been an anxious witness of the first rising of trouble from the East, as a member of the Assembly of 1814. He had sat in the Assembly of 1817, and saw the indications of growing error and an increasing spirit of false charity, tolerant of innovation, but intolerant of faithfulness in defence of the truth. He had enjoyed abundant opportunity, as a member of the Synod of Pittsburgh, to watch the working of the Plan of Union, there and in the Western Reserve. In the concurring incidents of this year, he recognized a crisis in our history. "The year 1826, was an eventful year,"—so he afterward wrote,—"as relates to this subject. The formation of the Home Missionary Society,—in our opinion the most formidable machine for the subversion of Presbyterianism, that was ever invented,—the transfer of the missions of our Church to the American Board, and the cases of Messrs. Chambers and Bissell, deeply impressed the minds of some of the members of that Assembly, and soon began to create just and well-founded apprehensions, that there was, in fact, a design to sap the foundations of Presbyterianism, by systematic, underground approaches."*

With such views, Mr. Baird, upon his return from the Assembly of 1826, drafted an overture, on the state of the Church, for the consideration of the Synod of Pittsburgh. In this document, after a citation of some of the general principles, which are stated in the Introduction to the Form of Government,—the dangers threatening the Church, and the remedy, were pointed out in the following terms:—

"Notwithstanding the adoption and promulgation of the above, among other general principles, with all the

* Pittsburgh Christian Herald, 1837, p. 115.

care that has been taken, and all the means that have been employed, for their correct application, they are oftentimes evaded, or violated, by the admission into this Church of ministers, who have not given that security which its Constitution expressly demands. Ordained ministers of other denominations, with whom we are on terms of friendly correspondence, coming, with dismissions as ministers in good standing, are, by a number of our Presbyteries, received, as a matter of course, without incurring those obligations by which we ourselves are bound; nor does even the form of installment provide for the omission. There is also abundant reason to apprehend that the admission of such is becoming still more common; from which, encouragement has been taken, even to require their reception, as a privilege they have a right to demand.

"Although it is believed that, with every correct mind, the very act of uniting with any church, constitutes a tacit adoption of its doctrines and discipline; and ought to be deemed *primâ facie** evidence of the sentiments of the party being in accordance with those of the body with which he unites; yet we are too well aware of the evasions, which are often used on such subjects, as well as with facts, which have transpired, not to see the absolute necessity of the *most explicit avowals*, where ministerial consistency, harmony and soundness in the faith are so deeply involved.

"It cannot, for a moment, be supposed, that our ecclesiastical reputation, or even our strength, depends on, or consists in, the number of our adherents; but, under the guardian care of our Church's Head, on our unity, purity, and piety. Where, then, shall we find a reason,

* Presumptive.

or even an excuse, for the anomaly which now appears in the Presbyterian Church? Here, we see her sons, nurtured in her bosom, fostered by her care, and instructed in all her doctrines and rites of worship, *justly* required, before entering into the ministry, by a public profession of their faith, to give a pledge of the purity of their sentiments, and the correctness of those doctrines they are likely to inculcate; while those who have been raised under the influence of other principles, forms, and prepossessions, are admitted, without any such assurance. Surely if an explicit and solemn guarantee be requisite from those who have been instructed in all our doctrines and the forms of our ritual, much more is it necessary from those who are in a great degree strangers to us and to them: but if it is not proper or necessary from the latter, then they are right who would exterminate all creeds and confessions from the Church of God.

"We do not, therefore, attempt to conceal our deep and growing concern under the apprehension of that danger to which our constitutional standards, ecclesiastical institutions, and doctrinal purity are exposed, by receiving ministers of religion, as constituent members of our judicatories, and committing to their government and instructions our rising congregations, who have not incurred the same obligations by which their brethren have plighted their faith.

"Although we can, without any dereliction of principle, or reluctance of feeling, cherish the most friendly sentiments toward those who differ from us in many particulars, and cultivate a friendly intercourse with them, we do not, therefore, believe, that either principle, prudence, or courtesy, requires us to invest them with the direction of our ecclesiastical concerns; and the harmony, order, and beauty of this branch of the Zion of God imperiously forbid it. Indeed, when our judicatories shall have been, in a great measure, composed, as, from the present practice, may, at no distant period, be realized, of those who have not submitted to our regulations, do not feel our obligations, and whose attachments to our doctrines may frequently and justly be questioned, we may see our schools, our funds, and all our resources transferred to other hands, and employed for other purposes than those for which they have been bestowed and accumulated, and we may, in vain, regret the apathy which has been indulged, while surrendering, inch by inch, the very foundations on which our ecclesiastical institutions are based.

"To guard, therefore, as far as practicable, against consequences of so serious a character as those to which we have adverted, the Synod of Pittsburgh, respectfully, yet most earnestly recommends to the General Assembly the adoption of the following, or some other, adequate rule, for the more effectual application of the 'general principles' avowed and published in the Constitution of our Church.

"*Resolved*, 1. That it shall, henceforth, be the duty of every Presbytery under the care of this Assembly, to keep a book, in which shall be transcribed the obligations required of ministers of this Church, at their ordition; which shall be subscribed, in the following form, viz.: 'I, A. B., do, *ex animo*,* adopt, receive, and subscribe, the above obligations, as a just and true exhibi-

* From the heart.

tion of my principles and faith; and do resolve and promise to exercise my ministry in conformity thereto.'

"2. That every minister of the Presbyterian Church shall be required to subscribe the above obligations; and that every individual, who shall hereafter become a minister of this Church, whether by ordination or admission from any other ecclesiastical body, shall, before taking his seat in Presbytery, in like manner, subscribe the same.

"3. That the books or catalogues, thus formed, shall be annually submitted to the inspection of the respective Synods, as the other minutes of Presbytery are; and the Synods shall form the rolls of their members from the catalogues, thus formed, and laid before them.

"4. That, as, in the opinion of this Assembly, no minister of this Church, who is not unfriendly to our doctrines and discipline, will refuse to subscribe the above obligations, it is the manifest duty of all who cannot conscientiously enter into these engagements, promptly and peaceably to withdraw."*

This overture was adopted, by the Synod of Pittsburgh, "*nemine contradicente*,"† and ordered to be sent up to the General Assembly. When the Assembly of 1827 met, the paper was placed in the hands of the Committee of Bills and Overtures. The Rev. Dr. Francis Herron, of Pittsburgh, was Moderator of the Assembly. He called together the commissioners from the Synod, and proposed to them to suppress the overture. This they declined to do. He, thereupon, assumed, personally, the responsibility, of withdrawing it

* Minutes of Synod of Pittsburgh, p. 253; Digest, p. 658.

† No one dissenting.

from the Committee, on which there were members whom that paper would have excluded from the Presbyterian Church.

Some years after the controversy had ended, in the division of the Church, and when the author of the overture was sleeping in the dust, it was the privilege of the writer of this history to meet with the venerable Herron. He, at once, referred, in terms of affection, to the memory of Mr. Baird, and remarked,—"Had I and others possessed the same appreciation of the condition of things, and the same clear forecast, which, at an early day, Mr. Baird displayed, our Church might have been saved from years of distraction and strife, and final division."

The above overture was revived by the Synod of Pittsburgh, in 1831, with some modifications, and again sent up to the Assembly. That body had, at its preceding meeting, adopted an order, upon the motion of Dr. Green, that licentiates and ministers, coming from corresponding denominations, into the Presbyterian Church, should be required to answer, affirmatively, the same questions, respectively, which are proposed to our own candidates for licensure and ordination.*

The Synod, highly approved this measure; yet, observing that it made no provision for the cases of the large numbers who had already gained unconstitutional admittance into our Church, and for other prevalent disorders, urged the Assembly to take further action. It stated that "common fame loudly proclaims, that in some of the congregations and Presbyteries, constituting the Synod of Western Reserve, and in some other

* Minutes, 1830, p. 12; Digest, 254.

sections of our Church, our constitutional forms and constitutional obligations are disregarded, in the organization of churches, and in the admission of members of Presbyteries; and that there is reason to fear that there are but few exceptions, in such regions, to this remark."

To obviate these disorders, the Synod proposed to the Assembly the adoption of the following regulations:

"*Resolved,* That every church session, and Presbytery, under the care of this General Assembly, shall be, and hereby is, required to keep a book, in which the following formula shall be recorded, viz.: 'I, A. B., do sincerely receive and adopt the Confession of Faith and Catechisms of the Presbyterian Church in the United States of America, according to the plain and obvious meaning of the words in which they are expressed, as a just and candid exhibition of my principles and faith; and I do promise and oblige myself to exercise my ministry, (or eldership, as the case may be,) in conformity thereto. I do, also, approve the Form of Government and Discipline of the said Church, and do promise to exercise and perform my official duties according to the principles and rules therein contained.'"

The other regulations of this overture were, also, essentially the same as those of 1826, except the last, which anticipated the disowning acts of 1837.—"Resolved, That any Synod, Presbytery, Minister or Elder, refusing to comply with the above conditions, or such other adequate provision as may be adopted by the General Assembly, shall be considered as renouncing the jurisdiction of the Presbyterian Church, and consequently no longer to be considered in connection with that body."*

The answer of the General Assembly to this overture, assumed two directions. On subscription to the Confession of Faith, the Assembly declared no further action necessary. It, however, decided that subscription includes the Catechisms. As to the Synod of the Western Reserve,—it was, by the Assembly, directed to review the state of its churches, and report to the next Assembly, touching any existing disorders.

In the Assembly of 1831, the question respecting committee-men again came up, upon occasion of the delegation of Clement Tuttle who was designated in his commission, a "committee-man," from the Presbytery of Grand River. The Committee on Elections, to whom the case was referred, declined to express any opinion, on the constitutional question. The Assembly, however, determined to enroll him as a member.

Against this decision, a protest was entered, by R. J. Breckinridge, and sixty-six others. Mr. Daniel W. Lathrop, now a minister, reported a reply, which was adopted. This reply admits that the case involves "an appearance of departure from the letter of the Constitution;" but not its spirit; because the definition of Ruling Elders, in the Form of Government, chapter v., describes exactly the character of the committee-men. To have refused the committee-man a seat would have been to violate "a solemn compact,"—the Plan of Union,—"as that instrument has been construed and acted on by the Assembly, during the last ten years. To refuse such commissioners a seat, would also be to

* Minutes Synod of Pittsburgh, p. 354.

wrest from the Presbytery a constitutional right to a representation in the Assembly; inasmuch as the practice of the Assembly for the last ten years, afforded a full warrant to Presbyteries to expect that a representative of this character would be received as a member." "The conventional agreement expressly provides that laymen, of the character there contemplated, shall be admitted to the Presbyteries, on an equality with elders. If, therefore, there is, in connection with this subject, an infraction of the Constitution, it is, in *the treaty itself; and the only proper remedy for the supposed evil, would be, in a regular proceeding to amend or annul the said treaty*."*

Toward the close of this Assembly, the withdrawal of members, upon leave of absence, gave a majority to the Old School, and a resolution was submitted, as follows:

"Resolved, That, in the opinion of the General Assembly, the appointment, by some Presbyteries, as has occurred in a few cases, of members of standing committees to be members of General Assembly, is inexpedient, and of questionable constitutionality; and, therefore, ought not in future to be made."

In the discussion on this subject, Dr. Spring showed that the Plan of Union never contemplated the right of Presbyteries sending committee-men to sit in the Assembly. He pointed out the evils resulting from the system, and stated that these Presbyteries sometimes send delegates to the Assembly who are not even committee-men; that there might be a number of them on this floor, and but for their influence, in the decisions

* Minutes, 1831, p. 195.

of this house, we might this day be at peace. He intimated that he did not speak upon surmise; and being called upon for facts, he appealed to the Rev. Dr. Snodgrass, who rose, and named a member of the Assembly, who was represented in his commission as an elder, but who had confessed himself to be not even a committee-man. This was in that famous Assembly of 1831, in which Dr. Beman presided. He wished the privilege of taking part in this discussion. But his suggestion being opposed was withdrawn. The resolution was then adopted, by a vote of eighty-one to fifty-three.

But the great controversy, the history of which is here traced, concerned not only, the doctrinal purity of the Church, and the maintenance of the divine order of God's house. It, also, involved the evangelic office of the Church, itself,—her right and duty, with her own hands, to minister to the wants of the needy, and carry the gospel of salvation to a perishing world. To that topic we shall next address ourselves.

CHAPTER XVII.

EARLIER EVANGELIC AGENCIES.

The General Presbytery organized as an evangelic society—Such its office and work—The fund for pious uses—Its home missions—Its attention to ministerial education—Rev. John Brainard's mission—Indian missions, at the beginning of this century—Missions of the Synod of Virginia—Western Missionary Society, of the Synod of Pittsburgh—Missions of the Synod of the Carolinas—Sandusky mission—Its transfer to Maumee—Mode of the Assembly's management of its missions—The standing committee of missions—Ministerial education.

We have already seen, that the General Presbytery was organized, as an evangelic society; and so viewed, distinctly, by its members. Its founders conceived the Church to have been constructed by her Head to be his chosen and sufficient instrumentality, to fulfill the great commission and carry the gospel to every creature. Whilst yet unorganized, and scattered abroad, as isolated lamps in surrounding darkness,—when planning the increase and diffusion of the light, they, at once, recognized their own organization, after the scriptural model of our Presbyterian standards, as being the fundamental step in the whole matter.

Hence, they at once announced themselves, in this capacity. Their statement to Sir Edmund Harrison, we have already seen. To the Synod of Glasgow, they write to the same effect.—"We have, for some years past, formed ourselves into a Presbyterial meeting, and to our capacities, (considering our infancy, paucity, and the many oppositions and discouragements we have all along struggled with,) taken what care we could, that our meeting, though small, might be for the general good of religion in these parts."

The reader of the minutes of this body, at once feels, that, he is perusing the records of a missionary society. The business of their meetings, was, to devise and execute the most efficient means of spreading the gospel. Their correspondence with Europe was opened with that object and occupied with that theme. They feelingly exhibit the destitutions around them, and plead with their more favored European brethren, for more men, to supply the want, and for money to support them, when sent out.

As early as 1717, they, out of their own poverty, laid the foundation of a "fund for pious uses," to which they solicited the annual contributions of their people. It began with the sum of "eighteen pounds, one shilling, and sixpence," given "by the members of the Synod themselves," and "weighed and delivered into the hands of Mr. Jedidiah Andrews, treasurer for the time being;"—a most liberal contribution, in their poverty, from those faithful and zealous servants of Christ. There were present, thirteen ministers and six elders; who thus gave a fraction less than a pound each; equivalent to much more, in the present day; a sum which well justified the moving appeals urged by them for aid from Europe. "We ourselves," say they, "have begun a small fund, for this and other religious purposes among us. But, alas! it is yet so small that little or nothing can be done by it." Men of God, well done! "The little one shall become a thousand, and a small one a strong nation."

The first appropriation, from this fund, was made in 1719, when "a tenth part of the neat produce of the Glasgow collection" was given to the Presbyterian congregation of New York, toward the support of the gospel among them. The foundations of the magnificent churches of New York city all rest on this appropriation, made in faith, out of the depth of poverty, in that day of small things.

In 1722, the first formal appointment of itinerant missionaries was made. The Rev. Messrs. Hugh Conn, John Orme, and William Stewart, were directed, severally, to visit some Protestant dissenting families in Virginia, who were desirous of supplies from the Synod, to preach four Sabbaths each. From the date of that appointment, the missionary exertions of our fathers were constant and untiring, commissioning, sometimes, settled pastors, sent on tours of a few weeks; and, sometimes, missionaries destined to permanent settlement, in the new churches, founded in the wilderness. They were the first home missionaries on the continent.

For the first century of her existence, until the Plan of Union had time to work out some of its proper effects, the right and duty of the Church to fulfill those functions, which are now entrusted to the immediate charge of her Boards, were never questioned; whilst they constituted, in fact, the principal business, in the annual meetings of the supreme court. From the first hour of her existence, we have seen that domestic missions were her immediate charge, and received, in all her sessions, the most earnest attention. When the General Presbytery was but four years old, she took authoritative control of the ministerial training of David Evans. And, from that day, the charge of education, academic and theological, was among her recognized and most active functions. In that office, the Old Side Synod patronized Mr. Alison's school, established at New London, in 1741; whilst the New Side were laying the foundations, broad and deep, of New Jersey College.

A general and systematic plan was adopted, by the General Synod, in 1771, for the support and education of candidates for the ministry; and means taken to obtain the requisite funds, from the liberality of the churches. The expected results, however, were greatly diminished, by the occurrence of the Revolutionary war. After the close of the war, the subject received comparatively little attention, in the deliberations of the supreme court, until 1805, when the incipient steps were taken, which, in a few years, resulted in the organization of the Board of Education.

Whilst devoting its utmost energies to home evangelization, the General Synod was not indifferent to the condition of the heathen. In 1751, a standing rule was adopted, in view of the "exigencies of the great affair of propagating the gospel among the heathen," that a collection be taken, in each of the churches, for that object, once a year. On this fund, the Rev. John Brainard was sustained, among the Indians of New Jersey, until his death, in 1781.

With the beginning of the present century, new

efforts were made by the courts of our Church in behalf of the aborigines. In 1801, the Assembly and its Committee of Missions, each, published an appeal for missionaries to labor among the Indians. That same year, the Commission of the Synod of Virginia reported to the Assembly, that besides the labors expended within the bounds of the Synod, it had sent two missionaries to Detroit, two to Cornplanter, chief of the Senecas, and two to the settlements on the Muskingum. The next year, it reported nine missionaries, sent west of the Alleghanies, for different periods of time. Of these, three were sent to the Shawanese and other Indians, about Detroit and Sandusky. These were temporary laborers. It also sent a pious young man, to instruct them in agriculture. Blue Jacket, an Indian boy, instructed in Virginia, under the direction of the Commission, had given evidence of a work of grace, and was to go out as an interpreter; and the prospect of success in this mission was favorable.

That same year, the Synod was divided, and the Synod of Pittsburgh erected. At its first meeting held in Pittsburgh, 1802, the following constitution was adopted by the Synod, in order to facilitate its missionary operations :—

"1. The Synod of Pittsburg shall be styled, The Western Missionary Society.

"2. The object of the Missionary Society is, to diffuse the knowledge of the Gospel among the inhabitants of the new settlements, the Indian Tribes, and, if need be, among some of the interior inhabitants, where they are not able to support the gospel.

"3. The society shall annually appoint a Board of

Trust, consisting of seven members; a majority of whom shall be a quorum, whose duty it shall be to transact all missionary business, which may occur, necessary to be done, between the annual meetings of the society; which Board shall meet quarterly.

"4. It is required of the Trustees, that they employ none as missionaries, except those who give credible evidence of being the subjects of special grace, and of their Christian zeal, wisdom, information, and experience, in ministerial labors; which may enable them to do the work of evangelists, in the most self-denying circumstances.

"5. The Board of Trust shall have authority to draw money from the Treasury, to pay the missionaries whom they have appointed. It is expected, also, that the Board of Trust will give directions to the missionaries, how long they shall be out, and where their mission shall be.

"6. The Board of Trust are required to lay before the society, at their annual meeting, in fair records, all their proceedings, together with the journals of the missionaries; and, if it can be, to have the missionaries attend, themselves.

"7. That the society engage a suitable person, annually, to preach a missionary sermon, on the Thursday, next after the opening of the Synod; at which, a collection shall be made, 'for the support of missionaries.'

"Agreeably to the above plan, the Synod proceeded to the election of members as a Board of Trust, when the following persons were duly elected, viz.: The Rev. Messrs. John McMillan, David Smith, Thomas Marquis, and Thomas Hughes; together with Messrs.

James Edgar, William Plummer and James Caldwell, Elders."*

About this time, also, the Synod of the Carolinas, entered upon the same work, in the Southern field. At its sessions, in 1802, it appointed two missionaries to visit the Natches, and also created a Commission to attend to the missionary business; by which the Rev. William C. Davis was sent to the Catawbas. Thus began the labors of that Synod, among the Indians of the South, the history of which remains to be written.

The Indian missions of the Pittsburgh Synod were conducted, at first, by the agency of itinerant and temporary laborers. But the results soon demanded closer attention and permanent missionaries. In 1805, the Rev. Joseph Badger was appointed a stated missionary to the Wyandots, at Sandusky. Two white men, as laborers, one of whom was ultimately to be engaged as a teacher, and one black man and his wife, were also employed; live stock, household furniture, farming tools, and a boat were sent on; and the foundations laid for a permanent and vigorous mission. In 1806, the Synod applied to the Assembly to assume the charge of this mission. This the Assembly declined, but granted it pecuniary aid thenceforward, for a series of years.

The Sandusky mission was continued, until the war of 1812, when, that region becoming the scene of hostilities, it was necessarily suspended. After the war, it was partially resumed. But the multiplying of the white population, and the gradual dispersion of the In-

* Printed "Records of the Synod of Pittsburgh" from 1802 to 1832, p. 11.

dians, induced its transfer to Maumee, in 1822. Here, buildings were erected, a mission organized, and the foundations of a prosperous future laid. The ultimate destination of this mission we shall see hereafter; as also the history of the Assembly's own mission to the Cherokees of the South.

It is not, however, our present object to trace the details of the plans and administration of the Synods and Assembly, in the evangelic enterprise; but merely to illustrate the thoroughness with which this was, from the beginning, appreciated by our Church, as the peculiar and paramount office of her courts.

After the organization of the General Assembly, the rapid enlargement of the Church, and increase of its business induced great embarrassment in managing the various branches of evangelic enterprise, from the long intervals between the sessions of the Assembly, and the brief time allotted to deliberation, when convened.

Still, for a time, the proper remedy did not suggest itself, or may have been, in the circumstances, of doubtful practicability. Until 1802, the whole missionary business was performed by the Assembly, while in session. The field covered by the Synods of Virginia and the Carolinas was, at their request, remitted to the charge of those Synods; the Assembly reserving the right to send missionaries there, at its own discretion. The rest of the country was under the immediate administration of the Assembly; and, by it and the Synods, the work was conducted in the same manner. The missionaries were all itinerants. They were often settled pastors, who were sent on prescribed tours, among the destitute settlements. The Assembly, whilst in session, received the reports of those who had been sent out the year before; approved or censured them; audited their accounts; nominated missionaries for the ensuing year; defined their route of service, and determined their compensation.

In 1802, a standing committee of missions was appointed, consisting of seven members of the Assembly. Its business was merely to collect and digest information for the Assembly during the recess. It was continued, until the close of the Assembly following that by which it was appointed, when the members were superseded by others. Gradually, the powers of this committee were increased, and its organization perfected. In 1816 its name was changed to the Board of Missions, and the whole business was assigned to it, subject to the annual supervision and control of the Assembly.

Whilst the energies of the Assembly were so strenuously given to the supply of the destitute with the Gospel, her attention was arrested, in 1805, by an overture written by the Rev. Dr. Ashbel Green, showing the necessity of greater efficiency in the education of candidates for the ministry. The subject was transmitted to the Presbyteries, for consideration, and referred to the next Assembly.

In 1806, the Assembly, after hearing the reports of the Presbyteries, and anxious deliberation on the subject, determined to recommend to every Presbytery, "to use their utmost endeavors to increase, by all suitable means in their power, the number of promising candidates for the holy ministry;—to press it upon the parents of pious youth, to endeavor to educate them for the Church;—and on the youth, themselves to devote their talents and their lives to the sacred calling;—to make vigorous exertions to raise funds, to assist all the youth who may need assistance;—to be careful that the youth they take on their funds give such evidence as the nature of the case admits, that they possess both talents and piety;—to inspect the education of these youths, during the course of both academic and theological studies,—choosing for them such schools, seminaries, and teachers, as they may judge most proper and advantageous; so as, eventually to bring them into the ministry well furnished for their work."

The Assembly, further, ordered the Presbyteries to make annual report to it, "stating what they have done in this concern; or why,—if the case shall be so,—they have done nothing in it; and that the Assembly will, when these reports are received, consider each, distinctly, and decide, by vote, whether the Presbyteries, severally, shall be considered as having discharged or neglected their duty in this important business."

The Assembly of 1817, attempted to remedy some defects which were found in the working of this plan, by recommending, to Presbyteries which have funds but no candidates, to correspond with other Presbyteries or the Assembly, for the purpose of obtaining beneficiaries. The inadequacy of this attempt soon became apparent; at the same time that it arrested attention, anew, to the whole subject involved.

CHAPTER XVIII.

THE EDUCATION QUESTION.

Causes of uneasiness—Organization of the American Education Society—Origin of the Presbyterian Education Society, of Philadelphia—Presbyterian Education Society of New York—Proposed union of the two—Erection of the Board of Education in 1819—Endowed with efficient powers, after five years—Reorganized, with Dr. John Breckinridge as Secretary, in 1831—Auburn Seminary—Maryville Seminary.

Coincident with the occurrence of the question as to the education of ministerial candidates, were the agitations which divided the New York Missionary Society; the dissatisfaction in the Synod of Philadelphia, at the spread of Hopkinsian doctrines; and the opposition to Princeton Seminary, which was manifesting itself, in connection with the inaugural pledge of the professors, to which we have already referred.

In 1815, the American Education Society had been organized, in Boston; and was already putting forth its energies, to possess and control the Presbyterian Church; giving occasion, to anxious fears, on the one hand, and, on the other, to high expectation, as to its influence, in forming the future character of her ministry.

Under the influence of such considerations as these circumstances were calculated to induce, a conference was held, in Baltimore, at the close of the sessions of the Synod of Philadelphia there, in October, 1818, to consult on the formation of an education society. As the result, the Rev. Drs. Janeway and Neill, and the Rev. James Patterson, were appointed, to mature a plan for such a society; and the Rev. R. F. N. Smith, the editor of the Religious Museum, published at Milton, Pa., was requested to announce the proceedings to the public; which he did, earnestly recommending the subject to his readers, and especially to the members of Synod; to each of whom he sent a copy of the paper.

The committee engaged in an extensive correspondence, on the subject. They found it to be the opinion of the Professors of the Theological Seminary at Princeton, and of many other ministers and members of the Presbyterian Church, that one general education society ought to be established; which should be under the immediate inspection of the General Assembly, and which should be a faithful representative of the whole denomination;—that this society ought to embody, systematize, and direct, all the energies of our Presbyteries and congregations, which may be devoted to the education of young men willing to consecrate themselves to the ministry, but unable to defray their own expenses, while preparing for the work;—that this society ought to carry the sons of her adoption through the whole course of their academical and theological studies, until they obtain licensure;—that the managers of this society should serve as a standing committee, or Board of Education, for the supreme judicatory of the Church; through which all the Presbyteries, and such auxiliary societies as might be formed, should annually report to the Assembly, what they have done on this subject;—and that this society should, from the surplus funds of the different Presbyteries, and such other resources as may be obtained, create a general fund, from which all co-operating Presbyteries and auxiliary societies, may derive such assistance as the number of their candidates, and other circumstances may demand.*

With a view to effecting such an organization, the committee called a meeting, in the Third Church, Philadelphia, on the 9th of December, 1818. This meeting appointed the Rev. Drs. Janeway, Neill, Wilson, Green, Alexander, and Miller, with the Rev. James Patterson, a committee to draught a constitution, to be reported at an adjourned meeting, to be held on the 17th of the same month. At that time, the constitution was reported and adopted, the society organized, and officers elected.

Simultaneous with this movement, in Philadelphia, was a similar one, in New York. On the 23d day of October, 1818, a number of ministers and laymen met in the session room of the Brick Church, New York, and resolved, unanimously, to attempt the formation of a society, for the education of poor and pious youth, for the gospel ministry. A committee was appointed, to prepare a plan for such a society. The committee met, on the 10th of November, in the session room of the Wall Street Church, and agreed upon the form of a constitution. This they reported to a meeting held at New Brunswick, New Jersey, on the 26th of November, when a society was organized, under the style of "The

* First Annual Report of the Presb. Ed. Soc., etc., May 29, 1819. Philadelphia, Printed by Jacob Frick & Co., 8vo. pp. 15.

Education Society of the Presbyterian Church in the United States of America."

Drs. Alexander and Miller, attended this meeting. But they found the prevalent feelings so hostile to the authority of the General Assembly, to the doctrines of the standards, in their strict acceptation, and to the plan of Princeton Seminary, that they withdrew, and returned home.

The essential difference between the two societies appears, distinctly, on the face of their constitutions. The society, organized at New Brunswick, the seat of which was New York, jealous of ecclesiastical control, and of doctrinal strictness, made no recognition, in its articles, of the authority of the Assembly, and no provision for any denominational relations, whatever; nor for the theological training of beneficiaries. "Article 1. This society shall be called—The Education Society of the Presbyterian Church, in the United States of America. Article 2. The object of the Society shall be, to assist indigent and pious young men, destined for the gospel ministry, in acquiring an academical education." —And that was all.

The constitution of the other society contained these clauses.—" Article 1. This Society shall be called—The Education Society of the Presbyterian Church, under the care of the General Assembly. Article 2. The object of this society shall be to furnish pious and indigent youth, of the Presbyterian denomination, who have the gospel ministry in view, with the means of pursuing their academical and theological studies. Article 8. It shall be the duty of the Board of Managers, every year, to communicate to the General Assembly, for their information, a copy of the report, required by the last article, [the annual report,] as soon as possible after it shall have been laid before the Society. Article 13. The annual meetings of the society shall be, always, held in the city of Philadelphia, on the Tuesday next after the commencement of the annual sessions of each General Assembly of the Presbyterian Church; at such time and place as the Board of Managers may direct."

At the third meeting of the Board of Managers of the Philadelphia Society, held on the 11th of January, 1819, their attention was called to a printed circular letter, signed by the Rev. Dr. James Richards, of Newark, New Jersey, and others, stating that an offer had been made, by some members of the New York society, through the brethren at Princeton, for the union of the two societies, on certain specified terms. The writer stated, that, pained at the existence of two rival societies, and anxious not to lose the benefit of a general and combined operation, some of the brethren had proposed to the gentlemen at Princeton, through a common friend, "so to enlarge the object of the society, as to include, according to their wishes, both a theological and academical course, and to locate the institution in Philadelphia,—as the American Bible Society is located in New York,—by choosing two-thirds of the directors there; thus making that city the chief seat of operations; retaining, however, the principle of alternation, in the anniversary."*

This circular, although not officially certified, was

* Extracts from the circular, in the MS. records of the Presbn. Ed. Soc., under the care of the General Assembly, deposited with the Board of Education.

sent out under the auspices of the New York Society; and was, therefore, supposed to be an authentic statement of what it was willing to do. The Board of Managers at Philadelphia, therefore, drafted a project of union, on the basis here indicated; in which, the only modification suggested, upon the New York overture, was, with respect to the annual meeting. Anxious that it should be held in the presence of the General Assembly, the Board proposed the holding of a semi-annual meeting, in New York, during the sessions of the Synod of New York and New Jersey. Should this plan not prove acceptable, they proposed that each of the societies "request the General Assembly, which is to convene in May next, to appoint an Education Board of the General Assembly of the Presbyterian Church, in the United States of America; and that, in case such a Board shall be established, each society shall alter its style, so as to become auxiliary to said Board."

These propositions were immediately communicated to the New York Society; but the response was not in the spirit anticipated. The New York Board replied that, as to these propositions, they "have not found in them that appearance of conciliation they had been led to expect;" and that, as the Philadelphia Board "could not be ignorant of the views of this Board, it may be matter of conjecture, what could be the motive, in submitting a plan of union, which yields nothing to their brethren." They intimate that it was incautiously, "in a moment of anxiety, and to prevent division," that "a number of members of this Board offered to the brethren at Princeton, to include the theological course." But, in view, especially, of doctrinal differences, they are, now, decidedly of the opinion that the object of the society "ought to be exclusively to assist indigent and pious young men, destined to the gospel ministry, in acquiring an academical education."

To the proposal, that the Assembly be petitioned to erect a Board, they replied that their Society, had "so far pledged itself to the public, in the choice of its officers, and in the organization of auxiliary societies, and executive committees, that it would be incompatible with that pledge, to abandon the essential features of its constitution, or to become, itself, auxiliary to any other body."

The New York plan, of abandoning candidates, when they were about to enter upon their theological studies, was a scheme, palpably, contrived to render these two societies mere feeders to the American Education Society and the New England Theological Seminaries. The pledge, which rendered it impossible that the New York society should become auxiliary to the Assembly's Board, proved no obstacle to a subsequent subordination, and ultimate union with the American Society.

In a final review of these negotiations, the Philadelphia Board remarked that it augured ill for the peace and prosperity of our Church, "to hear our brethren plead difference in theological views, as a reason for limiting the object.—And have matters come to this pass, that members of the same Church cannot associate, in assisting young men in their theological education? Why can they not associate? Is not the Confession of Faith a basis wide enough for us to walk together, in peace? All the ministers and elders belonging to this

Board have professed 'sincerely to receive and adopt the Confession as containing the system of doctrine taught in the Holy Scriptures.' And the ministers and elders belonging to the other Board have made the same profession. We are willing to go, heart and hand, with our brethren, in supporting the doctrines contained in our Confession. Are they willing? . . . If they are afraid to trust the matter in the hands of the supreme judicatory of our Church, this Board have more confidence in the wisdom and integrity of that venerable body."

The Philadelphia Board, further, as an act of justice to themselves, informed the New York society that they "would willingly have conceded the principle of alternation in the anniversaries, rather than prevent a union."

So ended this correspondence. At the meeting of the General Assembly, in May, 1819, an overture came in, for the organization of a Board of Education. It was referred to a committee, of five; every man of which, but one, belonged to that class of moderates, who opposed the decisive maintenance of the principles and polity of the Church. They reported a constitution for a General Board, which was adopted by the Assembly. And, so far, the "Calvinists" of the Church seemed to have succeeded. But the Board was left so entirely destitute of resources, and the means of obtaining them; and so restricted in its functions and objects, that the apparent success, availed nothing. The voluntary societies availed themselves, most diligently, of the interval, during which the Board had existence without powers. In 1821, it applied to the Assembly for authority to employ agents to solicit funds, and fulfill the designs of the organization. But the Assembly found it "inexpedient, for want of time, to act" on the application.

In 1824, that judicatory, was requested "to authorize the Board of Education to select such young men as are contemplated by the constitution of the Board, for the gospel ministry, and make provision for their support." For five years, the Board had existed without this power! The request was, at length, granted, and the Board began to exist, as a power for usefulness.

Still, however, there was a most deplorable want of efficiency, in the management. From 1824 till 1829, the duties of Corresponding Secretary were performed by the Rev. Dr. Ely, in connection with the multiplicity of his pastoral and other labors. The Rev. William Neill, D. D., was then called to that office. His second report, was made in May, 1831. It exhibited sixty-five beneficiaries on the roll; the treasury in debt; no funds on hand, and no attempt made, nor plan proposed, to supply the deficiency. A committee was appointed by the Assembly, to report on the expediency of making any alterations in the organization of the Board. A member of this committee, the Rev. Moses Chase, of Western New York, contemptuously remarked, that the Board was dead, and it would be well to leave its burial to the Philadelphia brethren. The suggestion was, in the same spirit, acquiesced in, by the party which was a majority in that Assembly, and now began to be designated as the New School. The opportunity thus given was seized upon by the Old School party; who, thereupon, proposed an enlargement of the

Board, which was granted. They were, also, allowed to make their own nominations for the vacancies, and the names proposed were elected. At the first meeting of the reorganized Board, Dr. Neill resigned his office. On the next day, the 8th of June, the Rev. Dr. John Breckinridge was elected his successor. He accepted, upon condition that $10,000 were, in the first place, put into the treasury; and that the Board should make it the basis of future operations, "to receive, at all hazards, every fit candidate, who may come, regularly recommended; trusting to God and his Church to sustain it in redeeming the pledge."

These conditions were complied with, and the policy thus inaugurated by Dr. Breckinridge, and the vigor infused into all its operations, by the personal energies of that eminent servant of Christ, at once lifted the Board out of the depth into which it had fallen; and started it forward on a career of prosperity and usefulness.

Such is the first chapter in the history of a succession of persistent plans, designed to bind our Church, hand and foot,—to "liberalize" and corrupt her divine and saving theology, and to enervate and subsidize the resources and efficiency of her scriptural polity.

We have seen the energy and zeal, displayed by the Hopkinsian party, in its endeavor to take charge of the education of the rising ministry; and the unfavorable light in which they viewed the Seminary at Princeton. In such circumstances, they did not overlook so evident a feature of policy, as the establishment of a Theological Seminary. The importance of such an institution had been the subject of private conversation for some time. In February, 1818, it was proposed to the Synod of Geneva, which was, at the time, the sole offspring and representative in New York, of the Plan of Union. The Synods of Genesee and Utica were formed, subsequently. After discussion, the Synod resolved to ask the advice of the Assembly. That body replied that it was not prepared to give any opinion or advice, on the subject of the overture, "which contemplates the establishment of an academical and theological seminary; believing the Synod are the best judges of what may be their duty, in this important business."

At a special meeting of the Synod, held in Auburn, in August of the same year, it was determined to proceed at once to establish a theological seminary; and, on certain conditions, to locate it at Auburn. The conditions were promptly complied with, and the institution so located. Application was then made to the Legislature, for a charter, which was obtained, in April, 1820.

This charter appoints certain persons, and their successors, "Trustees of the Theological Seminary of Auburn, in the State of New York." To them are entrusted the immediate care and management of the funds and property, for the uses of the institution; but "in such way and manner, only," "as shall be appointed by the Board of Commissioners hereinafter mentioned."

"A representation, annually to be chosen, of two clergymen and one layman, from each of the following Presbyteries, and such other Presbyteries as shall hereafter associate with the said Synod, for the purpose,— to wit:— . . . shall compose a Board of Commissioners, who shall have the general superintendence, management, and control, of the aforesaid institution; and who shall have authority to fill the places of the aforesaid Trustees, as they shall become vacant; to appoint the tutors, professors and other officers of the said institution; to fix and determine the salary and other compensation of the said officers; to authorize and direct all such appropriations of their funds as they shall think proper; to make by-laws and regulations, for themselves; to choose their own president and other officers; and to determine what number of their Board shall form a quorum, for doing business."

Under this charter, the Boards of Trustees and of Commissioners were constituted, and on May 2d, 1821, the institution was organized by the election of the Rev. Matthew La Rue Perrine, D. D., of New York, the Rev. Henry Mills, D. D., of Woodbridge, New Jersey, and the Rev. Dirck C. Lansing, of Auburn, professors. The last of these, was a temporary appointment. Two years after, the chair of theology was conferred on the Rev. James Richards, D. D., of Newark, New Jersey, who was inducted into office, on the 23d of October, 1823.

Whilst the Hopkinsians of New York and New Jersey were rearing the walls of Auburn, those of Tennessee were laying the foundations of Maryville.

The Hopinsianism of East Tennessee was of sporadic growth. The case of the Rev. Dr. Hezekiah Balch, who was tried before the Assembly, in 1798, on charges of doctrinal error, has already been noticed in these pages. Dr. Balch had acquired his new sentiments in the course of a tour to New England, in 1795, on behalf of Greenville College, of which he was the founder and president. As he was a zealous propagandist, his Hopkinsian sentiments were soon diffused to a considerable extent among his ministerial brethren, but few of whom possessed sufficient theological learning, to render them altogether proof against such specious innovations. And, as he remained at the head of the college, until his death, in 1810, and was succeeded by his friend and associate, the Rev. Dr. Coffin, a disciple of the same school, the result was the dissemination of his theological sentiments throughout East Tennessee, by means of the alumni of the college, who became the pastors of the churches. Such was the manner in which, through the casual visit of an individual to New England, the speculations which have corrupted the theology of the East gained footing in the only locality which they ever possessed in the South. The similar tendency, developed at a later period, in South Carolina, in the publications of the Rev. W. C. Davis, and the apparent sympathy of his Presbytery, was quickly suppressed, by the firm and judicious exercise of discipline.

In 1819, the Synod of Tennessee determined to found a theological seminary. The institution was opened in 1822, under the charge of the Rev. Dr. Gideon Blackburn, who was a pupil of the Rev. Dr. Robert Henderson, Dr. Balch's son-in-law. Dr. Blackburn was an ardent disciple of the school of Hopkins, and a devoted advocate of voluntary societies, and enemy of the Boards of the Church.*

* As Dr. Blackburn journeyed from Pittsburgh, after the Assembly of 1836, he gave my late venerated friend, the Rev. Dr. George W. Janvier, who was of the company, his interpretation of the three unclean spirits, like frogs, which John saw. They were certain great errors in the Church, one of which was, ecclesiastical Boards!

He was succeeded, in this post, by the Rev. Dr. Isaac Anderson. The latter had been early trained in the faith of his Presbyterian ancestors. But coming, as a student of theology, under the private tuition of Dr. Blackburn, some years before the establishing of the seminary, the latter set himself with extraordinary earnestness and diligence, and with complete success, to turn him from the doctrines of his youth, and establish him in the better way devised by the divine of Newport.

CHAPTER XIX.

OUR MISSIONS AND THE AMERICAN BOARD.

The United Foreign Missionary Society—Its missions—Cheering report, in 1825—Acquisition of the Maumee mission—Amalgamation with the American Board—The terms rejected by the Assembly—Appropriation of the Cherokee mission by the Board—Acquisition of the Chickasaw mission, from the Synod of South Carolina and Georgia—The Presbyterian Church not new to the work of missions.

WHEN the Board of Domestic Missions was erected, in 1816, the committee which reported its constitution to the Assembly, at the same time, recommended the organization of a Foreign Missionary Society, to be composed of members, not only of our own, but, also, of the Reformed Dutch and Associate Reformed Churches. A committee was, therefore, appointed, to correspond with those churches, and endeavor to secure the erection of such an institution. The result was, the organization, in 1817, of the United Foreign Missionary Society, which, although originated at the suggestion of the General Assembly, and under the patronage of the three denominations named, was a purely voluntary society, dependent, in no respect, as to its organization and management, upon the courts of the churches, by which it was orignated and sustained.

It entered, however, with considerable efficiency, upon

the work to which it was designated. The New York Missionary Society transferred to it the Tuscarora mission, commenced about 1801, and the Seneca mission originated in 1811, both in New York. The Northern Missionary Society surrendered to it, a mission at Fort Gratiot, on the river St. Clair, a little below the outlet of Lake Huron. Five missions were established by the society itself,—the Union mission, on Grand River, twenty-five miles above its junction with the Arkansas,—the Great Osage mission, on the Marias de Cein, six miles above its entrance into the Osage,—the Cataraugus mission in New York; the Mackinaw mission, in Michigan; and the Haytian mission, at Port au Prince, Hayti.

In the annual report of this society, for 1825, it was able to present the following flattering comparison:—

"The American Board of Commissioners for Foreign Missions, at its eighth anniversary, reported three missionary stations, twenty missionaries and assistants, two schools, sixty-four pagan children and youth, and one or two converts from paganism to Christianity. At its fifteenth anniversary, celebrated in September last, the same institution reported thirty-three stations, one hundred and forty-four missionaries and assistants, ninety schools, and three thousand scholars.

"At your eighth anniversary, you number eight missions, fifty-five missionaries and assistants, four schools, two hundred and thirty pagan youth, and more than forty converts to the faith and hope of the Gospel. Should the sphere of your operations be extended, in the ratio which has marked the progress of that important society, you will, in seven years, number seventy-eight stations, three hundred and ninety-six missionaries and assistants, one hundred and eighty schools, and more than ten thousand scholars. To this may be added,—should the blessing of Heaven descend, proportionally, upon your labors, you will behold a company of more than five hundred converts, rescued, through your instrumentality, from the dominion and degradation of paganism, and rejoicing in the efficiency of that grace, which had raised them to the high and holy character of children of God, and heirs of eternal glory. Carry your view forward, to the close of a few more septennial periods, and who can estimate the amount of temporal and spiritual benefit, that may redound to immortal souls! Who can compute the amount of revenue of glory, that may accrue to the kingdom of Immanuel?"

At the same time, the report of the treasurer announced an income of $20,975.45; all expenses paid; and a debt of $7,953.19, with which the year began, reduced to $257.62. And yet, with a situation so favorable and prospects so flattering, the Directors of this society were just about to consummate its extinction!

It was whilst this society was thus crowned with success, and seeming to glow with hope for the future, that, in the fall of 1824, the Board of Trust of the Synod of Pittsburgh advised, and the Synod consented to accept overtures received from it, proposing correspondence, with a view to becoming auxiliary.

The Synod, however, prescribed the following conditions:—1. That, until the Synod shall otherwise order, the title to the real estate at Maumee should remain in it. 2. The United Foreign Missionary Society shall establish a Board of Agency at Pittsburgh, to attend to the missions of the Synod. 3. The personal property, already acquired by the Synod, and any funds given by it, for the purpose, to be used in the support of Indian missions.

Should the society agree to these terms, and establish an agency at Pittsburgh, the Synod, under the name of the Western Missionary Society was to be, forthwith, an auxiliary of the United Foreign Missionary Society, "to the extent before described."

These conditions were unacceptable to the managers of the United Foreign Missionary Society. The Board of Trust, therefore, consented to further negotiations; and, finally, in June, 1825, agreed to an arrangement, by which the United Foreign Missionary Society engaged to take the station at Maumee, under their care and exclusive direction, "and pay the Board of Trust of the Western Missionary Society one thousand dollars, in cash, provided, the Synod of Pittsburgh shall duly and legally convey and transfer to them the said station, with all the real and personal property of the Board of Trust of said society, thereunto belonging; to be the property, and employed for the use of said United Foreign Missionary Society."

To this arrangement, the Synod yielded a reluctant consent, at its meeting in October, 1825,—a consent which would, surely, not have been given, could the developments of a few months have been anticipated. The thousand dollars, here stipulated, was not proposed as adequate compensation for the property; but was merely, a consideration, necessary to give the contract legal force; so as to place the whole matter beyond the further control of the Synod.

Whilst the Synod of Pittsburgh was considering and ratifying these terms, for the surrender of that cherished and promising mission, the United Society had already, one month before, made proposals to the American Board of Commissioners for Foreign Missions for the transfer of all its missions and property to that society, and its own dissolution. The ecclesiastical significance of this step is indicated, in the reasons adduced by the commissioners of the Society, in conference with the Board, in favor of union. They stated, that, "the spirit of controversy having subsided, the intelligent and candid of the Christian public are all satisfied that the same gospel which is preached in the Middle and Southern and Western States, is preached also in the Eastern States.

"That the missionaries of both societies preach precisely the same gospel to the heathen; and that the same regulations are adopted by both, in the management of missions.

"That both derive much of their funds from the same churches and individuals; that the great body of Christians do not perceive or make any distinction between the two institutions; and, consequently, do not perceive any necessity for two, and regret the existence of two; and that many churches and individuals, unwilling to evince a preference for either, are thus prevented from acting promptly and contributing liberally to either."

The considerations here exhibited, and which were the familiar reasons for incorporating the executive organizations of our Church with the New England Societies, never, by any accident, occurred, to prevent the organization of the latter, in view of the prior existence of the others; nor to induce the amalgamation of the Congregational Societies with the Boards of the Church. The argument was only good in one direction.

These reasons for the transfer were not, however, urged upon the Assembly. To it, the plea was, a lack of funds. Says Zechariah Lewis, Esq.,—"So far as I know, this was the only inducement. In May, 1825, having served the Board faithfully and gratuitously, for five years, as their principal Secretary, and finding that my health began to yield under my heavy labors, and having the satisfaction of seeing the Society, for the first time, free from debt; I resigned my office, in favor of Mr. Crane, and removed my family to the country for the summer. On my return to the city, in September, I found, to my astonishment, that the drafts upon the Board, and other expenses, had, in four months, exceeded the receipts, by nearly *ten thousand* dollars; that the Board, as well as the Treasurer, had become alarmed; that they had determined to offer the whole concern to the Eastern Board, on condition that it would assume our debt; and that Commissioners had gone to lay the proposition before that Board, then in session."*

Upon this, Dr. Green, justly, remarks, that "if the Society was out of debt, entirely, but four months before the transfer; and if the amount of the debt, at the time it took place, did not exceed ten thousand dollars; and if, as we know was the fact, three respectable denominations were morally bound and even solemnly pledged, to see the debt discharged, it cannot

* Dr. Green's History of Presbyterian Missions, p. 75.

be credited that there were not other, and more powerful motives, prompting to the transfer, than the fact that the United Foreign Missionary Society owed ten thousand dollars." In confirmation of this view, it may be added that the debt accrued at a season of the year when all experience, then, as well as since, taught the Treasurer to expect limited receipts; that it was in the midst of this pressure and alarm of debt that the Society negotiated the purchase of the mission of the Synod of Pittsburgh, at the expense of $1000, making a part of the debt; that this was done after declining the plan of the Synod, for a relation to be formed without any such expense; and that the property of the one mission thus acquired, was sufficient of itself to have paid the entire debt.

The motives governing the whole transaction, and which, especially, caused the anxiety of the Directors of the United Society to get absolute control over the mission of the Synod of Pittsburgh, may be surmised, from the insertion of a provision. in the plan of amalgamation with the American Board, designed to bind the whole Presbyterian Church to the permanent support of the Board. It proposed that "the highest judicatories, of the Presbyterian Church, and of the Reformed Dutch Church,* will recommend the American Board of Commissioners for Foreign Missions, as a National Institution, and entitled to the warm support and efficient patronage of the Churches under their respective jurisdictions."†

* The Associate Reformed Synod had been united, in 1822, with the General Assembly.

† See the terms. Preliminary, and Permanent, in the Digest, p. 339.

The proposal of union was immediately accepted, by the American Board. The Directors of the United Foreign Missionary Society unanimously adopted it; and the Society, at its annual meeting, in May, 1826, cordially approved and recommended it to the General Assembly, for its sanction. In such circumstances, the Assembly had no alternative. To compel a society to continue its operations, which unanimously sought extinction, and had already allowed a considerable debt to accumulate through inaction, pending these negotiations, was out of the question. The subject was referred to a committee, which brought in a report recommending amalgamation, "on the terms specified." "The Rev. Mr. McCalla," says Dr. Janeway, "began the debate. He spoke plainly, and was insulted, by many members passing out of the room occupied by the Assembly, into the gallery of the church. They went out between him and the Moderator,—Dr. McAuley. Seeing the impropriety, Dr. Junkin said,—'Moderator, do you see what is occurring?' The reply was, 'I know what I am about.' When Bro. McCalla, had finished, I arose, to speak a few words. There was a rush of the members, who had gone out, into the room. I paused, till they were seated. After expressing my regret, on account of the necessity of the case, arising from the debt of the U. F. M. S.,—I said, 'There is one term, to which I neither can, nor will, give my assent,—and that is, to recommend the A. B. C. F. M., as *a national society*,—although I should stand alone on the floor.' I, therefore, moved that the term should be stricken out. For the motion, I assigned *three reasons*. Then, Dr. Alexander, who was sitting at some distance on my right hand, said, 'Let all the terms go.' I hesitated to make a motion for the purpose. While deliberating on the probability of its carrying, Mr. Zachariah Lewis, a member of the committee of the U. F. M. S., who was sitting near me,—anxious for the amalgamation, rose while I was yet standing, and said, 'Moderator, I make the motion to strike out *all the terms.*' Then, I said, 'Moderator, I accept that, as my motion,'—and took my seat. To my astonishment, the motion was carried, with only two or three dissenting voices.

"Afterward, a member rose and observed,—'We have saddled the A. B. C. F. M. with a debt, and, have not even recommended our churches to aid in extinguishing it. I hold in my hand, a recommendation for the contributions of the churches, which you may recall next year, if you don't like it.' It was adopted. Thus, our Church was saved from being deprived of the privilege and duty of carrying on the work of foreign missions."*

Dr. Janeway's "three reasons" were,—that the endorsement of the Board as a national society would be offensive to other denominations;—that, the denominations which sustained the Society and the Board did not, together, constitute a majority of the religious public;—and, consequently, that, if the Assembly were to denominate it, a national society, it would dishonor itself by falsehood.

Beside striking out all the terms, the Assembly further amended the paper by declaring its "*consent to*" instead of "approval of" the amalgamation.

The casual recommendation given to the Board, in

* MS. Letter from Dr. Janeway to the author, of July 21, 1852.

the closing resolution, was afterward used, as we shall see, as a recognition of the claim of nationality, which was so expressly repudiated by the Assembly.

The Synod of the Reformed Dutch Church took action on the amalgamation precisely coincident with that of the Assembly. It acquiesced in it, with the express declaration, "that no pledge of support or recommendation to the patronage of our churches is understood to be implied in the consent of this Synod."

Already, fifteen years before, that Board had inexcusably taken possession of one of the early missions of the Assembly. In 1803, the Rev. Gideon Blackburn, whilst in attendance on the General Assembly, was invited to a conference with the Committee of Missions, and tendered an appointment, as missionary to the Cherokees. This, he accepted; and, soon, the foundations were laid for that Christian civilization, by which that people are now characterized. But, in the midst of a most prosperous career, Mr. Blackburn withdrew from the service, in 1810. The Committee had no thought of abandoning the mission, on which $8000 had been expended, with the most encouraging results. But, whilst they were looking for a suitable successor to Mr. Blackburn, the Rev. Cyrus Kingsbury passed through Philadelphia, under commission from the American Board, to occupy that field. He waited on the chairman of the Committee, to learn whether they had any objections to his mission. He was informed that the Committee could not object to his laboring for the benefit of that people; but was distinctly apprised of their design to resume the mission, as soon as suitable missionaries could be obtained. The claims of our

Church were, however, entirely disregarded, and the field, which was ripening to the harvest, since so abundantly realized, was, at once, occupied by the Board. Nor did that body, in any of its reports, ever make the slightest acknowledgment of its indebtedness to the Assembly, and its missionary, for the happy results which it was privileged to chronicle, on that field.

The appropriation of this mission took place, when the American Board was but five or six years old, and when "the world was all before them where to choose."

Upon the amalgamation of the United Foreign Missionary Society with the Board, there still remained one Presbyterian Mission, not absorbed. The Synod of the Carolinas, in 1802, had commenced a mission, among the Indians of that region; which was ultimately fixed among the Chickasaws, and had been successfully prosecuted, until the time of that union. The acquisition of this mission, by the American Board, was now easily accomplished. The matter was brought before the Synod of South Carolina and Georgia. That body had fallen heir to the mission, upon the division of the Synod of the Carolinas. At its sessions, in 1828, a proposition for transfer was adopted, and at the same time, a Committee appointed, to publish an address to the churches, on the subject.

"The American Board,"—So ran this address,—"is, truly, a national institution. In its support, are now cordially united, our own Church, the Associate Reformed, the Dutch Reformed, and the Congregational Churches of New England; forming a body of Christians, vastly more numerous and efficient than any in

America. Besides, the operations of that Board are extensive and magnificent, in a degree wholly unexampled on this continent."

Thus, with pæans, was celebrated the finishing stroke of a policy, which, for a time, stripped the Presbyterian Church, of every mission, which, with prayer and toil, she had established among the heathen; and transferred their control to a body over which the Church of God has not the slightest official authority. We have already seen the slender ground on which was founded the assertion, that the Board was sustained, as a national society, by the cordial support of the Presbyterian Associate Reformed, and Reformed Dutch Churches.

It is customary to celebrate the organization of the American Board, as the origin of American missions to the heathen. It is true, that the origin of that Board may, justly, be regarded as the era of missions, in New England. And it is, farther to be admitted, that, by virtue of its abundant treasury, and the process of absorption above illustrated, it quickly assumed a most commanding position, and acquired control over the work, on a much larger scale than ever before realized. For whatever, of advancement to the cause of missions and the promulgation of the gospel, has hence resulted, let God be glorified.

But let it never be forgotten, that the Church which we love was laboring, diligently, in this blessed cause, years before that Board had existence; and that some of the missions, which have most honored the Board and cheered the hearts of those who pray,—"Thy kingdom come,"—were founded, before her organization was conceived, by the labors, the contributions and the prayers of the fathers of our Church; whose deep poverty abounded unto the riches of their liberality. When the Presbyterian Church shall cease to be devoted to the cause of missions, she will be derelict, not to her duty only, but to all her holiest traditions. She will lose her identity and cease to be herself.

CHAPTER XX.

THE HOME MISSIONARY QUESTION.

Growth of the Church—Erection of the Board of Missions—Origin of the American Home Missionary Society—It opposes reorganization of the Board—Correspondence between the Board and the Society—Arrogant claims of the Society—Plan to amalgamate the Board and Society—Rejected by the Board—Persistence of the Society—Prosperity of the Board—Proposal for union in the West —Rejected by the Assembly—Question as to Hopkinsian missionaries—Dr. Peters' visit to Cincinnati—Correspondence of that Presbytery and the Board.

For nearly a century and a quarter, the various courts of the Presbyterian Church had been vigorously engaged in the work of domestic missions. As the result of her exertions, thus conducted, she had grown from the little handful which first convened in the church in Buttonwood street, in 1705, to a vast body, having under the care of its General Assembly, sixteen Synods, ninety Presbyteries, fourteen hundred and seventy-nine ministers and licentiates, and about one hundred and sixty thousand communicants, distributed among eighteen hundred and eighty-seven churches.

In 1816, the Committee was erected into the Board of Missions, and its powers greatly enlarged. And yet, for several years afterward, the receipts into its treasury were gradually declining. In 1816, they amounted to $4948. In 1828, they had fallen to $2996. The causes of this are readily traceable. From the date of the controversy, in the New York Young Men's Missionary Society, in 1816, the energies of the Hopkinsian party had been devoted to the organization and support of voluntary societies for missions; in which they could enjoy an indulgence to theological aberrations, which they could not expect from the Assembly's Board. The Moderates, or Peace men, were induced, by a false liberality, to co-operate, largely, in these enterprises. The result was, a number of local missionary societies; by which the resources were absorbed, and the missionaries sustained, which would, otherwise, have been available for the Assembly's Board.

In 1822, a number of these societies were joined in forming the United Domestic Missionary Society. They had, already, twenty-nine missionaries in the field, who immediately came under the charge of the United Society. In the fourth annual report of this society, made in 1826, it announced an income of $11,804, and 148 churches aided in the support of 127 missionaries. At this anniversary, the society adopted a new constitution, and resolved itself into the American Home Missionary Society. This institution was planned, in a meeting of delegates from the New England churches, held in Boston, early in the same year. They selected the United Domestic Missionary Society, to carry into execution the plan so formed. At their request, that Society adopted the new constitution, thus devised, and assumed the new name.

The connection of this movement is worthy of notice.

It is given by a writer in the New Haven Christian Spectator. After alluding to the origin of the United Foreign Missionary Society, he states that "after the experiment of a few years, it appeared, that the great body of those, in all parts of the country, who cared for the missionary enterprise, had a strong confidence in the skill and fidelity of the committee at Boston; and the United Foreign Missionary Society, with all its debts, engagements, and encumbrances, was, after careful deliberation, and with the full consent of the judicatories, aforesaid, merged in the American Board of Commissioners for Foreign Missions. While this union was in progress, and was on the point of being consummated, the American Home Missionary Society was formed, in the city of New York."* The amalgamation, in the one case, and organization, in the other, were parts of the same plan, to subsidize our Church, in the interest of New England.

No sooner was the Society organized, than, under the management of its Corresponding Secretary, the Rev. Dr. Absalom Peters, it aspired to be, in the domestic field, what the American Board was just about to become, for the heathen world. In the circular, calling the convention, by which the reorganization of the United Society was accomplished, this idea was distinctly presented. "We cannot entertain a doubt, that, in the good providence of God, American Christians, of the Congregational, Presbyterian, and Dutch Reformed denominations, are prepared to sanction the measure which we now propose, and to unite in one

* New Haven Christian Spectator, 1832, p. 145.

concentrated and intense effort, to build up the wastes of our common country, and supply all her destitute with the means of salvation."

Probably, few of those to whom this circular came, understood, that it was the announcement of exterminating war, against any domestic missionary institution, which should refuse to become subordinate to this Society. Such, however, it proved to be.

It was now deemed important to give the Board of Missions greater efficiency and success, in the work entrusted to it. An overture was, therefore, brought into the Assembly in 1828; with this object. It was referred to a committee, which reported, that the overture presented matter of the first importance, to the interests of the Church and the world; and strongly recommended it to the Assembly. While the subject was under discussion, a communication was received from the Executive Committee of the American Home Missionary Society, announcing the appointment of a committee of that body, to communicate to the Assembly its views in opposition to the reorganization. A warm discussion ensued; and the arts of strategy were employed to defeat the measure; and when the Assembly had grown weary of the discussion, a member of the New School moved the previous question. This motion, as the rule then stood, involved inevitable misunderstanding and confusion. When the question was propounded from the chair, "Shall the main question be now put?"—if answered in the affirmative, the debate proceeded! If, in the negative, the debate was arrested; but the whole subject was indefinitely postponed! In the present instance, the decision was in

27

the negative, many members being, in the hurry of the question, unable to decide its effect.

A protest was drawn up, and circulated for signature. The New School became alarmed. A committee of conference was appointed, of five members from each side of the house.

This committee reported "that the Board of Missions already have the power to establish missions, not only among the destitute in our own country, or any other country, but also among the heathen, in any part of the world; to select, appoint, and commission missionaries, to determine their salaries, and to settle and pay their accounts;—that they have full authority to correspond with any other body, on the subject of missions; to appoint an Executive Committee, and an efficient agent or agents, to manage their missionary concerns; to take measures to form auxiliary societies, on such terms as they may deem proper; to procure funds, and, in general, to manage the missionary concerns of the General Assembly. It is, therefore, submitted to the discretion of the Board of Missions, to consider whether it is expedient for them to carry into effect the full powers which they possess."

This was a recognition of prerogatives, never before allowed to the Board. It was adopted by the Assembly; and, in the exercise of the powers thus conceded, the Board soon attained to a greatly increased efficiency.

Soon after the reorganization, the Board addressed letters of fraternal salutation to the American Board, and the American Home Missionary Society. From the former, a cordial response was received. In the communication to the latter, the Board had expressed the hope "that we shall be mutually helpers of each other's joy, and joint-laborers together with God, in his spiritual husbandry. We shall, together, sow the seed of the everlasting, ever-living, Word; and, together, rear and prune the trees of righteousness, which are to be translated from our care, in the nursery here, below, to the paradise of God. Let there be no strife between us, we pray you; none between your and our husbandmen; unless it be in the Christian effort of spreading the Gospel; and in diligence, meekness, humility, and zeal according to knowledge, in the Master's service. We wish you all success, in the Lord's field, and abundant harvest."

In reply, the Home Missionary Society entered into an elaborate argument, to show the impossibility of the two societies continuing independent and harmonious. "One such general Board," they state, "in the opinion of the founders of the Home Missionary Society, was necessary, to prevent the interference and cross-action of a large number of local societies, occupying portions of the same field, without concert and without agreement. . . . Let each of the missionary societies, connected with the denominations named in the former part of this letter,"—the Presbyterian, Congregational, Reformed Dutch, and Associate Reformed,—"become auxiliaries, or branches, of the Home Missionary Society, on the terms recommended in the appendix to our last report; and we have the fullest confidence that they would all be greatly strengthened and stimulated, in their work; while we can conceive of no embarrassment, which could grow out of such a connection.

But the existence of two general Boards, acting independently of each other, seeking to extend their efforts over the whole, or any large part, of this country, and asking the co-operation of all the churches within certain bounds, must, we think, increase, rather than diminish the evils which rendered one such society necessary."*

To this extraordinary communication, the Board of Missions, wishing, if possible, to avoid controversy, made no reply.

In December of the same year, Dr. Peters visited Philadelphia, to solicit funds for the society. During his stay, he had repeated interviews with Dr. Ely, the Secretary of the Board, and author of its letter to the Home Society. In these conferences, the New York Secretary succeeded in completely winning Dr. Ely over to his views. The Doctor seems to have been dazzled with the magnificent conception of a great national Church, to embrace, at least, the four denominations enumerated in the Society's reply,—an idea which was ardently cherished by some of the leaders; which is the key to much of this history; and, to the consummation of which nothing was necessary, but the triumph of "liberal" views in theology, and the policy of *American* societies, instead of denominational Boards. From this date, Dr. Ely was the devoted ally of those societies and that policy, to the entire disregard of those doctrinal questions to which he had, before, attached so much importance.

Between the Secretaries, a plan was devised, for the amalgamation of the Board with the Society. It con-

* The letter in the Christian Advocate, vol. vi., p. 473.

sisted in the dissolution of the Board, and the inserting of an article, in the Constitution of the Society, providing that "The officers of the society shall be a President, Vice-Presidents, a Treasurer, an Auditor, a Corresponding Secretary, and a Recording Secretary, who shall be annually appointed by the society; and fifty Directors, to be appointed, annually, by the General Conference of Maine, the General Association of New Hampshire, the General Convention of Vermont, the General Association of Massachusetts, the General Association of Connecticut, the Evangelical Consociation of Rhode Island, the General Synod of the Reformed Dutch Church, the German Reformed Synod, and the General Assembly of the Presbyterian Church in the United States of America, in proportion to the number of ministers, severally, embraced in the above-named ecclesiastical bodies; which said Directors shall enter on their duties, at the close of the anniversary next succeeding their appointment; and the said officers and Directors, together with the Directors for life, shall constitute a Board, seven of whom shall be a quorum, at any meeting, regularly convened. And it shall be understood, that, should any of the above-named ecclesiastical bodies neglect or refuse to appoint their proportion of the said fifty Directors, it shall be the duty of the society, at its next annual meeting, after such deficiencies shall have occurred, to fill the vacancies occasioned by such neglect."

The third annual report of the Society, made in May, 1829,—the earliest date at which the plan, if adopted, could have gone into effect,—enumerates the names of one hundred and thirty-five life Directors. In the sixth report, they had increased, by one hundred dollar contributions, to one hundred and ninety-five. Should any one of the denominations neglect or refuse to elect its proportion of Directors, the right lapsed, not, to the other denominations, but to the society.

Thus, the plan would have placed, not the Presbyterian Church, alone, but all the designated churches, together, in a helpless minority, at the start; under circumstances which would render that minority, in a very few years, utterly insignificant, amidst the mass of the society, and its hundreds of money-titled Directors. Five thousand dollars would have purchased as many life Directors as were offered to all the enumerated churches together.

On such terms, the Presbyterian Church was expected to surrender the care of its feeble churches and destitute regions to the unrestricted control of this society and its secretary.

The only additional feature, in the plan, required the society to send a copy of its annual report to each of the ecclesiastical bodies named. This plan was unanimously adopted, by the Executive Committee in New York. The Secretary then, revisited Philadelphia, and requested an interview with the Board of Missions. A meeting was immediately called; the plan laid before it, and the Secretary admitted to a full and patient hearing. The Board then adjourned for four days. On reassembling, it was resolved that the Board had no power to entertain such a proposition; and that, were it otherwise, it was its deep conviction, "that the interests of the Presbyterian Church, and the sacred cause of missions, require, that the character and powers of the

Board should remain as they are; without any such modification as that which has been proposed."

This conclusion was immediately communicated to the Society in New York, and it was hoped that the subject would be allowed to rest, and the Board of Missions permitted quietly to fulfill the office to which it was erected. The Home Missionary Society, however, at once, issued a private circular, dated February 5, 1829, addressed to its officers and members, stating their determination to persevere in the hope of accomplishing the amalgamation, on the plan proposed. They declared their conviction that it was impossible for the two institutions to exist separately, without strife; and stated the intention of the Society in New York to place itself in an "attitude to invite the co-operation of the General Assembly, in effecting the proposed union."

Here was a voluntary association of gentlemen, which had not yet been in existence three years, and which had no more right to claim authority over the missions of the Presbyterian Church than had the United States Bank. Yet it, formally and persistently, assumes such a right; claims, in the Assembly, itself, a voice against that body giving efficiency to its own Board; and, now, openly demands its dissolution, and the surrender, by the Presbyterian Church, to the discretion of that society, of its dearest and most sacred interests and most responsible functions,—the care and nurture of its feeble churches, and the supply of the destitute regions with the gospel of salvation,—interests over which the Church had, for a century and a quarter, maintained, constantly and intimately, an unquestioned and unquestionable control.

Upon learning the contents of the Circular of the American Society, the Board of Missions published a rejoinder; setting forth the facts, and making its appeal to the candor and conscience of the Church.

The publication of the Society's plan and purpose was undesigned by it. The Circular had been intended for private distribution; and complaint was made, of a breach of confidence, by some one, in its being made known to the Board and to the public. Its publication was its defeat. The scheme was so utterly indefensible, that no mention of it seems to have been made to the Assembly, which met in May, 1829; although Dr. Peters had been at some pains, writing to a number of individuals, urging them to see to it that "men of enlarged views on the subject of missions were sent to the Assembly." That body, however, adopted a resolution, affectionately soliciting the co-operation of the churches with the Board of Missions; yet leaving them entirely free to their own unbiased choice, as to the channel through which their charities should flow.

The friends of the Board began to congratulate themselves, that the struggle was at an end, and they would be at liberty to pursue their work in peace. Their satisfaction was premature. It had, now, become the fixed policy of the Home Society and of its Secretary, Dr. Peters, to destroy the Board, as the only way by which to secure to itself that undivided possession of the field, with a view to which, avowedly, the society was organized. There was, sometimes, an affectation of denying this purpose. But, not only was that policy manifest, in their whole course of action, but the purpose was, by Dr. Peters, distinctly avowed; as we shall see before the end of this chapter. New plans were, therefore, devised, and a new campaign began.

In the mean time, the Board was pursuing, with unwonted success, the objects of its commission. In the first year after the reorganization, it accomplished twice as much as had been done in any year before. The next year, its income, number of missionaries, and amount of labor performed, were doubled; and the number of auxiliaries trebled. In 1828, its income was $2996; in 1829, $7665; in 1830, $14,440; in 1831, $19,773. In that year, the active hostilities were intensified, and in 1832, the increase was small. The receipts were $20,692.

The new plan of the American Society, contemplated a transfer of the question to the West. In 1829, the Rev. Dr. J. J. Janeway, walking in Nassau street, New York, was accosted by a ministerial brother, who requested an interview. "We met," says Dr. Janeway, "at the time and place agreed upon. 'I wish,' said the brother to me, 'to apprise you of the design of the Executive Committee of the Home Hissionary Society. They have determined to destroy, if they can, the Assembly's Board of Missions; and to accomplish this design, Mr. Peters will go to the West and South, in the close of the summer, or early in the fall. Do not inquire how I got the information. I know the fact. Let this suffice; and avail yourself of this information, to counteract their design. My name is not to be mentioned.'" The Board accepted the warning, and its Corresponding Secretary visited the West, in the fall, and there found Dr. Peters. Subsequent developments, sufficiently confirmed the nature of his errand.*

At a meeting of the Executive Committee of the Home Society, held in New York, on the 11th of January, following, a "Central Committee of agency, for home missions in the Western States" was appointed at Cincinnati, Ohio; to co-operate with the Society, in the work of missions, in the field assigned it. On the 22d of February, the Central Committee was directed by the Executive Committee, in New York, to suspend the commencement of its operations, for the purpose of waiting the result of overtures, about to be made to the Board of Missions and the General Assembly. The Committee stated the following as their intentions:

"1. They will request the General Assembly to concur with this Committee in the appointment of the above Committee of Agency, with such alterations in the same, as shall be mutually agreed on by this Committee and the said General Assembly.

"2. They will request the General Assembly to instruct its Board of Missions to transact its business, within such limits as shall be agreed on, through the said Committee of Agency, and to co-operate with the same, in such manner as shall then be prescribed."†

In pursuance of this plan, the Executive Committee of the Society appointed three of their number, to present to the General Assembly, the requests and propositions which it contains. The Presbytery of Cincinnati, was induced to overture the Assembly in favor of the plan of operations proposed, and to request the

* Dr. Janeway, in the Presbyterian, 1836, p. 197.

† Home Missionary, 1830, p. 55.

Committee in New York to appoint a delegation, to further the object, in the Assembly. These three delegates were, therefore, modestly announced to the Assembly, as present "at the request of the Presbytery." They united with the commissioners of the Presbytery, in laying the proposition before the Committee of Bills and Overtures. That committee reported it to the Assembly, with a recommendation that the delegates from the American Society be heard, in explanation of the plan. This recommendation, the Assembly does not seem to have adopted. After some discussion of the general subject of this overture, a special committee of five was appointed, embracing the two Cincinnati commissioners, to confer with the delegates of the American Society, and report to the Assembly. The committee reported, "that it was expedient for the Board of Missions of the General Assembly, and the Board of the Home Missionary Society to conduct their missionary operations, in the West, through a common Board of agency, in that part of the country."

This report was accepted, the committee was discharged, and the whole subject dismissed.

On another point, connected with the Board of Missions, this Assembly took action, exceedingly obnoxious to the New School party. The Board had declined applications from the Presbyteries of Union and French Broad, for commissions, on behalf of two young men from the Maryville Seminary; because,—so states Dr. Ely,*—"they held that God is the efficient cause of sin." The Presbyteries, thereupon, memorialized the Assembly; which replied "That though they do not

* Philadelphia, 1831, p. 102.

recognize, in the Board of Missions, the authority to sit in judgment upon the orthodoxy or morality of any minister who is in good standing in his own Presbytery; yet from the necessity of the case, they must exercise their own sound discretion, upon the expediency, or inexpediency, of appointing, or withholding an appointment, from any applicant; holding themselves amenable to the General Assembly for all their official acts."

The action of the Assembly, on the project of joint operations in the West, was sufficiently decisive, to have been accepted, as final. But in the July number of the "Home Missionary," the monthly organ of the Society, the whole scheme was published, and the hope expressed, "that when our brethren of the Board of Missions shall have examined the plan proposed, they will see it to be entirely practicable; and will unite with us, and all other friends of the common cause, in wishing its adoption, with such changes and modifications as may be rendered mutually acceptable."* In that same month, Dr. Peters met with the Cincinnati Presbytery, for the purpose of conference with it, "as to measures proper to be pursued to promote union of action, in the Western States between the American Home Missionary Society, and the Board of Missions."† In a discussion, running through parts of two days, he animadverted upon the course of the Assembly and the Board, in rejecting the plan for joint agency; declared his purpose to devote his whole future life, if necessary,

* Home Missionary, 1830, p. 57.

† Dr. Peters' Letter in reply to Dr. Green, of Nov. 15, 1831, Beman's Appeal, p. 59.

to accomplish the amalgamation of the Board with the Society; and urged the appointment of a committee by the Presbytery, to press the matter anew on the attention of the Board. The Presbytery adopted his suggestions, and appointed a committee, by which a letter was addressed to the Board. In it, the evils of division were insisted upon, and the Board was urged to adopt the plan, which had already been so decisively rejected by the Assembly. The letter, also, informed the Board that the Central Committee of Agency had been dissolved, and all action in the cause of missions arrested, to await the attempt at union.

To this communication, the Board, through its Secretary, the Rev. Joshua T. Russell, made a full reply; giving the history of the whole matter, and stating the reasons why, even aside from the decisive action of the Assembly, the measure was inexpedient and impracticable; and closing with the assurance that "the Board do most sincerely believe, that, if the churches in the West are left to make their own election of the particular channel through which their charities shall flow, to bless the perishing, and the Presbyteries, to adopt and pursue such plans as they may, severally, deem most expedient, to promote the cause of missions,—existing evils will soon be removed, and harmony and peace will pervade every section of the Church, in reference to future missionary operations."

This letter, at the request of a member of the committee to which it was addressed, was published in the Cincinnati Journal. It produced a deep and salutary impression, in favor of the Board; relieving misapprehensions, developing the facts, and awakening the attention of the Church, to the true character and ends of the policy so pertinaciously followed by the American Society. Could the Board of Missions be excluded from the Western field, its speedy extinction would be inevitable. The strategy of the Society was admirable. But what shall be said for its morality?

CHAPTER XXI.

THE SYSTEM OF CONGREGATIONALIZING AGENCIES.

All our troubles came from Congregationalism—American Education Society—Presbyterian Education Society—It becomes the Presbyterian Branch—It resumes the original name—Its real character—Influence of the American Society—New England men poured into our Church—Latitudinarians—American Home Missionary Society—Young men sent abroad for licensure and ordination—Centres of influence acquired—Lane Seminary—The Plan of Union—Moderation—A towering national Church aimed at—Confession of Faith to be altered—These agencies, beyond the control of the Church—Her divine vitality evinced by her triumph over their combined power.

It will have been observed, that all the difficulties and distractions, developed in these pages, resulted directly from the admission into our Church of a foreign,—a Congregational element. It remained unassimilated; and engaged in the most strenuous, varied, and persistent exertions, to accomplish the transformation of the Church, in doctrine and order, and to deprive her of her evangelic office.

The organization of instrumentalities to accomplish these objects was, now, most comprehensive, and complete; the energies devoted to them were untiring; and the resources at command abundant.

At the foundation, was the American Education Society. This society, organized in Boston, in 1815, and reorganized in 1826, was constructed with admirable skill, with a view to acquiring complete control over ministerial education, throughout the country. Its structure, as reorganized, was that of a close corporation. Contributors of one hundred dollars, if laymen, and forty dollars, if ministers, became thereby honorary members. But the right to vote was, after the reorganization, restricted to those already members, and to such others as, from time to time, were chosen by them. In the annual report of this Society, for 1831, it announced 604 young men aided, in ninety institutions of learning; 411 in New England, and 193, elsewhere. Its receipts were $40,450.34; its expenditures $49,892.80, and its permanent fund $53,933.27. Four hundred ministers of the gospel had already been sent forth from among its beneficiaries; and "one-sixth, if not one-fifth, of all the students connected with theological seminaries, in the United States," were claimed as under its care.

One conspicuous feature in its system of organization was, its Branch Societies and Boards of Agency. Of these, it had nine, distributed from Maine to Indiana and Illinois. The largest and most important of them, was the Presbyterian Branch. We have already seen the origin and attitude of the Presbyterian Education Society, organized in New Brunswick, and located in New York. When the Board of Education was formed, in 1819, this Society inserted the following article in its constitution.

"This Society shall be auxiliary to the Education Board established by the General Assembly; and shall annually report to them their proceedings; reserving to themselves, however, the full and unrestricted right of taking up any young man who may give satisfactory evidence of piety and talents."

This nominal relation continued, until the year 1826; when a proposition was made by the Board of Managers, to the Directors of the American Education Society, for union. "The Presbyterian Education Society agreeing with the American, in the great principles which form the basis of its operations, was accordingly united with it, under the name of the Presbyterian Branch of the American Education Society. This arrangement took place in May, 1827. From this time, till May, 1831, the Branch, by mutual agreement, confined its efforts within the States of New York, New Jersey, and Pennsylvania; except as assistance was occasionally rendered to the parent society, in sustaining the common cause."* The system announced by the Presbyterian Branch was this:—

"1st. In the selection of objects of patronage, the mere distinction of sect is to be wholly disregarded; but no young man is to be taken under the care of the Society, or can receive aid from its funds, until he has given satisfactory evidence, to an Examining Committee of three persons, one of whom is always appointed by the Directors of the American Society, of his piety, his talents, his indigence, and his determination to devote himself to the work of the gospel ministry;—which determination must be expressed in writing, and repeated quarterly.

"2d. All moneys, furnished from its funds, to young

* Address of the Presbyterian Education Society to the Christian Public. New York, 1831.

men under the care of the Society, are advanced as a loan, not a gift,—and for the repayment, without interest, (and as soon as God shall enable him,) of all the money so received by him, each young man shall give his bond.

"3d. All accounts must be kept in the name of the American Education Society, and transmitted, quarterly, to the Secretary of the Presbyterian Branch,, to be by him transmitted to the Secretary of the American Society, in time to be laid before the Directors, at their quarterly meetings.

"4th. Over all young men, aided from the funds of the Education Society, the Secretary of the American Education Society, the Rev. E. Cornelius, late of Salem, Massachusetts, is to exercise a constant paternal supervision; and part of his duty, it will be, to visit, and personally converse with each of them, at least, once a year."*

In a word, the Presbyterian Branch was a mere instrument, of the American Society, in the field assigned to it. The Presbyterian Church, at large, outside the three enuumerated States, was left under the immediate supervision of the Society. The experiment thus made, however, soon demonstrated that the Society, under its own name, could accomplish but little, within the bounds of the Presbyterian Church. The subject became, therefore, matter of consideration, in the Board of Directors, and it was concluded, by them, "that the interests of the Society would be promoted, by a reorganization of the Presbyterian Branch, so as to extend its operations, within the territorial limits of the Presbyterian Church."

* Report of the Presbyterian Education Society, 1827, p. 10.

It was, therefore, agreed by the parent Board, that hereafter, the administration of the affairs of the American Education Society, within the territorial limits of the Presbyterian Church, out of New England, be committed to the Presbyterian Branch; if agreeable to said Branch." The fundamental conditions of this union were that "the principles and rules of the American Education Society, as existing at the time of this arrangement, or, as they may be hereafter determined, with the concurrence of the Presbyterian Society, be received and observed, in all cases, where they are capable of being applied;"—and "The Secretary of the parent society to have the liberty of residing in New York, and superintending the affairs of the Presbyterian Society; if, in his judgment, he can better promote, by such an arrangement, the general interests confided to him;—in which case, his support to be provided for, by the two societies, in such manner and proportion as may be agreed upon, by their respective Boards, or Committees."*

The plan was adopted, in May, 1831; and, thereupon, the Presbyterian Education Society issued a circular, setting forth the objects and principles of the new arrangement. "As the American Education Society was located in the heart of the Congregational churches of New England, and the Presbyterian Branch had an annual surplus income, to be appropriated in the destitute parts of the country, it was judged best that the Branch should enlarge its sphere of operations, to its former dimensions, and appropriate its own funds; especially, as those most needing them were in the limits of the Presbyterian Church. This, beside being the

* Annual Report of American Education Society, 1831, p. 50.

most natural method, would be less likely to excite jealousies of denominational influence." "By virtue of this new arrangement, the Branch resumes the former name of Presbyterian Education Society, and occupies its former limits. It takes, as its own, the rules of the American Society, and assumes its engagements, within prescribed limits. The entire concerns of that Society, out of New England, are now committed to this, as a *co-ordinate* institution; under no other restriction, in the administration, than that of conforming to received rules, and reporting proceedings, regularly."*

"The name of the Society, it will be perceived, is *Presbyterian*. It is so, in fact. It has been nurtured in the bosom of the Presbyterian Church; and owes its success to the liberality of its members. But, though Presbyterian, it is not a sectarian institution."†

Such was the sole ground upon which this institution claimed to be Presbyterian. It had the name, and the money, of Presbyterians. But it was neither responsible to the Presbyterian Church, nor sought her welfare, nor trained the youth committed to its charge in her faith. It was a "catholic society," and her catholic spirit is the glory of the Presbyterian Church! And all this was written and published over the signature of "E. Cornelius, Cor. Sec'y." Dr. Cornelius, the Corresponding Secretary of the Boston Society, had been invited to fill the same office, for the Presbyterian Society; and had accordingly removed to New York, and, without going through the form of joining the Presbyterian Church, was become the controlling spirit,

* Address of Presbyterian Education Society, 1831, p. 2.

† Ibid., p. 9.

in the institution which, thus, assumed charge of her most vital interests.

When, in 1828, the Rev. William T. Hamilton, appeared before the Synod of Pittsburgh, as agent of the Presbyterian Branch of the American Education Society, a few pointed questions, propounded by Dr. Janeway, compelled the agent to confess to the Synod, that the title, "Presbyterian," was a "misnomer." Striking out the word "Branch" from the name, only rendered it more utterly untrue. But this was the mode by which the Boston Society transferred the seat of its operations to New York, and made the Presbyterian Church its special field.

Already, in 1829, Professor Stuart of Andover had assured the public, that, to his "certain knowledge," the Directors of that society, in and about Boston, were in the habit of recommending "all young men, who go from New England into the boundaries of the General Assembly of the Presbyterian Church, to unite with the Presbyteries, and not to hold on upon Congregationalism;"—and that "nearly one-half of the young men who have gone from the Andover Theological Seminary, have become Presbyterians."* We have already seen the sort of theology which those Andover youth were taught by Professor Stuart; and, in the very document in which he makes the above statement, the professor indulged in a style of remark respecting the General Assembly, very illustrative of the kind of sentiments, with which his pupils would enter it; alike hostile and contemptuous, toward its doctrines, its order, government, and institutions.

* Examination of Strictures upon the A. E. S., by M. Stuart, p. 30.

Such was the system, devised by our Congregational brethren, for training a ministry for the Presbyterian Church. Professedly, indifferent to the doctrinal diversities between Andover, New Haven, Princeton, Auburn, and Lane, it was immaterial whether the theology, which the candidates imbibed, and the system of order in which they were instructed, were in harmony, or at variance with those of our standards. That, on both of these subjects, they should generally be latitudinarian, arose, of necessity, from the circumstances in which they were placed, and the avowed indifference of the society by which they were sustained. The Secretary, in his paternal visitations, brought annually to bear upon them, influences, the more potential, because not too frequent to degenerate into familiarity. Every report which the young men made,—every dollar which they expended, directed their thoughts and affections toward New England, and the principles governing its various "catholic" and "national" institutions. Thus, the system was eminently adapted to gain control over the candidates, within the bosom of the Church, itself, and mould their principles to the purposes of the society and its patrons. But the great fountain of supplies for our ministry was New England, itself. Her youth, trained, whether by Taylor, or Woods, or Tyler,—it was immaterial which;—and held in pecuniary bonds to the society, as all its beneficiaries were, for the amounts expended in their education, were encouraged to enter the Presbyterian Church, by patrons, who could scarcely speak of its distinctive principles and character, without evincing their repugnance and scorn.

To usher these accessions into our bosom, and find

for them fields of labor and influence, the American Home Missionary Society stood ready, and prepared, at all points. "It was organized," says a writer, already quoted, "on the presumption, that, provided the land can be supplied with an intelligent and faithful gospel ministry, it is a matter of inferior moment, whether the churches be called Congregational, Presbyterian, or Dutch. . . . . The Board never asks the candidate for missionary work, What Seminary has instructed you? What shade of orthodoxy do you profess? What party do you march with? What shibboleth do you pronounce? It asks him, only, for his credentials, as a minister of the Gospel."*

If it was doubtful whether a candidate would stand the test of a Presbyterial examination, he was ordained, before being sent out; perhaps, by a Congregational council; but, more frequently, by the Presbytery of Newburyport, or the Third Presbytery of New York. Neither of these bodies was in any danger of hesitancy, upon the score of doctrine or order. The former of them, at one time, ordained nine young men, as evangelists, for the American Home Missionary Society. The latter, upon another occasion, at the request of the same society, set apart ten. Most of these were destined to fields in the Presbyterian Church, in Ohio and the West; where, in all directions, Presbyteries were organized, competent and entitled to try and judge the qualifications of those who felt called to labor among them. But, armed with "clean papers," these youthful cadets of liberal Christianity claimed and received admission into the Western Presbyteries, and whilst, in

* Christian Spectator, 1832, p. 146.

many cases, altogether ignorant of the Confession and order of the Church, assumed and exercised decisive control over all its dearest interests.

Coincident with these operations from without, was the policy pursued, within the bosom of the Church. "If a candidate for the ministry was rejected by an orthodox Presbytery," says Dr. Wilson, "for unsoundness in the faith, he was immediately sent off to New England, or to the Western Reserve, or to some other unsound region, and there invested with ministerial office, and sent back with clean papers; and was soon in our churches and judicatories. At the last meeting of the General Assembly, [that of 1834,] I heard a New School gentleman boast, that he had brought into the Presbyterian Church, about thirty-eight, in this way; some of whom were then members of the Assembly. The consumption of time, and the great trouble of manufacturing Presbyterian ministers in this way, was made a subject of grievous complaint; and was urged as a reason for the organization of "elective affinity Presbyteries," that they might proceed more expeditiously in this "good work!"* The New School gentleman was, the Rev. Mr. Patterson of Philadelphia.

With the facilities which were at their command, it would have been strange, if the managers of this vast system had overlooked the advantage of securing control, at such places as promised to become centres of great and extensive influence. Cincinnati was, of these, evidently, the first in importance. Dr. J. L. Wilson, the father of the ministry there, was a man of great

* "One proposition sustained against the New School," by Rev. J. L. Wilson, D. D., 1835, p. 10.

ability and influence, and of a warm and trusting spirit. His confidence was easily gained, on behalf of plans which purported to have nothing in view but the building of Christ's kingdom. The Presbytery of Cincinnati was speedily filled with young ministers from the East, fully imbued with the new theology, and eager to signalize their zeal by enterprises and triumphs on its behalf. The venerable Wilson awoke from his sleep; but it was, to find himself betrayed and bound.

Lane Seminary had been founded by the beneficence of an Old School minister, the Rev. James Kemper, who gave seventy acres of land, in the suburbs of Cincinnati, for the purpose of a theological seminary; provided, the professors should be in connection with the Presbyterian Church, under the care of the General Assembly of the Presbyterian Church in the United States of America. Subsequently, Mr. Lane, a Baptist gentleman, through Dr. Wilson, gave twenty thousand dollars to the institution; which were expended in erecting buildings. Measures were taken to endow the professorships of the Seminary. Mr. Arthur Tappan, of New York, President of the Presbyterian Education Society, and Auditor of the American Home Missionary Society, offered to endow the chair of theology, provided he were allowed to nominate Dr. Beecher to the post. The proposition was accepted, and the Dr. was transferred from Boston, and the perplexities of his position as the confidential adviser and apologist of Dr. Taylor, to preside over the interests of Presbyterianism, at the great centre of influence for the West. Soon, his son, the Rev. Edward Beecher, was translated from the tutorship in Yale, to preside over Illinois College.

While the fountains of education were being thus seized, a new impulse was given to the tide of ministerial immigration, from New England into the Church; and the fact began to be openly and unequivocably avowed, by the younger and more imprudent of the number, that they were coming, with the express design to gain control over, and revolutionize it.

In the system organized, under the auspices of the American Societies, the form of adopting the Confession of Faith was usually observed, by ministers, ordained within the Church; although it was divested of real significance. The Plan of Union threw the doors, yet more widely, open; and individual ministers, and entire associations were received, without any inquiry, as to doctrine, or allusion to the Confession of Faith. Thus, a great number of ministers were brought into the bosom of the Church, without even a pretence of attachment to it, or respect for its doctrines or order. On the contrary, the majority of them were not only Congregationalists, in their views of order; and, in their faith, held to one or other of the multiform phases of New England theology; but were under bonds to the Education Society, for the debt incurred in their preparation for the ministry; and dependent, for daily bread, upon the treasury of the Home Missionary Society, by which their fields of labor were selected and their subsistence provided.

To all this, is to be added, the silent but enormous moral power exerted by the American Board of Commissioners, by virtue of the mere fact that it, a New England institution, was the only representative of the spirit of missions in our Church,—the only channel through which our people could express their love to the souls of the heathen, and their reverence for the Saviour's last command. And, to crown the whole, the spirit of Moderatism was occupying almost all the high places of the Church, which were not possessed by the New School; presiding with few exceptions, over all our colleges; filling our influential pulpits; and occupying the chairs of instruction in our seminaries,—ready, always, to cry "Peace!" and to frown upon the first indications of any such active zeal for the truth as threatened to disturb the sinister tranquillity which they so fondly cherished. It was, under God, mainly due to the fidelity, courage, and faith in God, displayed by our unpretending country pastors and elders, that the Church was rescued from the devices which were formed respecting her.

Such is an outline of the system of organizations and influences, which conspired against the Presbyterian Church. It was not, indeed, designed to rend her to pieces, to dissolve her organization or diminish her numbers. On the contrary, the authors of the policy dazzled their imaginations with visions of a national Church, as comprehensive in its embrace as the ambitious "national societies" by which it was to be developed; and which were to shine and thrive in the light of its greatness. The churches of New England, the Presbyterian Church, the Reformed Dutch, the Scotch, German, and Associate Reformed,—these all, were to be included. And not these alone. Prospects undefined and boundless opened to the imaginations of the patrons of these schemes. But the magnificent conceptions thus pictured to fancy, were to be realized at the expense of all that is worth holding dear, in the Presbyterian Church,—her scriptural and saving faith, and her divinely originated and symmetrical order. The design was entertained and avowed to alter the Confession of Faith. On this subject, the Rev. Dr. J. L. Wilson thus testifies:

"The first declaration of this kind, which I shall notice, was made by an agent of the American Home Missionary Society; who, by his movements, first opened my eyes, to perceive the real designs of the New School. He said,—not to me, but to other persons; one of whom was so startled as to reveal the secret;—He said, holding the Confession of Faith in his hand,—'In a few years, we will have the majority; and then we will alter this book as we please.'

"Another declaration was made to me, in my own pulpit. I was speaking to the gentleman, about some erroneous opinions advanced in a sermon he had just delivered. He said, 'In less than twenty years, there will not be a Confession of Faith containing more than three articles.' This gentleman ranks with the moderates; and is a leading man, in some parts of the Church. This is in perfect accordance with the fact that so many brief Confessions of Faith have been recently published, both East and West, and, in some places, substituted for the standards of the Presbyterian Church."*

In fact, in many parts of the Church,—wherever the Plan of Union prevailed,—these abbreviated Confessions were in vogue, and, in a great measure, superseded the Westminster formularies. In 1836, a member of

* Wilson's One Proposition, p. 12.

the Assembly, from the Western Reserve, was found to be entirely unacquainted with the Confession of Faith; and was induced to purchase and take home a copy, by a member of the Presbytery of Ohio, who ascertained that the book would be a curiosity, not to him only, but to some of his Presbyterian neighbors.

The idea of an alteration of the Confession of Faith, so as to admit of a more easy comprehension of diverse sentiments, and consequent increase of accessions to the body, was not a mere passing suggestion of the less considerate and influential, but was seriously cherished, by some of the most considerable persons in the Church.

As the members were returning from the Assembly of 1836, two parties of them spent a night in rooms adjoining; separated by nothing but a plank partition. In one of these rooms were two of the most distinguished New School doctors; and in the other, the Rev. Samuel G. Winchester, and the Rev. James A. Peabody, Financial Secretary of the Board of Education. The attention of the latter was suddenly arrested, by a remark made in the adjoining room, in a tone so unguarded that they were involuntary hearers. "If the doctrine of election were out of the Confession of Faith," said the speaker, "what a glorious career would be before our Church!" "It is too soon," was the reply;—"The people will not bear it, yet." The interlocutory was here interrupted, by the voice of Winchester, warning the speakers, that they were overheard.

Such was the ulterior design; and in the mean time, the emphasis of the "*system*," in the ordination pledge served almost the same purpose.

Whilst a system so comprehensive was organized, for

ends so momentous to the Church, the structure was such as to be beyond the inspection and entirely independent of the control or interposition of its courts. The friends and officers of the American Societies were everywhere, in all the courts of the Church, ready and vigilant, to seize every opportunity to tease, and criticise, and harass her Boards; to encumber their organizations, embarrass their action, and neutralize their exertions. But the friends of the Church and of its Boards had neither voice nor hearing, in the councils of the societies. The condition of the privilege of speech, in those councils, was a liberal pecuniary pledge of devotion to their prosperity. And, even this was not sufficient, to confer a right to vote upon their affairs; unless the zeal of the giver was so well assured as to secure his enrollment, by a vote of those already in possession of the control.

Said a writer, in 1837: "The gratitude of Presbyterian candidates is secured, and a consequent modification of their sentiments effected,—the pecuniary obligations are held, and the influence consequent on such obligations preserved,—the young men from New England are systematically crowded into our Church, and our judicatories filled with those who, frequently, have not studied, understood, adopted, or even read our standards;—and, if our literary and theological institutions are free from the influence, it must be, because, if our Presidents and Professors are not more than *men*, they are, at least, more than *other* men. We ask, then, would any other sect or denomination, besides the Presbyterian Church, have ever endured the operation of such a tremendous moral power; operating, year after year, within its ecclesiastical jurisdiction? Could any other find, among themselves, a formidable party, to encourage and sustain such a foreign interference?"*

The history of the Church of God scarcely exhibits a more signal pledge of her heaven-born vitality, and the conservative power of the true principles of doctrine and order, with which Christ has endowed her, than is presented in the fact that our Church came off, wounded, indeed, and scarred, but triumphant, from the struggle with the tremendous system of agencies, without and within, by which she was beset, and seemingly overpowered. Bound, though she was, with seven green withes; when she awoke out of her sleep, they were as a thread of tow, touched by the fire.

* Rev. Thomas D. Baird, in the Christian Herald, 1837, p. 119.

CHAPTER XXII.

BARNES' FIRST TRIAL.

The Rev. Albert Barnes — His sermon on the The Way of Salvation—Call to Philadelphia—Opposed in Presbytery—Discussion on his reception—Dr. Ely writes Mr. Barnes' creed—Mr. Barnes received—Charges against him rejected—Action of Synod on complaint—Called meeting of Presbytery—Dilatory policy of Mr. Barnes' friends--Examination of the sermon—Committee to confer with Mr. Barnes—He refuses to hear them—Reference of the case to the Assembly—Complaints accompany it, from the friends of Mr. Barnes.

Dr. Taylor's Concio ad Clerum was preached in the chapel of Yale, on the 10th of September, 1828. On the 8th of February, following, a discourse was delivered, in the Presbyterian church, in Morristown, New Jersey, which fills a place as important in this history, as did that of Dr. Taylor, in the annals of New England theology. The preacher, the Rev. Albert Barnes, was a young pastor, whose earlier years had been passed under the teachings of the Methodist Church. After passing through college, he made a profession of religion, and united with the Presbyterian Church. A few days afterward, he entered Princeton Seminary, as a student of theology. After entering upon the ministry, he became pastor of the church in Morristown. Here, in the midst of an awakening, Mr. Barnes preached, from Titus iii. 4–7, his discourse entitled "The Way of Salvation." In the following winter, it was published, "at the suggestion, and chiefly at the expense of a few friends; simply with the hope of giving a more fixed impression of the views then expressed." This "prefatory advertisement" was dated, December 26, 1829, more than ten months subsequent to the delivery of the discourse; a lapse of time, which, taken with the manner and avowed motives of the publication, precluded the plea of haste or inadvertence, as to the sentiments presented.

At this time, the name of Mr. Barnes was before the people of the First Church in Philadelphia, as successor to the Rev. Dr. James P. Wilson; who was then in infirm health, and, shortly afterward, died. This circumstance at once directed attention to the sermon. The Rev. Wm. M. Engles published, in the Philadelphian, some strictures, in which he placed the sermon and the Confession in juxtaposition, and showed that, on the fundamental points of original sin and the atonement, the two were irreconcilably at variance. A reply soon appeared, from the pen of Dr. Wilson; and a discussion of some length ensued, between the reviewer and the defender of the sermon.

In the mean time, a congregational meeting was held, in the First Church, and a call voted to Mr. Barnes. This call was submitted to the Presbytery of Philadelphia, at its stated meeting, in April; and leave asked to prosecute it, before the Presbytery of Elizabethtown. In opposition to this request, the venerable Dr. Green urged the erroneous doctrines of the printed sermon. An attempt was made to preclude any discussion on that discourse; on the ground that it was equivalent to an arraignment and trial of Mr. Barnes, for heresy, whilst he was beyond the jurisdiction of the Presbytery. This motion was, however, rejected, by a vote of thirty-seven to ten; and the discussion proceeded. The objections urged against the sermon were,—that, whilst it purports to state the way of salvation, no mention is made of the cardinal doctrine of justification;—that the author contemptuously rejects the doctrine of the imputation of Adam's first sin; that he intimates that the first moral taint of the creature is coincident with his first moral action; that he denies that Christ sustained the penalty of the law;—that he affirms that the atonement had no specific reference to individuals, and secured the salvation of no man;—that he limits the inability of the sinner, to an indisposition of will;—and that he declares his own independence of all formularies of doctrine; notwithstanding his professed adoption of the Confession of Faith.*

On the part of those who favored the call, there was a studied evasion of the doctrinal issue. The Rev. Dr. Thomas McAuley, the Rev. Mr. Sanford, Dr. Ely, and others, admitted, in general terms, that there were some things in the sermon, equivocal, and some erroneous. But, it was denied that the Presbytery had any right to inquire into Mr. Barnes' doctrinal views; and much was said of his excellent character and piety. The cry of "Persecution!" was raised; and the imprudence, of offending a church so influential and important as the First, was pointed out. Dr. Green and the Rev. Joshua

* Engles' True and Complete Narrative, p. 8.

T. Russell, the President and Secretary of the Board of Missions, were admonished that the Board, would suffer, in consequence of the part they took in opposition,—a threat to which the subsequent history gave profound significance.

Upon the question, permission to prosecute the call was granted, by a vote of twenty-one to twelve. The minority entered a protest, in which they set forth the errors in doctrine contained in the sermon. To this no reply was made.

On the 18th of June, following, a special meeting of the Presbytery was held, "for the purpose of considering the subject of the reception of the Rev. Mr. Barnes, and to do what may be deemed proper, in his installation." This meeting was not held in the customary place, but in the lecture-room of the First church, apparently with a view to exert an influence on the minority of Presbytery. Upon the presentation of Mr. Barnes' testimonials of dismission from the Presbytery of Elizabethtown, it was moved that he be received as a member. After some discussion, Dr. Ely moved, "that the motion now under consideration be postponed: that, before deciding on it, any brother of the Presbytery, who may deem it necessary, may ask of the Rev. Mr. Barnes such explanations of his doctrinal views as said brethren may deem necessary." This motion was rejected.

In the course of the discussion which followed, Mr. Barnes rose, and proposed to make some explanations of his doctrinal views. This, he said, he was willing to do, voluntarily, but not in compliance with a demand; which he held the Presbytery had no right to make.

In making these explanations, he occupied some five minutes. He acknowledged that his sermon was defective, through oversight, on the doctrine of justification. And yet, its theme was, the way of salvation! His further remarks, shed no light on the questionable passages; but only tended to confirm the conviction that his views were radically at variance with the Confession.

At another point in the discussion, Mr. Barnes joined with Dr. Ely, in a proceeding, but little to the credit of either party. Dr. Ely having constructed a series of ambiguous statements, on the points at issue; he was authorized by Mr. Barnes to submit them to the Presbytery, as an exhibition of the faith of the latter. The paper thus submitted, "with the approbation and signature of Mr. Barnes," was couched in the following terms:—

"That he does believe and teach,

"1. That God regarded and treated Adam, in the garden of Eden, not as an insulated individual, but as the head and father of all his race; so that his trial was a virtual trial of all his race, and his sentence a virtual sentence on his race.

"2. That, by a divine constitution, such a relation subsisted between Adam and every one of his posterity, that his first act of sinning was to secure, and, by acting in this relation, Adam did secure, the bringing of every descendant of Adam into an estate of sin and misery, in which it was rendered morally certain that they would righteously suffer all the evils which God actually brings upon them; and would, every one of them, so soon as capable of moral agency, commence a course of sinful moral agency, which would be interrupted by nothing but regeneration.

"3. That there is SOMETHING, whether it be called, *tendency, disposition, principle,* or, *depravity,* in man, which renders it certain, as a result from Adam's fall, that the first moral action, and every subsequent one, of every descendant of Adam, by natural generation, will be sinful, until the subject of this depravity is transformed by the Holy Ghost.

"4. That this depravity of man is such that no one of our race ever did, or ever will, repent and receive the Lord Jesus Christ, without being both PERSUADED and, spiritually and morally, ENABLED by the Holy Ghost so to do.

"5. That all men, in their native state, possess all the requisite natural faculties for serving God perfectly; but are wholly destitute of that right disposition, or moral nature, which is requisite to the serving of him acceptably.

"6. That Christ suffered, in the place and stead of sinners; and that believers are justified, or judicially declared to be righteous, solely and entirely on account of Christ's vicarious righteousness, and of his exclusive merits; which, after they have been *given* to the believer, are *judicially reckoned,* and in this sense IMPUTED to him.

"7. That the doctrine of justification should have been more distinctly and prominently brought forth, in his sermon; and that the omission of it was probably owing to this truth, that he had never any difficulty, in his own mind, on the subject, and that no controversy existed, in the place of his former charge, about this all-important doctrine.

"8. That Christ did not suffer the *identical pains*, which sinners would have suffered; and *in this sense* he was not *punished*; but that, in the stead of sinners, he a divine and human person, suffered for sinners, that which the wisdom and justice of God deemed an *adequate equivalent*, or vicarious suffering, to satisfy divine justice, in the place of the punishment merited by the ungodly."*

It was not until two years after these proceedings, that the "Hawes correspondence" took place; so that to Dr. Ely, is to be awarded, at least, the palm of originality, in the device here exhibited. One thing, it clearly demonstrated:—that Mr. Barnes and his friends did not oppose inquiry into his theological sentiments, so much because of the supposed infringement upon his liberty,—for that point was surrendered by the very presentation of this paper,—as, because of the embarrassing questions which might be proposed, should he be brought under examination; and the erroneous sentiments which he might, thus be constrained to avow. It was easy to construct phrases of very specious seeming; if no one were allowed to ask precisely what the language was meant to convey or conceal.

Dr. Ely's paper was evidently designed for popular effect; and no doubt served its purpose. To the theologian, who is at all familiar with the Pelagian controversy; especially, in its more recent New Haven phases,

* Complaint of the minority of the Presbytery of Philadelphia, (Dr. Ely and others,) presented to the General Assembly, May 20, 1831. pp. 14, 8vo., p. 5.

the creed here exhibited, when interpreted in the light of the circumstances in which it originated, is an avowal of essential agreement with the system of the New Haven divines.

After several days' discussion, Mr. Barnes was received; by a vote of thirty to sixteen.

The Rev. Brogun Hoff then submitted a paper of charges against him, for unsoundness in the faith, as a bar to the installation. This paper the moderator pronounced to be out of order; as being the introduction of new business, at a *pro re nata* meeting. In this decision, he was sustained by the house, against an appeal taken by Dr. Ely; who, on this point, sided with the minority. All obstacles being thus overcome, the requisite arrangements were made; and, on the 25th of June, Mr. Barnes was installed.

Against these proceedings, the minority complained to the Synod of Philadelphia. In the Synod, the case occupied nearly two days of deliberate investigation. In the course of it, a member put the following question,—"Mr. Barnes, it is stated in one of the answers of our Shorter Catechism that 'The sinfulness of that estate whereinto man fell consists in the guilt of Adam's first sin, the want of original righteousness, and the corruption of his whole nature, which is commonly called, original sin.'—Mr. Barnes, do you believe this?" To which Mr. Barnes replied, "I do not."

The Synod, after a full hearing of all the parties, including the reading of an elaborate paper, by Mr. Barnes, decided, by a large majority, to sustain the complaint; condemned the Presbytery of Philadelphia, for not allowing the examination of Mr. Barnes, in connection with his printed sermon, previously to his reception; and referred the complainants back to the Presbytery, with an injunction to it " to hear and decide on their objections to the orthodoxy of the sermon of Mr. Barnes, and to take such order, on the whole subject, as is required by a regard to the purity of the Church, and its acknowledged doctrines and order."

Such changes had now taken place, in the Presbytery, that the opposers of the new theology were in a decided majority. Upon the adjournment of Synod, a system of tactics was commenced by the minority, with the design to nullify the decision of Synod and defeat the majority of Presbytery, over the details of which we draw the veil of silence.

At first, the attempt was made to carry matters by a surprise movement, at an adjourned meeting, which, as it happened, was appointed for some purpose, twenty-five hours after the adjournment of the Synod at Lancaster. This failing, and the subject being made the occasion of a called meeting, nearly three days were spent in dilatory motions, designed to preclude all action, unless the Presbytery would surrender the principle, that it had a right to examine and judge the sermon of Mr. Barnes, apart from any judicial process against the author. When, at length, the obstacles thus interposed were overcome, and the Presbytery was about to proceed to an examination of the sermon, the minority entered a protest, declaring such a proceeding unconstitutional, and that, if persisted in, " the undersigned must withdraw from all participation in such proceedings, and complain to the next General Assembly." In the sequel, however, it appeared that this withdrawal merely meant silence on the doctrinal questions, involved in the discussion. The protesting members claimed, and exercised, freely, the right to take part in all questions of order; and, in a word, whenever any opportunity occurred, to embarrass the proceedings. They also asked, and the Presbytery granted them the right to dissent, protest and complain, against its proceedings; which, otherwise, they could not have done, as willfully refusing to take part in them.

As the discussion of the sermon was about to commence, Mr. Barnes inquired, whether he had a right to appeal to the Assembly, and thus arrest the proceedings. Being answered in the negative, he presented a paper, avowing the authorship of the sermon, and offering himself for trial; either on the ground of common fame, or, upon charges made by a responsible accuser, or accusers. This request the Presbytery declined to grant; for reasons which were entered at length on the minutes. Mr. Barnes, then, asked leave of absence from the remaining sessions. He stated that he was confident of being able to make such explanations of his sermon as would satisfy the Presbytery of its entire harmony with the Confession of Faith; but, that, upon advising with his friends, he had determined not, then, to do it! His request was granted, at the same time that he was most importunately entreated, by Dr. Green and others, to remain, and give the explanations, which he professed himself so able to do, and which were so necessary to the peace of the Church.

He had, previously, asked whether he was entitled to vote, upon the questions involved in the examination of the sermon. This question was answered in the negative,—a decision undoubtedly erroneous; and which was carried, by the the votes of his own party, with a few others, against the prevalent sentiments and votes of the majority.

At length, the Presbytery was allowed to proceed to examine the sermon, and a paper offered by Dr. Green was read by paragraphs, amended and adopted. In this paper, the sermon was charged with errors of a dangerous tendency, on some principal points of Christian theology; especially, on original sin, the atonement and justification.

It was now moved by Mr. Engles, "that Dr. Green, Mr. McCalla, and Mr. Latta, be a committee to wait on Mr. Barnes, to communicate to him the result of the deliberations of this Presbytery, in the examination of his sermon, and to converse with him, freely and affectionately, on the points excepted to, in that sermon; in the hope and expectation, that the interview will result in removing or diminishing the difficulties which have arisen in his case; and that they report at the next meeting of Presbytery."

The minority had been silent, during the doctrinal discussion. They now resumed activity, and opposed this motion, as involving a direct insult to Mr. Barnes. It was, however, adopted by the Presbytery; whereupon the minority gave notice of complaint to the General Assembly.

The committee took an early opportunity to wait on Mr. Barnes, at his study, in a body. He received them with courtesy; but refused to hold any communication with them, as a committee, on the subject of their appointment; but said that he was willing to converse with them, individually, and in a private capacity. After remaining about an hour, they rose to leave; when he handed them a paper, stating the reasons of his refusal. These were, in brief, the asserted unconstitutionality of the course of the Presbytery; and his unwillingness, by any act, to recognize it as of binding force.

The committee made report of these facts and submitted Mr. Barnes' written answer, to Presbytery, at the stated meeting, in April, 1831. After discussion, it was resolved to refer the whole case to the General Assembly. The reference was accompanied with complaints from Mr. Bradford and from the minority against these proceedings. In the latter paper, the former majority give the following account of the impropriety of their own action, in refusing to entertain the charges, as a bar to the installation:—

"No sooner had Mr. Barnes been received by this Presbytery, on the 23d of June, than a paper, containing formal charges against him, for unsoundness in the faith, and signed by Ashbel Green, D. D., the Rev. Wm. M. Engles, the Rev. George C. Potts, the Rev. Alexander Boyd, the Rev. Brogun Hoff, the Rev. A. H. Parker, the Rev. Charles Williamson, and others, was presented to Presbytery, 'with a view to arrest the installation; and it was decided by the Moderator, that the paper containing the charges could not be admitted, at a special meeting, as the commencement of a trial; because out of order.' This decision, the undersigned, of whom the Moderator referred to is one, now judge to have been incorrect; because that special meeting was called, not only to *receive* Mr. Barnes, but to transact *any business* relative to his installation. These charges should have been constitutionally disposed of, either by declaring them irrelevant, or by taking the requisite steps for trying Mr. Barnes on the same."*

It will be remembered that these charges were only tabled, as a last resort, in bar of the installation, after the Presbytery had utterly refused to allow an examination, either of Mr. Barnes or his sermon. These brethren now acknowledge that the refusal to entertain those charges was a violation of the rights of the members presenting them. Yet they now complain to the Assembly, because the brethren thus injured did not accept of the false position in which, by this confessedly wrongful act they were placed; and prosecute Mr. Barnes, after installation, upon charges which, upon the face of them, were seen to have been tabled "with a view to arrest the installation." Furthermore, these parties complain to the Assembly against their brethren, for exercising a right of examination, conferred upon them by a judicial decision of the Synod; against which, if these complainants felt aggrieved by it, their only proper remedy was in an appeal from the Synod to the Assembly. Failing of this, they were utterly without a reasonable pretext for opposing the proceedings of the Presbytery; much more, for complaint to the Assembly.

If the case was to be decided upon its merits, by the supreme tribunal, the complainants had small prospect of success. Their confidence was based on other grounds; and was not disappointed.

* Complaint from the Minority, etc., pp. 14, 8vo., p. 6.

CHAPTER XXIII.

THE ASSEMBLY OF 1831.

Preparations for the Assembly of 1831—Peters' "Plea for Union in the West"—Publications on Barnes' case—Dr. Beman's Southern tour—The New Haven Spectator—The Assembly of 1831—Dr. Beman, Moderator—His theological position—Clement Tuttle, a committee-man—Barnes' case—Committee of reference—The report—Demand of Mr. McCalla—The report forced through—Breckinridge's protest—Mr. Bacon's comment on this transaction.

As the time drew on for the meeting of the General Assembly of 1831, measures were skillfully adopted to give it such a complexion as would subserve the purposes of the apologists for Mr. Barnes, and the enemies of the Boards of the Church. The reply of the Board of Missions, to the communication of the Presbytery of Cincinnati, on the project of union, was published in the Cincinnati Journal, at the request of one of the committee to whom it was addressed, on the 12th of November. This publication was immediately seized as the occasion for a series of six letters from the pen of Dr. Peters, which appeared in the same paper, in the course of December and January. These letters were entitled, "A Plea for Union in the West," and purported to make developments of the most startling character, involving charges, against the Board and its officers, of a course of systematized chicanery, fraud and falsehood, running through its publications, and especially premeating its annual report. Respecting them, the writer says,—"We know that such an exposure may occasion a malignant satisfaction, in the minds of opposers, and we regret its necessity, especially, at the present time, when the eyes of an infidel world are watching with eagerness for the halting of Christians. But, if the enemies of Christianity, and of the benevolent efforts of the day, must have occasion to reproach the professed followers of Christ, let them be compelled to do so, in full view of the fact, that ourselves are the first to expose every error, in the Church, or its members, which cannot be otherwise corrected. It is our solemn impression, that no fears, as to the consequences, ought to bear the weight of a feather against our high and holy obligations as Christians, to *provide things honest in the sight of all men.* I cannot, therefore, convince myself that, on account of the delicacy of my official relations, it is, any longer, my duty, as an individual, to shrink from the responsibilities of a step, which a just regard to the honor and purity of our benevolent institutions appears so imperiously to demand."*

What shall we think of the state of mind of the writer who could pen such a sentence as this; and then set himself to work with the utmost ingenuity,—by garbled extracts, by torturing a foreign meaning out of the plainest language, and by suppression,—to make out a case that should persuade the Christian public and the world, that the Board of Missions, its Executive Committee and its Secretary, had conspired to im-

* Dr. Peters' Fifth letter, in his "Brief Answer," etc., p. 42.

pose upon the Church, by the most clumsy deceptions and palpable falsehoods? This, too, was at a time when, if the character of the venerable president of the Board, Dr. Green, were left out of the account, two of the most eminent of New School divines, were involved in all the responsibility,—the Rev. Dr. Thomas H. Skinner, one of the three officers of the Board; and the Rev. Dr. Thomas McAuley, one of the three ministerial members of the Executive Committee.

The officers of the Board were Rev. Dr. Ashbel Green, President, Rev. Joshua T. Russell, Corresponding Secretary, Rev. Thomas H. Skinner, Recording Secretary. The Executive Committee were Drs. Green and McAuley, and Mr. Russell, with Messrs. James Moore, Solomon Allen, Geo. W. Blight, and Furman Leaming.

In the sixth letter of this series, the writer stated that it had hitherto been a leading object of his endeavors "to persuade the contending parties," the Board and the Society, "to become ONE;" and says,—"on this object, '*my heart is fixed.*'" "What measures ought now to be adopted, I do not feel prepared even to suggest. So far as the Western States are concerned, I trust our brethren, on the ground, will be prepared to express their wishes to the next General Assembly; or, that they will adopt other measures to secure that harmony of action, so essential to the peace of the churches, and the permanent prosperity of the missionary work."

Thus, whilst a desperate assault was made upon the truth and integrity of the Board,—an assault designed utterly to destroy the confidence of the churches in the honesty and management of that institution,—its union with the Home Society was announced, as the fixed intent of the Secretary; and the rallying call was uttered, to all the dependants and friends of the Society, to be prepared to secure that union, in the West, through the General Assembly.

The "Plea for Union" was republished, in the New York Evangelist. The Board, under date of March 2d, 1831, published an "Official Reply," to the letters, in a pamphlet of 32 pages. Dr. Peters, at once, rejoined, under date of April 25, in a "Brief Answer," consisting of a 48 page pamphlet, including, in an appendix, the Six Letters and other papers.

Whilst the American Home Missionary Society was thus marshaling its forces for the Assembly, an equal activity was displayed by the advocates and apologists of Mr. Barnes and the New England theology. Shortly after Mr. Barnes' installation, in June, 1830, a pamphlet was published in New York, entitled, "A Sketch of the Debate and Proceedings of the Presbytery of Philadelphia, in regard to the Installation of the Rev. Albert Barnes." This pamphlet, was written in a thoroughly partisan spirit. It concealed the weak points of the advocates for Mr. Barnes, while it exhibited his opponents in the most invidious light, as, at once weak and malignant. At the same time, the religious papers, all of which were in the interest of the New School party, or of Moderatism, teemed with similar representations. Some three months after the publication of the Sketch, the Rev. Mr. McCalla appeared in a pamphlet narrative of the proceedings, and review of the Sketch. After the judgment of the Synod, and the final action of

Presbytery under it, Dr. Ely published, in his paper, the Philadelphian, such a history of the proceedings as was best calculated to vindicate Mr. Barnes and his friends. This drew from Mr. Engles, the Clerk of Presbytery, "A True and Complete Narrative," published in pamphlet form. Through the winter of 1830–31, the Philadelphian was occupied with this subject; two numbers of which, containing elaborate papers by Mr. Barnes, were scattered broadcast and sent to the most of the Presbyterian ministry, throughout the country.

Whilst, thus, in Philadelphia, New York, and Cincinnati, every nerve was strained, to secure an Assembly favorable to Mr. Barnes, and to the Home Missionary Society,—the Rev. Dr. Beman was spending the winter in an extensive tour at the South. He subsequently denied, most emphatically, any ulterior objects in that tour. "My *only* object in this tour, was the restoration of *my health*."* The fact, however, was developed, that whilst he and the Rev. Dr. Spring were in the lobby of the Assembly room, awaiting the vote which placed him in the Moderator's chair, he stated to Dr. Spring that he had known, three months before, that, if he should be a member of the Assembly, and present at its opening, an effort would be made to make him Moderator; and, that there were "eight votes he had lost, from the absence of members from Virginia." With reference to these statements, Dr. Green pertinently demanded, in reply to disavowals of preconcert made by Dr. Beman and others,—"Could this possibly take place, without preconcert, and a good deal of it

* Beman's Appeal, p. 28.

too? Could he be sure that eight members from Virginia would, if present, vote for him, if there had been no preconcert? Are we to believe that at the Synod in Winchester, he spent his whole time in religious exercises, and entered into no preconcert, in regard to 'men and measures,' in the next Assembly? Is it credible that he could know, three months before the Assembly, when he was far distant, in the South, what he says he did know, if there had not been some special communication between him and his party at the North? And does such a correspondence consist with an open, public, and honest denial of all plan and preconcert whatsoever?"

In addition to the other appliances, which were brought to bear upon this important Assembly, the influence of New Haven was called into requisition. Mr. Barnes was a contributor to the pages of the Christian Spectator; and, now, its editors identified themselves with his cause. The number for June appeared a month in advance, so as to anticipate the meeting of the General Assembly; to the members of which it conveyed a very earnest plea in behalf of Mr. Barnes and his theology. "We hope," said the Spectator, "it will not be thought unkind or improper to remind those who seem bent on driving Mr. Barnes from the Presbytery of Philadelphia, that they are taking upon themselves a responsibility of no ordinary character; since the principle on which they act, if carried into full operation, must create a total disruption in the Presbyterian Church throughout the United States; and a consequent sacrifice, to an immense extent, of some of the dearest interests of the Redeemer's kingdom, both at home and abroad. We state the subject thus strongly, because every one, we suppose, understands that the case of Mr. Barnes is not that of an individual. The real question at issue is *whether New England Calvinism shall any longer be tolerated in the Presbyterian Church of this country.*" To enforce this consideration, and to aid in the management of Mr. Barnes' case, in the Assembly, the Rev. Mr. Bacon, one of the New Haven gentlemen, was commissioned as delegate from the Association of Connecticut.

When the Assembly of 1831 convened, it presented the largest body of commissioners that had ever met, in the supreme court of our Church. Two hundred and twenty-seven members were in attendance,—fifty-two more than were in any previous Assembly. In it, the New School party first appeared, in distinct and embodied organization; marshaled, as were its forces, by the combined and powerful motives of zeal for the cause of Mr. Barnes, and hostility to the Board of Missions, originating in devotion to the system of voluntary societies, and intensified by the doctrinal position of the Board, as indicated by its rejection of the Tennessee Hopkinsians, and by the activity of the President and Secretary, in the case of Mr. Barnes.

The first test of party strength was in the election of Moderator. Dr. Beman was the nominee of the New School party; and it is remarkable, that the only Moderator whom that party ever succeeded in electing to the chair should have been this gentleman. His entrance into the ministry of the Presbyterian Church would appear to have been by one or other of the arrangements for the convenience of Congregationalists; as, the fact was, with some difficulty elicited from him, by Mr. Baird, in the Assembly of 1832, that he had never adopted the Confession of Faith. We have already seen how fully he was identified with the preaching and measures of Mr. Finney, which were nowhere received with more favor than in Dr. Beman's pulpit. He was already the author of a published volume of sermons on the atonement, in which the scheme of the younger Edwards is explicitly developed and defended. Repudiating the doctrine of the Confession, that justice was fully satisfied in the redemption of Christ, he accepts Dr. Edwards' argument that if this be so "grace and pardon are out of the question," salvation is of debt. He follows that divine in classifying justice, as, *commutative*, which has respect to commercial transactions, the payment of pecuniary obligations, etc.; *distributive*, which "respects the moral character and conduct of creatures; and consists in rewarding or punishing them, according to their merit or ill desert;" and *public*, or *general*, justice, which "has no direct reference to law; but embraces those principles of virtue and benevolence by which we are bound to govern our conduct; and by which God himself governs the universe."

According to Dr. Beman, this last kind of justice, which "has no direct reference to law," and is therefore, as Dr. Edwards confesses, properly, no justice, is that which, alone, is satisfied in the atonement. "Distributive justice, as expressed in the law, has received no satisfaction at all;" and its uncanceled sentence will for ever stand against the redeemed in heaven. "The whole legal system has been suspended, at least, for the present, in order to make way for the operation of one of a different character." Christ suffered "not on legal principles, but by express stipulation or covenant with the Father." And the design was, not to satisfy justice, but to make an *exhibition* of God's abhorrence of sin, which should exert such a moral influence on the created intelligences, that justice may be set aside, and sin may be pardoned, in consistency with the general welfare of the universe. In this sense, the atonement is represented as a substitute for the infliction of the penalty of the law; and the sufferings of Christ are therefore called "vicarious sufferings."

That this theory is at direct variance with the Confession of Faith, is apparent. That it completely overturns the gospel scheme, and renders the justification of the sinner impossible, is equally evident; as we have seen.

It is, also, in open contradiction to the plainest teachings of Scripture, and the very words of the Son of God, himself. Dr. Beman asserts that the "law has received no satisfaction, at all. The whole legal system is suspended, in order to make way for the operation of one of a different character." The prophet says, "He will magnify the law and make it honorable." The Son himself testifies, "I am not come to destroy, but to fulfill. For, verily, I say unto you, till heaven and earth pass, one jot or one tittle shall in no wise pass from the law, till all be fulfilled." And Paul declares that he was "made of a woman, made under the law, to redeem them that were under the law."

Such were the leading principles,—we do not trace the details,—of Dr. Beman's published theology. Yet was he, beyond question, the most honored and influential leader in the New School body. Dr. Peters, by virtue of his official patronage, might *control* more votes. Dr. Richards may have stood higher in personal character. But Dr. Beman was the trusted leader, the marshal of the host, on every occasion of emergency, from 1831, when he was called to the Moderator's chair, in view of the great interests then at stake, until 1838, when he was again called to that office, to preside over the incipient proceedings, in the withdrawal of the New School body from the Assembly and the Church.

In organizing the Assembly of 1831, no leader could have been selected, who was personally more interested, or one more prompt and skillful in the direction and management requisite to the purposes cherished by the party, in that Assembly.

At the very threshold of its proceedings, an illustration was presented of the growing confidence of disorder sheltering itself under the Plan of Union. Mr. Clement Tuttle appeared, with a commission from the Grand River Presbytery, designating him as "committee-man," to sit in the Assembly. The case was referred to a Committee of Elections, which declined to express any opinion as to the constitutional right of such a person to a seat. The Assembly, however, after considerable discussion, resolved that he be received and enrolled.

Immediately upon the organization, the case of Mr. Barnes presented itself, in the complaints made against the proceedings in that case,—and in the reference from the Presbytery. These papers were sent to the judicial committee; which, subsequently, reported the complaints as in order. A proposition was, at once, made to refer the matter to a committee, to see if the case could not be disposed of, without a hearing. The Assembly, however, proceeded to hear the complaint and the records in the case.

Dr. Miller, then, moved a reference, with the consent of the parties. Dr. Green, on behalf of the Presbytery, asked a postponement for a day, that he might have opportunity to confer with the other members of the Presbytery's committee. This, the Assembly refused to grant. A hasty conference was then had, among those members of the committee who happened to be in the house, and Dr. Green announced that they acquiesced in the reference. Judge Darling, one of the committee to prosecute the complaint, inquired,—"Is it to be understood, that the whole business is given up entirely into the hands of the Assembly? Is it understood that neither of the parties shall have anything further to say, in the business? Is the business placed precisely in that state in which it would be, had both parties, at this moment, spoken until they were satisfied?" The earnestness with which this point was urged, should have aroused the suspicions of the defence. But they seem to have been altogether blind to the trap into which they were about to fall.

To Judge Darling's questions, a member of the house replied, by explaining that the parties relinquish all claim to be heard,—the committee, in their report, will bring the subject before the Assembly, when it will be discussed and disposed of. The same justice will be done the parties as if they had been fully heard. "He was not for covering up questions of such importance as the case involved. Sooner than this should happen, he would see the Assembly divided this moment; and the ties by which they were now dubiously held, rent asunder."*

After this explanation, in which all acquiesced, "the parties agreed to submit the case, without argument. It was, then, resolved to refer it to Dr. Miller, Dr. Matthews, Dr. Lansing, Dr. Fisk, Dr. Spring, Dr. J. McDowell, Mr. Bacon, Mr. E. White, Mr. Jessup, and Mr. Napier, as a select committee."

The mouths of the parties being now sealed, this committee, and the Assembly, under its guidance, proceeded to dispose of the case, without any regard to the provisions of the Constitution, for judicial cases. Having got rid of that rule which provides that the parties shall be fully heard, all its further provisions were treated with indifference. The roll was not called; nor were the members permitted any discussion of the case. The question was not taken, upon sustaining the complaint; nor was any one point, involved in the case, brought to a judicial decision.

The committee brought in a minute, embracing the following resolutions:—

"*Resolved*, That the General Assembly, whilst it appreciates the conscientious zeal for the purity of the Church by which the Presbytery of Philadelphia is believed to have been actuated, in its proceedings in the case of Mr. Barnes; and whilst it judges that the sermon by Mr. Barnes entitled 'The Way of Salvation,' contains a number of unguarded and objectionable passages; yet is of the opinion, that, especially, after the explanations, which were given by him, of those pas-

* Presbyterian, 1831, p. 63.

sages, the Presbytery ought to have suffered the whole to pass without further notice.

"*Resolved*, That, in the judgment of this Assembly, the Presbytery of Philadelphia ought to suspend all further proceedings, in the case of Mr. Barnes.

"*Resolved*, That it will be expedient, as soon as the regular steps can be taken, to divide the Presbytery, in such a way, as will be best calculated to promote the peace of the ministers and churches belonging to the Presbytery.

"With respect to the abstract points, proposed to the Assembly, for their decision, in the reference of the Presbytery, the committee are of the opinion that, if they be answered, they had better be discussed and decided, *in thesi*, separate from the case of Mr. Barnes."

When this report was made to the Assembly, the Rev. Wm. L. McCalla handed the Moderator a paper, which he wished to read to the house. The Moderator, Dr. Beman, looked through it, and then stated to the house that it was a plea in Mr. Barnes' case; and, therefore, out of order. He admitted that it was perfectly decorous in its language; and a motion was made that it be read. This motion the Moderator refused to put. An appeal was taken, and the Moderator was sustained. Had the paper been read, it would have appeared that its nature had been misstated. It was not a plea in the case, but a demand to be heard. Mr. McCalla had been out of the house, when the other members of the committee waived their right.

"I now come before you," said he, in this paper, "humbly to claim an opportunity to perform the duty which it [the commission from Presbytery] devolves upon me. . . . Many of the members of the Assembly believe that the want of an authentic answer to the complaint will rob our judges of that information which they need, and have a right to demand. The complaint is a protracted and highly argumentative document. As the Presbytery never saw it, they will expect their commissioners, to answer it, for them. My colleagues neither possess nor claim the right of depriving me of this privilege, without my consent; any more than I have a right of compelling them to exercise it, without their consent. When my momentary absence, at the time, can be shown to be so disorderly or disrespectful as to deprive me of my commission, then, and then only, let my Presbytery be cut off from a hearing. . . . I am willing to be precluded from the handling of all books and papers, whatever; with the single exception of my interleaved copy of the printed complaint. . . . I am willing to see the complainants furnished with all the books and papers which they may think necessary; while I shall be allowed no other help than the Spirit of Jesus, and the complaint above mentioned. Let them be cheered with the smiles of popular favor, and let me appear under the lowering frowns of an overwhelming *majority*. Only allow me the constitutional right of speaking for Christ and his people, and I am satisfied. If refused, I call heaven and earth to witness, that the complainees are denied a hearing, which they earnestly solicit, and to which they are entitled, by the laws of God and man. May our covenant God direct to proper measures, and a proper decision."*

To this letter, the Assembly, misled as to its contents,

* The Letter, in the Presbyterian, 1831, p. 63.

refused to listen. Members attempted to canvass the report of the committee; but were arrested with the admonition that, to reopen the subject would involve deplorable consequences, which, however, were undefined. The body was blindfolded, and the report of the committee, which was satisfactory to none, was forced through, with but few dissenting voices.

It was then moved, that the Assembly unite in thanksgiving for the harmonious result to which they had come, and imploring the blessing of God on their decision. The motion was adopted, and Dr. Fisk led in prayer.

Amid these proceedings, one earnest voice was raised in indignant protest. Robert J. Breckinridge, a young lawyer and elder, from Kentucky, with a manner significant of profound emotion, expressed his horror at what had been done. He declared that both parties had acted against the dictates of their consciences; those who thought with Mr. Barnes, in voting to condemn, as "unguarded and objectionable" sentiments which they thoroughly approved, and had, in their speeches, endorsed;—and his opponents, in disapproving, as merely incautious expressions, what they believed to be dangerous errors; and in censuring the Presbytery, for what they, in their hearts, believed to have been a most proper course of action. "We have agreed to bury the truth," said Mr. Breckinridge; "and before two years, God will correct us for it."

It needed but one thing more to fill up the measure of indignity done to the Presbyterian order of our standards, and of humiliation to our Church,—thus bound hand and foot and presented, a voluntary sacrifice, in its doctrines and government, to the system of our Congregational brethren. The cup was filled, full and running over, when the delegate from Connecticut, the Rev. Mr. Bacon, who was one of the committee on Mr. Barnes' case—after assisting to betray the Assembly into the false position in which it was left,—went home, and published to the world his scorn for the Church which dare not treat the case according to its own principles; but had taken refuge in the Congregational mode of proceeding.

"I suppose," said he, "that the committee, on which I was named, was appointed, not to try the case, on Presbyterian principles; but rather, to act as a council, for the settlement of the controversy, as we dispose of difficulties in our churches. I profess myself unskilled in the peculiarities of Presbyterian discipline; but if I understand your book, your way is, to try such a case by hearing, not only the documents, but the parties, and to decide it, not by proposing terms of reconciliation, but by giving a direct, distinct, and conclusive answer, to every question involved in the reference, complaint, or appeal. This I suppose would have been the Presbyterian method of proceeding, in the case of Mr. Barnes. But this course was not adopted. There was a reluctance, in a part of the Assembly, against a regular trial and decision in the case. I was not very well acquainted with members or parties; but this I know, the men who feared the result of a trial, were some of them men of great respectability.

"Not even the venerable editor of the Christian Advocate, will charge the venerable professor on whose repeated motion the Assembly at last consented to waive a regular trial, with being engaged in any conspiracy against the purity of the Presbyterian Church. Yet the fact was, Dr. Miller did earnestly deprecate the evils which would follow a regular trial and decision; and, on that ground, persuaded the parties to forego their constitutional rights, and to submit their case, without a trial; in the expectaton that the Assembly would endeavor to find some ground on which the parties might be at peace. I was disappointed at this; and yet I rejoiced in it. As a curious observer, I was disappointed, because I had expected to see the practical operation of your system of judicatories and appeals, in a case in which, if it has any superiority over our system of friendly arbitrations, that superiority would be manifest. As a Christian brother, I rejoiced, because I verily thought that the proposal was a wise one, and that peace could be better secured thus, than by a judicial decision, after a regular trial. I came to the General Assembly disposed to learn what are the actual advantages of that towering system of ecclesiastical courts which constitutes the glory of Presbyterianism; and, of that power to terminate all controversies which is supposed to reside in the supreme judicature.

"Of course, I could not but be at once astonished and gratified, to see that unconscious homage which was rendered to Congregational principles, when Presbyterians of the highest form, pure from every infection and tincture of Independency, untouched with any suspicion of leaning toward New England, strenuously deprecated the regular action of the Presbyterian system, in a case which, of all cases, was obviously best fitted to demonstrate its excellence. I was astonished. I had, indeed, expected that the voice which was to answer the complainants and the Presbytery of Philadelphia, would answer out of the whirlwind; but I had supposed that consistency in those brethren would constrain them to acknowledge that voice, even speaking from the whirlwind, as the voice of the only legitimate arbiter.

"I could not but ask within myself,—What is this lauded system of power and jurisdiction worth—these judicatures, court rising above court, in regular gradation,—what are they worth, if you are afraid to try your system in the hour of need? Yet, when I heard those brethren arguing in favor of referring the matter to a select committee, which should endeavor to mediate between the parties, and to propose some terms of peace and mutual oblivion,—in other words, to act as a Congregational ecclesiastical council would act, in attempting the adjustment of any similar controversy, I was convinced that they were in the right. And when the Assembly and the parties at last acceded to the proposal, I supposed that the general conviction was, that it was best to go to work, on that occasion, in something like the Congregational way, rather than in the Presbyterian way.

"Taking this view of the object for which the committee was appointed, and entering, as I did, very happily into the design, I never suspected that my not being a Presbyterian disqualified me from serving. I supposed that, being a Congregationalist, and therefore not wholly unacquainted with such methods of proceeding, I was only the better fitted to assist in the labors of such a committee; and, accordingly, I took hold of the work, with a disposition to assist in the humble measure of my ability."*

Such was the first great triumph of New School policy, in alliance with the party of moderation and peace.

* Christian Advocate, 1832, p. 20.

CHAPTER XXIV.

THE WESTERN MISSIONARY QUESTION.

The subject in the Assembly of 1831—Report of the Board—Proposal for union in the West—Attempt to elect a hostile Board—Excitement in consequence—Committee of compromise—Its report adopted—Plan of correspondence in the West—Mr. Thompson's circular—Plan of the West Lexington Presbytery—Pittsburgh conference—Cincinnati Convention—Letter from ruling elders in Portage Presbytery—Proceedings of the Convention—"Report" published by the minority—The Old School committees of correspondence—The "secret circular"—Mr. Baird's review of the Convention—Result of the Convention—The Old School employ the press.

THE subject of Domestic Missions came before the Assembly of 1831, through several overtures, on missions in the West, and through the annual report of the Board. In the report, the Assembly was informed of a year of most successful operations. It also communicated a resolution just adopted by the Board, that "in humble reliance on divine Providence, the Board of Missions will use their best endeavors to supply, in the course of five years, every vacant Presbyterian congregation, and destitute district, which may be disposed to receive aid from this Board, with a faithful and devoted minister of the gospel of Christ; and they do hereby pledge themselves to extend prompt and efficient aid to all feeble congregations, throughout the

Valley, which shall apply to them for assistance, with suitable recommendations; and, also, to send into this particular field, every well-qualified licentiate or minister of the Gospel who may hereafter be willing to engage in this work."

Three "friends of the present Board of Missions" had promised the sum of fifteen thousand dollars, in five annual payments, to aid in fulfilling this pledge. The evidence thus given by the Board and its friends, of a purpose to enter with determined energy into the great Valley of the West, which the American Home Missionary Society was so earnestly striving to possess, elicited strong indications of displeasure, from the majority of the Assembly. The usual vote of approval was withheld. Members insisted upon the striking out of that part of the report which respected the pledge; but it was, at length, resolved that with the suggestions made by the committee, which denied the accuracy of the statements of the report, on these points, "it be returned to the Board for its disposal."

The overtures on missions in the West were referred to a committee, which reported a plan for union with the American Society, upon the basis of Dr. Peters' Cincinnati scheme.

A substitute for this proposition was moved, recommending the Western Synods to correspond with one another, and agree upon some plan, to be reported to the next Assembly. Pending the decision, the movements hostile to the Board reached a crisis.

A motion had been made, by Dr. Richards, that a committee should be raised to nominate a Board of Missions. Dr. William Wylie moved a postponement of this, to make room for a motion to reappoint the old Board. In the discussion, the Rev. E. N. Kirk, stated that he came to the Assembly, for the purpose of accomplishing two objects,—the vindication of Mr. Barnes, and the dismissal of Mr. Russell, from the service of the Board; on account of his course in the case of Mr. Barnes. He intimated that these were the objects of his party, and that candor required their avowal.

The means on which the party relied for the latter purpose, was the election of a new Board, which was expected to amalgamate with the American Society.

The motion to appoint a nominating committee prevailed, by a vote of 109, to 87. This committee, appointed by the Moderator, consisted of Rev. Dr. Asa Hillyer, Rev. D. H. Riddle, Rev. Moses Chase, Rev. Asahel Bronson, Rev. S. Y. Garrison; and Elders William Jessup and William Anderson. The chairman, Dr. Hillyer, was a member of the Board of Directors of the Home Missionary Society, and the other members were, without exception, hostile to the Assembly's Board. This committee soon reported a list of nominations, in which the friends of the Home Missionary Society, and enemies of the Boards of the Church had an overwhelming majority. The Old School were allowed a respectable representation, in the distant parts of the Church. But of the members from the two Synods of New Jersey and Philadelphia, which lay immediately adjacent to the office of the Board in Philadelphia, the New School were assigned a majority of nearly two to one. Dr. Green, Mr. Russell, and a few others of the old friends of the Board were retained. But so few that they could have done nothing; and their continuance was believed to be with the expectation that they would resign, as soon as the changed complexion of the Board became apparent.

It was understood, by the Old School members of the Assembly, that the plan was to have the new Board meet, at once; while the Assembly was still in session, and enter into such a treaty with the American Society as would bind the Church to that institution. When, therefore, the report of the nominating committee came in, it occasioned a scene of intense excitement and confusion. Various motions were made; and many speakers at once claimed the floor. The Moderator's authority was disregarded, and at length a recess of ten minutes was resorted to, as the only means of restoring the house to order.

After the recess, the Assembly engaged in prayer for the divine direction. The Rev. Dr. William Patton, then, offered a proposition, upon which he and Dr. Spring had agreed, during the recess, as a compromise. It consisted in reappointing the old Board, and the adoption of the resolution then pending, as to the plan for missions in the West. The Rev. Elipha White, of Charleston, S. C., opposed the continuance of the old Board, because they were so devoted to the West that they would neglect the South. To obviate this objection, Dr. Spring proposed to endeavor to raise a thousand dollars, to be expended by the Board in the South. This, Mr. White resented, as an offered bribe!

A committee of compromise was at length appointed, consisting of the Rev. F. A. Ross, Dr. Peters, and Mr. Jessup; Dr. Green, Dr. Spring, and Mr. Breckinridge.

The committee, almost immediately, reported the following minute:—

"In view of existing evils, resulting from the separate action of the Board of Missions of the General Assembly, and the American Home Missionary Society, the General Assembly recommends to the Synods of Ohio, Cincinnati, Kentucky, Tennessee, West Tennessee, Indiana, and Illinois, and the Presbyteries connected with the same, to correspond with each other, and endeavor to agree upon some plan of conducting domestic missions, in the Western States, and report the result of their correspondence to the next General Assembly; it being understood that the brethren of the West be left to their freedom to form any organization which, in their judgment, may best promote the cause of missions, in those States, and, also, that all the Synods and Presbyteries in the Valley of the Mississippi may be embraced in this correspondence, provided they desire it.

"Resolved, by this Assembly, that the present Board of Missions be reappointed."

An attempt was made to strike out of this report, the clause proposing to embrace all the Synods and Presbyteries, in the Valley of the Mississippi, provided they desire it;—but the motion was rejected. The report was then adopted, by a large majority.

The plan for a correspondence of the western judicatories was urged upon the Assembly, by the friends of the American Society, in the confidence of having the control in those bodies; and measures were at once taken to secure that object. Under date of June 6th, a communication was sent from Philadelphia, by a number of the western members of the Assembly to the

Rev. John Thompson and two other members of the Cincinnati Presbytery, appointing them a committee to organize and direct the correspondence. They were advised to secure the appointment, by the Presbyteries, at their fall meetings, of delegates to meet in Cincinnati, "with all other friends that might be disposed so to do," to determine the question which was submitted to them.

In fulfillment of this appointment and plan, Mr. Thompson issued a circular letter, in which he designated Wednesday, the 23d of November, as the time for the proposed convention. After indicating the design of the convention,—to determine whether any change was desirable; and if any, what,—he stated that, "as the convention meet only for obtaining information, for mutual prayerful deliberation, and counsel, it is thought best to leave it to every Presbytery to send as many delegates as they choose, or may find convenient; allowing, also, any intelligent members of the Presbyterian churches, who feel a deep interest in the missionary cause, in the West, to attend and aid, in the deliberations; if they observe the same order as will be expected of delegates appointed by Presbyteries."

Could this plan have been carried into effect, the Convention would have been controlled by the New School of Cincinnati. Upon the publication of Mr. Thompson's circular, a meeting of the Presbytery of West Lexington was immediately called. After two days' deliberation, it unanimously adopted a plan for the convention. It declared it desirable and expedient that all the Presbyteries in the Valley be represented;—that their representation be upon the ratio to which they are entitled in the Assembly—that if distant Presbyteries send a less number than their ratio, they be entitled to their full vote;—that if any Presbytery be unable to send delegates, it forward an answer to the question, "To what plan, for conducting missions in the Valley of the Mississippi, would your Presbytery give the preference?"—and that no delegate be sent, who has not been regularly ordained to the ministry or eldership, after taking the prescribed obligations to the Constitution. With these, were other subsidiary regulations.

The clerk was directed to publish this plan in all the papers; to send a copy to the stated clerk of each Presbytery in the Valley, and to request Mr. Thompson to co-operate with this modified arrangement. Several other Presbyteries endorsed the plan thus modified; and in accordance with it, the convention was organized.

On the 1st of September, a conference was held in Pittsburgh, in response to a published call to the members of the Synod, of that name, to consult as to their duty in the premises. There were present members from five of the Presbyteries of that Synod. They declared themselves "decidedly of the opinion that the General Assembly should not place the important and precious trust of missions beyond the control and authority of its judicatories; and that the exigencies of the case do not require the institution, within its bounds, of an additional Board of domestic missions." They also declared it to be "highly expedient to co-operate with the western brethren, on the plan recommended by the Presbytery of West Lexington."

Subsequently, a Pittsburgh delegate elect, addressed a written inquiry to Mr. Thompson, whether the presence of the delegation from that Synod was expected or desirable. The reply was in the affirmative.

At the appointed time, the convention met, in the Third Presbyterian Church, in Cincinnati. An opening sermon was preached by the Rev. James Gallaher. Rev. Messrs. T. D. Baird, and Gallaher, and R. J. Breckinridge, Esq., were appointed a committee of elections, and reported forty-five delegates in attendance, representing twenty Presbyteries. The Rev. Dr. James Blythe was chosen Moderator, and Rev. Messrs. Samuel Steel and A. O. Patterson, clerks.

The convention continued in session a week. Incidental to its main business, a letter was received and read from two ruling elders in the Presbytery of Portage, Messrs. Joseph Ewart and Robert Baird, elders of the congregation of Springfield. They stated themselves to be, so far as they knew or believed, the only elders in the entire Presbytery, the only persons therefore entitled to sit as such from that Presbytery, in the Convention, and, as they dissented from the mind of the Presbytery, on the missionary question, they took this mode of expressing their dissent. They held that "The location and removal of ministers and pastors belongs to the *Church as such*, agreeably to the Constitution of the Presbyterian Church; and we believe this accords with the Word of God. If this be proper and needful, in the case of regularly organized congregations, it is much more necessary, in sending missionaries to destitute regions." "Further, as we apprehend that it is contemplated to form a missionary organization or agency at Cincinnati; even though a majority of the Convention be opposed to it, and though the last General Assembly recommended that the result of the correspondence be reported to the next Assembly, for its decision, we do here record our entire disapprobation of such a procedure. We consider that such a measure would be a direct violation of order, rendering the Convention of none effect, and calculated to create and increase division in the Church of Christ, particularly in that branch of it over which we, by office, and solemn covenant obligations, are appointed as watchmen."*

The apprehension thus expressed, arose no doubt from the action of Grand River Presbytery, which was not represented in the Convention, but sent on a communication, proposing that a society be formed, independent of both those already existing, but "to co-operate with either or both of them, whenever they may think best,—have the centre of their operations at Cincinnati or some more convenient place; and that this society be formed during the sitting of the Convention, by such members as approve of the plan; and that measures be taken to commence immediate operations."†

It was apparent, however, from the first moment of the assembling of the Convention, that the Home Society had utterly miscalculated its strength in the West. Five agents and missionaries of the society were members of the Convention; and but two other ministerial delegates voted with them.

On the third day of the sessions, a proposition was made, that the Assembly organize a Western Board of Missions, to be under its control and supervision, independent, alike, of the Society and of the existing

* Minutes of the Convention, p. 5. † Ibid., p. 5.

Board; but to receive pecuniary aid from both. This motion was rejected, by a vote of twenty-eight to forty-one; the vote being counted according to the representative ratio of the Presbyteries. Another proposition was made, that the wrongs done on both sides be forgiven and forgotten, and both the Assembly's Board and the American Society recommended, as deserving the support and confidence of the churches; their amalgamation being pronounced undesirable, as the two would do more good, than one. This was rejected, by a vote of seventeen to fifty-two. The final result of six days' deliberations, was embodied in the following minute:

"Whereas, it appears from the report of the committee to receive and report all written communications to the Convention, that, of the Presbyteries in the Valley of the Mississippi, fifteen, entitled to forty-two votes, have not been heard from; that one, entitled to two votes, is in favor of the American Home Missionary Society; that one, entitled to four votes, is in favor of both Boards, as they now exist; that two, entitled to eight votes, are in favor of an independent Western society; that one, entitled to two votes, is in favor of ecclesiastical supervision; and that seven, entitled to twenty-two votes, are in favor of the General Assembly's Board, in its present organization; and whereas twenty Presbyteries, entitled to seventy votes, being actually present in the Convention, a plan for the establishment of a Western Board of Missions, under the care of the General Assembly, after a full discussion, has been rejected, by a vote of forty-one to twenty-eight; and as it appears to the Convention, from these facts, that no arrangement, into which we can possibly enter, is likely to reconcile conflicting views on the subject; that, so far from healing divisions, or restoring peace to the churches, by any new expedients, they would only tend to multiply the points of difference, and increase the evil,—therefore,

"*Resolved*, That, under these circumstances, they deem it inexpedient to propose any change in the General Assembly's mode of conducting missions; as they fully approve of that now in such successful operation; and that the purity, peace, and prosperity of the Presbyterian Church materially depend on the active and efficient aid the sessions and Presbyteries under its care may afford to the Assembly's Board."*

The minute was adopted; by fifty-four ayes, to fifteen noes. The following resolution was then offered:—

"That this Convention, notwithstanding the preference avowed for the Assembly's Board of Missions, unite with the General Assembly of the Presbyterian Church in feelings of regard and affection for the American Home Missionary Society; and rejoice in the hope that by the aid of that society many of the destitute churches in the Valley of the Mississippi will be supplied with the stated preaching of the gospel, and many souls converted to God."†

This resolution was indefinitely postponed, by a vote of forty-two to seventeen. After taking order for the publication of its proceedings, the Convention, then, adjourned.

Before separating the minority appointed a committee,

* Minutes of the Convention, p. 13. † Ibid., p. 16.

to draw up and publish a statement of reasons of dissatisfaction with the decisions. This committee, speedily issued a "Report," in a pamphlet of forty-eight pages. They complained grievously of "the paramount and controlling influence, in the Convention, of the Synod of Pittsburgh:" that Synod not being one of the seven specified in the minute of the Assembly, under which the Convention was called. One of the committee, by whom this report was prepared and published, was the Rev. Daniel W. Lathrop, of the Synod of the Western Reserve, which was no more specifically named in the Assembly's minute than was the other. But both were included in the provision, which the Assembly, expressly, refused to strike out of the minute, that any other Synods and Presbyteries in the Valley, besides those named should "be embraced in the correspondence, if they desire it."

Other complaints, made, in the report, were, that the Cincinnati Standard had opposed the Convention, and thus led the friends of the American Society to absent themselves, upon the supposition that its conclusions would not be regarded, by the friends of the Board; that the delegates came, under instructions as to their votes, and were therefore without discretion; and that the Board of Missions itself had violated a tacit expectation of the Assembly, that they would not interfere; by republishing its reply to the Cincinnati Presbytery; and by announcing to the public that its views remained the same.

But especial emphasis was laid upon "the Secret Circular, issued by a certain Central Committee in Philadelphia." "To that circular we are disposed to trace the singularly full representation of the Synod of Pittsburgh. It is, at least, a striking fact that the Convention at Pittsburgh, which resulted in so full a representation to the Convention at Cincinnati, was called by the *committee* of *safety* for that Synod, named in the circular; with the exception of one whose name was placed on that committee without his sanction."*

The Central Committee, here alluded to, was appointed by the minority of the Assembly of 1831. It consisted of the Rev. Dr. Green, Rev. Messrs. Potts, Engles, and Winchester, and Elders Matthew L. Bevan, Solomon Allen, and Furman Leaming. At the same time, committees of correspondence were appointed in each Synod. That of the Synod of Pittsburgh, referred to in the Report, consisted of Rev. Messrs. E. P. Swift, T. D. Baird, A. D. Campbell, Wm. Wylie, C. C. Beattie, and John W. Nevin.

The "Secret Circular" was a communication, under date of July 21, 1831, issued by the Central Committee, and sent to the Synodical committees, and to others throughout the Church, who were supposed to sympathize with the objects. After stating the nature of the crisis, resulting from the organization and action of the Assembly of 1831, the circular proposed and answered the question, "What ought to be done?" Under the solemn conviction that "this is the last year in which our Church will remain without essential changes, unless her children shall be roused to a sense of their danger, and call into vigorous action their united energies, in her defence," the following measures were recommended:—

* Report of the Minority, pp. 5, 6.

"First of all, look to God for his guidance and blessing. . . . . Let us also both pray and labor to promote vital piety. . . . .

"2. Let all lawful measures be used to rouse our brethren, both clergy and laity, to a just sense of their situation and their duty. With this view, we advise that you correspond with Presbyteries, as stated in the beginning of this communication. Make, also, a free, but discreet use of the press; and encourage liberally, and circulate as widely as possible those publications which maintain the real doctrines of our Church, and advocate the support of her institutions. . . . .

"3. Our Board of Education and Board of Missions, must both receive a liberal patronage and a decided support. This is essential;—without this, we are undone. The voluntary associations that seek to engross the patronage of our Church, and have already engrossed a large part of it, have taken the start of us, in the all-important concerns of education and of missions. They now labor to get the whole of these into their own hands; well knowing that, if this be effected, they will, infallibly, in a very short time, govern the Church; for education furnishes missionaries, and missionaries become pastors, and pastors, with their ruling elders, form Church Sessions, Presbyteries, Synods, and General Assemblies. . . . .

"Finally,—The several judicatories of our Church must be carefully and punctually attended, by every orthodox man, whose right and duty it is to hold a seat in them. . . . . Nor was it ever so important in our Church, as at the present time, that orthodox Presbyteries should choose wise men, and firm men, to represent them in the Assembly. But it is most important that every man elected, whether minister or elder, unless prevented by invincible hindrances of a providential kind, should attend that body, at the next meeting. For want of that, at our last meeting, we were left in a minority." . . . .

Such was the whole substance of the paper, stigmatized in the "Report," as a "Secret Circular," although it conveyed no injunction of secresy, and proposed no deeds of darkness. The New School party strove, by every means, to render it odious, with a zeal proportioned to the well-grounded apprehensions they felt of its influence in arousing and organizing the Old School party.

A reply to the Report, and a review of the Convention was published in the Presbyterian, by the Rev. Thomas D. Baird, in a series of articles, signed by "A member of the Convention." The developments and decisions of that Convention, terminated the active Home Missionary controversy. Thenceforward, the efforts of the American Society were directed, rather, to the silent acquisition of influence, by multiplying its missionaries; than, to open assaults upon the Board, or formal attempts to accomplish its amalgamation, by the authority of the Assembly.

One of the suggestions made in the Philadelphia Circular was that a free use of the press should be made by the Old School. Heretofore, the papers of the Church had all been under the control of the New School, or of the Moderates. But, on the 16th of March, 1831, the first number of the Presbyterian was issued,—a paper, the principles of which were sufficiently indicated by the statement at its head, that its profits would be divided between the Boards of Missions and Education. During the same season the Cincinnati Standard commenced its issues; and the next spring, the Rev. Thomas D. Baird succeeded to the editorial chair of the Pittsburgh Christian Herald. Mr. Baird and the Rev. Dr. Samuel Ralston, the Philo Evangelicus of the Herald, had early covenanted with each other to devote their pens to the maintenance of the doctrinal purity and the order of the Church; a covenant which both of them fully redeemed; and Mr. Baird was now, by the friends of sound order, selected to preside over the press, at the most critical position in the entire field; requiring, more perhaps than any other, the utmost prudence, sound judgment, and firmness. For, whilst the Scotch-Irish Presbyterians of that Synod were of the most determined loyalty to the doctrines and institutions of the Church, the positions of distinction and controlling influence in the Synod were, with a very few exceptions, held by men whose sympathies were altogether against the decisive course of policy, by which, under the smile of the gracious Head of the Church, she was finally rescued from the dangers which surrounded her.

CHAPTER XXV.

ELECTIVE AFFINITY CHURCH COURTS.

Memorial to the Assembly to divide the Philadelphia Presbytery—Petitions to the Synod refused—Complaint to the Assembly—Elective Affinity Presbytery erected—The Synod refuses to recognize it—Complaint to the Assembly—Dr. Beman's management—Committee of compromise—Discussion in Synod—It reunites the two Presbyteries, and subdivides them geographically—Complaint to the Assembly—It is sustained—Synod of Delaware erected—Third Presbytery of New York—Presbytery of Cincinnati.

THE Assembly of 1831 had given its opinion that the Presbytery of Philadelphia should be so divided as to promote the peace of its ministers and churches. After the final disposal of Barnes' case, a memorial was presented, in which the Assembly was requested to divide that Presbytery, at once, and to erect the New School members into a second Presbytery. Hereupon, a discussion arose, as to the power of the Assembly in the premises. Mr. R. J. Breckinridge argued, at length, against its constitutional right to touch the proposition. After some discussion, the previous question was called for, and decided in the negative, by a vote of 117, to 64; and thus, under the rule, the subject was indefinitely postponed.

At the next meeting of the Synod of Philadelphia, two petitions came before it, on this subject,—one from the Presbytery of Philadelphia, and the other from the New School minority of that Presbytery. The former proposed a geographical division of the Presbytery, making Market street the line. The latter requested the Synod to set off certain enumerated ministers and churches, whose sentiments were supposed to harmonize with the New School, to constitute a second Presbytery, without defined geographical boundaries.

In the Synod, it appeared that the project of division, submitted by the minority, was framed without consulting the parties concerned; and some of the ministers, enumerated in the petition, earnestly protested against being associated with the new organization.

The Synod, after full deliberation, declined to comply with either petition, declaring that whilst it regarded with respect the recommendation of the Assembly, it considered any division of the Presbytery to be in every point of view, inexpedient. Dr. Ely and others gave notice that they would complain to the Assembly, and look to it, to grant the desired division.

They accordingly brought before the Assembly, in 1832, a complaint and petition. These papers, however, were incongruous to each other. The one complained of the Synod for not erecting a Presbytery, to consist of twenty-three enumerated ministers, and certain specified churches.

The petition sought the erection of a Presbytery of thirteen enumerated ministers and as many specified churches, differing from the former list. In the Assembly, various causes combined to secure success to the complaint and petition. Some members favored them, from sympathy with the theological sentiments which sought harbor in the new organization. Some were actuated by a hope that, by the separation of the opposing parties, peace might be restored to the Church. Others regarded the recommendation of the Assembly of 1831, in favor of a division, as a compromise measure, by which they were bound. After a full hearing of the parties and a long discussion, the complaint was sustained; but without censure upon the Synod. Mr. Robert J. Breckinridge, now moved that, as the petition before the Assembly was different from that which had been rejected by the Synod, the decision upon the complaint closed the judicial case, and the Synod should, therefore be readmitted to sit and vote upon the petition. This motion was renewed, at different stages of the business, but always rejected. In the result, the Assembly erected a Presbytery to be known as the Second Presbytery of Philadelphia, to consist of fourteen enumerated ministers and as many churches, selected with a view to their doctrinal affinities. The body thus created neither corresponded with that contemplated in the rejected application to the Synod, nor with that described in the petition to the Assembly.

When the Synod of Philadelphia met, in the following October, communications were received from the Synods of Cincinnati and Pittsburgh, enclosing papers adopted by those bodies, remonstrating to the Assembly against the creation of the "Elective Affinity Presbytery."* Sustained by such countenance, the Synod adopted a respectful but earnest remonstrance to the Assembly. In this paper it represented that such a

* This very apt designation originated, during the discussion, with Dr. Skinner, who was an original member of the body.

division as the Assembly had made was inexpedient; as, if acted upon, generally, it would create utter confusion, in consequence of co-ordinate and hostile jurisdiction of Presbyteries over the same territory;—and unconstitutional, inasmuch as the Form of Government expressly declares, that a Presbytery consists of "all the ministers and one ruling elder from each congregation within a certain district." The Synod, further, held the act of the Assembly to be unconstitutional, because, "while the Constitution prescribes that the General Assembly has the exclusive power 'of erecting new Synods, when it may be judged necessary,' it explicitly prescribes that Synods have the exclusive authority in 'erecting new Presbyteries, and uniting and dividing those which were before erected.'" In view of these considerations and of the dangers impending over the Church, the Synod declined to recognize the Presbytery, and earnestly prayed the General Assembly to review the matter, and redress the grievances which it had occasioned.

Against this action, protest was entered, and complaints were carried up to the Assembly. To secure the desired results from that body, the faculties of Dr. Beman were again called into requisition. A printed circular letter was secretly issued, over his signature, and addressed to trusted parties. After alluding to the action of the Synod in the elective affinity case, as "a blow aimed at the fundamental principles of Presbyterial government," and stating that "it is time the question was decided, whether our Church is bound by the express provisions of the Constitution; or whether an inferior tribunal has a right to disannul the decisions of the highest court of appeals"—this gentleman, whose place on the roll of the ministry of the Church, was in contempt of the Constitution, which he had never adopted, proceeded to ask his correspondents,—"Will you look well to the Commissioners who attend the next General Assembly? Observe the following particulars: 1. Be sure to elect your full number, both lay and clerical. 2. Let them be peace and union men; men who will take correct ground, in relation to those movements which are intended to excite jealousies and divisions in the Presbyterian Church. 3. Be sure and have all the commissioners attend. 4. Insist on their being present, in Philadelphia, at least the day before the Assembly opens. 5. Request them to attend and report their names, at the lecture-room of Dr. Skinner's church, in Arch street, on Wednesday evening, the 15th of May, at half-past 7 o'clock.

"Affectionately yours,

"NATHAN S. S. BEMAN."*

Marshaled, thus, as an Assembly of "peace and union" men, that body, after the precedent of 1831, had recourse to a "Committee of Compromise," to whom all the papers in the Philadelphia case were referred, "to endeavor to effect a compromise, if practicable, between the parties concerned." The Synod had appointed a committee to represent it and protect its interests, in this case; consisting of the Rev. Messrs. McCalla, Hutchinson, Douglass, Junkin, James and William Latta, and James Williamson. The committee of compromise, instead of consulting these, the true and

* Presbyterian, 1833, pp. 63, 70

official representatives of the Synod, called a meeting of such members of that body as happened to be in Philadelphia. Of these, a majority belonged to the minority of the Synod, and readily voted that the remonstrances and other papers should be suppressed, the complaints withdrawn, and the Elective Affinity Presbytery remain intact. The committee, thereupon, reported to the Assembly "that they have had an interview with several members of the Second Presbytery of Philadelphia; and, subsequently, with the Presbytery, itself, on the subject of their complaint against the Synod of Philadelphia; and that they have had an interview with thirty-one members of the Synod, assembled at the request of the committee;—that, after a free conference with both these parties, during which the subject of their conference was treated with much tenderness and Christian affection, the committee are enabled to recommend to the Assembly the following resolution, viz.:

"Resolved, that the complainants in these cases, have leave to withdraw their complaints, and that the consideration of all the other papers relating to the Second Presbytery be indefinitely postponed."

"The above report was approved, and the resolution unanimously adopted. The Assembly then united in prayer, returning thanks to God, for his goodness, in bringing this matter to such an amicable adjustment." It is a painful feature in this history, that the most indefensible acts of outrage to the Constitution and to the rights, therein, guaranteed to parties,—as in 1831, so, now,—were followed by the attempt to sanctify them with the form of thanksgiving and prayer. In the present instance, the whole ground of gratulation was, that the Assembly had succeeded in devising a mode in which to ignore the remonstrances of the Synods of Cincinnati, Pittsburgh and Philadelphia, and in effect, to sustain the complaint against the latter Synod, without allowing it the opportunity of one word in its own defence.

The committee, on behalf of the Synod, immediately sent in a communication to the Assembly, remonstrating against the course pursued. An attempt was made to induce them to withdraw the paper. But the house was informed, through the Moderator, that the committee could not take that responsibility. Repeated requests to have it read were refused; and finally, it was referred to the committee of Bills and Overtures, there to be suppressed.*

Such was the state of the case which came before the Synod of Philadelphia, at its meeting in October, 1833. At the opening of the sessions, Mr. Gilbert moved that the Presbytery be recognized, and its members enrolled. Mr. Engles proposed a substitute for this motion, in the form of three resolutions. The first protested against the constitutionality of the erection of that Presbytery, yet recognized and enrolled it, as a constituent of the Synod. The second reunited it with the Presbytery of Philadelphia. The third divided the reunited Presbytery by the line of Market street, the ministers and churches south of that line to be known as the Presbytery of Philadelphia, and those north of it to be the Second Presbytery of Philadelphia.

Dr. Green offered a different paper, which asserted the exclusive right of Synods to erect Presbyteries;—

* Mr. McCalla, in the Presbyterian, June 12, 1833.

denounced the principle of elective affinity in the erection of church courts;—denied the constitutional existence of the Second Presbytery;—declared the Synod to be "deeply aggrieved, and as having been treated with peculiar disrespect," by the Assembly, in its refusal "so much as to hear the remonstrance and representations of this Synod;"—and proposed to recognize the members set off into the new Presbytery by the Assembly, provided they would now acknowledge that Presbytery to be a nullity. It also provided that none who, since its erection, had been received by the Presbytery, should now be admitted as members of Synod.

Dr. Green's motion was rejected, by a vote of twenty-two ayes, to forty-three noes. Mr. Engles' paper was then adopted, by thirty-nine to twenty.

This action of the Synod was entirely disregarded by the Assembly's Presbytery, which continued its meetings and business, as though no such action had taken place. In due time, the case again came before the Assembly, by appeal and complaint of the Presbytery. These were sustained by the Assembly, which pronounced the act of the Synod, "so far as it was intended to unite the Second Presbytery with the Presbytery of Philadelphia," to be void; at the same time that it fully recognized the validity of the Synod's act, by which the reunited Presbytery had been geographically divided into the First and Second Presbyteries, only recommending that the name of the latter be changed. It would seem that the most obtuse comprehension must have seen the utter disregard of the Constitution, by which this decision of the Assembly was dictated. Whatever ulterior powers any one might attribute to the Assembly, for the erection of Presbyteries,—it must be conceded that, once erected, they are but Presbyteries; like all the rest in their functions, powers, and responsibilities. To them, precisely as to others, must the authority of Synods extend. To Synods, the Constitution expressly attributes power over all Presbyteries, without exception, "to unite or divide those which were before erected." Yet, here, the act of Synod, thus expressly authorized by the Constitution, is not reversed, merely; but prônounced void; and that, for no reason, whatever, that appears, except that the Presbytery was created by the Assembly, and thus endowed with some extraordinary principle of vitality and independence of the Synod. There was certainly not another Presbytery, under the care of that Synod, the dissolution of which, by it, would have been thus declared void.

Having come to this decision, the Assembly, next, proceeded to provide for the permanent security of this extraordinary offspring. It was in the course of the discussion on the appeal of the Presbytery, at this time, that Mr. Patterson urged the necessity of its continued existence, for the convenience of licensing and ordaining men who could not pass the strict examination, on the doctrines of the Confession, to which they would ordinarily be liable. The argument equally indicated the necessity of the Presbytery being placed under the guardian wing of a Synod, which would abstain from those troublesome scrutinies, on such subjects, in which the Synod of Philadelphia was likely to indulge. The Presbytery of Wilmington had just been set off by the Synod of Philadelphia, from that of New Castle, and was composed of the very sort of material requisite for the purpose. The adjacent Presbytery of Lewes was also a small body, of very "liberal" sentiments. The Assembly therefore erected the Synod of Delaware, to be composed of the Philadelphia Second Presbytery, Wilmington, and Lewes. Of these, the first numbered twenty-two ministers; the second, ten; and the third, six; so that, in no event, was the Elective Affinity Presbytery liable to any danger, from Synodical action; as it constituted a majority of the whole body.

Thus were disorder and anarchy organized, in the bosom of the Church. Not only were the Presbyteries constituting the Synod of Delaware secure harbors for unsound ministers;—not only did they enjoy and use every facility for multiplying a heretical ministry;—but, could the right of examination of intrant ministers, having clean papers, be taken from the Presbyteries, the machinery now constructed was abundantly adequate to revolutionize every sound Presbytery in the Church, and fill it with propagandists of Pelagianism, and of new measure revivals. At the same time, the Elective Affinity Presbytery, having no territory, was, by that very fact, left unlimited in its sphere of operations. It stood at the door of every church in the two Synodical Presbyteries of Philadelphia; ready to seize upon any occasion, to nourish disaffection in their churches, to foster schism, and to erect the disaffected into new congregations, under its own care and jurisdiction. Such was the system constructed by the wisdom of Moderation for healing the disorders which had arisen out of the introduction of false doctrine. Such were the legitimate results of that false charity which was willing to purchase peace and unity at the expense of purity of doctrine and fidelity in the discipline of the Church. Strife, division and bitterness resulted everywhere, of necessity, from the introduction into the bosom of the orthodox churches and Presbyteries of Philadelphia, of such a disturbing element as was constituted by the Elective Affinity Presbytery.

Two distinct objects were avowed in the erection of that Presbytery. It was designed as a safe retreat for the theological sentiments of Mr. Barnes. And it was provided as a means of facilitating the introduction into the ministry of candidates whose doctrines were at variance with the Confession. In a word,—the object to which it was designated, from the first, was the corrupting of the theology of the Church.

The system of organizations which was completed by the erection of the Synod of Delaware, was the first in which the avowed principle of selection was, hostility to the doctrines and institutions of our Church; and its erection, despite the resistance of the Synod of Philadelphia, established, in the most offensive form, the principle, that such hostility conferred a title to special privileges and immunities. The existence of these courts was, of itself, decisive of the inevitable division of the Church. It was a fact which no sound Presbyterian, in his senses, could tolerate.

But although this was the most offensive case, of organization determined by doctrinal and party affinity, it was not the only one, nor the first. In 1830, application was made to the Synod of New York, by eight members of the Presbytery of New York to be set off into a new Presbytery. The request was granted, and the Third Presbytery of New York constituted, consisting of Drs. Cox, Peters, and others, selected with a view to congeniality of views and principles. This organization soon became a most active and powerful instrument for corrupting the Church. It was the favorite agency for the ordination of the young missionaries from New England, with whom the American Home Missionary Society was flooding the Presbyteries of the West; and through it, Dr. Beecher accomplished his extraordinary transit into the Presbyterian Church, in order to qualify himself for the presidency of Lane.

Whilst, thus, Philadelphia and New York, the two great centres of influence for the Church in the East, were provided for, the queen city of the West, the centre of influence for that region, was not disregarded. The Presbytery of Cincinnati was not originally formed on the elective affinity principle. But it was so skillfully stocked by Dr. Peters with his partisans and agents, headed, at length, by Dr. Beecher, that, to all practical purposes it was as competent and efficient as either of the others. The resistance of Dr. Wilson and a few others was an annoyance, and to some extent embarrassing. But their struggles were unavailing, against the overwhelming Congregational majority, which rendered the body an active agency for the increase of the party, at the expense of the Constitution and order of the Church.

CHAPTER XXVI.

THE ASSEMBLY OF 1834.

Causes of New School majorities—Spirit of the Assembly of 1834—The Western Conference—Its memorial—Action upon it—Jennings' resolution on doctrinal errors, rejected—Resolution of attachment to the system of doctrines—A protest rejected.

For four years, from 1831 to 1834, inclusive, the majority in the General Assembly was in the hands of the New School. Several causes co-operated to induce this result. The ministry at the South were removed from contact with the heresies which prevailed on the Northern border. They could not, at first, believe that the Church was threatened with any serious innovations upon sound doctrine. The idea was assiduously disseminated among them, that the whole trouble arose out of an unholy lust for power, among a few persons connected with the Boards in Philadelphia and its vicinity. The position taken by the editors of the Princeton Review, tended to confirm this impression. That periodical bore, on the title page, that it was "edited by an association of gentlemen in Princeton and its vicinity." It was regarded as the organ of the faculty of the seminary. Of that faculty, the venerable Alexander,—a native of Virginia,—possessed, more than any other man, the confidence of the ministry and churches of the South. And when the Review, supposed to reflect his sentiments, made light of the apprehensions, and condemned the policy of the Old School, the effect was, to quiet apprehension, and induce, rather, feelings of annoyance and displeasure at the agitators, who were charged with destroying the peace, and endangering the unity of the Church, by untimely alarms. The religious press of the South was under the control of the Moderate party, disseminated these sentiments, and thus operated effectually in the same direction.

The removal of Dr. McFarland, of Virginia, to Philadelphia, in the fall of 1835, as Secretary of the Board of Education, involved results tending, greatly, to correct this state of sentiment. His position gave him an opportunity to form a just estimate of the real character and designs of the several parties. A man, eminent for mildness and moderation of spirit, and soundness of judgment, he held a high place in the confidence of his brethren; and when he sounded the alarm, it was felt that there must be a real and serious danger. It was mainly, however, through the developments of 1834 and 1836,—which compelled conviction, as to the revolutionary designs of the New School,—that the Southern section of the Church became thoroughly aroused.

Another efficient cause of New School majorities in the Assembly, was inequality of representation in that body. This arose, partly, from the unequal subdivision of Presbyteries, in different parts of the Church; and, partly, from the greater facility of access to Philadelphia, enjoyed by some sections. The combined effect of these causes, gave the North-east an advantage equal to fifteen per cent. in the actual results, as compared with the South and West.

In the Assemblies of 1832 and 1833, the controversy had been confined, mainly, to the case of the Elective Affinity Presbytery; which, as we have seen, was terminated, in 1834, by the erection of the Synod of Delaware. In the latter Assembly, the controversy assumed broader grounds and a more threatening aspect. In previous Assemblies, the New School party had conciliated the support of the Moderates, by a cautious, temporizing policy. But, in that of 1834, a different style was adopted. Confident of being upheld by the majority of the Church; and assured of the triumph of all their cherished plans, the majority of that Assembly displayed an impatience of opposition, and an eagerness to seize at once the prize that seemed, at length, within their grasp, which, happily, discovered to the Church, in time, the real spirit of the party, and the nature and importance of the issues involved. Under God, the overbearing domination of the majorities of the Assemblies of 1834 and 1836, were essential to the salvation of the Church. These drove many of the Moderates from their position of practical alliance with the New School party; and changed the balance.

At an early stage, in the proceedings of this Assembly, an overture was laid before it, which was popularly known as the Western Memorial. The history of this paper illustrates the sources whence, under God, the deliverance of the Church arose.

On the 31st of July, 1833, a conference was held, at the house of Elder John Monfort, residing in Monroe township, Butler county, Ohio. The object of the meeting was, to confer respecting "the fearful decline of sound doctrine and faithful discipline in the Church, and the apprehension of its entire subversion." There were present, eleven Ministers and ten Ruling Elders. The Rev. Francis Monfort, was chosen Moderator, and the Rev. Sayrs Gazlay, Clerk. The original minutes of the meeting, attested by Mr. Gazlay, are in the possession of the author.

Immediately after the organization, the conference held a season of devotion, in which "the brethren, in repeated addresses to the throne of grace, implored the divine favor and guidance." A number of letters, from Dr. J. L. Wilson, Dr. Ashbel Green, and others, were read. Messrs. Thomas Barr, James Coe, and David Monfort, Ministers; and C. H. Spinning, S. Clendennin, and William Lowrie, Elders, were then appointed, to take into consideration the papers which had been read, and make notes during the calling of the roll, and prepare, from the suggestions thus obtained, a paper expressive of the mind of the brethren. The roll was then called, and each member invited to present his views. After which, and the appointment of the Rev. John L. Belville, as an additional clerk, the conference adjourned, till the next morning.

In the morning, two hours were spent in devotional exercises. The committee then reported, recommending that a memorial be addressed to the Assembly. They, also, submitted a draft of such a paper. It was approved, "as to general features," and committed to Thomas Barr, J. L. Wilson, D. D., and John Burt, Ministers; and Henry B. Funk, S. Clendennin, and J. Bigger, Elders; with instructions to revise it, without adding any new topic, and report it, at a meeting to be held during the approaching sessions of the Synod of Cincinnati. The conference then adjourned.

At Synod, the conference approved the paper, as finally submitted, and designated a committee to lay it before the Committee of Bills and Overtures of Synod. The latter committee refused to present it to the Synod, "on account of its length and the amount of business on the docket of Synod." A committee was, therefore, appointed, to have a thousand copies printed and to furnish a copy to each member of the next Assembly; and the conference adjourned.

The paper, as it came before the Assembly of 1834, "had been adopted, either in whole, or in part, by about nine Presbyteries and eight Sessions; it was also signed by about eighteen ministers and ninety-nine elders;"—so stated the committee, to whom it was referred by the Assembly.

In this very able document, the memorialists, set forth, in respectful and dignified language, but with plainness and decision, the various evils with which the Church was troubled; and the unwarrantable policies adopted by successive Assemblies.

"We feel alarmed," said the memorialists, "at the evidences which press upon us, of the prevalence of unsoundness in doctrine, and laxity in discipline; and we view it as an aggravating consideration, that the General Assembly, the constitutional guardian of the Church's purity, even when a knowledge of such evils has been brought before it, in an orderly manner, has, within a few years past, either directly or indirectly, refused to apply the constitutional remedy. Appeals, references, complaints, and memorials, from individuals, Presbyteries, and Synods, have been dismissed on some slight grounds; perhaps, not noticed at all, or merged in some compromise, which aggravated the evils intended to be removed." They then proceed to enumerate "certain acts and proceedings, in our opinion, unsound and unconstitutional in themselves; some of which have been the precursors and inlets of other evils." They point out the Plan of Union; subscription to the Confession, with reservation; the ordaining, in the East, of candidates designed for the Western field; the encouragement given to voluntary societies; the favor shown to Mr. Barnes, by the Assembly of 1831; and "the compromising plan, brought into signal operation in 1831, in the case of Mr. Barnes, and on the question of the election of the Board of Missions, for that year. In both cases, this plan was evidently resorted to, in order to avoid the direct and decided course, which would have been agreeable to the spirit of pure Presbyterianism."

The memorialists then remonstrate and testify against nine specified doctrinal errors, which they attribute to the writings of Messrs. Duffield, Beman, Beecher and Barnes; and request the Assembly to exert all its powers for the suppression of them. They urge the redress of these various grievances, by the absolute repeal of the Plan of Union, and of any special arrangements with the Congregational churches; by using decided measures to restrain such Presbyteries as are perverting their opportunities to the propagation of error; and by employing the proper means to suppress erroneous doctrines in the Church. They "insist upon it, as a matter of constitutional right to your memorialists,—as well as, of obligation, on the part of your reverend body, and of duty to the whole Church,—that the Assembly express an unequivocal opinion, upon the following points, concerning which conflicting sentiments exist; creating difficulties, perplexities, and tendencies to division."

The points here propounded were, as to the right of Presbyteries to examine intrant ministers, coming with clean papers; the right to examine and censure heretical publications, irrespective of proceedings against the authors; and the question of adopting the Confession with mental reservations.

The memorial closed with a request for the repeal of the act erecting the elective affinity Presbytery of Philadelphia.*

It became, at once, a matter of the first importance to the party majority, in the Assembly, to break, as much as possible, the force of a document, so ably written; so respectful, yet earnest, in its style; and so weighty in the matters which it presented. When reported, therefore, by the Committee of Bills and Overtures, it was put upon the docket, without a hearing. It there remained, until the ninth day of the sessions. It was then, referred to a special committee. The committee, after three days, made a report, consisting of a series of resolutions. The first of these illustrates the arbitrary and intolerant spirit which prevailed in the majority. "Resolved, That this Assembly cannot sanction the censure contained in the memorial, against the proceedings and measures of former General Assemblies."

* See the Memorial, in the Digest, p. 670.

The report refused to abrogate the Plan of Union; referred the memorialists to previous action of the same Assembly, which advised against the ordination, in the East, of candidates destined for the West; and stated that the duty of guarding the doctrinal purity of the ministry belonged to the Presbyteries. On the subject of missions, it denied the Assembly to have any right to establish an exclusive system; but, whilst leaving the inferior judicatories to their own discretion, recommended the Board of Missions "to their willing co-operation."

On the subject of doctrinal errors, the report, bore "solemn testimony against publishing to the world, ministers in good and regular standing, as heretical or dangerous, without having been constitutionally tried and condemned."

With respect to the examination of intrant ministers, it, at first, stated, that "The Assembly do not deny the right of any Presbytery, when it is deemed proper to do so, to examine into the qualifications of persons, applying for membership;" yet urged that a due regard to the order of the Church and bonds of brotherhood, required their reception upon the faith of "constitutional testimonials," unless these have been forfeited, after being received. The first clause was stricken out, by the Assembly, before adopting the paper.

The report condemned the passing of censures upon heretical books, except in proceedings against the authors. It declared that the adoption of the Confession by ministers, should be accepted, as in good faith, unless there was evidence to the contrary. And, in fine, the inferior courts were urged, "in the spirit of charity and forbearance, to adjust and settle, as far as practicable, all their matters of grievance and disquietude; without bringing them before the General Assembly."*

The writing of this report was attributed to Dr. Beman, who was present, although not a member of the Assembly. It was not until after the reading of its hostile conclusions, that the Assembly, at length, consented to hear the memorial, itself. During the reading, members gave expression to their contempt and hostility, by leaving the house, and in other unequivocal ways.

The report submitted by the committee was urged as a moderate and conciliatory paper! The time of the Assembly was too far past to admit of anything more than a very brief discussion. The vote was taken, upon the resolutions reported, and they were adopted. A protest against this action was submitted. It was admitted to record, and a committee appointed to prepare a reply. The committee, however, reported it to be inexpedient to assign any further reasons for the Assembly's action; as its course had been fully vindicated in the debate!

Immediately after the adoption of the report upon the memorial, the Rev. Samuel C. Jennings, of the Presbytery of the Ohio, offered the following resolution:—

"*Resolved*, That this Assembly, in accordance with a previous resolution, which allows this body to condemn error in the abstract; and in accordance with our Form of Government, which gives the General Assembly the privilege of warning and bearing testimony against errors in doctrine; does, hereby, bear solemn testimony

* See the Report, in the Digest, p. 679.

against the following errors; whether such errors be held in, or, out of, the Presbyterian Church, viz.:—

"That Adam was not the covenant head or federal representative of his posterity.—That we have nothing to do with the first sin of Adam.—That it is not imputed to his posterity.—That infants have no moral character.—That all sin consists in voluntary acts or exercises.—That man, in his fallen state, is possessed of entire ability to do whatever God requires him to do, independently of any new power or ability, imparted to him, by the gracious operations of the Holy Spirit.—That regeneration is the act of the sinner.—That Christ did not become the legal substitute and surety of sinners.—That the atonement of Christ was not strictly vicarious.—That the atonement is made as much for the non-elect, as for the elect."

This list of errors was a transcript of those enumerated in the memorial; with two or three verbal alterations. Immediately, the resolution was indefinitely postponed. On the question of postponement, the yeas and nays were called for, by the minority, for the declared purpose of bringing the paper into the record. This call was withdrawn, upon the expressed understanding that a protest would be admitted. The Assembly then adopted the following resolution:

"*Resolved*, That this Assembly cherish an unabated attachment to the system of doctrines contained in the standards of their faith; and would guard, with vigilance, against any departures from it; and they enjoin the careful study of it upon all the members of the Presbyterian Church, and their firm support by all scriptural and constitutional methods."

The key to this resolution must be sought in the word, "system," that word of such convenient flexibility. The Old School members refused to concur in this action; as, in view of the facts which had just occurred, they could only regard it as a mockery;—an opinion which subsequent proceedings confirmed.

In immediate connection with this, the Assembly adopted two other resolutions. The first condemned the publishing abroad of difficulties and contentions of local origin. The second, naïvely declared, that, "except in very extraordinary cases, this Assembly is of the opinion that Presbyteries ought to be formed with geographical limits." It was by such empty words as these, that the Moderates, or Peace men, were held in subordination by the party.

The minority subsequently brought in their protest. After reciting Mr. Jennings' resolution, they said,—

"We protest against the refusal to consider and act definitely upon the above resolution, 1. Because the errors alluded to are contrary to the Scriptures and to our Confession of Faith, and are of a very pernicious tendency. 2. Because the Assembly was informed that such errors, to a great extent, pervade our land, and are constantly circulating through our Church, in books, pamphlets, and periodicals. 3. Because in the refusal to consider, and amend, if necessary, and adopt the above resolution, this Assembly has, in our opinion, refused to discharge a solemn duty enjoined by the Confession of Faith, and loudly and imperiously called for by the circumstances of the Church."

In violation, both, of the constitutional right of protest, and of the express agreement, by which the call for the Yeas and Nays had been withdrawn, the protest was refused a place upon the record. A motion was then made to record the Yeas and Nays, on this question; the effect of which would have been to bring the paper into the record. This motion, Dr. John McDowell, acting as temporary Moderator, pronounced out of order. An appeal was taken; but the decision was sustained by the house, which thus excluded from the record every line of this transaction.

CHAPTER XXVII.

THE ACT AND TESTIMONY.

A conference of the Old School—The crisis—Miller's Letters to Presbyterians—Organization and action of the conference—Committee to draft an Act and Testimony—Their report—Doctrinal errors specified—Remedies proposed—The signers covenant with each other—Publication of the Act and Testimony—Its reception, by the New School,—by the Moderates—Opposition of the Princeton Review—Dr. Wilson's "Moderates and Ultra Partisans"—Effect of the discussion.

WHILST the Assembly of 1834 was in session, a meeting was called, of the Old School members, and others, who sympathized with their views, "for the purpose of deliberating on the best method of promoting the interests of the Church, in the present crisis." For four years, the power of the Assembly had been in the hands of a revolutionary party,—a party thoroughly organized and disciplined,—managed with consummate skill, and guided with the farthest forecast, and a concentration and persistence of purpose, which nothing could divert from its chosen and cherished object. The design was, so to liberalize the Church, as to render her comprehensive of all grades of theological opinions, nominally evangelical; and a common receptacle, for the ingathering of an indefinite number of evangelical denominations, into one, grand, undiscriminating fold. The extent of the resources engaged, and the completeness and efficiency of the auxiliary machinery, we have seen. The ranks of the party were swollen, by all, with rare exceptions, whom the efficient and systematic operations of thirty years had drawn into the Presbyterian Church, from New England,—by those who had become infected with the contagion of New England theology, in any of its many phases; or, who had imbibed any form of lax principles on church government and discipline; by that large class who, themselves, knew and believed, or, rather, did not disbelieve, the truth, as to the doctrines of grace; but so little appreciated its value, that they did not consider it worth contending for, and preferred, therefore, a supine and shameful alliance with its enemies, rather than to be at the trouble of sharing in the toilsome and self-denying office of its defenders; and by many who believed and loved the truth; but, through a mistaken charity, could not be persuaded that evil devices were formed,—that the departures from the faith were really many and serious, and the danger great and imminent. From this class, mainly, the party of innovation derived moral power and character. Without them, it would have been comparatively impotent for evil. At each advancing step, in the progress of the movement, when the bosom of the Church throbbed with startled apprehension, in view of some new and menacing development, and when wise and faithful watchmen uttered the notes of alarm, and called the Church to wakefulness and action,—these good and trusted men were always at hand, ready to sing the lullaby, in the name of brotherly kindness, charity, and peace, and to hush the Church back to apathy and slumber.

The plans of the party were now advancing, fast and surely, to completion; and, unless the remedy is soon found and applied, it will shortly be too late. In the writings of Pearson and Anderson, Gilbert and Duffield, Barnes and Beecher, Beman and Cox, and others, heresy now vaunts itself, fearless of rebuke. In the person of Mr. Barnes, the Assembly has not only, judicially, conferred on it impunity, but, in contempt of the Constitution, itself, has made provision for its security and comfort; thus, practically establishing the principle, that departure from the doctrines of the Constitution, entitles the party to special immunities, and honor. In the elective affinity Presbyteries and Synod, and the judicatories, in New York and the West, built up under the operation of the Plan of Union, and through the agency of the American Education and Home Missionary Societies, and sustained by them, the requisite organizations are provided, to corrupt the theology of the Church, and supersede its Constitution. The Plan of Union, instead of being used as a temporary expedient, is treated as a sacred and time-honored covenant and constitution, paramount to the Constitution of the Church itself, and more venerable and binding every day. And now, the denial to the Presbyteries, by the Assembly of 1834, of the right of examination of candidates for admittance, exposes every Presbytery in the land, helplessly, to the infusion of a corrupt theology. The elective affinity Presbytery may send Mr. Barnes; that of Troy, Dr. Beman; and Oneida, Messrs. Finney and Burchard; with a sufficient number of others, armed with clean papers, to reconstruct any selected Presbytery. They may come, with the demand made on behalf of Mr. Chambers,—"We expect you to receive him, as one of us;" and there is no remedy. It was thus, Cincinnati Presbytery and Lane Seminary were lost and won.

And, the General Assembly, having pursued "the compromising plan," for several years, to the neglect and violation of its own constitutional duties, and the rights of those who are under its jurisdiction, and appeal to its bar,—it now sends forth to the inferior judicatories its admonition, to settle their difficulties among themselves; and not bring them up to the supreme court;—an admonition which, interpreted in the light of all the circumstances, must be understood to indicate a wish on the part of the Assembly, to abdicate its judicial office, and descend to the position of an advisory General Association; with a like transformation, in the inferior courts.

Nor have the plans, formed of old, respecting the Boards, been abandoned. But all things are tending to the desired end; and when the proper time shall come to strike the blow, it will be easy to elect to each of the Boards, and to the Directory of the Seminaries, such persons as will take the requisite action. Already, intimations are given of a design to make some changes in Princeton; and the names of McAuley, Mason, Hillyer, and Barnes, among the Directors, give reason to ponder the possibilities of the future.

In another direction, recent indications were calculated to cause anxiety. During the preceding spring, in a series of "Letters to Presbyterians," published in the Presbyterian newspaper, the Rev. Dr. Miller had assumed ground which was presumably indicative of the position to be taken by the Moderate party. In these Letters, the questions in agitation were brought under elaborate review. The conclusions, however, which were attained, were disproportioned to the argument, and altogether inadequate to the emergency. As to doctrinal differences, the Professor declared his conviction that "nineteen-twentieths of the whole number of our ministers are sufficiently near to the Scriptures and to each other, in respect to all the essentials of truth, to be comfortably united in Christian fellowship and co-operation;" and that the great mass of the ministry were as united in sentiment as were the fathers of the Church, in 1741. The schism of that year he regarded as having been condemned by the reunion of 1758. He, therefore, gave his voice, "not for division, but for peace and continued union;" "for softening asperities, for reconciling differences, for putting away all bitterness, and wrath, and evil-speaking." He insisted that the Church, in conducting the business of missions and evangelization, was engaged in her proper and peculiar work; yet wished her sons to sustain the voluntary societies, too; and, whilst expressing pleasure at the formation of the Western Foreign Missionary Society, uttered the hope that the attempt would not be made to induce the Assembly to undertake the work. He condemned and showed, very clearly, the evil and danger of erecting church courts upon the principle of elective affinity; and yet declared that, had he been in the Assembly, he would probably have voted for that measure. In fact, the venerable Professor was the leading promoter of the "compromising policy" of the Assembly of 1831, by which a judicial decision, in Mr.

Barnes' case was evaded; and he was chairman of the committee, which recommended the erection of the elective affinity Presbytery, for the accommodation of that gentleman, and his friends.

As the result of the entire discussion, the Professor opposed himself decisively to any really effectual measures, and proposed, as the remedy for the evils which were harassing the Church, that the extremists, on the one hand, should cease giving cause of uneasiness to their brethren; and that those, on the other, should no longer agitate the Church, with their apprehensions and alarms!

Such was the situation of the Church, and such the view of it taken by some of the most honored and revered of her ministers; when the conference was called, in the lecture-room of the Seventh Church, on the evening of May 26, 1834. The Rev. Dr. William Wylie was called to the chair; and the Rev. D. R. Preston appointed secretary. After an appeal to the throne of grace, and a free interchange of views, a committee of six was appointed, to prepare a protest against the action which had been taken that day, restoring the elective affinity Presbytery. But this was comparatively an unimportant matter. The great question was, to find a really practicable and effectual remedy for the evils threatening the Church. Protests in abundance were already on record; and served to acquit the consciences of the signers; but gave no relief to the Church. Prosecution for heresy, remonstrances, memorials, petitions, references, appeals, and complaints,—every form of ordinary remedy had been tried, in vain. To all, it was evident, that unless some means could be devised to arouse the Church, effectually, from the unconsciousness and stupor, into which she had been so assiduously nursed,—to convince her of the magnitude of the peril which impended; and so to draw the lines as to constrain those, who really loved her and the truth, to rally to her aid,—unless the honest and orthodox portion of the Peace party could be dislodged from their false position, and induced to take a stand, either for or against her, all else was in vain. Those who loved the doctrines of her standards might prepare to abandon the Church, and seek an asylum in some other fold.

One measure remained, which had been tried and blessed in other times of peril. To it recourse was now had. Upon motion of the Rev. Dr. W. D. Snodgrass, a committee of nine was appointed, to prepare an Act and Testimony, on the crisis. The names on this committee are worthy of a place on the page of history. They were the Rev. R. J. Breckinridge, Rev. Drs. Green and Snodgrass, and the Rev. Messrs. John Gray, Alexander McFarlane, Samuel Boyd, S. G. Winchester, H. Campbell, M. D., and the chairman, the Rev. Dr. Wm. Wylie. By these brethren' the duty of drawing up the paper was laid upon Mr. Breckinridge.

In preparing this document, Mr. Breckinridge consulted with the Rev. Dr. Charles Hodge; by whom, with one exception, were dictated the statements, under the head of "Errors" of doctrine. The clause under the head of "Imputation," was inserted by Mr. Breckinridge, contrary to the mind of Dr. Hodge. Other modifications were made, in the original draft of the paper, under the mistaken impression that it would, thereby, secure the approval and support of the Professor. As thus constructed, the document was reported, at an adjourned meeting of the conference, held on the evening of the 28th. It was, then, referred to a new committee, for revision. On the morning of the 30th, at six o'clock, this committee reported several amendments, which were approved; and, then, the paper was, finally, adopted and signed.

The Act and Testimony, thus carefully framed,—after a suitable introduction,—proceeded to testify against the various evasions employed in adopting the Confession; against a list of enumerated doctrinal errors, taught in the Church; and against irregularities in discipline and violations of order, which were prevalent. It closed with recommending to the churches certain measures of reform. As to doctrine, it bore witness against the following, as "a part of the errors held and taught, by many persons in our Church."

"1. Our relation to Adam.—That we have no more to do with the first sin of Adam, than with the sins of any other parent.

"2. Native Depravity.—That there is no such thing as original sin; that infants come into the world, as perfectly free from corruption of nature, as Adam was, when he was created; that, by original sin, nothing more is meant, than the fact that all the posterity of Adam, though born entirely free from moral defilement, will always begin to sin, when they begin to exercise moral agency; and that this fact is, somehow, connected with the fall of Adam.

"3. Imputation.—That the doctrine of imputed sin and imputed righteousness is a novelty, and is nonsense.

"4. Ability.—That the impenitent sinner is, by

nature, and independently of the aid of the Holy Spirit, in full possession of all the powers necessary to a compliance with the commands of God; and that, if he labored under any kind of inability, natural or moral, which he could not remove himself, he would be excusable for not complying with God's will.

"5. REGENERATION.—That man's regeneration is his own act; that it consists, merely, in the change of our governing purpose, which change we must ourselves produce.

"6. DIVINE INFLUENCE.—That God cannot exert such an influence on the minds of men as shall make it certain that they will choose and act in a particular manner, without destroying their moral agency; and that, in a moral system, God could not prevent the existence of sin; or, of the present amount of sin; however much he might desire it.

"7. ATONEMENT.—That Christ's sufferings were not truly vicarious."

The practical recommendations, embraced in the Act and Testimony, proposed to discountenance the propagators of error; to use all lawful means to bring them to discipline; to labor to re-establish sound discipline and order; and to hold elective affinity courts to be unconstitutional, and those who voluntarily belong to them to have, virtually, departed from the standards of the Church. It advised that all ministers, elders, and church courts give their public adherence to the Act and Testimony; and that importunate supplications be addressed to the King in Zion, for the restoration of purity and peace. It also recommended that, on the second Thursday of May, 1835, one week before the meeting of the General Assembly, "a convention be held in the city of Pittsburgh, to be composed of two delegates, a minister and ruling elder, from each Presbytery, or from the minority of any Presbytery, who may concur in the sentiments of this Act and Testimony, to deliberate and consult on the present state of the Church, and to adopt such measures, as may be best suited to restore her prostrated standards."

The paper closed, with the following earnest and decisive language: "And now, brethren, our whole heart is laid open to you, and to the world. If the majority of our Church are against us, they will, we suppose, in the end, either see the infatuation of their course, and retrace their steps, or they will, at last, attempt to cut us off. If the former, we shall bless the God of Jacob; if the latter, we are ready, for the sake of Christ, and in support of the testimony now made, not only to be cut off, but, if need be, to die also. If, on the other hand, the body be yet, in the main, sound, as we would fondly hope, we have, here, frankly, openly, and candidly, laid before our erring brethren the course we are, by the grace of God, irrevocably determined to pursue. It is our steadfast aim, to reform the Church; or, to testify against its errors and defections, until testimony will be no longer heard. And we commit the issue into the hands of him who is over all, God blessed for ever. Amen."

Thus solemnly and in the presence of God, did the signers of this paper pledge themselves to each other, to consent neither to peace nor truce with the corrupters of her doctrines and order; but to strive, by every lawful and scriptural means, for their reformation, or exclusion from the Church; until the object thus announced should be accomplished, or the witnesses themselves cast out of the body. Solemnly was their purpose announced; and well and faithfully was it fulfilled. History will cherish their names; and the Church of God, in coming ages, will honor their memories. Under God, the testimony and resolve thus recorded, and the measures adopted in pursuance of this pledge, were the means blessed to the recovery of the Church. It is evident to the intelligent and candid reviewer of the history, now, that without some such decisive action, her reformation was, humanly speaking, beyond hope; and that had the measure been delayed, but one or two years longer, it would, in all probability, have come too late. In fact, the futile prosecutions of Messrs. Duffield, the Beechers, and Barnes, and the proceedings of the Assembly of 1836, demonstrated that, already,—had the New School party known how to temper their triumph with moderation,—the Church was in their power, and the day for effectual resistance to their policy was past.

The Act and Testimony, as originally published, on the 19th of June, 1834, was signed by thirty-seven Ministers, and twenty-seven Elders. It ultimately received the signatures of about three hundred and seventy-four Ministers, seventeen hundred and eighty-nine Elders, and fourteen licentiates. It was also adopted, either entirely or substantially, by five Synods, and thirty Presbyteries.

The publication of this paper, after the rising of the Assembly of 1834, was received with various emotions, by the different parties, into which the Church was divided. By those who had been long struggling against growing corruption and defection, it was hailed, as a pledge of hope. By many, it was accepted, as an occasion of aroused attention, and of ultimate conviction, as to the reality of the emergency, and the necessity of active exertions, for the recovery of the Church. By the New School party, it was received with expressions of mingled derision, apprehension and displeasure. But it was among the Moderate party, that the decisive position taken, in the Act and Testimony, produced the profoundest impression, and elicited the strongest feelings, and the most intense opposition. Many of these made this the occasion definitively to commit themselves to the New School party. Others who saw with regret, the impossibility of retaining, much longer, the attitude of serene superiority, which they had sought to maintain; who felt that they must soon take a definitive position, on one side or the other, were excited to express their displeasure at the authors of this necessity, in terms which did not, always, keep within the bounds of that dignified moderation, which they, so much, affected.

But the most powerful and stunning blows dealt against the Act and Testimony, and its friends, came from a quarter whence they were least expected. Mr. Breckinridge had so modified the first draft of the document as to meet, as he supposed, the views of Dr. Hodge; with the hope of securing the sanction and co-operation of Princeton. In the end, it appeared that there had been a total misapprehension, between the parties, on this subject. In the Princeton Review, for October, the conductors of that periodical, in an elaborate article, planted themselves in determined opposition to the Act and Testimony, and the measures proposed by its advocates.

In this article, the document was condemned, as being, not a testimony, but a test,—divisive in its tendency,—as unjustly charging the General Assembly with giving countenance to error and disorder,—as exaggerating the extent of the evils complained of,—and as "a revolutionary proceeding," "an appeal from the constitutional government," in undertaking to call a convention to deliberate on these questions.

Replies to this article were made in the Presbyterian by Messrs. Engles and Breckinridge. The Review for January, 1835, pursued the discussion, in two several articles. In the first, the reviewer, went so far as to assert that, instead of the Assembly being, justly, chargeable with giving countenance to disorders or error, the Old School men themselves were responsible for the obnoxious measures, by reason of their clumsy management. "We have no doubt," said the writer, "that sound, Old School principles would have fared far better, in the General Assembly,—nay, they would have invariably triumphed, IF THEY HAD BEEN MANAGED AND PRESENTED WITH, EVEN, TOLERABLE DISCRETION."* The reviewer, still insisted that error and defection did not prevail to such an extent as to justify the representations of the Act and Testimony, or give occasion for serious apprehension. "If a few dozen men, whom we could name, had either the honesty to withdraw from a Church, whose formularies they never really believed; or, the discretion to keep their specula-

* Princeton Review, 1835, p. 65.

tions to themselves; we are fully persuaded, we should have occasion to hear little more, on this subject, in the Presbyterian Church."*

In the second article, the same views were pursued, with special reference to the defensive publications of Breckinridge and Engles. In closing his remarks, the reviewer pronounced, the Act and Testimony "confessedly a failure. It is announced that its object was to unite all the orthodox. This it has not done. It has received the sanction of but one Synod in the Presbyterian Church. It has not, even as a general declaration, been adopted by one-sixth of the ministers of our communion. It has, therefore, failed in its avowed object. More than this. By failing to unite, it must, of necessity, divide. If a certain portion only of the sound part of the Church adhere to this document, and its policy,—of course, the remaining portion is separated. Whose fault is this? The fault of those who proposed and urged the signing of a paper, as a test of orthodoxy, which few, comparatively, can conscientiously sign. It is no longer a matter of conjecture or opinion; but a matter of fact, that the Act and Testimony has divided the ranks of the Old School men. It has filled the mouths and hearts of their most open opponents with rejoicing. It is, to them, the most certain presage of triumph; the most welcome of all services."†

Happily, the reviewer was mistaken. The Act and Testimony was no failure. And, if the enemies of sound doctrine were disposed to imagine, in it, cause of triumph, their exultation was of brief continuance.

* Review, p. 65. † Ibid., p. 133.

To these articles, of the Repertory, the Rev. Dr. Wilson, of Cincinnati, published a pamphlet reply. A remark, of the Review, that "Moderate men have always fared badly between ultra partisans," suggested the title of his paper,—"The Moderates, and the Ultra Partisans." In playful reference to the nominal incognito, under which the reviewer insisted upon veiling himself behind the "Association of gentlemen in Princeton," by whom the Repertory was conducted,—Dr. Wilson suppressed his own name, and signed himself, "A Gentleman." "Hitherto," said he, "I have chosen the open field; but, now, I must 'take to a tree.' Some departure, therefore, from the strictest rules of polite warfare may be tolerated." In a mingled strain of pleasantry and satire he examined and replied to the points made against "ultra Old School men," and the Act and Testimony. With reference to the assertion that the cause of failure, before the Assembly, had been the mismanagement of the Old School, themselves, by whom, according to the reviewer, no case had been presented fairly upon its merits, "A Gentleman" pungently and most justly demanded,—"Why have not the *Moderates* done their duty, and showed the Old School how this thing can be done? Why have they not brought up *fairly* before the Assembly, some of the 'few dozen' heretics of their acquaintance, unconnected with 'peculiar, personal, local, or exciting circumstances;' so that the Assembly might have given, at least, one 'calm and dispassionate' decision?"

Whilst these various discussions were going on, and by means of them, the Act and Testimony was doing, most effectually, its expected work. And upon none did it operate with more evident power than upon a large class of persons who spurned the idea of submitting themselves to the bondage of its test; but were impelled, all the more earnestly, to demonstrate, otherwise, that they were not behind any, in their devotion to the faith, and zeal for the order of the Church.

CHAPTER XXVIII.

THE CONVENTION AND ASSEMBLY OF 1835.

Organization of the Convention—Proceedings—Memorial to the Assembly—Opening of the Assembly—Committee on the Memorial—Its report;—on examination of intrant ministers;—on the censure of books and publications;—on elective affinity—Dr. Elliott's motion—Dr. Ely's compromise—Voluntary societies—The Plan of Union—Proposition to the Association of Connecticut—Doctrinal errors condemned.

THE Convention, called by the Act and Testimony, met in the Second Presbyterian Church, in Pittsburgh, on the 14th of May, 1835, at 12 o'clock. It was the privilege of the author of this history to witness its proceedings. It was called to order, by the Rev. Thomas D. Baird. The Rev. John Witherspoon was appointed temporary chairman, and the Rev. Messrs. I. V. Brown and Thomas Alexander, temporary clerks. The Rev. Dr. James Blythe was appointed to preach before the convention.

In the afternoon, after sermon by Dr. Blythe, the permanent organization was effected, by the election of the Rev. Dr. Ashbel Green, President, the Rev. J. Witherspoon, Vice President, and the Rev. Messrs. James Culbertson and Ashbel G. Fairchild, Secretaries.

During the sessions, there appeared and were enrolled as members, forty-seven ministers and twenty-eight elders, representing thirty-six Presbyteries, and thirteen minorities.

The Rev. Drs. Blythe, Magraw, Montgomery, and Phillips; with Elders Robert Wray, M.D., of Pittsburgh, James Lennox, Jr., of New York, and Archibald George, of Baltimore, were appointed a committee, to prepare and report whatever business should come before the Convention.

Friday, the second day of the sessions was given, wholly, to fasting, humiliation, and prayer.

On Saturday, the Rev. Messrs. George Junkin, John Witherspoon, and J. L. Wilson, and Elders Boyd, Owen, and George, were appointed to prepare a respectful memorial and petition, to be addressed to the Assembly, "with our signatures as individuals, together with such other ministers and elders as may choose to unite with us." Messrs. Stuart and Steele and Elders McPherson and Ferguson were afterward added to this committee.

During the subsequent sessions, various subjects were brought in by the committee on business, discussed, and referred to the committee on the memorial. This committee made report on Tuesday afternoon. After full discussion, by paragraph, and amendment, the memorial was unanimously adopted, on Wednesday afternoon. It was signed by seventy-two ministers, and thirty-six elders. Many more signatures could have been obtained. But the time was limited, and the object did not require a display of numbers.

The memorial was, in its spirit and purport, identical with the Act and Testimony. It presented to the notice of the General Assembly certain grievances, for which redress was sought. These were,—the denial of the right of Presbyteries to examine applicants for admission; and to censure printed publications, irrespective of the authors,—the erection of elective affinity courts, —the favor shown to the American Home Missionary and Education Societies,—the operation of the Plan of Union,—the admission of Congregational delegates to the right of deliberation, on all questions coming before the Assembly,—and the prevalence of unsound doctrines in the Church. The doctrines enumerated, were essentially the same as those presented in the Western Memorial, and in the Act and Testimony. Of the tendency of these errors, the memorialists thus testified,—"Now, Reverend Fathers and brethren, we humbly conceive that this is 'another gospel,' entirely and essentially different from that laid down in the Bible and our Confession of Faith. And we do, most solemnly and sorrowfully, believe, that, unless the Spirit of the Lord raise up a standard against it, it will be followed, in our Church, as it has been elsewhere, by the entire system of Pelagianism, and ultimately, of Socinianism. If the atonement is not, essentially, vicarious and penal, why demand a *divine* Redeemer? If an *exhibition* is all that is required, why not hold up Stephen, or Peter, or Paul, or John Huss, or John Rogers? This tendency toward Socinianism, we think, is plainly manifested, in the denial of the eternal filiation of the Son of God. Again, if the Spirit's work is, merely, a moral suasion, why a divine and almighty Spirit? Must not the mind, which denies the necessity of an omnipotent influence, be strongly tempted to disbelieve the existence of an omnipotent Agent?"

Having finished its business, the Convention adjourned, after making record of its conviction that, "under the smiles and blessings of God," the Act and Testimony had been "of marked and extensive benefit to our beloved Church." This minute was made, and the Convention closed its sessions, a few moments before the opening of the Assembly of 1835. The proceedings of that body very soon demonstrated that the Act and Testimony had, indeed, exerted a most potent and salutary influence, throughout the Church.

The Rev. J. H. C. Leach, of Virginia, and the Rev. W. W. Phillips, D. D., of New York, a signer of the Act and Testimony, were the nominees for Moderator. Dr. Phillips was elected, by one hundred and seventeen votes, to eighty-three.

The principal business, transacted by this Assembly, grew out of the memorial of the Convention. This paper was early submitted to the Assembly, and referred to the Committee on Bills and Overtures. That Committee made an early report, recommending a reference of the several subjects included in the memorial, to appropriate committees. Upon the motion to adopt this report, Dr. William Hill wished time to consider. He thought it was giving the memorialists undue advantage, to have their memorial, at once, committed, to men, perhaps, who were familiar with the whole subject. "We are not on an equal footing. The memorialists have used a new system of tactics." Dr. William Wisner demanded, "To whom are we to commit this memorial? To committees appointed by one of the memorialists (the Moderator)? One of the committee of overtures, too, is a memorialist. While the house is acting on the subject, the chair should be occupied by one who is not a memorialist; and every memorialist should withdraw. Is it not evident how the memorialists will act? Will they not sustain the memorial? Ought they, then, to be on the committee, or to appoint it?"

This extraordinary mode of securing impartiality, by excluding from the house all who had avowed themselves in favor of reform, did not commend itself to the approval of the Assembly. The memorial was referred to a committee, consisting of Drs. Miller and Hoge, and Rev. Messrs. Elliot and McElhenny, and Elders Stonestreet and Banks.

This committee, after several days' deliberation, presented a report, embodying deliverances on each of the points embraced in the memorial; which, after full discussion and amendment, were adopted by the Assembly.

The first point, embraced in this report, had respect to the examination of intrant ministers, by the Presbyteries to which they apply. The right of such examination had been undisputed in the earlier history of the Church. It was not until the occurrence of Mr. Barnes' case, in 1830, that the authority of the Presbytery, in this matter, seems to have been seriously called in question. In the discussions which arose, then and subsequently, it was frequently the case that the two parties mutually assumed strangely false positions, in opposite directions. The Congregationalizing New School men, anxious to protect their partisans from the dreaded examination, ran to the extreme of denying, altogether, the peculiar rights and duties of Presbyteries, with respect to the guardianship of their own particular folds, and merged all in the unity of a consolidated Church; asserting that good standing in one Presbytery entitled the party to the same standing everywhere.

On the other hand, Old School men, in their zeal to protect themselves from the spreading sore of doctrinal error, sometimes assumed ground utterly destructive of the authority of the superior courts, and of the whole Presbyterian system; claiming for the Presbyteries, an original, independent, and unlimited right to judge of the qualifications of their own members. This right was deduced from the false assumption, that the Presbyteries had originally created the Assembly and endowed it with such functions and powers as they saw fit; retaining to themselves all such as they did not thus expressly alienate. It is the less surprising that ideas so entirely at variance with the facts of the Church's history, should have gained prevalence; because the earlier records had been but recently recovered, after having been long lost; and their contents were almost wholly unknown.

The General Assembly avoided the extremes of both parties, and planted itself upon the true principles of scriptural Presbyterianism. In determining the question in discussion, there were several points to be taken into the account. The Church is one body, of which the particular Presbyteries are but fractional parts. The whole Church has, in its Constitution, set forth the qualifications to be required of its ministry, and enjoined them upon the various judicatories, under an obligation, by which all alike are bound, to enforce them, in all cases. Those judicatories are not infallible; neither as to judgment, nor fidelity, in applying these rules. Each particular Presbytery has a field of its own, within which it is bound to see that the laws of the Church, as to the qualifications of her ministry, are faithfully obeyed. This does not imply any right of Presbyteries to establish new terms of ministerial fellowship; but simply the duty of enforcing those already established by the Church. In every Presbyterial district there are special and peculiar considerations, additional to those involved in general ministerial fitness, which may determine for or against the propriety of admitting a given individual. Every worthy minister does not suit every church, nor promise to be useful in every Presbytery.

A Presbytery is not, therefore, to assume, that all ministers who may be entitled to the confidence of other Presbyteries, are, therefore, qualified and entitled to exercise the ministry among its churches. It should be satisfied, not only, that the party is possessed of the prescribed qualifications for the ministry, but that he has such as give reasonable promise of edifying the churches under its charge. And as, in this, it is acting as a member of the whole body, any irregularity or error in its action, is subject to revision and correction, by the higher courts.

In accordance with these principles, the Assembly pronounced it to be the right of every Presbytery to be fully satisfied as to the qualifications of all applicants; and that, if there be a reasonable doubt, they may examine them, or take other methods of gaining the necessary satisfaction; and if it be not obtained, may decline receiving them. "In such case, it shall be the duty of the Presbytery rejecting the applicant, to make known what it has done, to the Presbytery from which he came, with its reasons. It being always understood, that each Presbytery is, in this concern, as in all others, responsible for its acts to the higher judicatories."

The decision thus adopted by the Assembly, in 1835, was re-enforced in 1837, with the injunction requiring Presbyteries to examine all applicants "at least on experimental religion, didactic and polemic theology, and church government."* By thus enforcing examination, in all cases, greater vigilance is secured; men of unsound views are warned of inevitable detection, and thus deterred from seeking admission; and, where just occasion of suspicion arises, and examination is necessary, the appearance of anything invidious is avoided.

Respecting books and publications, the Assembly pronounced that it is the right, and may be the duty of any judicatory, to bear testimony against them, if erroneous, "and this, whether the author be living or dead; whether he be in the communion of the Church or not; whether he be a member of the judicatory expressing the opinion, or of some other," and whether he be arraigned or not.

Touching elective affinity courts, the Assembly was, at first, greatly perplexed. The report of the committee was not consistent with itself. It, in the first place, decided "that the erection of church courts, and especially of Presbyteries and Synods, on the principle of 'elective affinity,' that is, judicatories not bounded by geographical limits, but having a chief regard, in their erection, to diversities of doctrinal belief, and of ecclesiastical polity, is contrary, both to the letter and spirit

* Minutes, 1837, p. 429; Digest, p. 253.

of our Constitution, and opens a wide door for mischiefs and abuses of the most serious kind. One such Presbytery, if so disposed, might, in process of time, fill the whole Church with unsound and schismatic ministers; especially, if the principle were adopted that regular testimonials must, of course, secure the admission of those who bore them, into any other Presbytery. Such a Presbytery, moreover, being without geographical bounds, might enter the limits and disturb the repose of any church, into which it might think proper to intrude; and thus divide churches, stir up strife, and promote party spirit and schism, with all their deplorable consequences. Surely, a plan of procedure in the Church of God, which, naturally, and almost unavoidably, tends to produce effects such as these, ought to be frowned upon, and, as soon as possible, terminated by the supreme judicatory of the Church."

The evils here enumerated had been realized, in all their enormity, by the churches of Philadelphia and its vicinity. Of this, the Assembly, itself, had abundant evidence, in the coming up of several judicial cases arising out of the intrusions of the Assembly's Second Presbytery, and consequent distractions and divisions, in the churches of the other Presbyteries of the vicinity. The subject was illustrated, by facts developed in the speeches of the Rev. S. G. Winchester, and Dr. Miller. The latter had become fully satisfied, from actual observation, of the unconstitutionality of the plan and the unmitigated evil of the consequences. The resolution was adopted.

Here, however, a very perplexing question presented itself,—what to do with the elective affinity Presbyteries already existing. The logical conclusion from the premises, *laid down in the foregoing resolution*, was very evident. Dissolve them, and connect their members and churches with the Presbyteries to which they belonged, geographically. But there were members of the Assembly, of the orthodox-moderate class sufficiently numerous to command consideration, who objected, most earnestly, to giving, thus, practical effect to the principles which they had just united in adopting. Besides, the members of the regular Presbyteries in Philadelphia desired, indeed, an end to the disorders incident to the elective affinity system. But they were alarmed at the prospect of the discomfort and embarrassments, which would result to them, from the introduction into their Presbyteries of the uncongenial and unsound elements, which had gained strength and organization, under the fostering wings of the obnoxious Presbytery.

These various considerations prevailed in the committee; which recommended to the Assembly a resolution, recommending that the Assembly's Second Presbytery "ought, for the sake of peace and order, to confine itself to those churches which were expressly included in the original act of erection; and ought not, hereafter, either to add to the number of its ministerial members, or to receive, as candidates for license, any others than those who naturally belong to some one or more of the churches already under their care."

The committee also advised that the Assembly allow any members or churches of this Presbytery, who may wish to join either of the other Presbyteries, to do so; and that the Synod of New York be requested to readjust its Presbyteries so as to obviate the evils of elective affinity there realized.

As a substitute for these resolutions, the Rev. Dr. Elliot moved the dissolution of the Synod of Delaware, and the Assembly's Second Presbytery, and the restoration of their elements to their proper relations. After a full discussion, when it was evident that Dr. Elliot's paper was about to be adopted, Dr. Ely brought in a proposition, as a compromise :—

"*Resolved*, That at and after the next meeting of the Synod of Philadelphia, to be held in York, Pa., in October next, the Synods of Philadelphia and Delaware shall, and hereby are declared to be united and one, embracing all the Presbyteries belonging to the two Synods, and to be known as the Synod of Philadelphia; and that the Synod of Philadelphia, thus constituted, by the union, aforesaid, shall take such order concerning the organization of its several Presbyteries as may be deemed expedient and constitutional; and that said Synod, if it shall deem it desirable, make application to the next General Assembly, for such a division of the Synod as may best suit the convenience of all its Presbyteries, and promote the glory of God."

The olive branch thus tendered, in a spirit so seemingly commendable, was, at once, cordially accepted, by the Old School majority. Dr. Miller proposed an amendment to the first clause of the resolution, in these words :—

"*Resolved*, That at and after the meeting of the Synod of Philadelphia, in October next, the Synod of Delaware, shall be dissolved, and that the Presbyteries constituing the same shall be, then and thereafter, annexed to the Synod of Philadelphia."

The amendment was readily accepted, and the resolution, thus modified, was passed by a unanimous vote; unless there may have been one feeble, "No." Several papers, with reference to some of the divisive proceedings of the Elective Affinity Presbytery, were then withdrawn, and all further proceedings thereon dropped, by common consent, amid mutual congratulations, and general joy.

We shall hereafter see the use subsequently made of Dr. Miller's amendment, and how little ground there was for the pleasant anticipations now realized.

As to the operations of voluntary societies, the Assembly, declared it inexpedient to prohibit them, but pronounced it "the first and binding duty of the Presbyterian Church to sustain her own Boards;" and admonished voluntary societies "neither to educate, nor send forth, as Presbyterians, any individuals known to hold sentiments contrary to the Word of God and the standards of the Presbyterian Church."

With respect to the Plan of Union, the report of the committee recommended that it be repealed, as unconstitutional and injurious to the peace and welfare of the Church.

Dr. Fisher announced himself in favor of rescinding the compact with the Congregationalists, if it were done in a decorous manner. He gave a history of the matter, according to which it appeared that, formerly, the Congregationalists from New England being active and enterprising in the Western country, the General Assembly had invited them to throw in their strength, to build up and enlarge the Presbyteries in that region. A mutual compact having thus been made, courtesy required that a committee be appointed to confer with the Association of Connecticut and secure its consent, before proceeding to repeal the plan.

Dr. Miller confirmed the account of Dr. Fisher. He was a member of the Assembly of 1801. "The offer came from us."

Other members objected to the proposed repeal, that it would involve the dissolution of the Presbyteries and Synods which had grown up under it. Mr. Hanford, of the Western Reserve, deprecated the measure, on this ground. "It would strike at the root of the existence of his Synod."

Dr. Miller explained, that the design of the resolution was wholly prospective; and Dr. Beman hoped that this would be distinctly indicated in the minute.

Drs. Fisher and Miller, were mistaken as to the history of the Plan. It was no "compact," and did *not* originate with the Assembly. Their statements, however, determined the action of the Assembly; which adopted a substitute proposed by the latter,—

"*Resolved*, That this Assembly deem it no longer desirable that churches should be formed in our Presbyterian connection, agreeably to the plan adopted by the Assembly and the General Association of Connecticut, in 1801. Therefore, resolved, that our brethren of the General Association of Connecticut be, and they hereby are, respectfully requested to consent, that said plan shall be, from and after the next meeting of that Association, declared to be annulled. And resolved, that the annulling of said plan shall not, in any wise, interfere with the existence and lawful operation of churches which have been already formed on this plan."

This was, to request the General Association to permit us to cease from introducing disorderly churches into our bosom; it being a covenant condition, that we will never attempt to correct the disorders, already introduced.

The Stated Clerk of the Assembly neglected to communicate this proposition to the delegate appointed to the Association of Connecticut. That body, therefore, took no action on the subject, and our Church thus providentially escaped the snare of the proposed covenant.

The Assembly declined to terminate the system of correspondence then maintained with the New England churches, as proposed in the memorial.

As to doctrinal errors, it declared the painful conviction that the errors specified in the memorial do exist; that they "are not distinguishable from Pelagian or Arminian errors;" and the holding of them is wholly incompatible with an honest adoption of the Confession. The Assembly, therefore, bore solemn testimony against them; and enjoined the inferior courts "to exercise the utmost vigilance in guarding against the introduction and publication of such pestiferous errors."

On the subject of foreign missions, action was taken, which will appear in another place.

When the Assembly of 1835 adjourned, the prevalent feeling among the Old School men of the Church, was one of thankfulness and congratulation, that the battle was fought and the purity and peace of the Church vindicated. Bright hopes were cherished for the future,—hopes doomed to disappointment. Dark and troublous days must yet be seen, before the return of peace and prosperity.

CHAPTER XXIX.

THE WESTERN FOREIGN MISSIONARY SOCIETY.

Conferences in Baltimore respecting Foreign Missions—Action of the Presbytery—Application to Dr. Rice—Published circular—Dr. Rice's overture to the Assembly—A committee to confer with the American Board—Dr. Swift's overture to the Synod of Pittsburgh—Western Foreign Missionary Society organized—Report of the committee of conference—Dr. Miller's resolution in the Board—Discussion and action of the Assembly—State of the Society in 1835—Proposed transfer to the Assembly.

We have seen the process of absorption by which, in 1828, the Church had been stripped of its Foreign Missions, for the benefit of the American Board. The condition of things thus induced was not viewed without profound emotion, by many, throughout the Church. In Baltimore, it immediately became a subject of anxious deliberation, in the weekly conferences of the pastors. After more than a year of private discussion, the subject was brought into the Presbytery, under the conviction and desire that the Presbyterian Church, as such, should exert itself, more directly, and efficiently in the cause of foreign missions. "It was felt to be her imperative duty, which she could not neglect, without great guilt; and absolutely essential to her piety and permanent prosperity. It was believed that the only organization which then existed,—the American Board,

—could never call into action the latent energies of the whole Church; and that something was required from among ourselves, to accomplish this transcendently important object. Accordingly, the Rev. Dr. John Breckinridge introduced the preamble and resolution of the 6th of October, 1830, which were unanimously adopted by the Presbytery."*

This first minute was as follows: "Whereas, in the view of this Presbytery, the Presbyterian Church, with which we are connected, in general, and we as a Presbytery, in particular, have to a most inexcusable degree, neglected the claims of Foreign Missions; and whereas, the present state of the heathen world, as well as the last command of our Divine Redeemer, most urgently call us to exert ourselves in this noble cause; therefore

"Resolved, That we, as a body, will make the attempt, from this time, to support at least one missionary, from year to year, in the foreign field."†

The views of these brethren, however, contemplated nothing less than bringing up the whole Presbyterian Church, in her organic capacity, to this blessed work. A few days after the adoption of the above resolution, the Rev. Dr. John H. Rice passed through Baltimore. In the parlor of Dr. Nevins, he was waited upon by a committee to which the subject had been referred by the Presbytery, and urged to prepare a paper, which might arouse the attention of the Church, and secure, in some form, the contemplated end. For no one was, as yet, clear, as to the precise mode of action to be

* Rev. Dr. G. W. Musgrave in the Baltimore Magazine, 1838, p. 222.

† Baltimore Magazine, 1838, p. 221.

adopted. All venerated the American Board, and were embarrassed, in considering the duty and privilege of the Church on the subject, by respect to the plans and policy of that institution. Dr. Rice promised "to think of it;" and fulfilled the promise, by his overture to the General Assembly, which was dictated from his death-bed a short time afterward.

It was at this conference, in Dr. Nevins' study, that the phrase,—"*the Presbyterian Church a Missionary Society*,"—true as it was to the facts of her history, was fixed upon as the rallying-call to the Church.*

On the 18th of March, 1831, the committee of the Presbytery published a circular letter on this subject. "Our Church," say they, "affords peculiar facilities for combined, uniform, and powerful operations, in this way. It is organized already, and only needs to be set in motion, in order to make it a most efficient missionary institution. The plan proposed above, of operating through the Presbyteries, seems to be at once the most simple and effective."

Again, "In proposing this plan, it is by no means intended to interfere with other societies, already engaged in missions. On the contrary, the object is, to co-operate with them, as far as possible to do so. But the Assembly's Board of Missions is fully occupied on our own continent, and has no purpose of effort beyond the two Americas. The American Home Missionary Society is exclusively domestic, as its name imports; and the American Board of Commissioners for Foreign Missions needs some such combined effort as this, to bring up 'to the help of the Lord against the mighty,' the

* Foote's Virginia, vol. ii., p. 497.

whole Presbyterian Church. The details of the plan may be left for future consultation. But the principle of operation might be at once adopted; the whole Church might be simultaneously excited through the Presbyteries; and the way be thus prepared to send forth, from one hundred Presbyteries, one hundred missionaries to the foreign field. Dear brethren, we are wedded to no peculiar plan; but we feel that something must be done; that it must be done at once; and that it must be done by all the Church; and with all our heart, and soul, and mind, and strength."*

This circular, signed on behalf of the Presbytery, by William Nevins, George Morrison, George W. Musgrave, and John Breckinridge, prepared the way for the overture of Dr. Rice, and excited the hope and expectation that the Church would be induced to make a proportionate response to the call of duty, so impressively urged.

Dr. Rice had already indicated the hold which the subject had taken on his mind. On the 22d of November, 1830, he wrote to the Rev. Dr. B. B. Wisner, Secretary of the American Board. In this remarkable letter, he surveys with anxiety and alarm the undeveloped indications of the coming strife in the Church, and the growing estrangement between the Congregational and Presbyterian elements. "I do think, that, in a year or two, there has been a considerable increase of local and sectarian feelings among Congregationalists and Presbyterians. That these two denominations are further apart than they were some years ago, is manifest. I thought, too, that during my visit to Boston, I saw tokens of a

* Baltimore Magazine, 1838, p. 223.

growth in the strength of *New England* feeling. *Presbyterian* feeling also is considerably roused up."

"I want some of my beloved New England friends to come to Philadelphia, [to the Assembly,] just to try to get good, and to do good; to come without feeling that they belong to New England, but that they belong to Christ and his Church; not to say one word about any matter in dispute among Christians, but determined to know nothing but Christ and him crucified. . . . . I wish, too, that some plan might be devised for kindling up in the Presbyterian Church, the true spirit of missions, and rousing this sluggish body from sleep. Here is a subject of delicacy and difficulty. The *Presbyterian* spirit has been so awakened up, that I begin to apprehend that no power of man will ever bring the whole body to unite under what is *thought* to be a Congregational Board. But the Church must not be under the guilt of letting souls perish, who might be saved. What can be done? Here we want wisdom. I never will do anything to injure the wisest and best missionary society in the world, the American Board. But can no ingenuity devise a scheme of a Presbyterian Branch of the American Board,—co-ordinate,—sufficiently connected with the General Assembly to satisfy scrupulous Presbyterians, yet in union with the original Board,—having the same object, and tending to the same result? Do think of this. Something must be done; but I cannot say what."*

"A Presbyterian branch, co-ordinate, sufficiently connected with the General Assembly, yet in union with the original Board;"—such was the conception of this

* Maxwell's Memoir of Rice, pp. 380, 383.

departing servant of Christ. On the next Sabbath he preached his last sermon. Had the men to whom he addressed himself been worthy, what a sublime spectacle would the Congregational and Presbyterian Churches have now presented,—one in faith and love; independent, yet united; together laboring for the world's conversion, through the instrumentality of organizations, co-ordinate, and operating each freely, in its own sphere, yet maintaining mutual understanding, concert, and co-operation in their plans, to the furtherance of the one end!

To Rice's call for New England men in the Assembly, who should "come without feeling that they belong to New England," and "not to say one word about any matter in dispute," the response was the presence and labors of Mr. Bacon, on behalf of Mr. Barnes, and his subsequent insults over Presbyterianism as a failure. To the proposition for a co-ordinate Board, the reply was,—without alternative,—the American Board, and that only.

In fulfilment of his sublime conception, Dr. Rice dictated to an amanuensis, from his sick-bed, the overture on missions, which was laid before the Assembly of 1831.* This paper, in the preamble, set forth the evangelization of the world as being the pre-eminent office of the Church, according to the institution of Jesus Christ. It recognized the divine favor, bestowed upon the American Board, and expressed an earnest desire to co-operate with it. It then proposed a series of resolutions, predicated upon the proposition "that the Presbyterian Church in the United States is a missionary

* The overture will be found in the Assembly's Digest, p. 363.

society, the object of which is, to aid in the conversion of the world; and that every member of the Church is a member for life of said society, and bound, in maintenance of his Christian character, to do all in his power for the accomplishment of this object." The plan provided that the Assembly appoint from year to year a "Committee of the Presbyterian Church in the United States, for Foreign Missions," "to whose management this whole concern shall be confided, with directions to report all their transactions to the churches. The Committee shall have power to appoint a Chairman, Corresponding Secretary, Treasurer, and other necessary officers. The Committee shall, as far as the nature of the case will admit, be co-ordinate with the American Board of Commissioners for Foreign Missions, and shall correspond and co-operate with that association, in every possible way, for the accomplishment of the great objects which it has in view."

We have already seen the complexion and spirit of the Assembly of 1831, before which this overture came. It was controlled by those who, in 1826, had attempted to bind the Assembly by solemn covenant to the American Board. Dr. Miller states, that, a year or two later, "a proposal was privately made, by some of the friends of the American Board, that the General Assembly should pass a solemn act, binding itself, or, at least, resolving, not to undertake any separate foreign missionary enterprise. This proposition, however, was firmly resisted," and, for the time, defeated.* The attempt was now made to use the occasion of Rice's overture to accomplish this cherished object.

* Miller's Letters to Presbyterians, Letter V.

The overture was referred to a committee of five, who recommended that a committee of three be appointed to confer with the American Board, as to measures to be adopted for enlisting the Church more fully in the work of foreign missions, and report to the next Assembly. This proposal was adopted, and the committee of conference elected by ballot. The Rev. Drs. John McDowell, Thomas McAuley, and James Richards, were the New School nominees, and were elected; while the Rev. Drs. A. Alexander, John Breckinridge, and E. P. Swift, the Old School nominees, were appointed alternates. Dr. Rice was still living. When he heard the names of the committee, he remarked that "some of the alternates, he thought, understood his views better than some of the principals."*

After the result of this vote had been ascertained, two commissioners from the Synod of Pittsburgh,—the Rev. W. C. Anderson, and the Rev. E. P. Swift,—happened together, on the steps of the church where the Assembly met. "What is now to be done?" said the former. "We must go home," was the reply, "and revive our Western Missionary Society." Upon the return of these members from the Assembly, this suggestion was anxiously weighed by brethren of the Pittsburgh Synod, first among whom, in these consultations, beside those already named, were the Rev. Thomas D. Baird, and the Rev. Alan D. Campbell. The result was the introduction, by Dr. Swift, of an overture to the Synod of Pittsburgh, in pursuance of which that body resolved to resume its missionary organization and work.

* Foote's Sketches of Virginia, ii. 439.

In this overture, a survey was taken of the aspects of Providence, as calling the Church, in every land, to the work of missions. The efforts already put forth, and labors and results accomplished by the servants of Christ, were recognized. Especially and with pleasure "the truly splendid operations of the American Board" were referred to "with none but unmingled feelings of respect and affection."

"Nor do the Synod regard it as improper to recur, with grateful sentiments, to those humbler efforts which they have been enabled, in departed years, to put forth, through the Western Missionary Society, in this great and good cause. Still, however, much remains to be done. The resources of large districts of the Presbyterian Church are slumbering in inaction, and experience, for a few years past, has demonstrated the fact that they cannot be drawn forth by a society so remote as the American Board; or by any that does not involve an ecclesiastical organization, comporting with the honest predilections of many of our people."

It was, therefore, resolved "that it is expedient forthwith, to establish a society or board for foreign missions, on such a plan as will admit of the co-operation of such parts of the Presbyterian Church as may think proper to unite with it, in this great and important concern."

The first article of the Constitution provided that "This Society shall be composed of the Ministers, Sessions and Churches of the Synod of Pittsburgh, together with those of any other Synod or Synods, Presbytery or Presbyteries, that may hereafter formally unite with them; and shall be known by the name of

The Western Foreign Missionary Society of the United States."

A Board of Directors was immediately chosen, consisting of six Ministers and six Ruling Elders, residing in the vicinity of Pittsburgh, together with one minister and one elder from each Presbytery belonging to the Synod. Provision was also made for the admission of a Minister and Elder from each Presbytery belonging to any other Synod, which might enter into cooperation on this plan.

The first officers of the Society were the Hon. Harmer Denny, President, Rev. Thomas D. Baird, Vice President, Rev. E. P. Swift, Corresponding Secretary, Rev. Elisha McCurdy, Treasurer.

In the Assembly of 1832, Dr. McAuley, from the committee of conference with the American Board, submitted a report, signed jointly by the committee and by the Rev. Drs. Jeremiah Day, Lyman Beecher, and B. B. Wisner, a committee on behalf of the Board. This report entered into an elaborate argument, to prove that the Board is "properly a national institution;"—that it "sustains the same relation to the Congregational, Presbyterian, and Dutch Reformed churches, and fairly represents each of these religious denominations;"—and, in short, that there should be but one foreign missionary institution, sustained by those denominations, and the Board should be that institution.

The conclusions to which the joint committees of conference came were, "that it is wholly inexpedient to attempt the formation of any other distinct organization, within the three denominations, for conducting foreign missions; and that it is of the highest importance to their own spiritual prosperity, and to the extension of the Redeemer's kingdom, in the earth, that the ecclesiastical bodies and the individual churches in these connections should give to the American Board of Commissioners for Foreign Missions their cordial, united, and vigorous support.

"In reference to the particular topic, named in the resolution of the General Assembly of the Presbyterian Church, appointing their committee, viz.: 'Measures to be adopted for enlisting the energies of the Presbyterian Church more extensively in the cause of missions to the heathen,' the committees of conference are of opinion that but two things are wanting, to secure the desired result;—that the Prudential Committee of the American Board should take prompt and efficient measures, by agencies and other ways, to bring the subject of foreign missions, in its various relations, before the individual congregations and members of the Presbyterian body; and that the General Assembly and subordinate judicatories of that Church give their distinct and efficient sanction and aid to the measures that shall be adopted, for this purpose."

With the report, were submitted a series of resolutions, which do not appear in any of the published accounts of the proceedings. Their purport may be gathered from what follows. When this report was under consideration before the American Board, the Rev. Dr. Miller, who was present, as a member of the Board, offered the following minute, as further expressive of its mind on the subject,—

"While this Board accept and approve the foregoing

report, as expressing their firm opinion, on the subject referred to the Committee of Conference,—

"*Resolved*, That if the General Assembly of the Presbyterian Church, or any of its subordinate judicatories, shall eventually think proper to form any association for conducting foreign missions, separately from the American Board, this Board will regard such association with fraternal feelings, and without the least disposition to interfere with its organization or proceedings."

"This amendment," says Dr. Miller, "was very unceremoniously negatived; two other members of the Board, only,—so far as I recollect,—viz.: Dr. Spring, of New York, and Dr. Carnahan, of Princeton, rising in its favor."*

This took place, at the meeting of the Board in October, 1831; and occurred in view of the fact, which was publicly known, that the Synod of Pittsburgh was, at that very time, about to revive the Western Missionary Society.

When the report of the committee came before the Assembly of 1832, it is possible that, had matters remained as when the committee was appointed, the Assembly might have been induced to accept the bonds forged for them, by the committee and the Board. But, in the mean time, the Western Society had been organized. Already, it had chosen Africa as its first field of operations. The funds were in its treasury, and the first missionaries chosen. And the announcement of these facts,—the report that the Presbyterian

* Dr. Miller's Letter to Dr. McElhenny, in the Presbyterian, 1837, p. 62.

Church was about to be known again among the heathen, had excited in the bosom of the churches an interest and aroused emotions which commanded respect, and set a ban upon the present proposal.

In the discussion that ensued, Mr. Baird, the Vice President of the Western Society, gave voice to these sentiments,—"I am a friend of the American Board. But passing those resolutions will do it more hurt than good. There is a spirit rising, in the West, for a separate movement, on ecclesiastical principles. The Synod of Pittsburgh has, already, organized a foreign missionary society. The missionaries are selected, and the funds secured, to commence their operations. This is so organized that it may be transferred to the General Assembly, and placed under its ecclesiastical supervision, whenever it shall be judged expedient for the Assembly to take up the work of foreign missions. Those who are opposed to the whole principle of voluntary associations may here be enlisted under an ecclesiastical organization; and feelings will be awakened in favor of foreign missions, which the Board never could reach. But if these resolutions are passed, in view of the fact that a Western Board has already been established, many will feel that the Assembly and the American Board have set up too high and exclusive a claim in behalf of that institution."

Dr. Alexander objected to the resolutions, "because they will so commit the Assembly, that we cannot with propriety, at any time, or for any reasons, organize a Board of foreign missions. It also contains a virtual censure of the society already formed at Pittsburgh. So long a report ought never to be adopted as the act of the Assembly. I am in favor of the American Board. I am a member, and have confidence in it. I am willing to recommend it, and invite its committee to send their agents into our bounds, whenever the churches are willing to receive them. But I am not willing that the Assembly should thus bind themselves and their successors for ever, from acting by themselves. Suppose the charter members, who all reside in Massachusetts, should hereafter fall into great errors, in regard to the manner of conducting missions; or, into fundamental errors of doctrine.—I have no suspicion of the kind. But we have no security that such a thing will never take place. And is this supreme judicatory of the Presbyterian Church to be so committed, that it cannot withdraw the control of its foreign missions from such a Board?"

The resolutions were rejected, and it was resolved, "that while the Assembly would express no opinion in relation to the principles contained in the report, they cordially recommend the American Board of Commissioners for Foreign Missions to the affection and patronage of our churches."

Whilst the Board was thus strongly endorsed, the Western Society was no otherwise recognized than by a sentence in the Narrative, in which "the Assembly hail, with pleasure, the appearance of a deeper interest in the subject of Foreign Missions, recently manifested in the churches of the West, by the establishment of a Western Foreign Missionary Society. We would that all our churches might have a strong sense of their obligation to send the gospel to every creature, and afford fairer evidence of the sincerity of their daily prayer, 'Thy kingdom come.'"

But, although the Western Society shared so little in the favor of the majority of the Assembly, it enjoyed the smiles of the Head of the Church, and the growing confidence and support of his people. When its third annual meeting was held, in May, 1835, it had already established missions in Western Africa, in Northern India, and among the Wea, Iowa, and Omaha Indians. The Synod of Philadelphia had united with that of Pittsburgh, in its control. It had about twenty missionaries under its care, and was well sustained by the contributions of the churches.

By the Assembly in session in Pittsburgh, in that year, a committee was appointed to confer with the Synod of Pittsburgh, on the transfer of the society to the care of the General Assembly; and to devise and digest a plan for conducting Foreign Missions. By a subsequent resolution, the committee was authorized, should the terms of the transfer be approved by them, "to ratify and confirm the same with the Synod, and report the same to the next General Assembly."

Under this commission, the committee proposed to the Synod, at its next stated meeting, certain "Terms of Agreement," in reference to the transfer, which were accepted and ratified by the Synod, and reported accordingly to the Assembly of 1836.

CHAPTER XXX.

DISCIPLINE ATTEMPTED.

The Act and Testimony proposed a resort to discipline—Duffield's case—His book examined and condemned—Proceedings against him—Dr. Beecher's accession to the Church—Opposition of Dr. J. L. Wilson—He tables charges—Dilatory course of Presbytery—Decisions in Presbytery and Synod—Appeal to the Assembly—Illinois College planned and organized at New Haven—The case of Edward Beecher, Sturdevant and Kirby.

THE signers of the Act and Testimony, therein covenanted with each other, respecting disseminators of doctrinal errors, to "make every lawful effort to subject all such persons, especially if they be ministers, to the just exercise of discipline, by the proper tribunal." In accordance with this announcement, several prosecutions took place, resulting in a demonstration of the futility of expecting to restore an extensively corrupted Church, by means of personal process against individuals. In every instance, the whole party at once made common cause with the accused. Every art of party management was brought into requisition, to confuse and embarrass the proceedings, to weary out the prosecution, to create side issues, and distract the public attention from the real questions; to prevent calm and candid investigation, and secure the immunity of the accused. And the success of these measures demonstrated, beyond question, that the signers of the Act and Testimony did not exaggerate the extent of the danger,—that the evil was already beyond correction by the ordinary remedies of the Constitution.

Already, before the Act and Testimony was written, the case of the Rev. George Duffield had been tried before the Presbytery of Carlisle. This gentleman published, in 1831, an octavo volume, of 613 pages, on "Spiritual Life, or Regeneration." The dedication tendered the work to the people of his charge, "as an atonement for occasional attempts, in the early periods of his ministry among them, to explain the great fact of a sinner's regeneration, by the aid of a philosophy, imbibed in his theological education, interwoven in many of his exhibitions of scriptural truth; but for years past repudiated, by their much-attached pastor." The philosophy and explanations thus repudiated, were those of the Westminster standards; as the author distinctly indicates in the course of his discussions.

It being a common fame that the book contained grave doctrinal errors, the Presbytery of Carlisle, in 1832, appointed a committee to examine it. This committee made report, at an adjourned meeting, held on the 27th and 28th of June, setting forth the errors of the book.

The errors enumerated were twelve in number, metaphysical and theological: 1. As to the nature of life; that it "consists in the regular series of relative, appropriate, characteristic, action, in an individual being."* 2. That the soul is produced *ex traduce*,† from the

* The quotations are from Duffield, as cited by the committee.

† By generation.

parents. 3. That the image of God in which man was created consists, principally, in his threefold life, vegetable, animal, and spiritual. 4. That Adam was related to his posterity, as parent, only. 5. That the death of infants is not penal. 6. That depravity consists, exclusively, in the acts and exercises of the will. 7. That infants have no moral character. 8. That the inability of sinners is wholly of the will. 9. That regeneration consists in a voluntary act of the will, under the influence of moral suasion, in which the soul is active, not passive. 10. That, by election, the Scriptures mean nothing else than the actual conversion of men to God. 11. The human nature of Christ possessed no personal, characteristic holiness, irrespective of and previous to his moral acts and exercises. 12. The author speaks unguardedly and erroneously on being filled with the Holy Spirit.—"We have seen already," he remarks, "that ideas of personal inhabitation, of infused grace, and of any mystic agency of the Spirit, form no part of the scriptural doctrine of his influence."

Of these opinions, the first was designed to constitute a psychological basis for the doctrinal scheme which follows. The enumeration, among doctrinal errors, of the traducean theory, as to the origin of the soul, was certainly an indiscretion; as that doctrine has been held, from the days of Tertullian and Augustine, by many of the ablest and most orthodox men who have blessed the Church. Says Turrettin, "not a few of the old divines believed it, and Augustine himself, more than once, seems to incline to it. And it is not to be questioned, that its admission relieves the subject of original sin of every difficulty."*

The Presbytery adopted the report, and warned all her ministers, elders, and people against the errors of the book. It, also, appointed Messrs. Williams and Wilson a committee, "to confer with Mr. Duffield, in a friendly manner, respecting the erroneous doctrines contained in his book."

Mr. Duffield had protested against the committee of examination, as unconstitutional. Upon the same ground, he refused to take any part in the discussion of the report. He and Mr. Dewitt complained to the Synod of Philadelphia, against these entire proceedings.

In Synod, it was decided, that as the principal complaint of Mr. Duffield, and that on which the other two rest, and from which they spring, is "that without the preferring of charges, citation, and other steps of judicial process, the Presbytery have in fact condemned him, as heretical," and the Synod are distinctly informed, that the Presbytery intend, as soon as practicable, to commence and issue such process, therefore,

"*Resolved*, That further progress in the present complaint is unnecessary, if not improper, until the Presbytery shall have brought the contemplated trial of Mr. Duffield to an issue; which they are hereby enjoined to do as soon as possible."

Accordingly, the Presbytery, on the 20th of October, appointed a committee, which, on the 28th of November, reported a list of charges, identical with those pre-

* Turrettin IX., xii. 6. My late friend and instructor, the Rev. Dr. James Wood, author of "Old and New Theology," firmly held the traducean view.

viously made against the book, except that the twelfth was omitted, and the eleventh combined with the seventh. The case came on for trial, on the 11th of April, 1833.

Thursday, Friday, Saturday, and the forenoon of Monday were expended by Mr. Duffield in pleas to the competence of the Presbytery, and of members of it, to the sufficiency of the charges, denying the existence of common fame, and so on. Particular emphasis was laid upon the fact that the charges did not write the name, "*heresy*," against the errors charged. Upon various points, he entered Protests, Complaints, and Appeals.

Presbytery, at length, proceeded to hear the charges and evidence, the prosecuting committee, and Mr. Duffield; whereupon, the vote was taken, and the charges were sustained, except the third and tenth, which were rejected.

It was then resolved that, "as to the counts, in which Mr. Duffield has been found guilty, Presbytery judge that Mr. Duffield's book, and sermons on Regeneration, do contain the specified errors, yet as Mr. Duffield alleges that Presbytery have misinterpreted some of his expressions, and says he does in fact, hold all the doctrines of our standards, and that he wishes to live in amity with his brethren, and labor without interference, for the glory of God and the salvation of souls, therefore,

"*Resolved*, That Presbytery, at present, do not censure him, any further than warn him to guard against such speculations as may impugn the doctrines of our Church; and that he study to maintain the unity of the Spirit, in the bonds of peace."

Against this decision, Mr. Duffield gave notice of an appeal to the General Assembly; which, however, he did not prosecute. Under the name of an appeal, however, he published an elaborate document, in which, taking up the charges, one by one, he tried to show that he had not maintained or propagated opinions or doctrines, at variance with the Confession of Faith.

When these proceedings came before the Synod of Philadelphia, in review, in October, 1833, action was postponed, in consequence of the sickness and absence of Mr. Duffield. The next year, it was taken up, and a minute adopted, censuring the leniency of the Presbytery. And so ended the case. Light has been recently shed upon it by the exposition made by Dr. Duffield, of the "Doctrines of the New School Presbyterians," in the Bibliotheca Sacra for July, 1863.* The reader who will compare the charges, of which the Doctor was convicted, with the article in that quarterly, will see that the doctrinal system, involved in those charges, is precisely that, in all its essential features, which he describes with approbation as the theology of the New School.

We have already seen something of the theological position and relations of Dr. Lyman Beecher. In 1832, upon the nomination of Arthur Tappan, Esq., as the condition of a gift of $25,000 to the Lane Seminary, he was chosen to the presidency of that institution; to which, none but ministers of the Presbyterian Church were eligible. Whilst he was holding this appointment in consideration, the Rev. James Weatherby, of Mississippi, visited New England, as delegate from the Gen-

* See, also, Princeton Review, 1867, p. 655.

eral Assembly to the General Association of Connecticut. Dr. Beecher sought an interview, in the course of which he informed Mr. Weatherby of the appointment, and expressed some doubt of being able to come up to the requirement as to Presbyterianism. Mr. Weatherby told him that any doubts on that subject admitted of easy solution. If he could, with a good conscience, answer affirmatively, the questions put to candidates for the ministry, he was a Presbyterian. Dr. Beecher, at once, brought a Confession, and placing it in the hands of Mr. Weatherby, requested him to propound the questions. This he did, and received affirmative answers, to all except the second, "Do you sincerely receive and adopt the Confession of Faith of this Church, as containing the system of doctrine taught in the Holy Scriptures?" The reply was, "Yes, but I will not say how much more it contains." Mr. Weatherby closed the book, saying that he was no Presbyterian. After some conversation on the subject, the process was, at the request of Dr. Beecher, repeated; but with the same result. Again the subject was discussed, Mr. Weatherby remarking that no such Yankee answer would do.—That it was idle for Dr. Beecher to pretend to be a Presbyterian. Finally, the Doctor proposed a third trial; when he passed successfully through the ordeal, giving the answer in simple affirmative.* He, soon after, wrote to the Third Presbytery of New York, declaring his affirmative answer to those questions,—was thereupon received as a member,—and, immediately, at

* MS. memorandum, from the late Mr. Weatherby, dated May 13, 1853. Mr. Weatherby stated these facts to the writer, and, by request, gave him a written note of them.

his own request, dismissed to join the Presbytery of Cincinnati.

Such was the début of this distinguished leader, in the Presbyterian Church. At the time of his arrival in Cincinnati, that Presbytery had been for some time suffering distraction, from the success of the policy of Dr. Peters, by which it was filling with New School men, and being pervaded with New School doctrines, measures, and policy. Dr. Beecher had been selected as the leader of this party, and was, at once, recognized in that office. "I have been chosen and come," said he to a distinguished gentleman, then connected with a literary institution in that region, "to make the West what New England is; and I can do it. I have pledge of the co-operation of such and such eminent men; and I want you to help me."

When he was admitted into the Presbytery of Cincinnati, upon dismission from the Third Presbytery of New York, Dr. J. L. Wilson offered a protest, which was refused a place on the record, on the ground that he was moderator, and not entitled to vote, and, therefore, had no right to protest.

A motion was, thereupon, made, for a committee to inquire as to a common fame charging the Doctor with doctrinal error. This motion was rejected. A similar motion was made, in April, 1833, postponed until the fall, and, then, indefinitely postponed. Against this conclusion, complaint was made to the Synod; which decided, that Presbytery could not be compelled to proceed, judicially, unless a responsible prosecutor appeared. Appeal was taken to the Assembly of 1834, which threw it out on technical grounds.

40

At length, in November, 1834, Dr. Wilson presented himself at the bar of Presbytery, and tabled charges against Dr. Beecher, under four general heads and numerous specifications. These exhibited the New School theories, as to man's native depravity, ability, and the work of the Holy Spirit in regeneration. They further charged the Doctor with teaching a doctrine of perfection, contrary to the standards,—with slander, in belying the whole Church of God, by representing these as being its accepted doctrines,—and with hypocrisy and dissimulation, in professing attachment to the Confession of Faith.

Upon the presentation of these charges, the Presbytery entered them on record, but postponed the consideration of the subject, till the next stated meeting,—from the 11th of November, 1834, till the 10th of April, 1835. At that time, it ordered the citation of the witnesses, warned the prosecutor, solemnly constituted as a judicial tribunal of the Lord Jesus Christ; and then—adjourned for two months, till the 9th of June! At the June meeting, the case was, at length, taken up and issued. The discussion was protracted through more than a week, and resulted in the acquittal of the accused, and, a reference to the Synod of Cincinnati, to decide what censure should be inflicted on the prosecutor. Against this decision, Dr. Wilson took an appeal.

Before the Synod, such explanations and statements were made by Dr. Beecher as satisfied the majority of that body. It however decided, that the appeal be sustained; 1st. Because there was no reason to censure Dr. Wilson. 2d. "Because, although the charges of slander and hypocrisy are not proved; and although Synod see nothing in his views, as explained by himself to justify any suspicion of unsoundness in the faith; yet, on the subject of the depraved nature of man, and total depravity, and the work of the Holy Spirit in effectual calling, and the subject of ability, they are of the opinion that Dr. Beecher has indulged a disposition to philosophize, instead of exhibiting, in simplicity and plainness, the doctrines as taught in the Scriptures; and has employed terms and phrases, and modes of illustration, calculated to convey ideas inconsistent with the Word of God, and our Confession of Faith; and that he ought to be, and hereby is, admonished to be more guarded in the future."

Dr. Beecher declared his ready acquiescence in this decision of the Synod; which, thereupon, expressed its satisfaction, and advised him to publish, "at as early a day as possible, in pamphlet form, a concise statement of the argument and design of his sermon on native ability, and of his views of total depravity, original sin, and regeneration, agreeably to his declarations and explanations, made before Synod."

Dr. Wilson appealed to the Assembly. When, however, the case came before that body, in 1836, he was induced by the advice of brethren, to waive the prosecution; as Barnes' case was then pending, the decision upon which, it was hoped, would determine the questions involved in this.

In response to the advice of Synod, Dr. Beecher published,—not a concise pamphlet statement, as recommended,—but a volume of "Views on Theology," a work comparatively orthodox.

That Dr. Beecher had held and taught the leading points of New School theology, is unquestionable. And, that there is an irreconcilable difference between his various statements on the subject, is equally certain,—a difference to be accounted for, perhaps, to a great extent, by the idiosyncrasies of an intellect, intensely active, but capricious, illogical, and, seemingly, almost devoid of memory.

About the time of Dr. Beecher's removal to Ohio, there existed in Yale Seminary an association of young men whose attention was turned to the West, with a view to the same object which brought him to Cincinnati. They originated the plan of Illinois College, and organized themselves into a board of trustees, before they had ever seen Illinois. As fast as the associates entered the ministry, they removed to that State, united with the Presbyterian Church, and located around the institution, which with the Rev. Edward Beecher, late a tutor in Yale, at its head, they destined to be the Yale of the West. Dr. Taylor and the other divines of New Haven were the counselors of the enterprise; the American Education and Home Missionary Societies afforded all the requisite means; and the wealth of New England was freely bestowed upon an enterprise so full of promise.

In 1833, the Rev. Wm. J. Fraser tabled charges, before the Presbytery of Illinois, against President Beecher, and the Rev. Professors J. M. Sturdevant, and William Kirby, for teaching erroneous doctrines. The witnesses relied upon were mostly students of the college. After considerable progress had been made, in taking testimony, the accused proposed, as a substitute for all testimony, a statement of their faith, in writing. This the prosecutor accepted. It was as follows :—

"We believe and teach, that the sinner has power to make himself a new heart, without the influence of the Holy Spirit; but, that such is his voluntary aversion to his duty, that he never will do it, without those influences; and that, of course, he is dependent on them for salvation.

"That the nature of sin is such, that no man can become a sinner, except by his own act; and yet, that all men sin, in all their moral conduct, from the commencement of their moral agency; and that the reason of this fact is to be found in the original fall of the human race.

"We believe and teach, that God, foreseeing from all eternity that such would be the character and condition of men, determined to interpose, for the salvation of a certain part of the human race, and to make them willing to do their duty; not from any foreseen good in them, as the exciting cause of his conduct, but from a regard to his own glory and the general good. That those whom he does not thus interpose to save, are left to deserved ruin, as the natural result and just punishment of their own voluntary depravity; but we do believe, that if men were the subjects of an absolute inability to obey the law of God, or accept the offers of the gospel, such that nothing but the influences of the Spirit of God could give them ability, it would then be tyrannical in God, to withhold from a certain portion of the human race those influences, and yet damn them to all eternity, for not obeying his law, or accepting his gospel.

E. BEECHER,
J. M. STURDEVANT,
WM. KIRBY."

Upon this profession of faith, the Presbytery, after protracted discussion, decided that "The accused brethren do not teach doctrines, materially or essentially, at variance with the standards of the Presbyterian Church and the Word of God." Mr. Fraser appealed to the Synod. But he was induced to drop it, in the expectation that the other cases then pending would lead to a settlement by the Assembly, of the questions involved.

CHAPTER XXXI.

BARNES' SECOND TRIAL.

Charges entered before the Assembly's Presbytery—The charges—Action of Presbytery—Jurisdiction of Synod denied—Action of the Synod, and suspension of Mr. Barnes—The principle of his defence—His explanations—New School identified with him—The decision—Protests, and Reply—It attested Mr. Barnes' orthodoxy—The evidence—Assembly's professed devotion to the Confession—Old School distrust—Parody on the New England Primer.

THE case toward which all eyes now turned, and on the decision of which all the interests of orthodoxy seemed, for the time, to hang suspended, was the second trial of Mr. Barnes. The prosecutor was the Rev. Dr. George Junkin. The charges were based upon the doctrines contained in Barnes' Notes on the Romans, which had just issued from the press. They were entered before the Assembly's Second Presbytery, on the 23d of March, 1835; and the prosecutor entertained the hope and expectation that the trial would be issued, with a reasonable promptitude, so as to enable him to carry the case at once to the Assembly of 1835; and thus secure a decision of the vital questions involved, with as little delay and consequent agitation of the Church as possible. Such, however, was not the policy of Mr. Barnes and the Presbytery. From the entering of the charges, until the 30th of June, more than three months, the time was consumed by the Presbytery in evasive measures, designed to avoid altogether a trial of the case. At length, when, apparently, every such resource had failed, the latter date was set for the trial. At the appointed time, the Presbytery met. The parties were present and ready to proceed. But a new evasion had been discovered. The charges were in the following terms:—

"The Rev. Albert Barnes is hereby charged with maintaining the following doctrines, contrary to the standards of the Presbyterian Church. 1. That sin consists in voluntary action. 2. That Adam, (before and after his fall,) was ignorant of his moral relations to such a degree, that he did not know the consequences of his sin would or should reach any further, than to natural death. 3. That unregenerate men are able to keep the commandments, and convert themselves to God. 4. That faith is an act of the mind and not a principle, and is itself imputed for righteousness.

"Mr. Barnes is also charged with denying the following doctrines, which are taught in the standards of the Church, viz.: 5. That God entered into covenant with Adam, constituting him a federal or covenant head, and representative to all his natural descendants. 6. That the first sin of Adam is imputed to his posterity. 7. That mankind are guilty, *i. e.*, liable to punishment on account of the sin of Adam. 8. That Christ suffered the proper penalty of the law, as the vicarious substitute of his people, and thus took away legally their sins, and purchased pardon. 9. That the righteousness, *i. e.*, the active obedience of Christ to the law, is imputed to his people for their justification; so that they are righteous in the eye of the law, and therefore justified. 10. Mr. Barnes also teaches, in opposition to the standards, that justification is simply pardon."

In all this the word, heresy, is not to be found. Presbytery, therefore, after deliberation, assumed that no offence was charged, in the accusation, as it stood; and resolved to allow the prosecutor to withdraw his charges, for the purposes of emendation, or, otherwise, Presbytery would not proceed to the trial. This Dr. Junkin refused to do; and was about to retire; when further reflection convinced the Presbytery that it would be utterly impossible to defend the position which it had taken. The action was reconsidered, and Dr. Junkin allowed to proceed. The trial lasted for a week, and resulted, according to expectation, in the acquittal of Mr. Barnes; only the Rev. Mr. (now Dr.) Boardman, and Elders Bradford and Stillè voting in the negative.

Dr. Junkin now proposed to appeal directly to the General Assembly. To this, however, Mr. Barnes strongly objected. Dr. Junkin, therefore, waived this intention, and inquired whether the appeal could go to the Synod of Delaware,—would it ever meet again? To this inquiry several voices responded,—"No, it can't meet,—Its time of meeting is after the time to which the Synod of Philadelphia stands adjourned; and, of course, it cannot meet." "Then," said the Dr., "the appeal must be to the Synod of Philadelphia." In this view, all tacitly concurred; and to that Synod, the appeal was taken.

The Synod met, in York, on Wednesday, the 28th of October. On Thursday, the appeal of Dr. Junkin was reported, and the Synod resolved to issue it. The next morning, Dr. Ely presented a minute, which had been adopted by the Assembly's Presbytery, the day before:—

"Whereas, the General Assembly of our Church dissolved the Synod of Delaware, *at and after* the meeting of the Synod of Philadelphia, which occurred yesterday; whereas, the said Assembly passed no order for the transfer of the books, minutes, and unfinished business of the Synod of Delaware and of the Presbyteries then belonging to the same, to any other Synod or judicatory; and whereas, it is utterly inconsistent with reason and the excellent standards of our Church, that any Presbytery should be amenable to more than one Synod, at the same time, therefore, resolved, That the Presbytery will, and hereby does decline to submit its books, records, and proceedings, prior to this date, to the review and control of the Synod of Philadelphia, until the General Assembly shall take some order on the subject."

Rev. Dr. John Breckinridge asked Dr. Ely if he did not draft the minute of the Assembly, and suggest the plan therein proposed; and now, if there was a trap in it, was it not strange that he, the author of it, should plead it against the Synod?

Dr. Ely replied that he did draft the original minute; but the Assembly did not order the Presbytery to put the records into the hands of this Synod. He was thankful that a slip had been permitted in the legislation. Dr. Miller had amended his minute; and thus "in the providence of God, they had been permitted, in their very anxiety to secure their end, to do that which protects the Assembly's Second Presbytery in their rights."

The use here made of Dr. Miller's amendment, was very extraordinary. It must be admitted that the amendment,—taken by itself, without respect to the circumstances, and the unquestionable design of the Assembly,—did give some color of ground for the position now taken by Dr. Ely and the Presbytery. It was, however, entirely neutralized by the well-understood and unquestioned design of the Assembly,—a design invested with all the sacredness of a solemn covenant of peace. The interpretation now adopted was, further, forbidden by the anomalous and unconstitutional attitude, in which it would have placed the Presbyteries concerned, subject to no synodical supervision, whatever, for the year which was now closed. In fact, that interpretation seems to have been a mere afterthought, which occurred to some one, a day or two before it was plead at the bar of Synod.

The attitude assumed by the Presbytery was, the more extraordinary, as Mr. Barnes himself did not pretend to deny the jurisdiction of Synod; professed to be ready for the trial of the appeal; and yet sheltered himself behind this action of his Presbytery, and refused to plead, unless the official records of the Presbytery were obtained; although, he was well aware that authentic copies were before the Synod.

The attitude of the Presbytery and of Mr. Barnes was not permitted to arrest the proceedings, in the Synod. Dr. Junkin produced and authenticated a copy of all the evidence and of the judgment of Presbytery. The Synod, thereupon, proceeded to try the appeal, notwithstanding the refusal of Mr. Barnes to plead. Five days were spent in the hearing, when the vote was taken, the appeal sustained, and Mr. Barnes found guilty of errors, some of them fundamental, and all contrary the doctrines of the standards and Word of God. He was suspended from the ministry, " until he shall retract the errors hereby condemned, and give satisfactory evidence of repentance."

Against this decision, Mr. Barnes took an appeal to the General Assembly. It came up early in the sessions of the Assembly of 1836. Constitutionally, this appeal could not lie; as Mr. Barnes had not submitted to trial. But this was not regarded. The case occupied the most of nine days of the sessions. The general principle on which Mr. Barnes based his vindication, is thus stated, in his published " Defence."—

" Of the Confession of Faith of the Westminster Assembly, I may be allowed to say, that when I expressed my assent to it, as 'a system of doctrines,' I did it cordially; and that I have never had occasion to regret the act. I then regarded it, as I do now, and ever have done, as the best summary of the doctrines of the Bible which I have seen. . . . . The *system of truth* contained there, as distinguished from all other systems,—the Socinian, the Pelagian, the Arian, the Arminian, etc., has appeared to me the true system; and without hesitation or fluctuation, I have received it. I have not forgotten, however, that nearly two hundred years have elapsed, since it was formed; that language often varies its meaning; and that views of philosophy, which insensibly insinuate themselves into theology, seldom continue the same two hundred years. I have thought that there was perhaps, somewhat too much harshness and severity of language in the general cast of the Confession; and that a few expressions do not convey, without much labored exposition, the meaning of the Scriptures. To a few of those expressions, small in number, and not affecting the *system* as a system, I have always taken the exceptions which others have been allowed to do."*

In the course of the proceedings, on the appeal, there appeared, at one time, to be a prospect of amicable adjustment of the whole matter. So ample seemed the explanations of Mr. Barnes; so full the retractions which he was understood to make, and so hearty apparently, his acceptance of the teachings of the Confession, on the questions at issue, that Dr. Junkin was induced, to say to the Assembly,—"If the concessions which we heard yesterday can be put in a form that is satisfactory, I shall be willing to take a course that will save the time of this Assembly." Had Mr. Barnes been willing to put upon record the acknowledgments which he had made, on the floor, the case would there have ended, and the peace and unity of the Church might possibly have been preserved. This fair prospect was, however, quickly closed, by the announcement of Mr. Barnes that he had not retracted anything; and that he never would.

In the discussion which followed the hearing of the parties, the attitude assumed by the New School leaders was as arbitrary and uncompromising as was that of Mr. Barnes. While some of the members affected to see no irreconcilable difference between the sentiments of Mr. Barnes and the doctrines of the standards, others recog-

* Barnes' Defence, p. 111.

nized and openly gloried in the difference, only complaining that Mr. Barnes was *too orthodox*. The body of the New School made Mr. Barnes' case their own, and avowed that with him they must stand or fall. Dr. Peters, their unquestioned leader, took the position that Mr. Barnes was not merely to be tolerated, but entitled to all confidence and honor. Dr. Skinner avowed that he was himself on trial, in the person of Mr. Barnes, and was unwilling that "the slightest censure" should be inflicted on him. And, said Dr. Peters,—"I honor the design of preparing a doctrinal book that shall be divested of technical language and hard names; and I not only adhere to the doctrines, but for the most part, to the very language of Mr. Barnes' book."* In his estimation, not Mr. Barnes, but Dr. Junkin, if any one, must be held dependent upon the toleration of his brethren; since he denied the doctrine of natural ability.†

On the final question, the appeal was sustained, by a vote of 134 to 96; six declining to vote; the Synod of Philadelphia being, of course, out of the house. The suspension of Mr. Barnes was then reversed, by a vote of 145 to 78; eleven declining to vote.

Dr. Miller then offered a resolution pronouncing the judgment of the Assembly, that some of Mr. Barnes' published opinions are materially at variance with the Confession of Faith and the Bible, "especially with regard to original sin, the relation of man to Adam, and justification by faith in the atoning sacrifice and righteousness of the Redeemer;" censuring the manner in

* Quoted in his anonymous Plea for Voluntary Societies, p. 143.

† Ibid. p. 141.

which he had controverted the language and doctrines of the Confession; and admonishing him to review his work, on the Romans, and to rectify its objectionable statements; and "to be more careful, in time to come, to study the purity and peace of the Church."

This resolution was rejected by a vote of 109 to 122; three declining to vote.

Two protests were entered, against the decisions of the Assembly, in Mr. Barnes' case. One of these was signed by one hundred and one members, and the other, by sixteen; all of whom, but two were signers of the first. To these protests, a reply was adopted, which was, perhaps, the most extraordinary feature of the whole case. It was reported by a committee consisting of the Rev. Drs. Skinner and Allen, and the Rev. Mr. Brainard. Dr. Beecher was understood to have had a principal hand in its preparation. Mr. Duffield seconded Dr. Skinner's motion for its adoption; and it would seem to have received the unanimous vote of the New School majority of the Assembly. In this paper, the Assembly declared that the phraseology of Mr. Barnes had not been always sufficiently guarded, but that, even in the first edition of his Notes on the Romans, "the language is, without violence reconcilable with an interpretation conformable to our standards;" much more, therefore, the revised edition, in the light of "all his disclaimers before the Assembly, and all his definite and unequivocal declarations of the true intent and meaning of his words, in the first edition."

To substantiate this position the reply proceeded to give "a careful analysis of the real meaning of Mr. Barnes, under each charge, as ascertained by the language of his book and the revisions, disclaimers, explanations and declarations which he had made." For example, it asserts that "Mr. Barnes nowhere denies, much less, 'sneers' at, the idea that Adam was the covenant and federal head of his posterity. On the contrary, though he employs not these terms, he does, in other language, teach the same truths which are taught by the phraseology."

But Dr. Junkin's charge was, that Mr. Barnes denied Adam to be the federal head *and representative* of his natural posterity; and, among the proofs cited from the book, were the following:—"Nothing is said here, [Romans v. 19] of the doctrine of representation. It is not affirmed that Adam was the representative of his race, nor is that language used in regard to him in the Bible. (2.) Nothing is said of a covenant with him. Nowhere in the Scriptures is the term *covenant* applied to any transaction with Adam. (3.) All that is established, here, is the simple *fact*, that Adam sinned, and that this made it certain that all his posterity would be sinners. Beyond this, the language of the apostle does not go; and all else that has been said of this is the result of mere philosophical speculation. . . . . Various attempts have been made to explain this. The most common has been, that Adam was the representative of the race; that he was a covenant head, and that his sin was *imputed* to his posterity, and that they were held liable to punishment for it, as if they had committed it themselves. But, to this, there are great and insuperable objections. (1.) There is not one word of it in the Bible. Neither the terms, representative, covenant, nor, impute, are *ever* applied to the transaction, in the sacred

Scriptures. (2.) It is a mere philosophical theory; an introduction of a speculation into theology, with an attempt to explain what the Bible has left unexplained."* Again:—"A comparison is also instituted between Adam and Christ, in 1 Cor. xv. 22, 45. The reason is, not that Adam was the representative or federal head of the race; about which the apostle says nothing, and which is not even implied, but that he was the first of the race; he was the fountain; the head, the father; and the consequences of that first act introducing sin into the world, could be seen everywhere. The words *representative*, and *federal head*, are never applied to Adam, in the Bible. The reason is, that the word *representative* implies an idea which could not have existed in the case,—*the consent of those who are represented.* Besides, the Bible does not teach that they acted in him, or by him; or that he acted *for* them. No passage has ever yet been found that stated this doctrine."†

On Romans v. 12, he says:—Paul "was inquiring into the cause why death was in the world; and it would not account *for that* to say that all sinned *in* Adam. It would require an *additional* statement to see how that could be a cause. The expression 'in whom all have sinned' conveys no intelligible idea. As men had no existence then, in any sense, they could not then sin. What idea is conveyed to men of common understanding, by the expression, 'they sinned in him'?" This looks not unlike a sneer.

It was in the presence of such language as this, cited by Dr. Junkin, from Mr. Barnes, that the majority of the Assembly entered it upon record, that he "nowhere

* Barnes on the Romans, 1st edition, p. 128. † Ibid., p. 120.

denies, much less sneers at, the idea that Adam was the covenant and federal-head of his posterity;" that in fact, he teaches the same truths, in other language! How were the prosecutor and the Church to understand this assertion, so plainly contrary to truth, and to the evidence staring them in the face?

As remarkable as the assertion of Mr. Barnes' orthodoxy, was the statement of the reply, as to the doctrinal views of those who were pronouncing his acquittal. "So far," said they, "is the Assembly from countenancing the errors alleged in the charges of Dr. Junkin, that they do, cordially, and *ex animo** adopt the Confession of our Church, on the points of doctrine in question, according to the obvious and most prevalent interpretation; and do regard it, as a whole, as the best epitome of the doctrines of the Bible ever formed. And this Assembly disavows any desire, and would deprecate any attempt to change the phraseology of our standards, and would disapprove any language of light estimation applied to them; believing that no denomination can prosper whose members permit themselves to speak slightly of its formularies of doctrine;—and are ready to unite with their brethren in contending earnestly for the faith of our standards."

What meant this remarkable statement? Had Drs. Skinner, Duffield, and their associates been suddenly converted into the soundest of Old School men? Did the phrase—"the obvious and most prevalent interpretation,"—contain a hidden meaning? Or, must the Old School conclude that the leaders of the Assembly began to find, or to fear, that they were drawing too

* From the heart.

heavily upon the good nature of their Moderate allies,—that the avowals, which had been so boldly made, in the discussion of Barnes' case, were in danger of alienating them, and of opening the eyes of the people? Was it thus, that a necessity arose for such a testimony of reverence for the Confession? and was that testimony to be understood, not as expressing the private sentiments of individual leaders of the party, but what they knew to be those of "the Assembly,"—that is, of the majority of the members, all parties included? Such were the questions which forced themselves into notice, in view of all the facts connected with the case.

Whatever its meaning,—so earnest a protestation of orthodoxy, coming from such a quarter, and in such circumstances,—entirely failed to conciliate the confidence, or quiet the alarms of the minority. They read this declaration, in immediate connection with the incredible assertion that Mr. Barnes' contradictions were in perfect harmony with the doctrines of the standards. They could not but reflect upon the avowals of indifference to the authority of the Confession, and rejection of its teachings, which they had heard so freely uttered, during the discussion of the appeal. They remembered the written avowals of Messrs. Edward Beecher, Sturdevant, and Kirby, when on trial, and the finding of their Presbytery thereupon. They remembered the writings of Beman and Cox and Duffield, and many others. In the light of such facts and recollections it was impossible for them to believe that the history of a quarter of a century of controversy and rebuke, in defence of the doctrines of the gospel, was all an unreal figment of the imagination, a troubled dream. Nothing in the whole history so shocked the conscience of the Church, or so prepared it for the action of 1837, as did this attempt to cover the doctrinal derelictions of Mr. Barnes and the party.

The real sentiments of this Assembly were more truly illustrated by an anecdote which was related by Mr. Finney, when, subsequently, his cordial relations with the New School had been terminated, by his advance to perfectionism. Whilst, in the progress of the trial, the subject of original sin was under discussion, one of the New School doctors penciled a couplet on a card. It was passed, in succession, to three others, each of whom added a line; so that, when the circle was completed, it read thus:—

"In Adam's fall, We sinned all.
In Abel's murder, We sinned furder.
In Tubal Cain, We sinned again.
In Doctor Green, Our sin is seen."

Mr. Finney states that "the above occurrence was a matter of common talk, among the New School members of the Assembly, at the time; and not an individual, so far as was heard, expressed his disapproval of it."

Whatever else, however, was still doubtful, one thing was now apparent. Discipline, as a means of vindicating the doctrines of the standards, against the incoming flood of error, had been fully tried, and utterly failed. The disease was too inveterate and pervasive for that remedy.

CHAPTER XXXII.

THE ASSEMBLY OF 1836.

New School majority—Report respecting the Western Foreign Missionary Society—Dr. Skinner's resolution—Letters from one of the Secretaries of A. B. C. F. M—Discussion in the Assembly—The Society rejected—Attempts to revolutionize the Boards of Missions and Education—Board of Education's report mutilated—Appeals of the elective affinity and Wilmington Presbyteries—Newark Church—McKim's case—The Presbyteries restored—Evening conferences of the two parties.

We have seen the action of the Assembly of 1836, in the case of Mr. Barnes. When that body met, the election of Dr. Witherspoon, as Moderator, over Dr. Peters, the New School nominee, seemed to indicate the presence of an Old School majority. But the arrival of a steamer, crowded with commissioners from Illinois and Missouri, turned the scale, and gave the New School party the absolute control. In fact, the majority of the body was the offspring of the Plan of Union, and the American Home-Missionary Society. Of this, the vote on the acquittal of Mr. Barnes was an illustration. Of the majority on that vote, sixty-three were from Western New York and the Western Reserve, and the larger part of the rest were the employés and friends of the Home Society, in Illinois, Missouri, and elsewhere.

Beside the case of Mr. Barnes, the most important

business that came before the Assembly, was the report of the committee appointed to negotiate the transfer of the Western Foreign Missionary Society. The committee reported that they had proposed certain terms of agreement, to the Synod of Pittsburgh, which had been duly ratified by that body. These terms provided that "the General Assembly will assume the supervision and control of the Western Foreign Missionary Society, from and after the next annual meeting of said Assembly, and will thereafter superintend and conduct, by its own proper authority, the work of Foreign Missions of the Presbyterian Church, by a Board especially appointed for that purpose, and directly amenable to said Assembly. And the Synod of Pittsburgh does hereby transfer to that body, all its supervision and control over the missions and operations of the Western Foreign Society, from and after the adoption of this minute; and authorizes and directs said Society to perform every act necessary to complete said transfer, when the Assembly shall have appointed its Board;—it being expressly understood that the said Assembly will never hereafter alienate or transfer to any other judicatory or Board whatever, the direct supervision and management of the said missions, or those which may hereafter be established by the Board of the General Assembly."

The terms of agreement further embodied a plan of organization for the Board of Foreign Missions of the Assembly.

After some discussion, this report was referred to a committee of five, with instruction "to review the whole case, and present it for the consideration of the Assembly."

In the report of this committee, after a review of the history, they state it, as the conclusion, from the whole, that "the Assembly have entered into a solemn compact with the Synod of Pittsburgh, and that there remains but one righteous course to pursue; which is, to adopt the report of the committee appointed last year, and to appoint a foreign missionary Board. To pause now, or to annul the doings of the last Assembly, in this matter, would be obviously a violation of contract,—a breach of trust,—and a departure from that good faith, which should be sacredly kept between man and man, and especially between Christian societies,—conduct which would be utterly unworthy of this venerable body, and highly injurious to the Western Foreign Missionary Society."

As a minority of the committee, the Rev. Dr. Skinner made a counter report, that,—"Whereas, the American Board of Commissioners for Foreign Missions has been connected with the Presbyterian Church from the year of its incorporation, by the very elements of its existence;—and, whereas, at the present time, the majority of the whole of that Board are Presbyterians; and whereas it is undesirable, in conducting the work of foreign missions, that there should be any collision at home or abroad; therefore,

"Resolved, That it is inexpedient that the Assembly should organize a separate foreign missionary institution."

Not only was this proposition strongly in the interest of the American Board. The argument came from the office in Boston. Pending the negotiations with the Synod of Pittsburgh, by the Assembly's committee, there issued from the press a twelvemo pamphlet of 24 pages, entitled, "Letters on the Constitution of the American Board of Commissioners for Foreign Missions. Addressed to the Rev. Dr. Abeel, of the Reformed Dutch Church, by one of the Secretaries of the Board." Of these letters, Dr. Rufus Anderson was the writer. They proposed to give an exposition of the title of that Board to the confidence and support of the Presbyterian, Congregational, and Reformed Dutch Churches.

"The American Board," says the writer, "had an ecclesiastical origin, and had its first existence, as did the foreign missionary enterprise, in this country, among the Congregational churches of New England. . . . . Its patrons, however, have never been confined to that denomination, nor to New England; although the United Foreign Missionary Society was formed with express reference to the Presbyterian, Reformed Dutch and Associate Reformed Churches, as early as the year 1818. This society was amalgamated with the Board, in the year 1826, at its own request. In the same year, according to the terms agreed upon for the amalgamation, the General Assembly of the Presbyterian Church and the General Synod of the Reformed Dutch Church gave the Board their official sanction and recommendation. In 1831, the General Assembly appointed commissioners to confer with the Board, relative to the measures best adapted to enlist the energies of the Presbyterian Church more extensively in the cause of missions to the heathen; who met and conferred with the Board, in the autumn of the same year. These commissioners reported to the General Assembly, that in their judgment, the Board was a national institution, belonging as much to one section of the country as to another;" etc. After recapitulating the argument of that committee against the erection of any other missionary organization; and in favor of united and vigorous support of the Board; and mentioning a similar report made to the Reformed Dutch Church, the Secretary proceeds:—

"Such, in brief, is the manner in which the Board has acquired its *official relations* to the *general ecclesiastical bodies* of the Presbyterian, Reformed Dutch and Congregational Churches." That is to say,—by an amalgamation, which both the General Assembly and the Reformed Dutch Synod expressly refused to approve, and the terms of which they formally rejected; although the Secretary intimates that they were adopted and fulfilled; and by a report, prepared jointly by the Assembly's committee and the Secretaries of the Board, the arguments and conclusions of which the Assembly, also, refused to sanction; a fact which the Secretary, for some reason, neglects to mention.

The Secretary then proceeds to the statement to which Dr. Skinner was indebted for his preamble:—"There is, however, another, and highly important view of its relations to these churches. The Board has been connected with the Presbyterian Church, from the year of its incorporation, *by the very elements of its existence.* The members originally incorporated were in number eleven. These, immediately after receiving the act of incorporation, elected thirteen others, eight of whom were from among the most distinguished members of the Presbyterian Church. The Board now became, by its very nature, connected with the Presbyterian Church. . . . . Now, the Board is to be regarded as being, in fact and in effect, what its corporate members are. Of these, there are eighty-three; and forty-four are Presbyterians, thirty-one are Congregationalists, and seven belong to the Reformed Dutch Church."

The reader understands that, in the selection of these numerous Presbyterian members of the Board, the Church was not consulted; that many of them were Presbyterian only in name; and that they were scattered from New England to Georgia, in accordance with a policy admirably adapted to secure the confidence and contributions of the people; but which did not even purport to give the organized Church any authority or voice, even, in the management of her missions; whilst the members, thus accredited to her, and thus scattered abroad, were certain never to meet with the Board in such numbers as to supersede or endanger the control exercised by the Congregational members, who were clustered around the seat of operations, in Boston. The subsequent experience of our New School and Reformed Dutch brethren has shed light on this subject.

The Letters of the Secretary were published in the winter of 1835–6, and the time and circumstances, the diligence with which they were circulated, and the coldness which the officers of the Western Society realized from those of the American Board, demonstrated that the Western movement was looked upon with displeasure and apprehension, in the office at Boston; and that the American Board still clung to the hope of acquiring the undivided control of the missions of the Presbyterian Church.

On the discussion of the subject in the Assembly, the entrance of the Church, in her organized capacity, upon the work of Foreign Missions was opposed, upon various grounds. It was denied that the Assembly had authority to organize a Board, or engage in this work. It has never received any such authority from the Presbyteries. The commission to send the gospel to every creature belongs to the Church universal, which is an unorganized body, and is, therefore, of no avail, as proof of the authority or duty of the Assembly, in the case. True, the Constitution does state that the General Assembly may, "of its own knowledge, send missions to any part, to plant churches, or supply vacancies."* But, "Here, there is no provision for the appointment of a permanent Board, for this purpose. The missions must be sent, *by the Assembly, of their own knowledge.* This can be done only while the Assembly is in session.. To direct a permanent Board to act with the *knowledge, as well as power* of the Assembly, would be for the Assembly to perpetuate itself, after its own dissolution; which is absurd. And the Assembly cannot delegate the power of acting, of their own knowledge, to any Board. It is impossible."†

The organizing of a Foreign Board was opposed, because the gospel is not sectarian, and should not be so exhibited to the heathen; and because two organizations operating in the same cause would be sure to come into collision.

The obligation to accept the Western Society was denied, upon the ground that the last Assembly had

* Form of Government, ch. xviii.

† Peters' Plea for Voluntary Societies, p. 80.

not the power to enter into a contract binding its successor; and should not have done it, if it had possessed the power. Yet, at the same time, it was asserted by the speaker, Dr. Peters, that the Assembly was bound to the American Board, by the treaty of amalgamation of 1826. A rejected treaty was held strong enough to bind the Assembly to abstain from the missionary work. But a treaty actually consummated was of no force, since it required the Church to engage in that work.

Special objection was urged against the proviso contained in the terms, prohibiting the alienation of the missions,—a condition suggested by the past impressive experience of the Synod of Pittsburgh and its missions.

The arguments of the nationality, the catholicity, and the Presbyterianism of the American Board, as embodied in the Letters of Dr. Anderson, were all exhausted, in demonstration that it, and it only should receive the confidence and support of the Presbyterian Church.

On the other hand, the right and duty of the organized Church to take charge of this great business,—the anxious hope with which many of her people were looking to her to enter upon it,—and the duty of fidelity to the obligations of covenant made with the Synod of Pittsburgh, were urged in vain.

The question was called, and, by a vote of 110 to 106, the Assembly refused to fulfill the covenant, or enter upon the work. A protest against this decision, penned by Dr. Miller and signed by eighty-two members of the Assembly, was entered, with a reply, drafted by Dr. Peters.

Coincident with the rejection of the Western Foreign

Missionary Society, was an attempt to revolutionize the Boards of Domestic Missions and Education. For the former Board, a ticket was nominated, composed of such names as Dr. Skinner, and Messrs. Duffield, Patterson, Eddy, and Adair; men than whom there were none more hostile to the institutions of the Church, or more thoroughly devoted to the Congregational Societies. This attempt was justified by Dr. Peters, upon the ground that there should be but one such institution. The attempt only lacked a few votes of succeeding. It failed through the defection of some of the more moderate men of the party, who revolted at the injustice and dishonor of the course pursued.

In the Board of Education a similar change was attempted, by secret treachery. It was the rule of the Assembly, that all nominations should be made in open Assembly, and posted at the door, a certain time before the election. The regular nominations had been made, and no opposition ticket presented. But when the time of election drew near, Mr. Peabody, the Secretary of the Board, was accosted by a gentleman, who informed him, that a secret ticket would be run, with the expectation of taking the friends of the Board by surprise, and so carrying the election. Mr. Peabody at once took such measures as time permitted, to secure a full vote of the friends of the Board. The secret ticket received so large a vote, that the Board barely escaped. How such measures were planned and arranged, will appear below.

In another form, the hostility of the majority of the Assembly, to the Board, and to the distinctive interests of the Church, was strikingly evinced. Dr. William Patton, the General Agent of the so-called Presbyterian Education Society, and the friends of that institution, had been in the habit of insisting upon the unnecessary expenses and other evils resulting from the operation of two similar institutions, in the same field. They, also, took pains to produce the impression that the Society was anxious to obviate the difficulty, by some plan of union with the Board; but, that the latter was so filled with the spirit of a narrow sectarianism, as to discourage all overtures toward that end. Dr. Patton, had, in fact, repeatedly introduced the subject, in personal interviews with officers of the Board. At length Dr. Breckinridge, the Secretary, with the informal sanction of the Board, addressed a letter to Dr. Patton, in which he referred to these conversations, and disavowed for himself and the Board any power to act definitely on the subject. He then proceeded to state the terms on which he had no doubt the Board would cordially recommend, and the Assembly sanction, a union. These were,—ecclesiastical supervision; the abandonment of the system of loans to beneficiaries, secured by bonds, for the return of the money advanced to them; and the sustaining of the doctrines and standards of our Church. In the annual report of the Board, a full account, of this whole matter was embodied, including Dr. Breckinridge's letter to Dr. Patton. The account closed by stating that this letter "was written in October last, and although the Corresponding Secretary of the Presbyterian Education Society has been since waited on and an answer requested, none has yet been received. If, therefore, the rival action of the two Boards produces evil consequences, to our Church, we trust our Board is not to be held responsible."

It was impossible for the Presbyterian Society to have replied to Dr. Breckinridge's letter, without demonstrating the anti-Presbyterian spirit which controlled it, and the falsehood of its Presbyterian name. There was, therefore, no reply. And in the same spirit, the Assembly ordered this whole statement to be erased from the Report of the Board!

Another subject of consideration and action was the case of the Presbytery of Wilmington, and the elective affinity Presbytery of Philadelphia. These bodies had been dissolved, by the Synod of Philadelphia. This action was in precise accordance with the express understanding had, and the instructions embodied in Dr. Ely's compromise resolution, for dissolving the Synod of Delaware; by means of which, the Assembly of 1835 had been cajoled into waiving the decisive measures, which it was about to take, respecting those Presbyteries. It was, furthermore, a step not only justified by the contumacy of those Presbyteries, in refusing to produce their records, upon the call of Synod, but imperatively demanded, in order to the peace of the Churches. From its origin, as we have already seen, the elective affinity Presbytery had maintained its growth, by intruding into the other Presbyteries, amidst whom it was planted, invading and dividing their churches, and creating constant distraction and disorder.

The Presbytery of Wilmington, although possessed of geographical boundaries, had entered upon a similar course of action. On this subject, two complaints came before the Synod, in the fall of 1835; one from the Presbytery of New Castle, and the other from that of Carlisle. In the former case, it appeared that the New

Castle Presbytery, having heard that a committee of the Wilmington Presbytery had been appointed to organize a church in the village of Newark, within the bounds of a church under the care of the New Castle Presbytery, the latter appointed a committee of its members, to be present and remonstrate against the proposed measure. In defiance of the remonstrances and entreaties of this committee, the Wilmington committee proceeded to organize a church of nine members; several of whom had no fixed residence.

From the complaint of the Carlisle Presbytery it appeared that Mr. J. M. McKim had been a candidate of that Presbytery, on trials for ordination. Having passed successfully certain parts of his trials, he submitted a popular discourse, on 2 Cor. v. 17: "If any man be in Christ, he is a new creature;" which, and his examination on systematic theology, were not sustained. Presbytery then assigned him Eph. ii. 1: "You hath he quickened, who were dead in the trespasses and sins," for another sermon; and recommended him "to pursue his theological studies at some approved theological seminary." He was a pupil of Mr. Duffield.

At a meeting of the Presbytery, held a short time after this action, a request was received from Mr. McKim, for a dismission to place himself under the care of the Presbytery of Wilmington; although he was living in the centre of Carlisle Presbytery. This request was not granted; but a committee was appointed to confer with Mr. McKim. To this committee he declared his purpose to submit himself to no further trials before that Presbytery, and renewed his request for a dismission. This not being granted, he was received, without dismission, by the Presbytery of Wilmington; although it was fully informed of the facts of the case. He was licensed by it, and appeared in Synod, as an ordained member of that Presbytery. In the mean time, he had been habitually preaching, by authority of the Presbytery of Wilmington, in the midst of the Presbytery of Carlisle, which had refused to license him, on account of his doctrinal unsoundness.

Upon the trial of these cases before the Synod, the Presbytery of Wilmington refused to produce its records, —taking the same ground with the Philadelphia Presbytery, as to the jurisdiction of Synod. The Synod, then, called upon Mr. McKim, as in a court of conscience, to state at what time and place he was ordained. It appeared, from his answer, that he had been ordained, on the morning on which the Synod met, in another church in the same village; the Presbytery thus treating with contempt the pending complaint, and forestalling the action of the Synod. Mr. McKim, some years later, addressed a letter to the Presbytery of Wilmington, in which he repudiated the doctrine of the atonement and other cardinal truths of the gospel,—traced his sentiments to the elementary principles which he had learned from Mr. Duffield,—and abandoned the Presbyterian Church.

The Synod censured the recusant Presbyteries for contumacy, in withholding their records. It dissolved the church organized in Newark; censured the conduct of the Presbytery with respect to Mr. McKim, and dissolved the two Presbyteries of Wilmington and Philadelphia, and appropriately distributed their ministers, churches, and other elements, to the adjacent Presbyteries.

Against this action, the two Presbyteries appealed to the Assembly; and, in the mean time, treated the act of dissolution as a dead letter. Commissioners were sent, by the elective affinity Presbytery of Philadelphia, to the General Assembly. They were at once enrolled, and held their seats undisturbed, till the adjournment of the Assembly.

Upon the appeal, the Presbyteries were restored. The elective affinity Presbytery was assigned a geographical territory and boundary, and its name changed to the Third Presbytery of Philadelphia. Hitherto it had held the name of Second Presbytery, in common with that erected by the Synod.

During the exciting and anxious sessions of this Assembly, the Old School members held one or two meetings for consultation, in the Second Church. They were convened, by public announcement, by the Moderator, in the Assembly, inviting the presence of those who voted with the minority on Dr. Miller's resolution in Barnes' case. Before the business of the conference had commenced, the youthful pastor of the church, without consultation, announced that any who did not sympathize with the objects of the meeting, were requested to retire. This suggestion was at once repudiated, by a general cry of "No! no!" Dr. Miller emphatically stating that they had nothing to conceal, and no wish that any one should retire.* This suggestion, which was thus, at once, repudiated, by acclama-

* The author, then a collegian, was present with several young friends.

tion, was made the occasion of much invidious remark among the New School members of the Assembly, as to secret conclaves, and conspiracies.

At the very time that the Old School were thus stigmatized, the other party were holding meetings in the basement of the Third Church, which convened without public notice, and from which the public were actually excluded. Here, the reconstruction of the Boards was discussed; and here the question was anxiously considered whether the seminary at Princeton should not be remodeled. But the conclusion was, that the Church was not yet ripe for a step so decisive.

CHAPTER XXXIII.

THE CRISIS.

Committee of Correspondence—Causes of anxiety—The Committee's circular letter—Their address—Separation must be had—Anxiety respecting the Moderates—Conference with the Princeton professors—Proposed abandonment of Princeton—New York Union Seminary founded—Convention called, for the second Thursday of May—Published warning of separation.

In the conference of the orthodox, held during the sessions of the Assembly of 1836, some of the members were inclined to proceed at once to extreme measures. Recoiling from the prospect of hopeless strife and growing disorders, and startled and disgusted with the developments of that Assembly, they were urgent for immediate division or secession. The larger number, however, although indignant at the haughty spirit, the clandestine management and doctrinal contradictions, of the majority, were opposed to so extreme a step; regarding it as only justifiable when the redemption of the Church was demonstrated to be hopeless. They proposed a committee of correspondence, who should consult with the orthodox brethren throughout the Church, and if it should be judged expedient, call a Convention, preliminary to the next Assembly; so that the whole orthodox part of the Church might be represented and consulted, and any final measures be adopted by common consent, after full conference and deliberation. This proposition was adopted, and a committee accordingly appointed. It consisted of the Rev. Drs. W. W. Phillips, Joseph McElroy, George Potts, John Breckinridge, Francis McFarland, W. A. McDowell, and John M. Krebs; with elders, Henry Rankin, Hugh Auchincloss, and James Lenox.

The duties of this committee were of the most responsible and delicate nature. The crisis was pressing. The rejection of the Western Foreign Missionary Society was not only a criminal breach of covenant, but, in view of the facts and the arguments used, indicated a fixed purpose for ever to exclude the Presbyterian Church, through its own organization, from the foreign missionary field. The mutilation of the annual report of the Board of Education, the treacherous attempts to revolutionize it and the Board of Missions, and the denial to the Assembly of the constitutional power to erect Boards, at all, or to organize any standing executive agency, evinced a persistent hostility to those institutions, which threatened their utter destruction. The arbitrary temper manifested by the leaders of the party, when they found themselves sustained by a clear majority of the Assembly, indicated how little was to be expected from their forbearance, if once possessed of decisive control. The avowals boastfully and defiantly made, in the discussion of Barnes' case, of doctrinal identification with him, of contempt for the authority of the Constitution, and of the embrace of doctrines at variance with it, were none the less significant, because of the zeal, afterward, so strangely aroused and unanimously expressed for the doctrines of the Confession, by men whose names were identified with life-long labors, in behalf of the doctrines of the new divinity.

The attitude of the Moderate party, and its influence in inducing the present condition of things, were, also, subjects of painful and anxious thought. It was felt that, however unintentionally, their influence had operated, directly and most powerfully, to discourage, embarrass, and enfeeble the friends of the Constitution, and to strengthen the hands of the authors of innovation; and that, unless they could, by some means, be dislodged from their present position and brought to co-operate actively with their brethren, the salvation of the Church was almost beyond hope.

A few weeks after the adjournment of the Assembly, the committee issued, in lithograph, a circular letter to leading ministers, in all parts of the Church, designed to elicit facts and ascertain their sentiments, as to the steps to be taken in the crisis. Answers were solicited to the following queries:—

"1. With so great a diversity of sentiment, in regard to doctrine and order, in the Presbyterian Church, can we continue united in one body, and maintain the integrity of our standards, and promote the cause of truth and righteousness in the earth?

"2. If you think *we can*, then please to say how the causes that, at present, distract us can be removed.

"3. Do you believe that there are ministers in our connection who hold errors, on account of which they ought to be separated from us?

"4. If you think such errors are held, please to name them, particularly.

"5. If you believe that persons holding the errors

you name ought to be separated from our communion, what, in your judgment, is the best way of accomplishing it?

"6. It was repeatedly avowed, by ministers in the last General Assembly, that they received the Confession of Faith of our Church, only 'for substance of doctrine,'—'as a system,' or, 'as containing the Calvinistic system, in opposition to the Arminian,' etc. Hence, we know not how much of our standards they adopt, and how much they reject. Is this, in your opinion, the true intent and meaning of receiving and adopting the Confession of Faith?

"7. It is believed, by many, that much of the evil of which we now complain has come upon us in consequence of our connection with Congregational churches, within our own bounds and represented in our judicatories. We would ask you, whether, in your judgment, it would not be better for us, as a Church, to have no other connection with Congregationalists, than the friendly one which we now have with them, as corresponding bodies?"

It has been denied, of late, that the division of 1837 grew out of doctrinal questions. But it will be observed, that the attention of this committee, in this confidential development, was occupied almost wholly, with the doctrinal errors which prevailed. It will also be seen, that, in the seventh question, they approximate the very solution which was reached by the next Assembly.

The issue of this paper elicited a burst of indignation from the New School leaders, by whom it was stigmatized as a secret conspiracy against the peace of the Church. It, however, accomplished the end had in view, by developing a vast amount of information, as to the precise nature and extent of the evils complained of, and the mind of the most judicious men in the Church, as to the crisis.

Predicated upon the light thus obtained, the committee then published "An Address to the ministers, elders, and members of the Presbyterian Church," in a pamphlet of 41 pages. In this publication, as introductory to the main design, it was maintained "that the prosperity of the Church, and her efficiency, in securing the great objects of her institution, depend, under God, on the purity of her faith." "That to the successful maintenance of the truth of God,—to union of effort in its maintenance,—creeds, confessions of faith are indispensable;"—and, that the Confession is not to be received "for substance," nor "as a system;" but sincerely as "containing the system of doctrine taught in the Holy Scriptures."

As illustrative of a different view of this subject, the Address then proceeded to a review of the case of Mr. Barnes. This was followed by an exhibition of the missionary question, as discussed and determined in connection with the repudiated treaty with the Synod of Pittsburgh.

The result of the whole survey was expressed, in one word.—"Fathers, Brethren, Fellow-Christians, whatever else is dark, this is clear,—*We cannot continue in the same body*. We are not agreed, and it is vain to attempt to walk together. That those whom we regard as the authors of our present distractions will retrace their steps, is not to be expected; and that those who have hitherto rallied around the standards of our Church, will continue to do so, is both to be expected and desired. In some way or other, therefore, these men must be separated from us." How this should be effected, the committee did not venture to suggest.

In fact, a feeling of discouragement and despondence began to infect the ranks of the orthodox, and to beget a disposition to seek peace and a pure gospel and scriptural order, in the bosom of the Reformed Dutch Church. Particularly disheartening was the attitude maintained by the Princeton professors, who, while they were recognized as doctrinally with the Old School, were found in opposition to almost every measure proposed or attempted by it, for the reformation of the Church. So serious was the embarrassment hence resulting, that "a company of gentlemen were designated by a large and respectable number of the Old School, to proceed in a noiseless and unobserved manner, to wait upon the professors at their homes, to reason and remonstrate with them, on the subject of their position, and, if possible, to induce them to concur with their brethren, in the public action of the Church. These gentlemen, agreeably to the arrangement made for them, assembled at Princeton, in the autumn of 1836, and met the professors, in Dr. Hodge's study, whither they had been invited to repair. At this conference, the three professors of the Seminary attended; and the Rev. J. W. Alexander was also present. The following members of the Old School deputation were in attendance:—Rev. Dr. James Blythe, of South Hanover, Indiana; Dr. C. C. Cuyler, of Philadelphia; Dr. George Junkin, of Easton, Pennsylvania; Dr. W. W.

Phillips, of New York; and last and least, the humble penman of these pages,"—the Rev. Dr. Isaac V. Brown.

"Nothing important or decisive was exhibited in this interview. The parties, respectively, with much moderation, stated their views, but without any decisive result. In the course of these remarks, a gentleman in company took liberty to observe that, to him there did not appear to be any great or serious obstacles between them; and that it really seemed very deplorable that so great an interest should be left in suspense, when the only difference appeared to be a mere matter of church policy. After an interim of silence, perhaps five minutes in duration, the Rev. James W. Alexander, then, comparatively, a young man, in a very unassuming and respectful manner, repeated the suggestion, that there was really very little difference or distance between the parties; and manifested a strong desire that an entire reconciliation should take place. He urged, very gently, that the parties both desired the same thing; and they differed merely as to the best manner of accomplishing it. This, said he, is not a sufficient ground upon which to jeopardize so great an interest. Wise men do not act in this manner. In a strain somewhat like this, and of very little greater extent,—the remarker did more, probably, toward adjusting the difficulty, than any one who had preceded him. The tone, as well as the temper, of his remarks, seemed a little above his years; and that gave to them a peculiar emphasis."*

In connection with this Princeton conference, Dr. Brown relates a fact which illustrates the extremity of

* Brown's Historical Vindication, p. 175.

the situation and the nature of the apprehensions felt by the best men in the Church. He states that, in New York, at this time, lived a wealthy, intelligent, and devoted ruling elder. In common with many others, he was apprehensive that, in consequence of the mistaken course of the moderate men, the policy of the New School party was about to acquire permanent control over the Church and its institutions. He was, therefore, anxious to ascertain, through the committee of conference, whether the Princeton gentlemen were determined to persist in the active opposition heretofore maintained by them to the reforming policy of the Old School. He was opposed to scandalizing the cause of religion, by protracting a hopeless controversy; and unless some favorable indications could be elicited from that quarter, "he, and others like-minded, had resolved to abandon Princeton, immediately, to the control of the adversary, and take measures to establish another seminary, on ground entirely out of their reach. For this purpose, the money was ready in bank; a beautiful site, with appropriate grounds and edifices, was selected; the principal officers of the institution were designated, from among the most prominent in our Church, and everything ready for action. But the delegates did not, upon the whole, consider the condition of the seminary at Princeton, exposed as it was, sufficiently desperate to warrant so great a sacrifice, and so decisive a change, at that time. In this feeling, our highly respected friends in New York cordially acquiesced."* The ruling elder here referred to was Robert Lenox Esq., the father of that eminent servant of Christ and

* Brown's Historical Vindication, p. 176.

benefactor of our Church, James Lenox, Esq., of New York.

The Committee of Conference left Princeton, greatly disheartened at the seeming failure of their mission. And yet the result showed that they had not labored in vain. Influenced, no doubt, partly, by the considerations urged in this conference, and partly, by convictions, subsequently reached, as to the plans and policy of the New School, Dr. Alexander was found among the foremost in the next Assembly, in devising and executing the measures, which brought deliverance to the Church.

It was about this time, that New York Union Theological Seminary was founded, upon a plan expressly devised to keep it out of the control of the General Assembly, should a majority of that body, at any time, prove to be Old School. "It was felt that, sustained by the patronage and confidence of the pastors and churches of the city of New York, and those who sympathized with them, throughout the Church, the proposed institution might be competently endowed, ably officered and well sustained. It would, at least, in the hands of directors independent of the Assembly, remain under the control of men who would promote its interests, without reference to an accidental majority in the Assembly. It was consequently, established and placed under the care of a Board of Directors appointed by its founders."*

The institution was projected in 1835. In October of that year, nine persons met at a private house, to consult as to the proposition,—four ministers, of whom

* Gillett's History, vol. ii., p. 501.

Erskine Mason was one, and Dr. Thomas McAuley and Henry White, probably two of the others; and five laymen. The institution was founded in January, 1836, and went into operation before the close of the year.

The original faculty were Dr. Thomas McAuley, President and Professor of Pastoral Theology and Church Government; Henry White, Professor of Theology; Dr. Edwin Robinson, Professor of Oriental and Biblical Literature; Dr. Thomas H. Skinner, Professor of Sacred Rhetoric; Dr. I. S. Spencer, Professor of Biblical History and its Connections; and Dr. Erskine Mason, Professor of Ecclesiastical History. George Bush was temporarily engaged to supply the place of Dr. Robinson.*

As the time approached when the General Assembly must again convene, the most anxious thought and expectations were directed to its deliberations and their probable results; as all felt that, for weal or woe, its decisions would and ought to be final. Should the New School party prove to be in the majority, those who had so long and faithfully contended against their innovations were determined to withdraw from the Church and erect, on independent ground, the same standard, around which they had always rallied. Should the Old School have a majority, their purpose was fixed, to adopt such decisive measures as would terminate controversy, and put an end to the schemes of innovation.

In fulfillment of the design of their appointment, the Committee of Correspondence, on the 12th of January,

* Gillett, p. 501.

issued a call for a convention, to meet in Philadelphia, on the second Thursday of May, 1837, one week preceding the meeting of the Assembly. In their circular, the committee stated the result of their correspondence to be "a conviction that the real friends of the doctrines and of the institutions of our Church are now satisfied that the present state of things ought not, longer, to continue; and that the time has come when effectual measures must be taken for putting an end to those contentions which have, for years, agitated our Church, by removing the causes in which they originated." As to the measures to be adopted to accomplish this object, the committee declined making any suggestions. They, however, recommended "ministers and churches that mourn over the false doctrines so industriously propagated, by many in our connection, the contentions and strife thereby engendered, and the consequent withdrawal of the influences of the Holy Spirit, to observe the second Thursday of May, next, as a day of fasting, humiliation and prayer, in view of these evils, and to implore the Divine direction in the present crisis."

This call was published in all the old School papers; and full warning was thus given to all parties, of the momentous issues depending upon the decisions of the approaching Assembly.

In the mean time, publications made by such men as Dr. Miller, of Princeton, Dr. John Breckinridge, and Dr. Francis McFarland, and the editors of the Princeton Review,—men of the mildest spirit and most moderate sentiments, attested the reality and greatness of the danger, indicated the modified views of Princeton, and did much to unite men of like sentiments and spirit, in approval and support of the decisive measures which were about to be employed for the reformation of the Church.

CHAPTER XXXIV.

THE REFORMING ASSEMBLY OF 1837.

The Convention of 1837—Its testimony and memorial—The Assembly—Committee on the Memorial—Abrogation of the plan of union—Citation of judicatories—Committee on Amicable Separation—Purposes of the New School—The disowning acts—Certain Synods admonished—Other measures of the Assembly—Protests and replies—Provisions as to the roll of 1838—Character of this Assembly—The majority and the slavery question.

THE convention called by the Committee of Correspondence, met at 10 o'clock, on the 11th of May, 1837. The Rev. Dr. James Blythe was appointed temporary chairman, and the Rev. Thomas D. Baird, temporary secretary. The entire day was consecrated to humiliation and prayer. On the next day, the Convention was organized by forming the roll, and appointing as permanent officers, the Rev. Dr. G. A. Baxter, President; the Rev. Dr. C. C. Cuyler, Vice President; the Rev. Thomas D. Baird, Recording Clerk; and the Rev. H. S. Pratt, Reading Clerk.

There were in attendance, one hundred and twenty members, representing fifty-two Presbyteries, and thirteen minorities. The course pursued by the previous Assembly, with respect to the foreign missionary question, the facts in connection with the case of Mr. Barnes, and the other causes mentioned in the last chapter, had operated powerfully, to arouse the attention of the Southern churches, and to convince them of the true character of the controversy, and the vital nature of the interests at stake. They were, therefore, largely represented in the convention, and the developments there made brought them generally to decisive co-operation with the Old School, in the measures of reform adopted by the Assembly.

The sessions of the Convention were occupied, mainly, with inquiry as to the nature and extent, of the heresies and disorders which were prevalent. The roll was called, and each member, in turn, invited to state the facts of his knowledge. The developments thus received were of such a character as to banish doubt from the minds of the most skeptical, and confirm the entire body in the conviction of the necessity of some immediate and adequate remedy. Particularly emphatic and precise was the testimony respecting Western New York, the Western Reserve, and Illinois, where contempt and hostility to the doctrines of the Confession were freely avowed, and the heresies of Taylor and policy of Finney were openly cherished.

The results of the discussions and deliberations were embodied in a Testimony and Memorial to the Assembly. This most able and impressive paper was prepared by a committee, consisting of the Rev. Messrs. R. J. Breckinridge, George Potts, and Thomas Smyth, and Elders, Nathaniel Ewing, and David Fullerton.

The Memorial, after the opening address to the General Assembly, proceeded to justify the course of the Old School, under the circumstances of the times.—"That we have not been rash and hasty, nor manifested a factious opposition, to errors and disorders, which were only of small extent, or recent introduction, is manifestly proven by the fact that these evils have been insidiously spreading through our Church for many years—and that they have at length become so mature, and so diffused, as not only to pervade large portions of the Church, but to reign triumphantly over the body itself, through successive General Assemblies. On the other hand, that we have not been wholly faithless to our Master and to truth, we appeal to the constant efforts of some, through the press and pulpit—to the firm and consistent course of some of our Presbyteries and Synods—to the faithful conduct of the minorities in the Assemblies of 1831–2–3–4, and 6—to the Act and Testimony—to the proceedings of the Conventions of Cincinnati in 1831, and Pittsburgh in 1835, and to the noble Assembly of 1835."

The memorialists then testify, in the following impressive language, that it is the corrupting of the pure gospel of Christ against which they have contended, and that all the other questions are subordinate to this. "We contend, especially and above all, for *the truth*, as it is made known to us of God, for the salvation of men. We contend for nothing else, except as the result or support of this inestimable treasure. It is because this is subverted that we grieve; it is because our standards teach it, that we bewail their perversion; it is because our Church order and discipline preserve, defend, and diffuse it, that we weep over their impending ruin. It is against *error* that we emphatically bear our testimony,—error dangerous to the souls of men, dishonoring to Jesus Christ, contrary to his revealed truth, and utterly at variance with our standards. Error, not as it may be freely and openly held by others, in this age and land of absolute religious freedom; but error, held and taught in the Presbyterian Church—preached and written by persons who profess to receive and adopt our scriptural standards—promoted by societies operating widely through our churches—reduced into form, and openly embraced by almost entire Presbyteries and Synods—favored by repeated acts of successive General Assemblies, and at last virtually sanctioned, to an alarming extent, by the numerous Assembly of 1836.

"To be more specific, we hereby set forth in order, some of the doctrinal errors against which we bear testimony, and which we, and the churches, have conclusive proof, are widely disseminated in the Presbyterian Church.

"1. That God would have prevented the existence of sin in our world, but was not able without destroying the moral agency of man; or, that for aught that appears in the Bible to the contrary, sin is incidental to any wise moral system.

"2. That election to eternal life is founded on a foresight of faith and obedience.

"3. That we have no more to do with the first sin of Adam than with the sins of any other parent.

"4. That infants come into the world as free from moral defilement as was Adam, when he was created.

"5. That infants sustain the same relation to the moral government of God in this world as brute animals, and that their sufferings and death are to be accounted for, on the same principles as those of brutes, and not by any means to be considered as penal.

"6. That there is no other original sin than the fact that all the posterity of Adam, though by nature innocent, or possessed of no moral character, will always begin to sin when they begin to exercise moral agency; that original sin does not include a sinful bias of the human mind, and a just exposure to penal suffering; and that there is no evidence in Scripture, that infants, in order to salvation, do need redemption by the blood of Christ, and regeneration by the Holy Ghost.

"7. That the doctrine of imputation, whether of the guilt of Adam's sin or of the righteousness of Christ, has no foundation in the Word of God, and is both unjust and absurd.

"8. That the sufferings and death of Christ were not truly vicarious and penal, but symbolical, governmental, and instructive only.

"9. That the impenitent sinner is by nature, and independently of the renewing influence or almighty energy of the Holy Spirit, in full possession of all the ability necessary to a full compliance with all the commands of God.

"10. That Christ does not intercede for the elect until after their regeneration.

"11. That saving faith is not an effect of the special operation of the Holy Spirit, but a mere rational belief of the truth, or assent to the word of God.

"12. That regeneration is the act of the sinner himself, and that it consists in a change of his governing purpose, which he himself must produce, and which is the result, not of any direct influence of the Holy Spirit on the heart, but chiefly, of a persuasive exhibition of the truth analogous to the influence which one man exerts over the mind of another; or, that regeneration is not an instantaneous act, but a progressive work.

"13. That God has done all that *he can do* for the salvation of all men, and that man himself must do the rest.

"14. That God cannot exert such influence on the minds of men, as shall make it certain that they will choose and act in a particular manner, without impairing their moral agency.

"15. That the righteousness of Christ is not the sole ground of the sinner's acceptance with God; and that in no sense does the righteousness of Christ become ours.

"16. That the reason why some differ from others in regard to their reception of the Gospel is, that they make themselves to differ.

"It is impossible to contemplate these errors without perceiving, that they strike at the foundation of the system of Gospel grace; and that, from the days of Pelagius and Cassian to the present hour, their reception has uniformly marked the character of a Church apostatizing from 'the faith once delivered to the saints,' and sinking into deplorable corruption."

This statement of prevalent errors, after being framed by the committee, was, at their request, carefully revised by the Rev. Dr. Miller, than whom no man in the Church was less open to the charge of giving countenance to false accusations, or imaginary alarms. The above is the form in which the paper was adopted by the Assembly; differing, by three or four mere verbal alterations, from the original, as embodied in the Memorial.

The memorial presented a similar statement of "departures from sound Presbyterian order," and discipline. It then proceeded to indicate necessary measures of reform. These were,—the abrogation of the Plan of Union;—the discountenancing of the operations of the American Home Missionary and Education Societies within the ecclesiastical limits of the Church;—the bringing into order, dissolution, or separation from the Church, of every inferior court, not regularly organized;—the requiring of Presbyteries to examine applicants from other denominations, on theology and church government, personal piety, and ministerial qualifications, and to require of them an explicit adoption of the standards;—the enforcing of discipline against heretical ministers, and courts that tolerate them; and the adoption of measures "that such of these bodies as are believed to consist chiefly of decidedly unsound or disorderly members may be separated from the Church," provision being made for any cases of orderly members or churches among them;—and the admonition of such voluntary societies as were not expressly condemned.*

This paper was drafted in the name of the Convention, and signed by its officers.

The regular sessions of the Convention continued until the meeting of the General Assembly, when they were merged in conferences held from time to time, as occasion indicated.

Upon the opening of the Assembly, the election of Moderator and clerks showed a decided Old School majority. The Rev. Dr. David Elliott was chosen Moderator, by 137 votes, against 106 cast for the Rev. Baxter Dickinson. On the second day of the sessions,

* For this paper, in full, see Digest, p. 710.

the memorial was presented, and referred to the Committee of Bills and Overtures. The next day it was reported back to the Assembly, and was, at once referred to the Rev. Drs. Alexander, Plumer, Green, Baxter, and Leland, and Elders Walter Lowrie and James Lenox.

On Monday, the 22d, this committee reported, in part, the doctrinal testimony of the Convention, with a few verbal alterations, as above copied. The adoption of this paper was designed as a basis for whatever further action the Assembly might take; as all recognized this to be the fundamental issue, out of which all the others had sprung and derived their importance. To defeat this purpose, the New School had recourse to the policy of so overloading the doctrinal testimony, by additions proposed, on points disputed by no one in the Church, as to deprive it of any practical significance or value. To avoid, therefore, a protracted discussion, the report was, for the present, postponed.

The committee, also, reported resolutions, recommending the cultivation of friendly relations with the Congregational churches; but proposing the abrogation of the Plan of Union. The former was, immediately, adopted. The proposed abrogation of the Plan, elicited earnest discussion. Its unchangeable authority was urged, upon the false assumption, that it was not a mere "Regulation" of the Assembly, and subject to its discretion, but a solemn "compact," or covenant, with the Association of Connecticut, which could not be set aside, without a gross breach of faith.

In the course of the discussion, Dr. McAuley asked, whether the abrogation would be retrospective, or prospective only. Dr. Alexander replied, that he could speak for himself only,—that he regarded the proposition as having respect to the future, rather than to the past;—that as to the churches already formed under the Plan, he presumed some arrangement would be adopted to allow them a year or so, to choose, between Presbyterianism and the Congregational system.

The abrogation was discussed, till the close of Tuesday's sessions, when, upon a call for the previous question, the resolution passed, by a vote of 143 to 110.

On the morning of Thursday, the 25th, the committee on the Memorial reported in full; and on the afternoon, Mr. Plumer, in accordance with its suggestions, moved that the proper steps be now taken to cite to the bar of the next Assembly any inferior judicatories charged with disorder;—that a committee be appointed to digest the plan of procedure;—and that, as citation is the commencement of process, the judicatories involved be excluded from seats in the next Assembly, till their cases are decided.

In the discussion on these resolutions, it was urged by the New School speakers, that the doctrinal diversities which prevailed were merely different modes of *explaining* the doctrines of the Confession; and that the Assembly had no right to try inferior courts, nor to exclude them from their seats, pending process. Dr. Beman warned the house, that this Assembly is a very different body from the next. There may be a change of all its members. The members composing it will come with commissions in their pockets, and cannot be excluded. "The men you propose to exclude are Thermopylæ men. They are Smithfield men. This resolution will blow a blast which will bring fifty men to this place, who might now, rightfully, be here. They will meet the question at Philippi, and there will they settle it."

The warning and defiance thus given were not unheeded. The resolutions were adopted, on Friday evening, upon a call for the previous question, by a vote of 128 to 122. A committee was then appointed, consisting of Dr. Cuyler, Mr. Breckinridge, Dr. Baxter, Mr. McKennan, and Mr. Baird, to ascertain the judicatories charged with disorders, and report a plan of procedure, in the matter.

Mr. Breckinridge then gave notice that he would, on the next morning, propose the appointment of a committee of equal numbers from the majority and minority, to consult upon a voluntary division of the Church. This motion, upon being presented, in the morning, was adopted. The committee consisted of Rev. R. J. Breckinridge, Dr. Alexander, Dr. Cuyler, Dr. Witherspoon, and Nathaniel Ewing, Esq., on the part of the majority; and Dr. McAuley, Dr. Beman, Dr. Peters, Dr. Dickinson, and William Jessup, Esq., on the part of the minority. The committee and the subject referred to it were then commended to God, in prayer, led by Dr. Baxter.

On the afternoon of Tuesday, the 30th, this committee reported, through Dr. Alexander, that they had not been able to agree. It appeared from the papers submitted, that the two sub-committees were agreed as to the propriety of a voluntary separation; and as to the corporate funds, the names to be held by the two denominations, the records, and the Boards and institutions of the Church. It was agreed that the Old School should retain the name, the Boards, the seminary at Princeton, (Alleghany seems to have been overlooked,) and the records of the Assembly. It was, also, agreed that the New School Assembly should be known as the General Assembly of the American Presbyterian Church; that a certified copy of all the records of the Church should be made for its use, and that the corporate funds of the Church, not belonging to Princeton Seminary, should be equally divided. These amounted, in all, to less than twenty thousand dollars.

The committee disagreed as to the propriety of entering at once upon the division;—as to the power of the Assembly to do it;—and as to breaking up its succession,—the New School insisting that neither of the bodies should be recognized, as, in law, or in fact, the lineal successor of the existing Assembly.

At one stage in the consultations of the committees, they seemed to be about to agree. The minority committee proposed that the points on which they disagreed should be submitted to the Assembly, for its decision. But it appeared, upon explanation, that they did not intend to hold themselves bound by the action of the Assembly, on the points thus to be submitted, should it be contrary to their views. The majority committee, therefore, concluded that a *voluntary* separation was altogether impossible, and informed the minority that, unless they had something else to offer, this proposition must be considered a virtual waiver of the whole subject. The position maintained by the minority committee was, that they could not assent to any division, by the present Assembly; "as it would, in no wise, be obligatory on any of the judicatories of the Church, or any members of the churches. The only effect would be, a disorderly dissolution of the present Assembly, and be of no binding force or effect upon any member who did not assent to it." They insisted that, in order to separation, the plan must be sent down to the Presbyteries and receive their sanction, as an amendment of the Constitution.

The motion for the appointment of the joint committee, had been made by Mr. Breckinridge, at the suggestion of Dr. Peters; and it became evident, from the result, that the object was, to postpone action, so as to enable the minority to call the phalanx of "Thermopylæ" to the plains of "Philippi,"—to gather a majority for the Assembly of 1838.

The report of the committee put an end to all hope of an amicable division. The committee was, therefore, discharged, and the subject laid on the table.

The Old School were now placed in a most critical situation. "We have responsible names," said the Rev. Thomas D. Baird, a man whose candor and truth were attested by his opponents, themselves,—"without any restraint of confidence, except what our own sense of propriety may impose, and we have not the slightest shadow of doubt, that, for the General Assembly, there was a reforming process prepared, on the opposite side, no less severe and decisive than that which was applied by the orthodox. Many, however, are so easily scandalized, by an exposition of names, that we shall, at present, forbear; and only state what we distinctly understood to be a part of the contemplated process. 1. The removal and change of *at least* two of the Princeton professors. This has sometimes been the subject of conversation, for years, and had now become ripe for execution. 2. The entire change of the Boards of Missions and Education. A partial attempt was made at this alteration, last year, which was to have been carried out, at the late Assembly, had not a wise and kind Providence interposed to defeat it. These two acts would have entirely changed the face and character of the Presbyterian Church; had nothing else been done; but the process was not to end there. 3. Individuals and judicatories were to be subjected—according to the invidious phraseology now adopted—to the guillotine; and, no doubt, in the hands of New School men, it would have been a lawful and wise expedient."*

The alternative now presented to the majority was, to take decisive steps for the reform of the Church, or supinely surrender her to the patrons of the new theology.

In the discussion, on the citation of inferior judicatories, Dr. Beman had so ably exhibited the embarrassments to which that proceeding would be liable, as to create very serious apprehensions, as to the result. These were increased, by the closeness of the vote on the measure, the majority being reduced to six, in consequence of distrust in the practicability of the plan. Pondering upon the situation, Dr. Baxter was led to reflect that those inferior courts which were infected with unsound doctrine, had, almost without exception, been organized and still remained under the Plan of Union; and that as all that has been done upon an unconstitutional basis falls with it, the abrogation of the

* Pittsburgh Christian Herald, 1837, p. 103.

Plan operated to the dissolution of those courts. Pending the conference upon amicable separation, a meeting of the Convention was called, the suggestion laid before it and approved, and action in accordance with it decided upon.

Upon the discharge, therefore, of the Committee of Conference, Mr. Plumer moved,

"That, by the operation of the abrogation of the Plan of Union of 1801, the Synod of the Western Reserve is, and is hereby declared to be, no longer a part of the Presbyterian Church in the United States of America."

During the discussion of this resolution, Dr. Junkin was interrupted, in a statement of the heresies and disorders prevalent in the Western Reserve, by Mr. Seward of that Synod; who offered himself, as a witness in its behalf.

He was asked, "Did you assent to the Constitutional questions, prescribed for ministers, at your ordination?"

To this he refused to answer.

Dr. Beman.—"Mr. Seward has been interrupted by questions."

The Moderator.—"Mr. Seward requested that he might be questioned."

Mr. Seward.—"I do adopt the book."

Question.—"Did you do so, at your ordination?"

No reply.

Mr. Brown, Elder from the Presbytery of Lorain.—"We have been greatly misrepresented. There are thirty Presbyterian Churches in our Synod."*

* Those churches had twenty Commissioners on the floor of the Assembly.

Dr. Cuyler.—"There are one hundred and thirty-nine churches in the Synod."

Mr. Brown.—"The Confessions used in these churches are abstracts of the Presbyterian Confession. My Presbytery consists of twelve churches; I do not know of more than one, that is strictly Presbyterian."

Mr. H. Kingsbury, an elder from the Cleaveland church, said,—"I have a substantial copy, made by myself, of a certificate given me by the Rev. S. C. Aikin, and which I have carried for two years, to show that I am an elder. I got it, because I was once a committee-man, and sat in the Assembly, where my seat was challenged."

Mr. Breckinridge.—"Is he a ruling elder, ordained according to the Book?"

Mr. Kingsbury.—"I will answer no questions. I am not on trial."

Mr. Breckinridge.—"I am credibly informed that he never was an elder; and that there is no board of elders in his church. I ask Mr. Kingsbury now, if he *ever* adopted the Book?"

Mr. Kingsbury.—"I answer no questions."

Subsequently, Dr. Peters stated that Mr. Kingsbury authorized him to explain, that he had declined to answer, because he was not on trial; but that he was ordained a ruling elder, two years and a half ago.

Mr. Breckinridge.—"Will Mr. Kingsbury now say whether he ever adopted the Constitution of the Presbyterian Church?"

Mr. Kingsbury.—"I answer no questions."

Mr. Breckinridge.—"That's enough."

After an able discussion, the resolution was adopted, by a vote of 132 to 105.

The same rule was subsequently passed, with reference to the Synods of Utica, Geneva, and Genesee, by 115 to 88.

The Assembly, at the same time, recorded that its solicitude on the subject and urgency for its immediate decision, were greatly increased, "by reason of the gross disorders which are ascertained to have prevailed in those Synods; it being made clear to us, that even the Plan of Union itself was never consistently carried into effect, by those professing to act under it." It declared that it had no intention to affect, in any way, the standing of ministers or members, as such, nor the mutual and several relations and duties of pastors and people; but only to declare their relation to the Assembly and the Presbyterian Church.

It also directed, that any orderly ministers and churches which might be within the bounds of the four disowned Synods, should apply for admission into such Presbyteries belonging to our connection as may be most convenient; and that any orderly Presbyteries, in similar circumstances, report themselves to the next Assembly, for direction.

The elective affinity Presbytery of Philadelphia, which had been the occasion of so much controversy and evil, was now dissolved, and its ministers, licentiates, and churches directed to apply to the proper surrounding Presbyteries for admission.

Late in the sessions, the committee on the citation of inferior judicatories, reported. Its chief functions had been superseded by these measures of the Assembly.

It, however, recommended that the Synods of Albany, New Jersey, Michigan, Cincinnati, and Illinois, be admonished to take order, respecting errors in doctrine, and disorders, which were charged, by common fame, against certain of their Presbyteries, and to report thereon to the next Assembly. The report was adopted.

These were the principal measures of this Assembly. The testimony of the Convention, against doctrinal errors, and violations of order, was also, adopted; and the American Education and Home Missionary Societies were requested to cease to operate within the Church; a Board of Foreign Missions was appointed; and a pastoral letter to the churches, and a circular letter to all the churches of Christ, with respect to these transactions, were issued. Protests against these various measures were entered, and replies made.

In the protest against the testimony on doctrinal error, the minority arrayed, in opposing paragraphs, the errors condemned by the Assembly, and the doctrines embraced by the protestants. The profession of faith thus presented was, on some essential points, ambiguous, and, on others, palpably erroneous.

The Assembly made no other answer to this paper than to require the attention of the Presbyteries to which they respectively belonged, to the avowals thus made by the subscribers to the protest.

Two other measures, of a cautionary nature, were adopted. To guard against a possible policy, the clerks were directed to enroll no newly-formed Presbytery, until it shall have been reported to the Assembly and recognized by it. Should it appear that any new Presbytery had been formed with a view to unduly increase the representation, the Assembly declared that it would refuse to receive its commissioners, and might order the Presbytery to be reunited to that from which it had been taken.

It was further moved to require of the Assembly's clerks, the Rev. Drs. J. McDowell and J. M. Krebs, a pledge to conform their action to the regulations at this time passed by it. Those officers anticipated the adoption of the motion, by severally, stating, that, as they were merely administrative officers, they held themselves bound to conform strictly, in their official action, to the determinations of the Assembly. The motion was, thereupon, withdrawn.

Such were the proceedings of this Assembly, which has been the object of an extraordinary amount of obloquy and reproach. The design of this history does not permit a detailed exposition of the arguments presented in the discussions, and the various incidents of the proceedings. But one remark may not be suppressed. Whether estimated by the number of eminent and venerable names to be found on its rolls, by the peril to the cause of Christ which called them together, the difficulties and embarrassments with which they were called to contend, the ability of the discussions, the moderation and prudence, the firmness and courage, displayed, the wisdom and fitness of the measures adopted, or the peace and prosperity, for so many years enjoyed, as the blessed results,—the reforming Assembly of 1837 ranks with the most illustrious of the faithful councils with which God has blessed his Church. Memory fondly lingers over the record of their beloved and venerable

45 *

names, whilst they sleep peacefully in the dust. It drops a tear upon the recent graves of an Engles and a Junkin, and reverently counts up the three or four who still remain, last relics of the former age. And now, a new generation has arisen. The attempt is assiduously made to disparage the wisdom and fidelity of those men of God, to whom our Church owes such a debt of undying gratitude. Men whose glory it once was to shine in their reflected light, are heard with patience, whilst assuming an apologetic tone, on behalf of those great men gone. They were good men, indeed; but, borne away, by the excitement of the time, to acts of unjustifiable violence and wrong! Their work is disparaged and maligned. All the arts of management and enginery of excitement are brought into requisition, to hurry the Church into a temporary forgetfulness, and persuade her to destroy all that they so painfully and prayerfully wrought. The same ambition for a vast communion, with which they had to contend, gives impetus to the present movement; and there seem to be many who are anxious to revive and restore to honor, those latitudinarian principles and that Broad Church policy, which they cast out of the sanctuary, as unclean things.

Who can witness these portentous facts, without emotions of alarm, and the distressful ejaculation of the bereaved prophet of Israel.—my "father! my father! The chariot of Israel and the horsemen thereof!"

The Assembly of 1837 had not yet adjourned, when an attempt was made to stigmatize the majority, by the pretence that it was acquired by a corrupt alliance with the South, in the interest of slavery. To this charge, the answer is decisive. The agitation of the slavery question, in connection with abolitionism, was then new in the Church. The first Assembly which took action on it, subsequent to 1818, was the New School Assembly of 1836. The action taken by it was, to postpone indefinitely the whole subject; and that, on the ground that "no church judicatory ought to pretend to make laws, to bind the conscience, in virtue of their own authority;" and that the shortness of the Assembly's sessions rendered it "impossible to deliberate and decide judiciously, on the subject of slavery, in its relations to the Church." A majority of the affirmative votes on this postponement was composed of members who voted for the acquittal of Mr. Barnes. In the Convention of 1837, the subject came up, incidentally, upon occasion of its mention in a paper, communicated to the body. It elicited no action, however, and seems to have been alluded to by none but Southern members,—Mr. Smyth and Mr. Plumer expressing the opinion that the Assembly ought to take no action on the subject; and Mr. Breckinridge taking the ground that no other subject should be allowed to mix itself with the reform of the Church; and, that, on the one hand, the spirit of abolitionism was to be exceedingly deprecated, as an absorbing and destructive fanaticism; and, on the other, the Assembly could not go back from the action formerly taken on the subject of slavery. As to any private understanding or compact, there is not a trace of evidence to sustain it. The Rev. Samuel Steele, of Ohio, was named as an Old School abolitionist, who was a party to the pretended covenant. But he emphatically and unreservedly denied the charge. The Rev. Thomas D.

Baird was one of the Secretaries of this Convention, and Vice President of that of 1838; and may be supposed to have been in the confidence, and possessed of any secrets of the Old School. He, in common with all the other members of the Convention, declared his entire ignorance of any understanding, whatever, with respect to slavery. In fact, no such arrangement was made. The votes of the Southern commissioners in the Assembly were determined by other causes, already indicated; and the fact that the Old School were unwilling to be diverted, by the question of slavery, from the great issues before them, and that the New School, who, in the preceding Assembly had avoided this subject, were anxious, now, that the South was lost to them, to press it on the Assembly, and willing to see their opponents distracted by it, needs no explanation.

CHAPTER XXXV.

THE DISRUPTION OF 1838.

New School meetings—Auburn Convention—Ann Arbor Convention—"Opinions" on the Disowning Acts—Conventions of 1838—Plan of the New School—Meeting of the Assembly—Group of New New School leaders—Dr. Patton's motion—Dr. Mason's motion—Mr. Squier—Mr. Cleaveland's paper—Dr. Hill's account—Dr. Beman moderator in the aisle—The withdrawal—The heralds—The end of the struggle—Four successive moderators—The New School stultify themselves—Strength of the parties—Doctrinal position of the New School—End of this History.

UPON the dissolution of the Assembly of 1837, Dr. Beman announced that a meeting of the minority would be held in Mr. Barnes' church, on the next afternoon, Friday, the 9th of June. At this meeting, a series of resolutions, submitted by the Rev. E. Cheever, were adopted. These resolutions denied that there were more doctrinal errors prevalent than heretofore, or greater irregularities in the disowned Synods than in other parts of the Church. They declared the reasons insufficient to justify the measures of the Assembly; and pronounced the abrogation of the Plan of Union, the cutting off of the four Synods and dissolution of the elective affinity Presbytery, null and void. They admitted that the alienation of parties in the Church was such as to render a division probably unavoidable;

yet recommended all the New School Presbyteries to be fully represented in the next Assembly,—that they "claim seats for the commissioners from those Presbyteries which have been unconstitutionally exscinded; and that, in case their seats shall be denied them, said commissioners take immediate measures for a separate and constitutional organization of the General Assembly, as constituting the only true General Assembly of the Presbyterian Church, in the United States of America."*

One danger threatened this policy. For several years, the Churches of Western New York and the Western Reserve had displayed a strong disposition to withdraw from the Church, and organize themselves as Congregationalists. It had required, heretofore, the utmost exertion of the influence and tact of the party to prevent a step so disastrous to their cause. To obviate such a course, at this critical moment, the meeting "earnestly requested" the churches in question, "to adhere to, and maintain their present organizations, and firmly to resist any and every attempt which may be made, by circular letters or otherwise, to change their present ecclesiastical relations." The allusion, here, was, to circulars, just before, issued, by certain Congregational bodies, which had been organized, recently, in Western New York.

The chief speakers, at this meeting were appropriately selected. They were Drs. Beman and Peters, and the Rev. Mr. Cleaveland. It was fitting, that Mr. Cleaveland, whose connection with the Church was a matter of mere temporary convenience,—Dr. Beman, who had never

* See the proceedings in the New York Observer, 1838, pp. 94, 98.

taken the oath of allegiance of a Presbyterian minister, and whose writings were in open antagonism to the standards of the Church,—and Dr. Peters, whose life had been publicly devoted to the destruction of our Boards, who denied the right of the Assembly to organize any permanent agency, whatever, and had labored, so long and so zealously, to cripple and destroy the Board of Missions,—should be the men to originate and direct this scheme, which proposed to seize possession of the Church which had so long borne with them, and assume charge of the institutions and funds which had been organized and accumulated, in spite of their opposition. The characteristic features of the New School, from its origin, had been, dislike to the strictness of the theology of the Confession, and to the system of government therein set forth; and consequent coldness or hostility to the seminaries and Boards of the Church, and preference for the voluntary societies and seminaries. The latter, therefore, were the recipients of their gifts; while the institutions of the Church were endowed and nourished by others. The New School, therefore, had no rightful ground for any pretence to property in those institutions. In the conferences of the joint committee on amicable separation, this was so clearly recognized, that the only claim which the New School members of that committee made, upon the property of the Church, was, to one-half of some twenty thousand dollars of permanent funds, not belonging to the seminaries. They were, also, ready to leave the chartered name of the Church to the Old School, and not anxious to retain the succession, provided the Old School would allow it to be destroyed, and not claim it to themselves.

Yet these were the men, who, having, deliberately and of purpose, placed their own seminaries and institutions beyond the reach of the Church, in any event, now form their plans and announce their purpose, to seize to themselves, alone, her name and succession, her funds and seminaries, her Boards and all her institutions. To this end, were all their measures, subsequently, directed; at first, in ecclesiastical conventions and the courts of the Church, and then, in the civil tribunals of the country.

The Philadelphia minority meeting was immediately followed by one in New York, which endorsed the resolutions passed by the former. Shortly after, a call appeared for a convention, at Auburn, New York, on the 17th of August, to deliberate on the proper measures to be taken "touching our grievances, and our duty, in relation to them."

At the time indicated, the Auburn convention met, and was organized by appointing the Rev. Dr. James Richards, President, with four Vice Presidents, and two Secretaries. About one hundred and eleven ministers, and sixty "laymen" were in attendance, representing some thirty-one Presbyteries and thirteen minorities. Most of these were from the disowned Synods. No regular report of the discussions was published. They continued until Monday the 21st, when the convention finally adjourned.

Whilst the larger proportion of the members were from the disowned Synods, the business of the convention was managed, mainly, by others, whose great labor it was to induce the disowned Synods to claim seats in the next Assembly. A decided disposition prevailed among the latter to abandon the attempt to revolutionize the

Church, and to enter into their own proper Congregational affiliations,—a disposition to which appeal was shortly after made in one of the expected "Circulars," from the General Association of the Congregational Ministers in New York.

With a view to this point, the principal resolutions of the convention were adopted. These declared that the disowning acts were unconstitutional, null and void; that the action of all judicatories "ought to be directed to the preservation of the *union and integrity of the Presbyterian Church;*" and that, "in accordance with these principles, it be recommended to the Synods declared to be exscinded, with their Presbyteries and churches, to retain their present organization and connection, without seeking any other; and that the Presbyteries send their commissioners to the next General Assembly, as usual."*

A great discovery was announced by this Convention,—that the churches in Western New York did not come in on the Plan of Union of 1801, but under the arrangement made with the Middle Association, in 1807 and 1808. It was, therefore, assumed, that the abrogation of the Plan did not affect these churches. Unfortunately for this conclusion, the history shows, as we have seen, that the arrangement of 1808 was merely an application of the principles of the Plan, on a large scale; and that the Plan was immediately adopted, by the bodies coming in under that arrangement, as their fundamental constitution; and so continued and was universally recognized, until the passage of the disowning acts, and the supposed discovery now proclaimed.

*Minutes of the Auburn Convention, pp. 36, 8vo., p. 7.

The convention adopted and published a series of reports, (1) upon the disowning acts; (2) a circular letter, on the same subject; (3) a Declaration of the Rights of Presbyterians; (4) a report on Doctrine, in which the doctrinal statement of the minority of the late Assembly was embodied; and (5) a statement of facts relative to the origin and character of the churches of the "excinded" Synods.

In the discussion on these subjects, the Rev. Dr. Joseph Penny stated, that there was a disposition to suppress the facts; that there was much more reason for the charge of doctrinal error and disorders, than many seemed willing to admit. Another member, whose disclosures threatened to be peculiarly damaging, was entreated to stop; but, refusing to do so, he was induced to yield to an adjournment, retaining the floor. When, however, the convention reassembled, he asked leave of absence, and desired to state his reasons for the request. The convention would not listen to the reasons; but granted the request; whereupon, the member took his seat among the spectators, and continued in attendance till the adjournment of the convention.

A similar convention of the Presbyterian and Congregational ministers and churches, who were connected with the Presbyterian Church under the Plan of Union, was held in the end of August, at Ann Arbor, Michigan, with like objects and like results. While the Stated Clerk of the Synod of the Western Reserve was advising the Synod, through the editorial columns of the Ohio Observer, "to declare itself an independent body, changing its name perhaps for, 'the Western Reserve General Consociation,' and modifying its rules as circumstances shall seem to require," the Presbyteries making like changes,—the convention determined "to retain existing relations, for the present."

In the mean time, the appeal of the New School to the civil tribunals was foreshadowed, by the procuring and publishing of "opinions" from various gentlemen of legal eminence, against the constitutionality of the measures of 1837. On the other hand, those measures were very ably vindicated, in two articles in the Princeton Repertory,—in a review of the Assembly's proceedings, which appeared in the July number; and an article on the State of the Church, in the number for April, 1838. They were from the pen of Dr. Hodge.

As the time for the meeting of the Assembly of 1838 approached, arrangements were made, by common consent, for a conference of the commissioners who were prepared to sustain the action of 1837, in the Seventh Church, on the morning of Tuesday the 15th of May, two days before the opening of the Assembly. A "meeting" was also called, by Drs. McAuley, Richards, and others, to be held in the First Church, on the evening of Monday, the 14th.

The Old School Convention of 1838 was organized with the Rev. Dr Wm. McPheeters, President, the Rev. Thomas D. Baird, Vice President, and the Rev. Messrs. Elias W. Crane, and Horace S. Pratt, Clerks.

On the evening of the first day's sessions, the Convention was waited upon by a committee from the New School "Meeting of Commissioners." They communicated a series of resolutions, which,—assuming the unconstitutionality of the disowning acts, and making the recognition of the regular standing of those Synods a fundamental condition,—proposed to the Convention "to open a friendly correspondence, for the purpose of ascertaining if some constitutional terms of pacification may not be agreed upon."

The reply of the Convention was drafted by a committee consisting of Dr. Baxter, Prof. John Maclean, of Princeton, and Wm. Maxwell, Esq., of Va. It declared the idea of regarding the disowning acts as unconstitutional, to be utterly inadmissible, and that the firm maintenance of those acts and the connected measures, presented the only prospect of securing the peace of the Church.

In the mean time, the New School meeting was engaged, with the assistance of legal counsel, in devising a plan by which to seize possession of the charter and the Church. Their scheme was ingenious. But it failed to take into account the cardinal fact, that, in the constitution and laws of the Church, express provision is made for the organization of the Assembly, designating precisely the officers by whom it is to be accomplished, and every step in the process.

Ignoring this fact, the plan devised went upon the assumption, that the assembled commissioners were in the predicament of a popular meeting, dependent for its organization upon the tact of such leaders as should most promptly seize the reins, and elicit the votes of their party;—or, at best, like an assembly of legislators, State, or National, whose only official assistant, in organizing, is a clerk, without legal authority, and liable to be superseded at any moment, by the will of the members.

This misconception of counsel, "learned in the law,"

but ignorant of the constitution of the Church, introduced confusion and perplexity into the proceedings of their clients; and rendered that absurd, which was already impossible.

At the hour appointed for opening the Assembly, the seats near the pulpit of the place of meeting, the Seventh Church, located in Ranstead Court,—were filled with the Old School members. They had been informed, the day before, by Dr. Nott, of Union College, of the plan of the New School, to attempt by a tumultuary movement to seize upon the organization of the Assembly; and, therefore, occupied the seats immediately in front, for the purpose of protecting and sustaining the moderator. The New School members came in, together, from the meeting in the First Church. They assumed seats in the body of the house, next to those already filled by the Old School. Foremost among them, was a group of eight persons, who sat in the middle aisle, nine or ten pews from the front. They were the master-spirits of the occasion, who had been designated to enact the leading parts in the drama of the disruption. First, of these, in place and responsibility, Mr. Cleaveland, was most appropriately selected, to await the critical moment, and, with hearty good-will and steady hand, strike the blow which should rend the Church. A year or two afterward, he had returned to the Congregational Church, from which he came. With him, were Dr. Beman, the veteran strategist of this cause, Dr. Samuel Fisher, Dr. Erskine Mason, of Union Theological Seminary, Dr. William Patton, of the Presbyterian Education Society, and the Rev. E. W. Gilbert, author of the diagram illustrating gradual regeneration by moral suasion. These were the actors, designated in the programme; and, as if, to complete the dramatic accuracy and fullness of the arrangement, Drs. Beecher, of Lane, and Taylor, of New Haven, who was present as the delegate from the General Association of Connecticut, sat immediately behind Mr. Cleaveland, ready at the moment of crisis, to stimulate his failing courage, and urge him on to his appointed office.

Thus curiously were brought together, as the conspicuous objects, at a moment so impressive, and in attitudes so significant, a complete exemplification of the strange conglomerate which was about to usurp the name and the authority of the Presbyterian Church. In Drs. Patton and Mason, the voluntary societies and seminaries were represented. Moderate orthodoxy and Presbyterianism recognized an honored exemplar in Dr. Fisher; whilst the Edwardean theology of Mr. Gilbert and Dr. Beman, the Plan of Union Presbyterianism of the latter, the Congregationalism of Mr. Cleaveland and the Pelagianism of Dr. Taylor, all contributed to the propriety and completeness of the exhibition; and the ambiguities and versatility of Dr. Beecher, his catholic affinities and schemes of comprehension, presented a solvent, to fuse and cement in one the entire mass.

The Constitution provides that the Moderator of the last Assembly, if present, "shall open the meeting, with a sermon, and preside, until a Moderator be chosen." In accordance with this rule, the Rev. Dr. Elliott opened the Assembly with a sermon from Isaiah lx. 1. After the sermon, he gave the usual notice, that as soon as the benediction was pronounced, he would proceed to organize the Assembly. The benediction was then pronounced, and the Moderator assumed the chair, and called upon the clerks, who, by a standing rule, were constituted the Committee of Commissions, to report the roll.

At this moment, Dr. Patton rose, and hastily calling, "Moderator! Moderator!" asked leave to offer certain resolutions, which he held in his hand. The Moderator declared him out of order, as the first business was the reporting of the roll. Dr. Patton stated that the resolutions had reference to that very business. But the Constitution expressly provides that "no commissioner shall have a right to deliberate or vote, until his name shall have been enrolled by the Clerk, and his commission examined and filed among the papers of the Assembly." Until the report of the Clerks, therefore, neither was Dr. Patton competent to introduce any business, nor was there a house to act upon his motion. The Moderator, therefore, pronounced him out of order. Dr. Patton attempted to appeal. But, as the Moderator informed him,—there was no house to appeal to. The appeal was, therefore, out of order; and Dr. Patton took his seat. The manifest propriety of the Moderator's decision, unexpected though it seems to have been, confounded and silenced him; although this was the precise point in the proceedings when the learned counsel had instructed them that these resolutions should be acted on, in order to accomplish the object.

Dr. Patton's resolutions were condemnatory of the disowning acts of 1837, and proposed to instruct the Clerks to include the names of the Commissioners from the disowned Synods, in the roll of the Assembly. It was the plan of the New School, to force action on this subject, before the organization; and, upon the resolutions being rejected, to proceed at once to organize the minority as the Assembly, thus anticipating the regular organization and superseding it. Dr. Patton's failure introduced confusion into the whole plan; which was, thus, already, defeated.

The Permanent Clerk, now, on behalf of the Committee of Commissions, reported the roll of members, present with regular and orderly commissions. He, also, reported the names of several persons, without, or with defective commissions; and the case of commissioners present from the Presbytery of Greenbriar, newly organized, by the Synod of Virginia. With the report, the documents belonging to these cases were submitted by the Clerk.

The Moderator, thereupon, announced that the persons whose names had been enrolled were to be considered as members of the Assembly; and stated that if there were any Commissioners present, who had not had opportunity of submitting their commissions to the Committee, they could now present them to the Clerks and be enrolled.

The Rev. Dr. Erskine Mason, here, rose and moved to complete the roll, by adding the names of the Commissioners from the disowned Synods, who, he said, had been rejected by the Clerks. Their commissions he now tendered to the chair. But the rule under which the Moderator was acting was imperative. "The persons whose names shall be thus reported shall immediately take their seats and proceed to business. The first act of the Assembly, when thus ready for business, shall be the appointment of a Committee of Elections, whose duty it shall be to examine all informal, and unconstitutional commissions, and report on the same, as soon as practicable."* The design of the Moderator's call was, to enable the Clerks to complete their report. No other business might interpose between that report and the "first act" provided for by the rule. After its performance, the house would be ready for business, and Dr. Mason's motion would then be in order. The Moderator, therefore, pronounced the motion of Dr. Mason "out of order, at that time." Dr. Mason appealed; but, for the same reason, the appeal was disallowed. The Rev. Miles P. Squier now arose and tendered a commission, and claimed a seat, as a member, from the Presbytery of Geneva. The Moderator asked, if the Presbytery belonged to the Synod of Geneva; and upon being answered in the affirmative, replied,—"We do not know you, sir."

The New School leaders now found themselves in a very embarrassing position. A part had been assigned them to perform. The last moment, when its performance would be possible, was passing. And yet the fact upon which it had been predicated had not occurred. Neither the Moderator nor the Assembly had refused to receive the "exscinded" commissioners. The question had been excluded by a strict compliance with the Constitution and rules. Evidently, these rendered it impossible to force upon the attention of the Assembly, in an inchoate and unorganized condition, a question so grave as that of treating as a nullity a solemn decree of a former Assembly. After the Committee of Elections has been appointed, it will be in order to raise the question now pressed. But the propriety, then, of a

* Digest, p. 295.

reference of the subject to that committee would be so evident as to admit of no question. And the Assembly would then be so manifestly and fully organized that an attempt at a tumultuary supersedure of it would have been absurd.

At this moment, Mr. Cleaveland seems to have been greatly embarrassed and agitated. His countenance was flushed and his frame trembled. Apparently, he hesitated, and held a hasty conference with those around him. With excited countenances and eager gestures, the voices of Drs. Beecher and Taylor were heard in low but earnest tones urging him, "Go on! Go on!"

In the mean time, the Rev. Joshua Moore, of the Presbytery of Huntingdon, had responded to the Moderator's call, and presented himself to the Clerks, for enrollment. But upon examination, finding that he had left his commission at his lodgings, he left the house, to procure it. A motion was then made, for the appointment of a Committee of Elections. But the question was interrupted.

Mr. Cleaveland arose, and without addressing the Moderator, proceeded, in a distinct, but trembling voice, to read, from a written paper, an apologetic preamble. The original of this paper was afterward, carefully suppressed, as were, also, the written affidavits of Mr. Cleaveland and Dr. Beman, as to this transaction. They were in possession of the New School counsel, on the subsequent trial before judge Rogers; but were not exhibited.

On the Minutes of the New School Assembly, what purported to be "the substance" of Mr. Cleaveland's preamble was stated in these words: "As the commissioners to the General Assembly of 1838, from a large number of Presbyteries had been refused their seats; and as we have been advised, by counsel learned in the law, that a constitutional organization of the Assembly must be secured at this time and in this place, he trusted it would not be considered as an act of discourtesy, but merely as a matter of necessity, if we now proceed to organize the Assembly of 1838, in the fewest words, the shortest time, and with the least interruption practicable."

He, therefore, moved, that Dr. Beman preside till a new Moderator be chosen. He proposed the question, which was responded to by a vociferous shout of Aye! It is impossible to determine from the testimony, amid a scene of excitement and confusion, whether upon this or any subsequent motion in the process, the question was reversed. Several of the New School witnesses testified that it was, and that there were negative votes. On the contrary, the New School Minutes stated that the questions were unanimously carried, and the Old School witnesses declared, that they heard no reversal, nor time allowed for it. However, amid calls to order, from the Moderator and members, Mr. Cleaveland put the question and pronounced Dr. Beman elected,—the Old School members sitting in indignant silence. Says Dr. Hill,—"I had determined to take no part, and was opposed to the proceeding from the first. I expected a riot would ensue. When Mr. Cleaveland made the motion, that Mr. Beman should take the chair, he put the affirmative,—'All those who are in favor will say, aye.' There arose a simultaneous burst of ayes, some of which were very indecorously and offensively loud.

I don't know that all the scattering ayes had ceased, when he reversed it. I heard a few scattering noes, only from the direction of the Old School. I was astonished at this, because I expected a thundering, 'No!' as they claimed to be the majority. I had expected that the noes would be of another character, and was agreeably disappointed. I had anticipated these events, and feared that a great riot would take place." *

Dr. Beman assumed his imaginary chair, by stepping out of the pew, and standing in the aisle. A general movement now took place in that part of the house, the members rising, mounting the seats, and even standing on the backs of the pews, as the only way in which they could command a view of the new Moderator, amid a crowd on the floor. At the same time, the excitement was transmitted to the crowded galleries and the spectators below, whose interest, on both sides, was expressed with less regard to decorum than that of the members. Amid such a scene, however, the Old School members only caught the sound of successive affirmative responses to questions which they could not hear. In a few moments, the throng which had clustered about Dr. Beman, changed its position to one about twenty feet farther from the pulpit and the Moderator's chair; and, some five minutes after the rising of Mr. Cleaveland, they retired from the house.

At this instant, another pair of actors presented themselves for a moment, to give a fitting ending to the scene. Dr. Edward Beecher, and the Rev. Eliakim Phelps, agent for the Presbyterian Education Society,—

* Dr. Hill's testimony, in Miller's Report, p. 212. Dr. Hill identified himself with the New School.

Congregational sojourners, both,—appeared at the several doors of the house, the heralds of the pageant, and announced to the members in stentorian voices, that the Assembly had adjourned, to meet immediately in the First Presbyterian Church! One of the gentlemen was a little hoarse, and his first effort being not quite satisfactory, he cleared his throat, and repeated the proclamation, in tones which left no room for any to plead ignorance.

And so, the anxieties and controversies of a quarter of a century were ended! The withdrawal of that mixed company from the house in Ranstead Court, was the retirement of the foreign and disturbing elements from the Church. The spirit of rest and peace breathed his influences upon the hearts of the members; and with mingled emotions, —tears trickling, from many faces, yet profoundly grateful for a great deliverance, the Assembly resumed its interrupted business. A Committee of Elections was appointed; and Dr. Plumer was elected Moderator and the Rev. E. W. Crane Temporary Clerk.

The next day, it appeared that after the call of Dr. Beman to the chair, Dr. Fisher had been chosen Moderator, and Dr. Mason and Mr. Gilbert, Temporary Clerks, and then, respectively, Stated and Permanent Clerks. Thus, the energies of four successive Moderators had been called into requisition with a magic promptness and facility, to get the "constitutional Assembly" upon its feet;—Dr. Elliott,—the only constitutional feature in the case,—by whose mandate the Assembly was convened and opened; Mr. Cleaveland, who, self-elected, gave place in a few moments, to Dr. Beman, as he, again, after two or three minutes' incumbency, to Dr. Fisher.

After the organization of the body had been thus completed, and the adjournment had taken place to the First Church, the seceding Assembly took up and adopted Dr. Patton's paper. In it, they declared, that "the Assembly cannot be legally constituted, except by admitting to seats, and equality of powers, in the first instance, all Commissioners who present the usual evidence of their appointment; and that it is the duty of the clerks, and they are hereby directed, to form the roll of the Assembly of 1838," by including the commissioners from the exscinded Synods and the dissolved Third Presbytery of Philadelphia.

They had just pretended to supersede the regular organization of the Assembly, because Dr. Elliott had refused to entertain this question, "*in the first instance.*" And now, after completing their own organization, without the essential enrollment of these members, they stultify themselves, by declaring that an organization *cannot* take place till after such enrollment, and therefore order it to be made, now that the Assembly is already organized!

After the retirement of the New School, and the completion of the organization of the Assembly in Ranstead Court, the roll was called and it was found that of the 220 commissioners who had been enrolled, 152 were present and answered to their names; and 5 were at the moment out of the house; but afterward appeared and acted with the Assembly. Four additional commissioners afterward arrived and reported themselves, whilst two of those who answered at the calling of the roll, afterward declined to recognize either Assembly. So that the whole number acting with the Assembly was 159.

The New School Minutes exhibit the names of 287 Commissioners. But these include 157 of those who were in attendance on the Assembly in Ranstead Court, the 2 neutrals who were there, 5 neutrals who went home, and 2 commissioners who were not in Philadelphia at all; leaving, thus, 121 in actual attendance on the New School Assembly. These included 58 Commissioners from the disowned Synods, and Third Presbytery of Philadelphia. Thus, in the united attendance on the two Assemblies, the Old School had a clear majority over the New of 38; and of 31 over New School and neutrals combined.

We have seen that the division grew out of doctrinal diversities. The New School Assembly hastened to define its position on that subjeet. In 1839, it published "A Declaration, setting forth the present position of our beloved Zion, and the causes which have brought us into our peculiar position." This paper purports to give a history of the subject; but it is a tissue of extraordinary inaccuracies. The reader, however, is possessed of the means of their correction, in these pages.

"It will be found," say they, "upon a reference to the history of bygone days, that, on the 6th day of April, 1691, the Presbyterian and Congressional denominations of Christians in Great Britain met at Stepney, and there, by the blessing of Almighty God, after talking over their differences and agreements, consummated a union of the two denominations, by adopting what was then called, 'the Heads of Agreement,' embracing a few cardinal principles, which were to govern them in their fraternal intercourse.

"The Presbyterian and Congregational Union sent over one of their number, by the name of Makemie, as a missionary to the new settlements in America; who, in connection with Messrs. Macnish, Andrews, Hampton, Taylor, Wilson, and Davis, in 1704, formed the first Presbytery which ever existed in America, by the name of the Presbytery of Philadelphia. This mother Presbytery was formed upon the liberal Christian principles which governed the London Association, by which Mr. Makemie was sent to this country, and was composed, partly of Presbyterian, and, partly, of Congregational, ministers and churches. Mr. Andrews, the first pastor of the Metropolitan or First Church in Philadelphia, was a decided Congregational Presbyterian; and the church over which he presided was under the care of the Presbytery *sixty-four* years, before they elected any ruling elders. This state of things continued until 1716, when the Synod of Philadelphia was formed out of the Presbyteries of Philadelphia, New Castle, Snow Hill, and Long Island; the last three having grown up, after the formation of the first, in 1704."

The "Declaration" traces the history down to the Adopting Act. But, under that name, it exhibits the Preliminary Act; whilst the Adopting Act itself is entirely ignored. It asserts that the "rash departure" of the Synod, in the Explanatory Act of 1736, "from the tolerant and fraternal principles of 1691, in England, and of 1704 and 1729, in America, led to the painful schism of 1741." This, however was healed, in 1758, when the two Synods were reunited, and in the sixth article of their union, they agreed to adopt the Confession of Faith, Catechisms and Directory, "as they had been adopted, in 1728."* It then relates the history of correspondence with the Congregational Churches, and of the Plan of Union; of which it says:—

"These Plans of Union between the two denominations, were a virtual recognition of the benign principles established in 1691, in England, and afterward adopted in America, and made the basis of Presbyterianism in the original Presbytery and Synod of Philadelphia.

"These fundamental principles continued to be recognized and acted upon by the Assembly of the Presbyterian Church, and the subordinate judicatories, with few exceptions, until 1837."†

The "Declaration" goes on to give an account of the transactions of 1837 and 1838, and the commencement of legal proceedings, designed, say they, if possible to restore the purity of the Church, "and secure religious liberty."

In a word, the division grew out of the question whether the Preliminary Act of 1729, erroneously called the Adopting Act, was the fundamental constitution of the Church. The issue was between the standards of the Church, and the "liberal principles" of 1691. The same issue is now anew presented to our Church.

Here we pause, leaving it to another occasion, should the Head of the Church graciously bestow the necessary leisure, to develope more fully the history here briefly sketched, in some of its aspects; and trace the results of

* See the Articles, above, pp. 115, 116.

† Moore's "New Digest," p. 549.

the measures of 1837 and 1838; the acts of the latter year for the pacification of the Church; the separation of the elements throughout the ecclesiastical limits; the proceedings at law; the charge of Judge Rogers and finding of the jury, and the final triumph of truth and righteousness, in the decision of the Supreme Court of Pennsylvania, in Bank, as set forth in the opinion of Chief Justice Gibson. It declared the disowning acts to be "certainly constitutional and strictly just,"—that "the Commissioners from those Synods were not entitled to seats in the Assembly, and that their names were properly excluded from the roll;"—that "an appeal from the decision of the Moderator did not lie; and he incurred no penalty for disallowing it;"—"that the Assembly which met in the First Presbyterian Church was not the legitimate successor of the Assembly of 1837; and that the [Old School] defendants are not guilty of the usurpation with which they are charged," in claiming the succession.

The blessings of thirty years have crowned the works of our fathers, and experience, in all those years, has attested the wisdom of their policy, and the manifest approval of the Head of the Church, through it, endowing her with prosperity and peace.

INDEX.

www.ingramcontent.com/pod-product-compliance
Lightning Source LLC
LaVergne TN
LVHW021231110826
845150LV00002B/300

9781425563073